Praise F

Handbook to Higher Health Consciousness
How to Transition to Plant-Based Eating to Heal Yourself and the Planet
By David A. Kater

David Kater has written a thoughtful indictment of the status quo, and an illumining road map that can guide many people to a better future. Read it, apply it, and thrive!

— Ocean Robbins, CEO, The Food Revolution Network

There's a food revolution underway with a rising awareness about the consequences of our food choices. The Handbook to Higher Health Consciousness is a beacon of helpful information that cuts through the fog and noise to provide you science-based facts about nutrition while raising awareness about how our food choices impact our health, the environment, and animal welfare. Complete with recipes from Tracy Childs, a leading Physicians Committee for Responsible Medicine Food for Life Instructor, it's everything you need to know to live plant-strong and thrive!

— Liz Gary, Founder, New Options Food Group

Moving to a plant-based diet is a journey. And like most adventures, you need a guide who has successfully traveled the path before you. In this comprehensive book, David takes you by the hand and walks you through the entire process. I'm happy the concept of recipe-free cooking has found a spot in this indispensable handbook, because it plays a pivotal role in moving away from processed meat and dairy substitutes. Instead, you'll learn to create meals based on whole foods, saving you time and money while keeping your taste buds happy and your tummy satisfied. Enjoy the journey!

— Patty "Sassy" Knutson, VeganCoach.com

A life changing book! I was educated, motivated, and even amused by it. I run a software company and travel a great deal. It is difficult to eat healthy at times. However, this book moved me much closer to completing my transition to a plant-based diet. The historical perspective, facts that have been purposely hidden by big companies, nutritional shocker facts, fun recipes, lots of resources—this book has it all. Kudos to David for this very well-written and comprehensive guide. Anyone can put this book to good use, become much healthier, and literally save the planet in the process.

— Randy Ozden, CEO, Streamlyne, Inc.

In this book, David offers a step-by-step guide for anyone who is wanting to include more plants in their diet as well as to someone who wants to transform their diet to one that is totally plant-based. He easily explains the whys as well as the how-tos of a plant-based diet and gives practical, doable advice on how to make plant-based eating easier and time-efficient. His enthusiasm for the benefits of following a plant-based diet makes the book an easy read as he encourages the reader to take small steps to ensure success. He includes many wonderful, easy recipes using real food that you can purchase at any supermarket. A very easy guide for someone who wants to know how to become a plant-based eater while living a real life.

To your excellent health,

– Jamie Davidson, Author, Health Educator, and Weight Management Coach

The Handbook to Higher Health Consciousness is a powerful tool on how to empower your life with a plant-based diet. David Kater has written a remarkable guide on how your food choices can better improve your health, save animals from torment, and preserve the planet. It's a must read!

– Jenn Nemeth, Clinical Cardiac Rehab RN with the Dr. Dean Ornish Prevent & Reverse Heart Disease Program & co-owner of Veg-Appeal

I was inspired by the story of how David Kater and his wife Donna adopted a vegan eating style. That's when I began my journey toward a vegan lifestyle, and it quickly became a priority in my world. I became a vegan without a struggle, and soon desired to share my passion with others. Two years ago, I decided to host vegan dinner parties at various local restaurants. I arranged for the restaurants to prepare fully plant-based meals for my guests. The dinners have been amazing and the idea has been a huge success, with over 400 members and counting on Meetup.com. A growing number of restaurants are accepting the idea that healthy vegan food is here to stay. Another way I share my passion for plant-based eating is by hosting monthly Lunch and Learn cooking classes in my home. The scale is small due to space limitations, but you never know where this might lead.

Thanks to David and Donna for the contagious love and energy they contributed to my world and many others as well. The Handbook to Higher Health Consciousness shares their story and is packed with information on health, nutrition, and how to make the transition to healthier eating. This book is a must read. You'll want to keep it on hand for reference, and to try out all the great recipes.

– Elizabeth Mansur, Health and Wellness Coach

A must read for anyone who wants to live and enjoy life with more energy and mental clarity than you have ever experienced. The best step-by-step how-to guide out there. Making one small change at a time, you will transition from eating the typical SAD (Standard American Diet) to experiencing the benefits of eating Real Whole Food.

– Kate, six-year vegan

Lucky me. I have the insider's look at the author's life, dedication, and daily activities. In addition to regular exercise and eating plant-based foods, one of David's daily habits is doing acrostic puzzles, both for the fun of it as well as to keep his vocabulary and thinking skills sharp. We are frequently delighted that the sayings that emerge from these puzzles often relate to our daily lives. Interestingly, today's acrostic puzzle is a quote from author Toni Morrison from *Write to the Heart*: "There's a difference between writing for a living and in writing for life. If you write for a living you making enormous compromises, and you might not ever be able to uncompromise yourself. If you write for life you'll work hard, you'll do what's honest not what pays." David definitely writes for life. He is very devoted to his writing and to the topic of plant-based nutrition in particular.

A good teacher simply presents concepts. A *great* teacher is a facilitator, one who makes the learning process easier. That's what David is. He has had a tremendous career as a professor, teaching mathematics to college students for several decades. He has influenced countless people, helping them learn basic math skills that opened doors to many life and career opportunities. One of his primary motivators is seeing the light going on in his students' eyes when they solve a particularly difficult math problem or finally understand an important math concept.

In a similar way, David understands that teaching people about plant-based nutrition, along with a few skills and techniques, will make a tremendous difference in their future health as well as the health of the planet. He has organized the current research and thinking in the whole food plant-based arena and has presented it in a thoughtful and sometimes humorous way so that it is easy to understand and implement. He and Tracy have collaborated to produce a smorgasbord of recipes that are delicious and satisfying! There are easy transitional recipes for readers just starting their journey as well as recipes that are optimized for health benefits for readers who are further along the path.

This book is very timely because we are at the beginning of a major paradigm shift. There is every indication that plant-based eating will go from a small percentage of the population to mainstream in the next couple of decades. Backed by solid science and research, the movement is growing strong, and people are feeling younger and healthier as they make better food choices. You see signs everywhere you look. It's exciting to be part of this food revolution, and this practical book will help those that feel the pull to catch the wave and give it a good ride.

I encouraged David to write about what he was learning as we journeyed into plant-based eating, because I know his teaching skills. I also knew that if David shared his journey and the discoveries he's made along the way, it would make it so much easier for those who chose to follow a similar path. He presents information in bite-sized pieces (pun intended!) so that people get it. He makes it easy to understand why one should consider eating plant-based food, and he encourages us all to try out fresh ideas and have fun with new recipes.

The vegan and whole food, plant-based paths to greater health and longevity are becoming better traveled. There is no need to reinvent the wheel. We are constantly learning from those who traveled the path before us. David is well along the path, and it's his dream to pass on his knowledge with lots of love, encouragement, and a sense of fun. There is no trudging along this path allowed; it's too enjoyable.

To your health . . . Enjoy the adventure and the journey!

– Donna H. Kater, Acupuncturist, Author, Coach, Speaker, aka the wife

Handbook to Higher Health Consciousness

Handbook to Higher Health Consciousness

How to Transition to Plant–Based Eating to Heal Yourself and the Planet

David A. Kater

The opinions expressed in this book have evolved from my years of research and learning as I have traveled the path toward a whole food plant–based diet. The information presented here is intended for general information only. It is not intended as medical advice. Do not rely on any information presented here as a substitute for professional medical advice, diagnosis, or treatment. Health information changes frequently as research evolves. Do not rely on any information presented here as a substitute for your own research. If you have concerns, consult a qualified healthcare provider before adjusting medications or making major diet changes. The author specifically disclaims all responsibility for injury, damage, or loss that the reader may incur as a direct or indirect consequence of following any directions or suggestions given in the book or participating in any programs described by the book.

To my loving wife, Donna H. Kater,
who inspired me to write this book.

CONTENTS

ABOUT THE AUTHOR

David A. Kater is an author, college professor, artist, and vegan enthusiast. After converting to a vegan diet in 2012, David has dedicated himself to expanding his knowledge about evidence-based nutrition and health. He learned how to prepare plant-based meals that are every bit as delicious as the Standard American Diet. With the help of cooking classes, online videos, and community support, David converted many of his favorite dishes to plant–based equivalents. In the process, he learned a tremendous amount about nutrition, and joyfully discovered that eating a plant–based diet also eases the pain of animals, conserves water, and is the only sustainable way to reverse the devastation to our planet, caused largely by industrialized food production.

David's journey as an author began in 1980 when he became a ghostwriter and researcher for the first Epson printer manual published in the United States. He learned the craft of clear communication from mentor Dr. David Lein, and soon became the sole author of several Epson printer manuals. This led to a book on TRS–80 Graphics for McGraw–Hill and RadioShack, a book on Microsoft Word for Microsoft Press, a book on desktop publishing for Sybex, and several others.

David started teaching at local community colleges after completing his Master's degree in Mathematics in 1976. After completing a second Master's degree in Educational Technology, David created a self–paced Math Center at San Diego City College in 1994. He directed the Math Center until his semi–retirement in 2012, and he now teaches online math courses for the college.

David is also a digital artist, displaying his works at Art Walk and other events in San Diego. He started his artistic journey with photography, and evolved into digital creations produced on a variety of media – metal, Plexiglas, canvas, photo paper, and 3D lenticular format. davidkaterart.com

Soon after retiring from full time teaching, David watched the food documentary *Forks over Knives* on the recommendation of a colleague. The documentary provided compelling evidence that many of the degenerative diseases that afflict our country can be controlled or reversed by eating a whole food plant–based diet. It was life–changing moment. That realization totally altered his relationship with food. It inspired him to learn the truth about food and transform his diet. His wife, Donna, joined him on this path of inquiry and experimentation. The insights that he gained over the years filled him with a desire to share his discoveries with others and provided the basis for this book. In 2017, David completed the Plant–Based Nutrition Certificate program from Cornell University to gain a deeper understanding of plant–based nutrition.

David is dedicated to helping people embrace a plant–based lifestyle for their health, for the health of the planet, and for the sake of the animals.

www.davidakater.com

ABOUT TRACY CHILDS

David asked me to share my motivation for providing recipes for this book and it's my pleasure to do so! After I read and contributed editing ideas for the first 3 chapters on my way to and from the July 2017 Physicians Committee for Responsible Medicine Nutrition in Medicine conference, I was hooked! It seems like I have always been passionate about the subject of plant–based diets and the many reasons we have to move toward adopting this way of eating, so I have eagerly read almost every book that has come out on the subject (or own it!). David's approach to the subject was new and fresh, and it's never been timelier to get the word out to a wider audience. So I was very excited to collaborate on the recipes, help with the editing and take a vested interest in its success.

Food has always been of utmost importance to me for many different reasons. I have long endeavored to use food as medicine for myself and others. I have changed the way I eat and cook dramatically over the years as I learn more and new nutrition research becomes available. I love sharing the empowering news that changing the way you eat can help combat many of the diseases that plague Western society today: obesity, cancer, diabetes, stroke, and heart disease to name just the most common. More and more, people and even medical systems are jumping on the bandwagon, which is encouraging to see!

I have been creating and tweaking recipes and food ideas to be healthier, tastier and better, for pretty much my entire adult life. I became vegetarian when I was 17, and have been exploring foods and cooking ever since. I love everything about food creation – the science behind it, the feeling of sharing foods and nurturing others through food, the pleasure of enjoying my own food creations, and the sheer creativity of it. It seems to be a bit of a lost art these days. People find it strange that I don't like to go out to eat much, but why go out when there are lovely foods waiting to be created at home that I'm more likely to enjoy? As my husband's Nanny Tillie would say, "Why go out, when there's food in the house?"

After years of food–fascination and having taught cooking and nutrition since 2005, I have compiled a lot of recipes on my computer that are used to create handouts and inspiration for my classes. Practically every recipe I present gets personalized in some way. I love sharing these gems with my local San Diego cooking class audience, and I am thrilled to now share them with the world at large. Thus, I am delighted to share, edit, perfect and contribute recipes for David's book.

Since becoming a certified Food for Life Nutrition and Cooking Instructor with the Physicians Committee for Responsible Medicine (PCRM), my cooking and recipe creation has been further refined to eliminate/minimize the use of non–whole/refined foods (oil, flour, sugar). These foods can be acceptable once in a while for treats, but excess amounts can be damaging to the body, especially while healing (as detailed in this book). I encourage everyone to seek out further resources and work to refine your taste buds over time, by minimizing refined foods, and learning to truly taste the food, using better quality ingredients.

I am grateful to David for allowing me to be part of this project. I have long wanted to share my recipes, to inspire as many people as possible to eat better for ourselves, the planet and the animals, but have been so busy with the day–to–day task of teaching classes, that I hadn't yet compiled my favorite recipes into a book format. This project has given me the impetus I needed to do it, and I'm glad to contribute, since this movement is truly a labor of love for me!

To find out more about my work, visit Veg–Appeal.com and plantdiego.com.
Bon Appetite and Happy Creating!

ACKNOWLEDGMENTS

I wish to acknowledge some of the champions of evidence–based nutrition who have inspired me: Dr. Michael Greger, Dr. Neal Barnard, Dr. T. Colin Campbell, Nelson Campbell, Dr. Thomas Campbell, Dr. Caldwell Esselstyn, Rip Esselstyn, Dr. Michael Klaper, John and Ocean Robbins, and my cooking coach, Patty "Sassy" Knutson.

My thanks to many local heroes who have contributed by teaching cooking classes, hosting meetups, posting videos, and spreading the word to local restaurants, schools, and companies – Tracy Childs, Liz Gary, Rochelle Harris, Joan Jackson, Elizabeth Mansur, Jennifer Nemeth, and Marina Yanay–Triner.

Thank you to those who reviewed early versions of the manuscript and gave thoughtful feedback: Tracy Childs, Donna Jacobs, Kathleen Kastner, Donna Kater, Elizabeth Mansur, Kate Woodward, and Carol Zurcher.

A special thanks goes to Jamie Davidson, a weight management coach, who did extensive review and editing of portions of the manuscript, especially the recipes. Having written a number of books on how to prepare healthy meals with Trader Joe's products, Jamie has a keen eye for the smallest out–of–place detail or inconsistency in a recipe. Her expertise was invaluable! Connect with her at jamiedavidsoncooks.com.

I'm deeply indebted to Tracy Childs for her contributions to the recipe chapter. Tracy has been a leader in the plant–based movement for many years, teaching cooking classes for cancer prevention and survival and for anyone wishing to adopt a "Food as Medicine" type of approach, while learning new ways to enjoy delicious as well as compassionate foods. She is also heading up the local PlantPure Nation pod in San Diego (PlantDiego.com), and extending her educational outreach and support services through Veg–Appeal (Veg–Appeal.com). She has been developing recipes and teaching about plant–based cooking for many years. Her expertise is undeniable. When we first talked about Tracy contributing recipes to this book, I thought it would be a few recipes here and there to fill in the gaps. Little did I realize the enormity of what she would bring to the table. As a result, there are now over 160 recipes in the book, covering a huge range of appetites and tastes. Thank you so much, Tracy.

Thank you to my wife, Donna Kater, for inspiring me to write this book. I had written quite a number of books and computer manuals back in the 1980s, but not much lately. When I helped Donna edit her first book, "I'm Still Alive, Now What?!? How to Survive and Thrive After a Life–Changing Event," it rekindled my interest in writing and refreshed my editing skills. As I amassed more and more information about plant–based eating and its global implications, Donna continued to encourage me to put that information into book form. Eventually, I saw the light and decided to go for it. That decision was a blessing. I've learned so much in the writing and research process. Thank you also, Donna, for your feedback, tireless editing, and support throughout the entire process.

I acknowledge you, too, my readers, for having the courage to expand your comfort zone and embrace the challenge of adopting a healthy plant–based diet.

FOREWORD

Congratulations! If you've opened this book, that probably means that you're thinking about giving a plant-based diet a try. It's a decision more and more people are making. We're seeing doctors prescribe a plant-based diet to their patients to prevent and reverse chronic diseases and other health problems. We're seeing top athletes, from the world of tennis to the NBA and NFL, choose plant-based diets to boost their recovery times and reduce inflammation. We're seeing leading scientists and policymakers dropping the meat and dairy to fight climate change.

Regardless of what first sparked your interest in a plant-based diet, you've made a wonderful choice. But now you might be wondering: *What next? Where do I start?* This book is the perfect place to dive in.

In *Handbook to Higher Health Consciousness*, David Kater takes readers on a step-by-step journey toward good health. As an educator and communicator who has taken this same journey himself, David will expertly guide you through the process, offering practical advice and words of encouragement along the way. You'll learn the basics, from navigating the grocery store to restocking your pantry. You'll learn the answers to all your questions: *Can I get enough protein? What about calcium?* And inevitably, as with any change in life, when obstacles arise, you'll learn to work through them, as David helps you navigate food cravings, social situations, and more.

The *Handbook* also contains more than 160 wonderful recipes that are worth the price of admission alone. In the book's recipe section, David teams up with certified Food for Life instructor Tracy Childs, who has helped countless people in her community transform their health through her nutrition and cooking classes. Now she's sharing her secrets with you. Whether you're a beginner or experienced cook, the *Handbook* meets you where you are. The book offers step-by-step recipes, but it also features creative "templates" that teach you to pair foods and experiment with new flavors to build salads, smoothies, and more. And if you're brave enough, David will even teach you how to cook without any recipes at all.

As you start experimenting with these recipes, you'll notice a few things. First, you'll realize how good they taste. And soon after, you'll notice how good you feel. Eating this way will boost your energy and elevate your health.

For three decades now, my colleagues at the Physicians Committee for Responsible Medicine and I have put these foods to the test and proven their power in our clinical research studies. We've seen the power of these foods to lower blood pressure and cut cholesterol. We've seen them tackle arthritis, hormone problems, and digestive problems. We've tested the effects of a plant-based diet on folks with type 2 diabetes and found that the pounds soon start to melt away, blood sugar begins to stabilize, and, in many cases, the need for medication is eventually reduced or completely eliminated. We've seen countless participants completely transform their lives.

And now it's your turn. I wish you the very best on your journey and encourage you to jump in, explore this book, test drive these recipes, and reap the benefits!

- Neal Barnard, M.D., PCRM.org

PREFACE

A change is coming. The world's population is exploding, projected to reach 9.7 billion in 2050 and 11.2 billion by 2100.[1] Even at 2017 population levels, our attempts to feed the populace using our current methods is devastating our planet. Our industrialized approach to food production, such as planting corn and soy to feed animals that will be eaten by humans, is simply not sustainable. The only way to feed the planet without destroying it is by adopting a plant–based lifestyle. Growing crops for direct human consumption is a far more efficient way to use our limited land and water resources compared to growing crops to feed meat and dairy animals. So, in the near future, eating plant–based meals will no longer be an option, it will become a necessity. A change is coming. You can either be part of the change, or be left behind.

There is a growing awareness in our society of how food choices affect human health, other creatures, and the environment. In June 2010, the United Nations recommended that a global shift toward a plant–based diet would prevent further global warning. In 2015, the World Health Organization classified the category of processed meats (bacon, sausage, hotdogs, salami, beef jerky, etc.) as a carcinogen, something that causes cancer.[2] These and other announcements are gradually helping to increase the awareness of the benefits of a plant–based diet, and the devastating effects of consuming meat, dairy, and eggs on our environment and our health. As more research comes to light and public awareness grows, masses of people will be converting to an entirely new way of eating. These people will have questions – questions about what it means to eat vegan, about nutrition, about how we got to our current SAD diet (Standard American Diet), about how to make the transition without giving up flavor, and about how to develop and maintain new and healthy eating habits. The Handbook to Higher Health Consciousness will help you explore answers to these questions as well as provide resources to support your journey to higher health consciousness.

Writing this book is a natural evolution of my journey towards a plant–based lifestyle. I changed to a vegan diet immediately after watching the compelling video, Forks over Knives, on Netflix in 2012. I did it primarily for health reasons, wanting to live to a healthy old age to enjoy my grandchildren. I immediately experienced the health benefit as weight loss, lower cholesterol levels, lower blood pressure, etc. I went from pre–diabetic to normal blood sugar levels. Yet, as I learned more, my eyes were opened to the far–reaching effects a change of diet can make. By eating plant–based, we are saving the lives and suffering of countless animals. We are also reducing the devastating effects that the animal agriculture industry has on our planet – deforestation, green house gas emission, water use, ocean pollution, and more. That's a lot of benefit from just being more purposeful about what we eat and a great motivator to investigate new ways of eating. The best part is that you can make the transition to more plant–based eating without feeling a sense of loss or deprivation. You can do it in a way that will make your taste buds sing and rejuvenate your body. I am passionate about sharing this knowledge with you.

As I researched healthy eating options, I also became aware of the huge economic and cultural forces that encourage people to mindlessly consume meat, dairy, eggs, and processed foods without thinking about the consequences. From a certain perspective, we as a people have subcontracted our meal preparation to companies whose primary purpose is to make a profit, with little or no consideration given to protecting or supporting our health. The issue of who controls our food is of paramount importance. It is too important to our health, the Earth, and the animals with which we share the planet to allow these influences to completely dictate our actions. This book is my contribution to help you break out of the mold and find your own path to a more healthy and sustainable, cruelty–free diet.

INTRODUCTION

I grew up in the 1950's as an all-American boy. I loved baseball with a passion. My friends and I played ball on the street, in a vacant lot, and in an organized league. I followed the Dodgers and collected and traded baseball cards. I participated in Cub Scouts and spent a lot of time outdoors with the YMCA. I was "blessed" with three younger sisters, and we fought and played, as kids are wont to do.

So, what were we eating in those days? My Mom was a serviceable cook, not with a lot of joy or passion, but she kept four kids and a husband fed. For dinners, we had spaghetti, salmon loaf, meatloaf, liver and onions (Yuck!), creamed tuna on toast, hamburgers, hotdogs, and lots of frozen TV dinners. Veggies and fruits were mostly canned or frozen. (Blah!) Breakfasts were mostly cereal or eggs, but Dad would sometimes whip up waffles or pancakes. Holiday meals and barbecues centered around meat: turkey, beef patties, sausage, hot dogs, ham, etc. Dinners out included Chinese food, pizza, barbecue, and burgers. My favorite meal was a Bob's Big Boy hamburger, Silver Goblet milkshake, French fries, and, of course, the tiny token salad with Thousand Island dressing.

My childhood eating habits laid the groundwork for my eating preferences as an adult. Your experience growing up with food may have been similar, or very different. Either way, the foods you ate growing up have a strong influence on your food preferences now. Your experiences helped to shape your individual food comfort zone. This comfort zone was also influenced by the attitudes and culture that you internalized from your family, friends, and community. These people were your food mentors. If you were raised in a primarily Hispanic community, you are more apt to be comfortable and familiar with refried beans, rice, and enchiladas. If your background was East Indian, your tastes will likely run toward Dahl, lamb dishes, curry, etc. If Chinese, rice, stir–fry, etc. You get the idea.

If your family and friends influenced your food comfort zone, who or what influenced your food mentors? Certainly, strong cultural traditions and foods were a factor, but changes in the way food was produced also played a part. As the food industry evolved in the mid-1900s, your mentors were influenced by increasing promotion and availability of meat, dairy, and eggs. They were also influenced by the lure of prepackaged convenience foods, addictive fast foods, and processed foods laced with sugar, fat, and salt. With the limited nutritional knowledge at the time, there was little to steer consumers away from these products, and plenty of advertising dollars to encourage them to eat convenience foods. Your food mentors developed habits based on readily available foods. They passed down their food traditions, you internalized them, and your body became conditioned to a particular style of eating.

Our collective individual experiences with food have culminated in what has become known as the SAD diet (Standard American Diet), or in some contexts, it is called the Western Diet. It refers to a diet rich in animal proteins and fats, and high in processed foods, cholesterol, and saturated fats. It is also generally low in fiber, complex carbohydrates, and vegetables. Unfortunately, this diet has led to rampant increase in obesity, heart disease, cancer, diabetes, and a host of other maladies. The SAD diet is ingrained in the psyche of those of us who grew up with it. Yet, it is in direct opposition to our current knowledge of healthy nutrition. The preponderance of scientific evidence indicates that the healthiest diet to mitigate all of these health issues is a whole food plant–based diet, one that is free of all animal products including meat, fish, dairy, and eggs.

With that knowledge in mind, you have a tough decision to make. Do you stick with your comfortable and traditional diet and risk progressive health issues, or do you give up all your favorite foods and settle for salads and broccoli in the name of better health? The good news is that you don't have to make that choice. There is another path. You can have delicious plant–based versions of your favorite foods. You can eat foods that you enjoy without sacrificing your health. And as your taste buds, eating habits, and knowledge evolve, you can move toward a more whole food plant–based diet. The benefits are compelling: flavorful food, better health, more energy, more clarity, less dependence on medications, and the comforting knowledge that you are contributing to reducing the suffering of animals as well as helping the environment.

This book is designed to guide you through the transition by redefining and expanding your food comfort zone. The goal is to always stay in your food comfort zone, and keep refining that zone as you continue to move toward an optimally healthy diet.

A major factor in your ability to transform your diet is motivation. Think about why you want to improve the way you eat. Is it to protect the environment, protect animals, improve your health, or all three? Whatever the reason, the more clear you are on your reason(s), the stronger your resolve will be. And while we are on the subject of clarity, being clear on your life's purpose can also affect the success of your journey as you develop and refine your healthy diet. If you are very clear on your mission in life, you will be highly motivated to achieve it, and you will need a vibrant and healthy body with lots of energy to support you in achieving that mission. Whereas, a body that is constantly fighting chronic disease and low in energy will inhibit you from pursuing your goals. So, spend some time, if necessary, to get clear on your life's mission. There are plenty of resources to help with the process. Search online for *Life on Purpose* or check out Chapter 7, Envision a New Mission, in *I'm Still Alive, Now What?!?* (on Kindle and Amazon) by Donna H. Kater.

We start in chapter 1 with a discussion of why people choose to eat a plant–based diet. Chapter 2 discusses how changing your diet can also change your awareness of both personal and planetary health. Chapter 3 addresses the nutritional aspects of eating plant–based. It reviews some of the key research and describes how to get all the nutrition you need to thrive. Chapter 4 discusses daily health and the healthcare industry. Chapter 5 is the crux of the matter. It describes ways to transition to a more healthy diet while maintaining your food comfort level. Chapter 6 describes numerous techniques to maintain a plant–based lifestyle for the long term. Chapter 7 introduces recipe–free cooking, which can help you change your focus from transitional products to whole foods. Chapter 8 has over 160 recipes and templates to help you prepare delicious and nutritious plant–based dishes. Chapter 9 provides resources for you to further your own knowledge and get support as you transition to a new eating style.

CHAPTER 1: WHY EAT A PLANT-BASED DIET?

A person who eats a vegan diet saves:
1,100 gallons of water,
45 pounds of grain,
30 square feet of forested land,
20 pounds CO$_2$ equivalent,
1 animal's life . . .
EVERY DAY!

– cowspiracy.com/facts/

There are many paths that can lead a person to embrace a vegan or a plant–based diet. The reasons are personal, largely influenced by an individual's life experiences as well as the timing of when they become aware of certain knowledge. Even though each person's journey is unique, there are similarities, and we will discuss those similarities in this chapter. Before we go any further, it will be helpful to clarify the difference between a plant–based diet and a vegan diet.

A whole food, plant–based (WFPB) diet is one that focuses on plant foods such as vegetables, fruit, legumes, grains, nuts, and seeds. It does not include any animal products such as meat, fish, butter, milk, eggs, cheese, or any other animal by–products. A WFBP diet recognizes that the combination of nutrients in whole plant foods act synergistically to nourish our bodies and protect us from disease. Whole foods contain phytonutrients, vitamins, minerals, fiber, and healthy fats. Processed foods strip off many of these nutrients in favor of shelf–stable, highly addictive foods. Heavily processed foods deplete healthful nutrients and concentrate on sugar, salt, and fat. As a result, a WFPB diet does not include any processed foods or any highly refined food such as refined sugar, bleached flour, and oil.

A vegan diet is similar, but the focus is generally less on eating whole–food plants and more on abstaining from eating any animal products. A vegan diet is less restrictive in a sense, because anything that does not contain animal products is considered vegan. An Oreo cookie, for example, is vegan, but you would never consider it as part of a whole food, plant–based meal. Similarly plant–based meats and cheeses are made without animal products. They are vegan, but they are processed to a certain extent and therefore don't fit into the whole food, plant–based category.

Being a vegan is more than just dietary choices. Veganism is deeply rooted in respect for animal rights, and it rejects the notion that sentient animals can be considered as a commodity. Full–fledged vegans not only exclude animal products from their plates, but also from their entire life. They exclude any products made from animals (leather, fur, wool, and silk), cosmetics that are tested on animals, and honey (made by bees).

According to a growing body of research, a well–managed whole food plant–based diet is the optimal diet for human health. In many cases, it is even more cost–effective than using medications.[1] By contrast, a vegan diet can range from very unhealthy to extremely healthy. It all depends on the food choices. The more processed foods, sugar, fat, and oils contained in a vegan diet, the less healthy it is. Yet, as these products are replaced by more whole food plant–based options, the healthier the diet becomes. This is the key – to crowd the less nutritious foods off your plate with more healthy options.

For the purposes of this book, we will view a vegan diet as a vital part of our transition away from the problematic Standard American Diet as we journey toward a whole food, plant–based diet.

Next, we look at some of the major reasons that people change to a plant–based diet.

Optimal Health

"Most deaths in the United States are preventable and related to nutrition."[2] According to the most rigorous analysis of risk factors ever published, the number one cause of both death and disability in the US is our diet. This replaced tobacco smoking as number one.[3]

So, if most deaths in the US are related to nutrition, what can we do about it? The verdict is in. The overwhelming evidence of scientific studies shows that eating a whole food plant–based diet is the best way to optimize your health. Not only that, countless individuals have cured themselves of life–threatening diseases such as cancer, heart disease, and diabetes by converting to a plant–based diet.

The food you eat can be either the safest & most powerful form of medicine
or the slowest form of poison.

— *Ann Wigmore*

Improved health and living a long life was my primary motivation to convert to a plant–based diet. I'd watched my parents and others suffer from chronic diseases. *Forks Over Knives* and other documentaries helped me realize that diet and lifestyle play a huge part in the development of these diseases. Chronic diseases are not preordained by our genetics, nor are they a required part of aging. The good news is that you **can** eat your way to good health.

What you eat every day is a far more powerful determinant of your health
than your DNA or most of the nasty chemicals lurking in your environment.

– *T. Colin Campbell*

Here are some sample studies. A study published in 2013 of over 73,000 participants compared mortality rates over nearly 6 years of 5 dietary patterns: non–vegetarian, semi–vegetarian, pesco–vegetarian, lacto–ovo–vegetarian, and vegan. All vegetarian groups had significantly lower mortality rates than the non–vegetarians. The vegans had significantly reduced risk of mortality in men for cardiovascular disease, ischemic heart disease, and all–cause mortality, and in both genders for "other" mortality.[4]

A 2003 study compared body mass index (BMI) of 38,000 participants over 6 years in four dietary patterns: meat–eaters, fish–eaters, vegetarians, and vegans. The age–adjusted mean BMI was significantly different between the four groups. The meat–eaters had the highest BMI and the vegans had the lowest, in both sexes.[5]

As you can see from these and other studies, eating vegan generally makes managing your weight easier. Vegans typically consume much less fat, especially saturated fat, than meat and dairy eaters. Those who eat a whole food plant–based diet (without processed foods) will naturally consume fewer calories and lose weight as a byproduct of healthy eating. Vegan foods are naturally high in fiber, something you don't get consuming meat or dairy. Fiber is filling, so a fiber–rich diet causes you to feel full sooner, and therefore consume fewer calories. Fiber also helps keep your internal plumbing clean and in working order. If weight loss is your goal, keep in mind that that you have to eat responsibly. Many processed foods are technically vegan, but if you eat nothing but sugary treats, fried veggies, and junk food, weight loss is simply not going to happen. Even if you eat unhealthy processed foods in addition to healthy food, your chances of weight loss are slim to none.

The health benefits of a plant–based diet are nicely summed up in The Plant–Based Diet booklet, produced by Kaiser Permanente, the nation's largest health care provider:[6]

- Lower cholesterol, blood pressure, and blood sugar
- Reversal or prevention of heart disease
- Longer life
- Healthier weight
- Lower risk of cancer and diabetes
- May slow the progression of certain types of cancer
- Improved symptoms of rheumatoid arthritis
- Fewer medications
- Lower food costs
- Good for the environment

The evidence for a plant–based diet being healthy is compelling and getting stronger all the time. It's the reason I changed my diet. I watched my parents, relatives, and even the general public increasingly struggle with obesity and a host of chronic diseases. Once I realized that most of these diseases are diet–related, the decision to change my eating habits was a no-brainer. The best part of deciding to eat more plant–based foods is that it has multiple benefits. It is healthier, it saves animals, and it helps the environment. The cherry on top, so to speak, is that the meals are tasty and satisfying.

I don't think I'll ever grow old and say, "What was I thinking eating all those fruits and vegetables?"
— *Nancy S. Mure*

Environment

Becoming vegan is the most important and direct change we can immediately make to save the planet and its species.

– *Chris Hedges*

It may seem like a stretch to think that what we eat every day can have much of an impact on the environment, but if you look more closely, the connection becomes crystal clear. Diet is not the only cause of the environmental issues we face today, but it is a major contributor and one that we can readily address. Let's look at the big picture.

We are all shepherds of planet Earth. It's up to all of us to sustain and nurture the planet. Unfortunately, there are three major problems that threaten to undermine our efforts to be good caretakers.

1. *Overpopulation.* There are approximately 7.5 billion people on the planet in 2017. That means there are three times as many people today as there were in 1950. The number of people on the planet is growing exponentially, and they all need to be fed.
2. *Overconsumption.* The global economy is based on massive consumption, yet we have finite resources to meet that demand. We burn fossil fuels at an alarming rate to power our excessive lifestyles.
3. *Food Choices.* Food choices that include meat, dairy, eggs, fish, and highly processed foods are unsustainable and put a burden on our resources. The typical Western diet requires over ten times as much land, water, and energy to produce the same number of calories as a plant–based diet.[7]

Overpopulation and overconsumption are enormous problems that could take centuries to resolve. However, the environmental impact of food choices is something on which each of us can have an immediate effect by simply eating more plant–based foods. It is really that simple. All we need to do is eat less animal products and more plants. In fact, a single individual can have an enormous impact. For example, it is estimated that it requires 1,000 gallons of water to produce the food that the typical American eats in one day. Yet, it only requires 400 gallons of water to produce the food that a person on a vegan diet eats in one day. That's a savings of 600 gallons of water every single day, just for one person.[8] Beef in particular has an overall water footprint of roughly 4 million gallons per ton produced compared to 85 thousand gallons per ton for vegetables. That's 47 times as much water used to produce beef as it takes to produce an equivalent weight of vegetables![9]

And it is not just water usage that is affected by the consumption of animal products. "… the livestock sector is a major stressor on many ecosystems and on the planet as whole. Globally it is one of the largest sources of greenhouse gases and one of the leading causal factors in the loss of biodiversity, while in developed and emerging countries it is perhaps the leading source of water pollution."[10] Regarding greenhouse gases, in 2010, UNESCO reported that "at least 51 percent of human induced greenhouse gas emissions" are attributable to livestock production.[11] Furthermore, raising animals for food is the leading global cause of rainforest destruction, species extinction, and ocean dead zones. [12, 13, 14, 15, 16]

To put the enormity of the issue created by our global food choices in perspective, consider this assessment from the Global Footprint Network. Our planet can only support a total of two billion people based on the lifestyle of the average European, and only one billion people based on the consumption level of the average American. Since there are currently 7.5 billion people on the Earth and counting, we have to find another way to feed the population without devastating the planet.[17]

Once you see the connection between food choices and the health of the planet, it's easy to see why so many people are inspired to adopt a plant–based lifestyle. Luckily, the same diet that can reverse climate change, end world hunger, and enable us to return billions of acres of farmland to more productive purposes is the same diet that can prevent or reverse most of our chronic diseases and reduce the needless suffering of animals. That diet is a whole food, plant–based diet.

Animals

*Veganism is not about giving anything up or losing anything;
it is about gaining the peace within yourself
that comes from embracing nonviolence and
refusing to participate in the exploitation of the vulnerable.*

– *Gary L. Francione*

For some people, reducing the suffering of animals is perhaps the most compelling reason of all to eat a WFPB diet. Animals raised for food are sentient beings. They suffer and are destined for an early death, even if they are raised in a "humane" setting rather than on a factory farm. The suffering is an integral part of the process, whether it is on a beef farm, dairy farm, or egg farm. There are plenty of films on Netflix that document this suffering as well websites like peta.org. Once you see videos of the cruel way "food" animals are treated, the choice becomes very simple. Either you eat meat, dairy, and eggs, and therefore condone and participate in the cruel treatment and killing of animals in the industrialized agribusiness, or you don't. Being healthy is not just about the food we eat. It is also about our conscious awareness of how our food choices affect spaceship Earth and our fellow passengers.

Cost

Before vitamins were discovered in 1912, it was common practice to consider food cost on a cost–per–calorie basis. It seemed reasonable at the time. The concept of a calorie and the need for calories in the human diet was well established in the early 1800s, so why not obtain the most calories you can for the least cost? It doesn't take more than a cursory glance at the highly processed foods available nowadays that are packed with calories (but devoid of nutrition) to realize that cost–per–calorie is no longer a useful measure of food quality. As our knowledge of nutrition has progressed over the decades, it has become evident that we should consider food cost on a cost–per–nutrition basis. By that measure, vegetables offer about six times more nutrition per dollar when you compare them to highly processed foods. Similarly, vegetables offer about three times more nutrition per dollar when compared to meat. So, eating plant based is a very efficient way to spend your food dollar and get the nutrition you need.

Inspiration (Because you want to look like Michelle Pfeiffer)

My intrepid research has uncovered yet another reason that people (mostly women) will want to eat a vegan or plant–based diet, namely to look like Michelle Pfeiffer, of course! In an interview with Urbanette, Michelle is asked about the secret of the incredible glow about her and her healthy–looking skin. She says, "Thank you! I definitely think it's because I'm vegan. Eating a vegan diet – it's just so much healthier – and you avoid a lot of toxins that could age your skin and your body. I really noticed a difference in my skin not too long after switching to fully vegan." Michelle saw Bill Clinton talking about the last heart attack that he had before becoming a vegan. She got inspired and followed up by reading a book by Dr. Esselstyn about the health benefits of eating a plant–based diet. The science was so compelling, that she gave herself eight weeks to try it out. The results were so great that it became her permanent lifestyle.

So, Michelle was inspired by Bill, and she in turn inspires others. Inspiration seems to be the key. Most of the people I've interviewed have something in common with Michelle. There was a pivotal moment in which they were touched by someone, something, some idea, an article, a website, or a documentary. It hit them at just the right time (when a parent developed dementia, a friend had a stroke, or they received a diagnosis of cancer in their body). It made such an impact that they made the decision to change their eating habits. Some, implemented the change right away, and others are still on the path of change.

I was inspired by one of the tutors at San Diego City College who lost 120 pounds over the course of a year or so. Every week, she kept looking healthier and more vibrant. When I finally asked her how she did it, she summed it up succinctly: "Watch Forks over Knives on Netflix." So, my wife and I sat down that night and watched. We were moved by the enormity of the health issues facing this country. We were convinced by the evidence presented in the documentary about the direct link between the Western diet and the present health epidemic. This link between diet and health was very obvious in the health issues experienced by our parents, family, and friends. We were encouraged by the efficacy of a plant–based diet to protect against chronic disease, and in some cases, reverse the damage and restore health. We looked at each other after absorbing the implications of the film, and immediately decided to start eating vegan. That was it. We never looked back.

There are plenty of sources for inspiration: scores of celebrities, books, documentary films, etc. If you want some moving stories, do an online search for "why I went vegan." For more inspiration, search for vegan athletes online. You'll be amazed at the top–notch athletes that eat nothing but plants. More than likely, you are already inspired. If not, find the thing that sparks your inspiration.

Is a Whole Food Plant–Based Diet for Everyone?

The simple answer is yes; it's the best evidence–based diet there is. However, that doesn't mean just avoiding animal products will guarantee you instant health. It's a crucial step, but there is more to it. If you load up on refined sugar, processed oil, and highly processed plant–based foods, you'll be eating "vegan," but not doing your body any favors. So, you need to eat a well–rounded diet consisting mainly of whole foods. And you need to balance your diet so that you receive an adequate amount of some key ingredients: vitamin B–12, calcium, vitamin D, iodine, etc. You may need to take supplements for some of these. These special nutrients and more are discussed in Chapter 3.

The most important factor in choosing what to eat is that each of us has unique and specific dietary needs. So, the best diet for you will be tailored to meet your individual requirements. For example, some people report difficulties with wheat/gluten, soy, or certain types of nuts. If you have sensitivity to any types of food, you need to limit or exclude these items from your plate. Part of your transition will be to experiment with different types of food to see what works best for your body and what doesn't. If necessary, you can get tested for food allergies. Consult with a health care specialist for specific advice, preferably one trained in integrative or functional medicine.

The other key factor is adopting a diet that satisfies you so that you will stick with it through thick and thin (hopefully thin). The ultimate goal for optimal health is a whole food plant–based diet, but there is definitely a learning curve to fashioning a diet that satisfies your appetite and fits your lifestyle. As you move toward that goal, you may include transitional vegan foods such as mock meats and non-dairy cheese to help you maintain you food comfort level. This was a key factor in my first exposure to eating vegan – the ready availability of transitional "unmeats" and "uncheeses" made it very easy to eat comfortably without missing a beat. As your comfort level increases, your palate adjusts, and your food preparation skills improve, you can incorporate more whole–food plants into your diet.

Realize that discovering your ideal diet is a journey. Be patient, and don't demand perfection. Take each positive step toward your goal as a success.

Focus on progress, not perfection.

– Josh Bezoni

What about other Diets?

Low–Carb Diets

Americans love to hear good things about their bad habits.

– T. Colin Campbell

People want to indulge in their pleasure behaviors without paying the price. Weight loss diets are often designed to take advantage of this human propensity. There are plenty of other diets – Atkins, Low–Carb, High–Fat (LCHF), Paleo, Ketogenic, Zone, South Beach, and more. Most of these are low–carb, high–fat, high animal–protein diets designed for weight loss, rather than improving your health. The entire diet industry is based on one thing: weight loss. As of 2012, there were 108 million people on a diet in the US, generating $20 billion annually for the weight–loss industry.[18] A low carbohydrate diet can induce weight loss for a few reasons. First, reducing the amount of processed foods containing refined carbohydrates will encourage weight loss. Second, reducing carbohydrates can reduce the overall calorie intake. The problem is that this weight loss is usually temporary, and low–carb diets are detrimental to your health. These diets usually result in high fat intake which overloads our systems and deposits unwanted fat in our liver, pancreas, and muscles, leading to diabetes. Low–carb diets are associated with higher death rates.[19]

The other problem with these diets is that our bodies have evolved to derive a significant portion of our calories from complex carbohydrates. This goes back to ancient times, when man began to cultivate a variety of healthy grains. Quinoa was a staple of the Inca culture. Amaranth was a cornerstone of the Aztec culture. Whole wheat and kasha sustained early Europeans. Quinoa and chia were also consumed in the Americas. The Egyptians cultivated farro (emmer). Asians cultivated rice. So, restricting your carbohydrate intake deprives your body of the primary fuel it has come to rely on for energy.

For me, one of the most compelling reasons for choosing a plant–based diet over the other diet choices is that it's the only diet that's ever been proven to reverse heart disease (the number one killer in the US) in the majority of patients. As a bonus, it is also easier to maintain, and it has been shown to prevent and treat a host of other leading killer diseases.[20]

Diets in the Blue Zones

It is extraordinarily important for us today to replace the prevailing image and reality of aging with a new vision – one in which we grasp the possibility of living all our days with exuberance and passion.

– John Robbins

The other thing worth considering when selecting a diet is what the healthiest and longest–lived people on the planet are eating. Doesn't it make sense to find out what they are eating and learn from them? That's exactly what John Robbins does in his book *Healthy at 100*. He investigates four distinctly different cultures around the world in which people live extremely long and healthy lives. These regions are often called *Blue Zones*. Robbins examines the factors for the longevity of people living in these Blue Zones. Their diets are largely whole foods, mostly complex carbs, little protein, and less fat. They consume very few processed foods. Some consume meat or dairy, but in very small amounts. They also get plenty of physical exercise, and lead active social lives within their families and communities. In other words, instead of suffering through their old age with debilitating diseases afflicted by dementia, these people are living rich and healthy lives, fully engaged right up to the end. That's a blueprint that I want to follow. If you want to be healthy, active, and vibrant in your 90s and 100s, this is a good lifestyle to emulate.[21]

Let's take a closer look at what they ate. As it turns out, the best–documented diets are also those of the most long–lived people. These are the people of Okinawa, the largest island of the Ryukyu Islands in Japan. The Okinawans are known for their high number of centenarians, long life expectancy, and very low incidence of age–associated diseases. Their dietary patterns are well documented, largely due to regular population surveys administered by local government. I will focus on the dietary patterns starting back in 1949, before the Western influence started affecting their diets in the 1960s.

The traditional Okinawan diet is low in calories (1785 calories per day), yet nutritionally dense. In particular, it is rich in phytonutrients (from plants) in the form of antioxidants and flavonoids. Overall, the Okinawans obtained 85% of their calories from complex carbohydrates, 9% from protein, and 6% from fat. Compared to the Western diet, the Okinawan diet is low calorie, low protein, and low fat.

The major sources of calories in their diet in 1949 were:[22]

FOOD	PERCENT OF TOTAL CALORIES
Sweet potatoes	69%
Other vegetables	3%
Rice	12%
Other grains	7%
Legumes	6%
Oils	2%
Fish	1%

The following foods each contributed less than 1% of total calories: nuts and seeds, sugar, meat, eggs, dairy, fruit, seaweed, flavorings, and alcohol.

Comparing the dietary intake of Okinawans with other Japanese circa 1950 highlights some of the significant differences that may account for their longevity. The Okinawans consumed: fewer total calories, less polyunsaturated fat, less rice, significantly less wheat, barley and other grains, less sugars, more legumes such as soy and other beans, significantly less fish, significantly less meat and poultry, less eggs, less dairy, tremendously more sweet potatoes, less other potatoes, less fruit, no pickled vegetables, and significantly less flavors and alcohol.

Food Consumed	Okinawans	Other Japanese
Total calories	1785	2068
Polyunsaturated fat (% of calories)	4.8%	8%
Rice	154g	328g
Wheat, barley, and other grains	38g	153g
Sugars	3g	8g
Legumes (Soy and other beans)	71g	55g
Fish	15g	62g
Meat and poultry	3g	11g
Eggs	1g	7g
Dairy	<1g	8g
Sweet potatoes	849g	66g
Other potatoes	2g	47g
Fruit	<1g	44g
Pickled vegetables	0g	42g
Flavorings and alcohol	7g	31g

The things that stand out from this comparison are the low overall number of calories, the very low consumption of animal products (meat, fish, dairy, eggs), and the astonishing amount of sweet potatoes. Sweet potatoes accounted for 849 grams of the 1262 grams of food that they consumed, which constituted 69% of their total calories.[23] I definitely ramped up the amount of sweet potatoes in my diet after learning about these amazing people. As you read the chapters on nutrition and health in this book, you'll see how this diet dovetails nicely with the recommendations of proponents of the whole food plant–based diet.

Eat Right for your Blood Type Diet

Another diet worth mentioning is the Eat Right for your Blood Type diet. It is not one of the high–fat diet spin–offs, but it gained considerable attention when it first came out in 1996, and still has some adherents. The book "Eat Right for Your Type" by Peter D'Adamo promotes the idea people should eat foods compatible with their blood type. It sounds intriguing, yet it doesn't hold up to scientific scrutiny. A literature review published in 2013 found that no evidence exists to validate the purported health benefits of blood type diets.[24] Even Wikipedia states that the consensus among dietitians, physicians, and scientists is that the diet is unsupported by scientific evidence. D'Amato and his publisher are rebuked for being deeply irresponsible and unethical to give readers the impression that blood type diets can cure or slow down deadly diseases in the article "Fakes and Frauds in Commercial Diets" in the Scandinavian Journal of Nutrition.[25] According to the article "Blood Type Diet Debunked", D'Amato claimed to be working on two scientific trials, one to show that the diet plays a role in cancer remission, the other to determine its effects on rheumatoid arthritis. Neither study has been published.[26]

Follow the blood type diet if you feel so moved, but I'm putting my money on the whole food plant–based diet as the way enlightened people will eat in the future.

Toxic Cleanse

Although it is not a diet per se, there is a lot of talk and marketing of products for removing toxins from our bodies. These products are sold on the premise that toxic chemicals build up in the liver and kidneys, and contribute to an array of symptoms and diseases. While it is true that our bodies are constantly exposed to a huge variety of natural and synthetic chemicals, it is also true that our bodies have evolved extensive defense mechanisms to counteract these unwanted substances. The liver plays a major role in combating this toxic invasion. Our kidneys, gastrointestinal system, lymphatic system, and our skin also collaborate in defending us against and removing these unwanted substances. The liver converts fat–soluble toxins into water-soluble substances that can be excreted from the body. The kidneys excrete waste products into the urine. So, our body is constantly cleansing itself of toxins.

The best thing we can do to support our bodies efforts to remove toxins is support our liver's own detoxifying enzymes. And the best way to do this is to eat our cruciferous vegetables such as broccoli, kohlrabi, cauliflower, cabbage, and Brussels sprouts. The cells in these vegetables contain an enzyme called myrosinase and a substance called glucoraphanin. These two substances are stored separately within the cells of the vegetable. They do not come into contact. However, when the vegetable is chewed or chopped, these two combine to form the compound sulforaphane, which just happens to be the best–known stimulant to the liver's detoxifying enzymes. Broccoli is a prime source of these ingredients and fresh broccoli sprouts are even better. Just like Mom said, "*eat your broccoli*!" Sulforaphane formation and cruciferous vegetables are also discussed in Chapter 4.

But I'm Super Healthy. Why should I change my diet?

If you are eating the standard Western diet, your physical exam and/or blood test results might not be a reliable predictor of your future health. For example, your blood pressure and cholesterol levels may be considered "normal" for the average American, but that just means that you are likely to develop the same chronic diseases that the other "normal" Americans are developing at record rates. Think about what your family, friends, and co–workers eat, and the diseases that they deal with. The bottom line is that the Western diet virtually guarantees some form of disease. If not now, soon enough. No one escapes the ravages of the Western diet. The likely manifestation will be one or more of the following: heart disease, hypertension, diabetes, erectile dysfunction, stroke, obesity, dementia, rheumatoid arthritis, or multiple sclerosis, not to mention increased risk of breast, colon, prostate, ovarian, and uterine cancers. You will see evidence of the association of the Western diet with many of these diseases in subsequent chapters. The most effective way to prevent these diseases from developing into major health concerns is to begin the process now of transitioning to a whole food plant–based diet to safeguard your future health.

The journey toward eating a plant–based diet can be healthy, joyful, and full of new tastes and culinary experiences. Whether you choose to go 100% plant–based in a single day, or take a leisurely approach, keep your goal in mind and enjoy the health benefits along the way. Each meal is an opportunity to improve your health, feel great about your contribution to healing our planet, and save another animal from being bred for a life of mistreatment. It's an opportunity to feel the satisfaction of knowing that you have freed yourself from the influences of big money interests and outdated information, and that you have chosen your own enlightened path to better health.

CHAPTER 2: HIGHER HEALTH CONSCIOUSNESS

When you make the choice to eat plant–based foods, you will likely find that you get more than you bargain for. Yes, you will get all of the health benefits, but you may find a shift in your conscious awareness as well. It turns out that choosing to eat plant–based is also choosing to use less water, reduce pollution and land use, and reduce the suffering of animals. For example, it takes more than 2,400 gallons of water to produce 1 pound of beef whereas it requires only 244 gallons of water to produce a pound of tofu. Regarding our global warming, a mind–boggling 51 percent or more of global greenhouse gas emissions are caused by animal agriculture. As far as land use goes, it takes almost 20 times less land to feed someone on a plant–based diet then it does to feed a meat eater.[1] The average vegan saves nearly 200 animals per year from slaughter.[2] All these benefits of eating plant–based are interconnected. As you learn more, you will likely experience an elevated awareness of these related issues, and how your food choices have a very real impact. So your journey to better personal health is also a journey to higher health awareness, not only for your own health, but for the health of the planet as well.

Your journey to higher health consciousness is strikingly similar to that described by Ken Keyes, Jr., back in 1972 in his seminal work, Handbook to Higher Consciousness. The Handbook to Higher Consciousness describes 12 pathways to achieve a higher level of consciousness. These pathways are grouped into four categories: freeing yourself, being here now, interacting with others, and discovering your conscious–awareness. In transitioning to a plant–based diet you go through many of the same stages. For example, you free yourself from many of the addictions that you had relating to food. You become more aware of the here and now in every meal that you have. You take more personal responsibility in your food choices and reinventing your personal programming. You share your challenges with other people and connect with them for mutual support. You learn to perceive yourself and others as awakening beings who are on their own journey to higher health consciousness.

> *If humanity will one day grasp the importance of natural food,*
> *this will be the beginning of a new era in the history of human life;*
> *it will simply be the PARADISE.*
>
> — *Arshavir Ter Hovannessian*

But do we, as a nation, really need to have our health consciousness raised? Of course we do! The majority of people in America are still eating like they are stuck in the twentieth century. They do not seem to be aware that our knowledge about nutrition has advanced significantly since then. They are not aware that millions of animals are living in horrifying conditions and being slaughtered for food. They are not aware that producing meat, dairy, and eggs costs millions of gallons of water, and dumps toxic materials into our lands, our oceans, and the atmosphere. They are not aware of the devastation of our forests and the oceans due in large measure to our industrialized system of animal agriculture. They are not aware that many of our health issues can be prevented or even reversed by eating a plant–based diet. I can relate to all of that, because I was equally unaware of these things before I watched the documentary *Forks Over Knives* and decided to change my eating habits. It felt as if I had blinders on, and suddenly, they were removed. I made the connection between diet and prevention of disease. I became aware of the way food choices affect the environment and the animals sharing the planet with us. As I became more aware of the issues involved, it felt like a fog lifting.

Indeed, it feels like I've achieved a higher level of health consciousness, and I continue to learn more each day.

In this day and age, it may be difficult to imagine the health consciousness of an entire nation being raised, but that's exactly what Simon Amstell portrays in his 'mockumenary' "Carnage: Swallowing the Past" (2017).[3] It's an often funny, sometimes serious look back at our current carnivorous eating habits as viewed from the future. The film is set in 2067 Britain, where meat, eggs, and dairy have been outlawed. It explores how public consciousness evolves from 1944 to 2067, driven by natural disasters (caused by climate change), performance art works, protests, and films. Eventually, the message solidifies in the public consciousness, and carnism (the ideology that conditions people to eat animals) becomes a thing of the past. Even though this film is mostly fiction, the message is real, and the future it presents is worth pursuing. The direction of that future is up to each of us, every time we choose what we put on our plates, and vote with our dollars in the supermarket.

> *Carnage: Swallowing the Past* was available online at one point. It appears that it is available exclusively on BBC iPlayer as of 8/2017. Check online for changes in availability.

CHAPTER 3: NUTRITION AND HEALTH

Your body has incredible healing powers. It can fight off disease if properly nourished and heal itself from years of dietary abuse. All you need to do as the custodian of your body is supply it with water, air, and the right combination of nutrients. Your body will do the rest.

So, what is the right combination of nutrients? Certainly, there is no one exact combination of nutrients that is optimal for every person. Each individual lives in a unique environment and has a unique genetic makeup. Even so, the preponderance of scientific trials and studies point to a whole food, plant–based diet as the optimal way to provide our bodies with the nutrients they need while at the same time avoiding toxins, carcinogens, and other harmful ingredients contained in animal–based foods. As Dr. Michael Greger of NutritionFacts.org says, "A significant convergence of evidence suggests that plant–based diets can help prevent and even reverse some of the top killer diseases in the Western world and can be more effective than medication and surgery."[1]

Kaiser Permanente, the nation's largest managed–care provider, echoes this sentiment in a nutritional update to physicians in 2013. It states that eating healthy may be "best achieved with a plant–based diet, which we define as a regimen that encourages whole, plant–based foods and discourages meats, dairy products, and eggs as well as all refined and processed foods." . . . "Physicians should consider recommending a plant–based diet to all their patients, especially those with high blood pressure, diabetes, cardiovascular disease, or obesity."[2]

Benefits of a Vegan Diet

There are many health benefits to eating a vegan diet. We'll look at some of the major benefits here.

Effective for weight loss

More than two–thirds of adults in the US are considered to be overweight or obese.[3] An estimated 45 million Americans diet each year, spend about $33 billion annually on weight loss products.[4] Many diets strive for weight loss by either eliminating one or more of the essential food groups or recommending consumption of one type of food in excess at the expense of other foods. These diets work in the short run, but they are not sustainable. "It's now well established that the more people engage in dieting, the more they gain weight in the long–term."[5] What is needed is a long–term sustainable diet that provides your body with all the nutrients it needs and promotes weight loss as a natural byproduct.

In 2006, a review of 87 published studies concluded that a vegan or vegetarian diet is highly effective for weight loss.[6] Other studies show similar results.[7,8,9,10,11] The beauty of a WFPB diet is that it is a lifestyle change that can help you transform your overall health, lose weight, and keep it off. Chapter 5 addresses how to make the transition to a vegan diet, and Chapter 6 addresses how sustain the diet and lifestyle.

Prevention and Management of Diabetes

Diabetes is a disease that causes chronically elevated levels of sugar in your blood. Type 1 diabetes results in antibodies in your body attacking your pancreas gland, which causes it to make insufficient insulin. Type 2 diabetes results in your body becoming resistant to insulin's effects. Type 2 diabetes has been called the "Black Death of the twenty–first century." It is rapidly spreading throughout the world, and it has devastating health effects. It can lead to blindness, loss of limbs, kidney failure, heart attacks, and stroke. The prevalence of diagnosed diabetes increased from 1.6 million (0.93%) in 1958 to a staggering 23.4 million (7.4%) in 2015.[12] The cause of type 2 diabetes is high–fat and high–calorie diets. In that context, diabetes is a disease caused by lifestyle choices rather than an infection. So, type 2 diabetes is almost always preventable and sometimes reversible by making appropriate diet and lifestyle changes.

I got to see the effects of diet on diabetes in a very personal way. My 90–year–old mother–in–law, Fern, came to live with us for a time. She started eating a mostly plant–based diet. She initially required 10 units of insulin every night to manage her diabetic condition. As the plant–based diet took effect, we were able to adjust her levels of insulin downward (all under a doctor's care). By the end of two months, she was totally free of the nightly insulin medication. It was an amazing demonstration of the power of plants.

Several studies show that people on a plant–based diet have significantly less risk of developing diabetes compared to non–vegetarians. For example, a 2009 study involving more than 60,000 men and women showed that the prevalence of diabetes in people on a vegan diet was 2.9% compared with 7.6% of the non–vegetarians.[13] See the book "Dr. Neal Barnard's Program for Reversing Diabetes" for more information.

Prevention of Heart Disease

Coronary heart disease is a benign food borne illness which need never exist or progress.
– *Caldwell B. Esselstyn, Jr., MD*

Coronary heart disease is the number one killer disease in the United States. According to the Centers for Disease Control and Prevention (CDC), heart disease kills over six hundred thousand Americans every year. That's more deaths than all of our past wars combined, every single year!

This is a slow disease that takes decades to develop. For Americans on the standard Western diet, fatty deposits called atherosclerotic plaque accumulate over time in the coronary arteries. If this process goes unchecked, the plaque builds up and begins to restrict blood flow to the heart. This can lead to chest pain during physical activity. If the plaque ruptures, a blood clot can form, blocking the flow of blood and causing a heart attack. Further, regular ingestion of meat and eggs changes the composition of your gut bacteria. When you continue to eat these animal products, your gut bacteria process them and produce TMA (trimethylamine). Then your liver converts the TMA into TMAO (trimethylamine N–oxide). TMAO is nasty stuff. Several studies have shown elevated levels of circulating TMAO in people with cardiovascular disease. [14,15] Other studies have shown that TMAO directly contributes to the narrowing of artery walls through plaque build–up.[16] It doesn't take a lot of animal products to affect your long–term health. Eating as little as 1 egg per day can have a profound effect. In the landmark Harvard Nurses' Health Study, eating one egg a day appeared to reduce life expectancy about the same amount as smoking 5 cigarettes per day for fifteen years.[17]

Heart disease is not an inevitable consequence of aging. There are communities around the globe in which heart disease is virtually unknown. It has been shown that their 'immunity' is not due to genetics, but due to very low cholesterol levels. They eat primarily plant–based foods such as grains and vegetables. Their diet is high in fiber and low in animal fat so that their total cholesterol levels averaged less than 150 mg/dL.[18,19] This is also what you expect for anyone who eats a primarily plant–based diet.

The insidious thing about heart disease is that there may be no external symptoms. You may be going about your usual business, and then suddenly have a coronary event. The alarming thing is that a 1981 study of American children found that the first stages of atherosclerosis were already present in nearly all children by age ten.[20] This has huge implications for those of us who are adults that grew up eating a standard Western diet. It means that we already have the beginnings of heart disease. Thus, our dietary goal should not be to prevent heart disease, but to reverse the heart disease that we already have. It's a sobering thought.

Is it even possible to reverse heart disease? Amazingly, the answer is yes! A study published in 1990 showed that 82% of the patients who adopted a plant–based regimen exhibited regression of their atherosclerosis.[21] Other studies show similar reduction of heart disease and death rates for those following a primarily plant–based diet.[22] Two long–range studies were conducted by Dr. Caldwell Esselstyn, who has been associated with the Cleveland Clinic since 1968. Esselstyn's studies showed that plant–based eating could help arrest and reverse heart disease in severely ill patients. In the first study published in 1995, 24 patients followed a plant–based diet with 10% of the calories derived from fat. They eliminated oil, and took cholesterol–lowering medication on an individual basis. Eighteen of the patients adhered to the diet during the 5–year study, and the disease was arrested in these patients, and even reversed in several patients. All but one of these patients were still following the program 7 years after the study. None of these patients experienced any coronary events or interventions. These are the same patients who had experienced 49 coronary events in the 8 years prior to the study. In the second study published in 2014, nearly 200 patients participated and confirmed the results of the initial study.[23]

Reduced Blood Pressure

High blood pressure kills nine million people worldwide every year.[24] It contributes to deaths in a number of ways including heart attacks, heart failure, kidney failure, and stroke. As with so many of the chronic diseases that we face in America, high blood pressure is a choice. If you eat a high-sodium, high-cholesterol Western diet, you increase the likelihood of having high blood pressure, especially as you age. Yet, if you adopt a low-sodium plant–based diet, you reduce your risk significantly. 1,800 Kenyans who followed a healthy plant–based lifestyle were studied over two years. There were no cases of high blood pressure.[25] None. And it is definitely possible to reduce high blood pressure in preexisting cases. A 1984 study examined patients who suffered from essential hypertension (high blood pressure) for an average of 8 years. All patients were receiving long–term medication for the hypertension. They were prescribed a vegan diet for one year. At the end of the year, all patients reported improvement. There was a significant decrease in systolic and diastolic blood pressure. In most cases, medication was no longer necessary or at least drastically reduced.[26]

An important aspect of managing your blood pressure is limiting sodium intake. It is well established that excess sodium increases blood pressure, because it holds excess fluid in the body. That creates an added burden on the heart. The body responds by raising your blood pressure to flush the excess fluid and salt out of your system. The American Heart Association recommends less than 1,500 mg of sodium daily. The average American adult consumes about 3,500 mg daily.[27] Why do we have this huge discrepancy? For one thing, salt is increasingly infused into virtually every kind of prepackaged food on the market. For another, salt can be addictive. It triggers the release of dopamine in the brain, giving our bodies a strong reward sensation.[28] Once you eat one potato chip laced with salt, your brain goads you into having more and more. On the other hand, we really don't need that much salt on a daily basis. The National Heart Lung and Blood Association reports that 500 mg is a safe daily minimum intake of sodium. That's one-third of the AHA recommendation! Furthermore, in an average climate, a normal adult may be able to thrive on as little as 115 mg of sodium each day.[29]

How can you lower your salt intake? First and foremost, avoid eating processed foods. Minimize dining out, or at least request low sodium dishes when you dine out. At home, don't add salt at the table. In fact, don't add salt when cooking. That may sound strange, but your tastes will adjust in time. You can compensate by adding any number of other delightful flavorings: onions, garlic, pepper, basil, lemon, chili powder, curry, etc. There is a wonderful book, *The Vegetarian Flavor Bible,* by Karen Page that pulls together favorite flavorings from leading experts for almost any vegetable, fruit, or other ingredient. You can also find flavor matches by searching online, and vegancoach.com has some great flavor matching recommendations. You can infuse your meals with rich flavor with little or no salt. By eating a varied diet of vegetables, fruit, beans, lentils, nuts, and seeds with low oil, the average person will get all the sodium required, without being exposed to the risks associated with high blood pressure. Your taste buds will adjust to taste the natural flavor of food without needing additional salt.

Prevention of Cancer

Cancer is a killer. No doubt about it. There are so many types of cancer (lung, digestive, liver, blood, kidney, breast, melanoma of the skin, prostate, . . .), it's hard to keep track of them all. Collectively, these cancers killed an estimated 595,690 Americans in 2016.[30] In fact, since 1999, cancer has surpassed heart disease as the primary cause of death for Americans younger than age 85.[31] The good news is that eating a healthy plant–based diet significantly reduces the risk of all types of cancer. Numerous studies are emerging to confirm this. A 2009 study at Oxford followed 60,000 people for 12 years. It found that those who consumed a plant–based diet were less likely to develop all forms of cancer.[32] In 2016, a comprehensive meta–analysis of 96 studies concluded that a vegan diet significantly reduced the risk of total cancer.[33]

One of the ways that a vegan diet can reduce the risk of cancer is by reducing the levels of a cancer–promoting growth hormone known as insulin–like growth factor 1 or IGF–1. High levels of IGF–1 signal the body to produce more cells. This is natural and necessary during childhood and puberty when you need to transition from about ten trillion cells to about forty trillion cells as an adult. But once you reach adulthood, the levels of IGF–1 normally diminish so that you maintain approximately the same number of cells throughout your adult life. However, the consumption of animal protein can trigger the release of IGF–1[34] The more IGF–1 in your bloodstream, the higher your risk of developing cancers.[35,36] The key to counteracting this effect is to eat a diet devoid of protein from any animal source, including meat, dairy, and eggs. Reducing the consumption of animal protein reduces the levels of IGF–1.[37]

Note that a diet too high in plant proteins can also raise your IGF–1 levels. That's why the goal of this book is to help you move through the transitional phase toward a more WFPB diet. Be cautious about including too many meat substitutes and other high–protein plant foods in your diet.

Reduced Risk of Death

One of the great benefits of eating plant based is the chance to have a longer, healthier life. A study published in the British Medical Journal concluded that lifelong vegans in the study had 57 percent reduced risk of death from heart disease.[38]

A massive study of over 130,000 participants over 26 years revealed that **every 3 percent increase** in calories from plant protein (vs. animal protein) reduced the risk of death from all causes (any of the major diseases) by 10 percent.[39] This is impressive. It means that participants who increased their plant protein by 6 percent (instead of eating animal protein), reduced their risk of death by 20 percent. Similarly, participants who increased their plant protein by 9 percent, reduced their risk of death by 30%.

Macronutrients and their Functions

There are three essential macronutrients that the body needs in large quantities to supply calories for primary functions: growth, reproduction, and metabolism. These are carbohydrates, protein, and fat. Water is not generally considered a macronutrient, but it is included here because it is the nutrient we consume most (by volume), and it is essential to maintaining and developing a healthy body.

Water

Most of the major systems in your body depend on water. Water dissolves minerals and other nutrients. It carries nutrients and oxygen to cells and removes waste through urine. Water regulates body temperature, and protects body organs and tissues. It lubricates joints and moistens tissues. Water is essential for human health. Inadequate hydration can lead to a host of unpleasant conditions such as kidney failure, muscle cramps, headache, and gout.

The Institute of Medicine recommends 15 cups of daily water intake for the average adult male and 11 cups for the average adult female. These numbers are meant to include water obtained from all beverages (water, coffee, tea, soda, juice) as well as the moisture content in the foods we consume. Most of our water intake comes from beverages, but about 20% comes from the food we eat, because many food items are full of water. That makes the recommended amount of beverages about 12 cups for men, and 9 cups for women. Again, that includes all beverages, not just water. If you are eating a plant–based diet with lot of fruits and vegetables, you will obtain an even larger percentage of your water from your food, and therefore need to consume fewer beverages.

The amount of water required will vary with several external factors. You may need to increase your water intake depending on the following conditions: level of physical exercise, hot or humid weather, illness, pregnancy, or breast–feeding.

A few guidelines will help you stay properly hydrated.

- Drink a glass of water one–half hour before or after each meal.
- Drink water before, during, and after exercise
- Be aware of your body's signals that it needs water and drink when you feel thirsty.

What is a good source of drinking water? Bottled water may be an option, but many people are concerned about BPA or BPS exposure from drinking bottled water. Opinions differ on using tap water. On the one hand, it is regulated by the Environmental Protection Agency to be safe when coming from the tap. This means that contaminants in the water are limited to levels that are considered "safe." Municipalities send an annual report to homes about drinking water quality. You can probably go online to view the report from your local water authority. However, chemicals such as fluoride and chlorine are routinely added to drinking water in some areas. Other chemicals such as lead can inadvertently find their way into the water system from corroded pipes. If you do not like the taste of the tap water in your area or are concerned about contamination, you can consider filtering your tap water. A carbon filter counter top pitcher can improve the taste and remove some of the common contaminants. A reverse–osmosis system can remove perchlorate and other toxins as well. These systems are historically installed under the sink, however they can be expensive to purchase and install. More recently, countertop reverse osmosis filter systems are starting to emerge for just a few hundred dollars.

Speaking of taste, there are quite a few ways to spiff up the taste of your water. You can add fruit or cucumber slices, a few mint or basil leaves, a cinnamon stick, or even fresh lavender. You can also replace ice cubes with frozen fruit (strawberries, blueberries, mangos, etc.). You can even add a few drops of juice concentrate like lemon or cherry. If you like the idea of flavoring your water, consider a water infuser. This is essentially a pitcher with a central infusing chamber in which you can place fresh or frozen fruit. When you fill it with water and let it sit in the fridge for a few hours, flavors and nutrients percolate from the central core into the water.

Carbohydrates

Carbohydrates are the body's main fuel source. All body tissues have the ability to break down carbohydrates for energy. The brain, kidneys, muscles, and heart require carbohydrates to function properly. Fiber, a form of carbohydrate, is essential for intestinal health. Carbohydrates are a particularly important fuel source for the central nervous system and red blood cells.

Carbohydrates include three types of sugars: glucose, fructose, and galactose. Glucose is the main sugar used by the body. It is used directly by the cells of the human body. The body regulates the breakdown of glucose to energy. As we consume more glucose, the body decreases the conversion of glucose into energy. Fructose, on the other hand, is not regulated. It is converted directly into energy. So, when you ingest fructose in the form of high-fructose corn syrup, it is converted to energy even if the body is satiated. This can lead to several unwanted side effects including risk of weight gain, type–2 diabetes, hypertension, liver damage, and exposure to mercury.[40] The main dietary source of galactose is lactose from milk and yogurt.

Carbohydrates are often classified as complex or simple. Complex carbohydrates are healthy for you; simple carbohydrates are to be eaten less often or avoided completely. The most common sources of complex carbohydrates are vegetables, fruits, legumes, grains, nuts, and seeds. Complex carbohydrates are digested more slowly than simple carbohydrates, and they are packed with fiber, vitamins, and minerals. Simple carbohydrates are readily digested, and as a result, raise blood glucose levels quickly. Simple carbohydrates occur naturally in fruits, milk, and some vegetables. They are also found in refined form in table sugar, high-fructose corn syrup, maple syrup, jams and jellies, fruit drinks, soft drinks, processed (white) flour, baked goods, processed foods, and candy. The refined carbohydrates provide energy, but they are stripped of their natural fiber and nutrients. The 2015–2020 Dietary Guidelines for Americans recommends that 45 to 65% of total daily calories come from carbohydrates, and primarily complex carbohydrates. However, plant–based nutritionists recommend more than 80% of total daily calories come from healthy complex carbohydrates.

Whole grains are a good source of complex carbohydrates. However, grains can also be highly processed. In a packaged food like cereal, it can be difficult to tell whether the grains are whole or not, despite the claims on the package. A good way to gauge of whether a product like bread or cereal is whole grain or not is to use the *Five–to–One Test*. Read the nutrition label. If you divide the grams of carbohydrate by the grams of fiber and get 5 or less (*Five–to–One Test*), that product is primarily whole grain. If the ratio is between 6 and 10 (*Ten–to–One Test*), the grains are more refined. If the ratio is 11 or more, any grains in that product are highly refined.

Uncle Sam Cereal, for example, has 36 grams of carbohydrates and 11 grams of fiber. Divide 36 by 11 to get 3.3, which is clearly less than 5. So, this product easily passes the Five-to-One test, which means that the wheat kernels and flaxseed in this cereal are primarily whole grain. Corn flakes, on the other hand, have 24 grams of carbohydrate and 0.9 gram of dietary fiber, for a ratio of 26.7. The corn in that product has been highly refined. Refined white flour has about 95 grams of carbohydrate and 3.4 grams of fiber for a ratio of almost 28.

The problem with refined grains is that the body handles whole grains and refined grains differently. Grains that are ground into a flour are digested more rapidly and completely. This not only increases the glycemic index, but the refined grains are digested almost entirely in the small intestine. There is very little to pass on to the colon. On the other hand, whole grains are only partially digested in the small intestine. The rest passes on to the colon for the good bacteria in your colon to feast upon and multiply. Eating whole grains containing plenty of fiber has many benefits, including reducing the risk of heart disease,[41] type 2 diabetes,[42] obesity, and stroke.[43] If a product passes the Five–to–One test, you can be reasonably certain that the product contains whole grains. The Ten–to–One test is less restrictive, but may still be a useful indicator in selecting packaged products that are primarily whole grain.

Remember, complex carbohydrates are your friends! It's only when they are overly processed and combined into products with fats and sugars that they become a problem and lead to weight gain.

Protein

Just as carbohydrates are an important fuel source for the body, protein is an essential nutrient to help the body build new tissues, antibodies, enzymes, hormones, and other compounds.

> *Don't ask me about my protein*
> *and I won't ask you about your cholesterol.*
>
> *T–shirt Slogan*

The number one question asked of most vegans is "where do you get your protein?" The surprising news is that over 97% of all Americans exceed the minimum daily requirements for protein. Even vegans exceed the RDA by 70%.[44] The RDA for protein is about 0.36 grams per pound of body weight for adult men and women. So, for a 170–pound individual, that's 61.2 grams of protein per day. The average American male consumes about 102 grams of protein per day; the average American female consumes about 70 grams of protein.

The RDA of protein equates to about 8–10% of total dietary calories. Note that the minimum amount of protein required for the average adult is much less, around 4–5%. By setting the RDA to the higher amount, the USDA provides a buffer that ensures that about 98% of the population will get more protein than actually needed.[45]

Clearly, protein deficiency is not a pressing health issue in America. So, it is amazing that so many people are obsessed about consuming protein, as if they can't get enough. I suppose that's a testament to the effective marketing tactics used by the purveyors of protein. If people examine the matter a bit more closely, they might revise their opinion. Consider John Robbins' book, *Healthy at 100*, which describes the diets and habits of four very different cultures that produce some of the world's healthiest and most long–lived people on the planet. There are several factors for the longevity and vigor of these populations, including regular physical activity, stress reduction, and engagement in family life. The common thread in their diets is that they all eat low protein, high nutrient diets.[46] Let that sink in. The healthiest people on the planet eat **low protein** diets. So, cramming the maximum amount of protein into your system isn't necessary, and it definitely isn't desirable, especially if you want to live a long and healthy life. In fact, excess protein has been linked with osteoporosis, kidney disease, calcium stones in the urinary tract, and some cancers.[47] Our bodies need protein, but moderate amounts will do nicely.

And the source of protein is critical. A recent large–scale study showed that high animal protein intake was positively associated with cardiovascular mortality while high plant protein was associated with reduced all–cause mortality and cardiovascular mortality.[48] In fact, Dr. T. Colin Campbell, in his book *The China Study*, states "dietary protein within the range of 10 to 20% is associated with a broad array of health problems (e.g. higher blood cholesterol levels, higher risks of cancer, osteoporosis, Alzheimer's disease, and kidney stones), especially when most of the protein is from animal sources."

In his article "A Fallacious, Faulty and Foolish Discussion About Saturated Fat," Campbell explains that heart disease is not caused by a single dietary factor such as saturated fat or a single clinical factor such as LDL cholesterol. Rather it is a complex sequence of events that is dependent on the consumption of animal–based protein. "It is far more important to focus on the avoidance of animal–based foods—and concocted 'foods' of plant parts—in favor of whole plant–based foods naturally low in fat and protein."[49]

Your daily protein requirement is readily obtainable from plant sources because plants contain a surprising amount of protein. The average green leafy vegetable has about 35–51% of its calories from protein. Other vegetables tend to be around 25% protein. Whole grains can range from 14% to 18% protein. Beans are around 25% to 27% protein. Fruits contain less protein, around 5% to 6%. So, if your goal is to consume between 6% and 10% protein, you can see that almost any combination of plant food sources will easily supply that.

The good news is that you don't need to obsessively mix and match plants in an elaborate production effort to assemble the perfect protein. Your body does it all for you. Every plant that contains protein, including vegetables, grains, legumes, nuts, and seeds, provides the body with amino acids. Eating a variety of plant foods provides all of the essential amino acids that we humans need. Your body breaks down protein from food sources into individual amino acid building blocks, and then reassembles them into proteins as needed. Even though some plants contain higher percentages of certain amino acids than others, as long as you consume protein from a variety of plants, your body can make as much protein as it requires. Of course, if you are aren't getting enough calories or eating all fruit, or eating large amounts of highly processed foods, all bets are off.

Keep in mind that when you replace animal protein with plant–based protein, you'll need to secure a reliable source of vitamin B–12. This is discussed in Nutrition Essentials for a Plant–Based Diet below.

Fat

Fat provides long–term energy storage, insulation to keep us warm, and protects our vital organs. It also helps in the absorption of fat–soluble vitamins A, D, E, and K. Fat is a very concentrated form of energy. Fat has 9 calories per gram, whereas carbohydrates and protein have 4 calories per gram. Your body cannot make certain types of fat, so you need to get some fat from your food.

The USDA recommends that adults consume between 20 and 35 percent of their daily calories from fat. However, studies have shown that such a high percentage of fat in the diet leaves you vulnerable to heart disease, cancer, and other diseases. On the flip side, a low fat diet is protective against these diseases. For example, a 2009 study published in the American Journal of Clinical Nutrition demonstrated that a low fat plant–based diet (about 10% of calories from fat) was more than twice as powerful at controlling and/or reversing diabetes than the American Diabetes Association diet, which recommends meat and dairy.[50]

Researchers at the Cleveland Clinic have shown that a low–fat plant–based diet (less than 10% of calories from fat) coupled with cholesterol–lowering medication is the single most effective way to stop progression of coronary artery disease.[51]

These and other results put the USDA recommendations on fat intake in a different light. Given that the mandate of the USDA is to promote agribusiness, it may be in our best health interests to opt for less fat in our diet. But, do we have to count calories? Not at all. Dr. T. Colin Campbell, celebrated author of the China Study[18], estimates that if one follows a whole food plant–based diet, the fat intake will naturally fall in the 10 – 15% range.

We need fat in our diet to help us absorb nutrients from food, but too much, and the wrong kind of fat can lead to complications. It's good to remember that fat is very calorie dense, but nearly devoid of nutrition.

Let's look at the types of fat. Fats are either saturated or unsaturated. Many foods have both types of fat, but one usually predominates.

Saturated Fat

Saturated fat is found mostly in animal products such as milk, meat, and cheese. It is also found in oils such as coconut oil and palm oil. Saturated fat is solid at room temperature. According to the American Heart Association, consuming saturated fat raises cholesterol levels in your blood, increasing risk for cardiovascular problems and Alzheimer's disease. Lowering your intake of saturated fat can reduce your risk of obesity, diabetes, and cancer.

Your body produces all the saturated fat it needs, so it is not necessary to consume any saturated fat in your diet.

Trans Fat

Trans fat is fat that has been hydrogenated to increase shelf life. This makes it the least healthy and most damaging of all the fats. You are well advised to avoid any food that contains trans fat. Check the labels of any processed foods, chips, crackers, cookies, and salad dressings.

Unsaturated Fat

Unsaturated fat is found mostly in oils from plants. It is liquid at room temperature, and better for your cholesterol levels than saturated fat. There are two types of unsaturated fat.

Monounsaturated Fat

Monounsaturated fat is found in avocado, nuts, and vegetable oils.

Polyunsaturated Fat

Polyunsaturated fat is found primarily in vegetable oils. It's also found in seafood. The two types of polyunsaturated fats are omega–3 and omega–6 fatty acids.

Omega–3 and Omega–6 Fatty Acids

Omega–3 fatty acids are found in plant foods and some seafood. Omega–3 fatty acids, such as EPA and DHA, can help the immune system, and support brain function. Omega–6 fatty acids are found mostly in liquid vegetable oils.

Human beings evolved consuming approximately equal amounts of omega–3 and omega–6 fatty acids. However, the Western diet today has a ratio closer to 1 to 15. That is, our Western diets are deficient in omega–3 fatty acids and are overloaded with omega–6 fatty acids. It's estimated that 90% of Americans are deficient in Omega–3 fatty acids.[52] This is a concern because 60% of the human brain is made up of fat. The imbalance between omega–3 and omega–6 fatty acids promotes many diseases including cardiovascular disease, cancer, inflammatory diseases, and autoimmune diseases.[53] Good sources of plant–based omega–3 fatty acids include ground flaxseeds, flaxseed oil, walnuts, hemp, and chia seeds. Sources of omega–6 fatty acids to be avoided or minimized include vegetable oil, salad dressing, potato chips, deep-fried fast foods, cookies, candy, pastries, beef, pork, chicken, dairy and eggs.[54]

Seek to increase the foods you eat that contain omega–3 fatty acids and reduce the foods you eat that contain omega–6 fatty acids.

Nuts and seeds deserve special mention. They are powerhouses of nutrition. Even though some nuts and seeds have high levels of omega–6 fatty acids, you'll see in the next chapter that regular consumption of nuts and seeds has been shown to both promote longevity and reduce the risk of chronic disease. For example, a small daily handful of nuts could add two years to your life span. The key is moderation. Eating more than one–quarter cup of nuts per day could negate some of the health benefits, so limit your intake. You especially want to avoid nuts and seeds that have been processed into oils.

High–Fat Diets

High–fat diets resurface periodically in various forms: Atkins, Zone, Paleo, Ketogenic, etc. While some individuals have achieved temporary weight loss on these diets, the health risks associated with these diets are not to be ignored. Here are some studies to illustrate the point:

A study of 301 subjects published in 2003 showed that increased animal fat is associated with the presence of diabetes.[55]

Study of over 337,000 women showed that a high saturated fat intake was statistically significantly associated with increased risk of breast cancer over 11.5 years.[56]

A study published in 2013 by the National Cancer Institute examined the relationship between high–fat dairy intake and mortality for 1,893 women. It showed that women who consumed the most high–fat dairy products were more likely to die during a 12–year follow–up, compared with those who consumed the least.[57]

Micronutrients

Micronutrients include vitamins, minerals, and phytonutrients. Unlike macronutrients, micronutrients do not contain any calories. Micronutrients are consumed in much smaller quantities than carbohydrates, protein, and fat, but they are just as vital to our health. According to Dr. Joel Fuhrman, "eating foods that are naturally rich in micronutrients is the secret to achieving optimal health and super immunity."[58]

Vitamins

Vitamins are organic compounds required in limited amounts for bodily functions. Vitamins facilitate the use of other nutrients. They are involved in regulating cell and tissue growth, manufacturing hormones, assisting enzyme–substrate reactions, and a host of other functions. The human body cannot synthesize vitamins, so they must be obtained through the diet.

Minerals

Mineral nutrients are inorganic elements found in food that the body cannot synthesize. There are five major minerals in the human body: calcium, phosphorus, potassium, sodium, and magnesium. Other minerals include iron, cobalt, copper, zinc, manganese, molybdenum, iodine, and selenium. Minerals perform a wide variety of functions. They help build bones and teeth, aid in muscle function and nervous system activity, assist in protein manufacturing and cell division, and facilitate the synthesis of hormones.

Phytonutrients

We've known about vitamins and minerals since the early 1900s, but phytonutrients have only become well known in the last two decades. Phytonutrients are compounds produced only by plants. There are an estimated 5,000 known phytonutrients, but a large number have yet to be identified. Phytonutrients are found primarily in fruits, vegetables, and grains, as well as nuts and seeds. Many phytonutrients act as antioxidants, neutralizing free radicals and preventing them from creating damage.

Some of the more familiar phytonutrients categories are:

Carotenoids (such as beta-carotene, and lutein) Beta–carotene is found in yellow or orange fruits and vegetables (cantaloupes, sweet potatoes, carrots) as well as dark green vegetables (broccoli, spinach). Beta–carotene protects the body from free radicals. Lutein is found in green leafy vegetables (spinach, kale, broccoli, romaine lettuce), and is linked to reduced risk of macular degeneration.

Flavonoids (such as resveratrol, luteolin, anthocyanin, myricetin, catechins, and quercetin) are powerful antioxidants, which support the immune system and have anti–inflammatory benefits. They can block enzymes that raise blood pressure. They can be found in almost all fruits and vegetables including apples, grapes, citrus fruit, strawberries, broccoli, kale, and many spices.

Ellagic acid decreases cholesterol levels. It is found in strawberries, blackberries, blueberries, kiwifruit, raspberries, and red grapes. Ellagic acid may help to remove carcinogens from the body.

Isoflavones potentially reduce the risk of some types of cancer. Sources of isoflavones include legumes, apples, carrots, garlic, potatoes, soybeans, and soy products.

Allium compounds protect the cardiovascular and immune systems. They are found in onions, scallions, leeks, chives, and garlic.

Lignans may decrease the risk of cancer. Lignans can be found in flaxseed, sesame seeds and whole grains.

As you might suspect, there have been attempts to isolate single phytonutrients and market them as a supplement. These efforts have met with little success. Rather, it appears to be the natural combination of phytonutrients in whole fruits and vegetables that is responsible for their antioxidant activity.

How Cooking Affects Micronutrient Availabiliity

Anyone adopting a vegan or plant-based diet will most likely eat a combination of raw and cooked food – raw for salads and whole fruit, cooked for most everything else. Cooking can be an exciting part of meal preparation, but high temperatures can destroy some of the micronutrients available in raw vegetables. For this reason, there are those who subscribe to a diet in which nothing is cooked above 104°F (though this number varies from 104° up to 118°).

The truth is that the bioavailability of nutrients in a cooked vegetable depends entirely on the vegetable and the cooking method. A study published in 2009 compared the antioxidant retention of 20 vegetables using 6 different home-cooking methods.[59] Artichokes retain their nutrients regardless of the cooking method, while beets, green beans, garlic, and onions do the same for most cooking methods. Carrots and celery actually increase in nutrient value when cooked. Likewise, cooking dramatically increases the bioavailability of the phytonutrient lycopene in tomatoes. On the other hand, bell peppers lose a large percentage of their nutrients when cooked, so they are best eaten raw.

As far as cooking methods go, microwaving retains more nutrients on average than other cooking methods. Steaming is effective as well, probably because of the short cooking times. Boiling and pressure-cooking are the least effective because nutrients leach out into the water during the cooking process. If you want to recapture some of the nutrients, you can put the water to use as a broth or in a soup.

Keep these results in mind if the topic of eating raw foods vs. cooked foods comes up. Do your own research. You may find yourself following Dr. Greger's advice of eating a mixture of raw foods and cooked foods. The good news for cooking enthusiasts is that even the most "harmful" cooking methods destroy less than 15 percent of the antioxidants. So, if you have a favorite cooking method, you can cook to your heart's content. Simply add a few more vegetables to make up for any potential loss of nutrients.

Microbiome

Your microbiome consists of the trillion bacterial organisms that live in your body. In particular, the organisms that surround your intestinal tract support your body's ability to absorb nutrients and fight infection. They act as an immune defense mechanism combating disease. Maintaining the correct balance between healthy bacteria and harmful bacteria in the gut is important because 80 percent of your entire immune system is located in your digestive tract. In fact, your digestive system is a large part of your neurological system. So, it is important to keep your digestive system healthy.

Your body naturally excretes beneficial bacteria daily, so it needs to be replaced on a regular basis. There are also other factors that can destroy our friendly flora. These include stress, toxins (pesticides, herbicides, and fertilizers), acidic foods, carbonated beverages, chlorine, and especially antibiotics. Fortunately, the gut's microbiome changes rapidly with a change in diet. The friendly flora can be replenished by eating foods with plenty of fiber and fermented foods containing *probiotics*. Some of these foods include natto (fermented soy bean dish), non–dairy kefir, kimchi, kombucha, miso, sauerkraut, and non–dairy yogurts.

My wife figured out how to make non–dairy yogurt, so that's how we get most of our daily probiotics. It's a pretty simple process (even a semi–retired math professor can do it!). See the recipe chapter for details.

Nutrition Essentials for a Plant–Based Diet

Before we investigate specific nutritional essentials, we need to discuss the RDA and its implications. RDA stands for Recommended Dietary Allowance. It is the estimated amount of nutrient per day considered necessary for the maintenance of good health by the Food and Nutrition Board of the National Research Council/National Academy of Sciences. The RDA is designed to meet the needs of 98% of the population. It's often called the Recommended Daily Allowance.

There is no RDA for carbohydrates, fat, or fiber, but there is an RDA for protein as well as some vitamins and minerals. The average requirement for protein is about 0.6 grams per kilogram of body weight. The RDA is set higher, at 0.8 grams per kilogram of body weight (or 0.36 grams per pound) so that it covers 97.5% of the population's needs.

A well–rounded WFPB diet with minimal supplements can provide all the nutrients you need to thrive. With some planning, you can get all the vitamins, minerals, and other necessary nutrients without all the saturated fats, cholesterol, and damage to the environment associated with animal products and their production. In this next section, we will cover the nutrients that require special attention for anyone eating a plant–based diet: Vitamin D, Calcium, Vitamin B–12, Zinc, Iron, and Iodine.

Vitamin D

Our bodies need vitamin D to absorb calcium and promote bone growth. Vitamin D also helps regulate the immune system and neuromuscular system. In fact, every cell in the body has a protein receptor for vitamin D.[60] Vitamin D deficiency has been linked to bone diseases as well as type II diabetes, cancer, and cardiovascular, autoimmune, and neurological diseases.[61] It is estimated that 64% of Americans don't have adequate vitamin D to keep their tissues operating at peak capacity.[62]

Clearly, it is important to ensure that we get enough vitamin D. In fact, it is so important to our health, that our bodies actually manufacture it as long as we get adequate sun exposure every day. However, getting enough sun is problematic for many people, and the further you live from the equator, the more difficult it is. There are a lot of factors involved including skin color, location, season, sun position, weather, and amount of sunscreen used as well as how often the sunscreen is applied. It is so involved that there are apps for your smartphone to help you determine if you are getting adequate sun exposure to satisfy your vitamin D needs. Unless you want to put a lot of energy into monitoring your vitamin D intake, you'll need to find an alternative source.

Very few plant sources provide vitamin D (mushrooms treated with UV light being an exception), so a person on a plant–based diet will have to look at foods fortified with vitamin D (nut milks, cereals, soy yogurt, and tofu) or take a vitamin D3 supplement. So, evaluate your typical sun exposure and consumption of foods fortified with vitamin D. If in doubt, take a daily vitamin D supplement. The recommended amount is 2,000 IU (International Units) per day, taken with the largest meal of the day.[63]

At each checkup, ask your doctor to test your vitamin D levels so you can find out if you need to adjust your supplement dosage to maintain optimal vitamin D levels. Many scientists recommend maintaining a level between 40–60 nanograms per milliliter in your blood, but this is still controversial.

Calcium

Calcium is one of the most important minerals to the health of our bodies. It helps form healthy teeth and bones as well as supporting muscle contraction, message transmission via the nervous system, and the release of hormones. In fact, almost every cell of our body uses calcium in some way. Fortunately, calcium is readily available from plant sources. If you think about it, huge herbivores like elephants and rhinos eat nothing but plant matter, and they get plenty of calcium to support their enormous bone structures. Calcium is also available from milk and other dairy products, but there is no good reason to expose yourself to the health challenges that come with consuming these animal products.

The RDA for calcium in the US is 1,000 mg per day for adults aged 19–50, 1,200 for older adults, and 1,300 for teens. However, these levels appear to be necessary to compensate for the high level of acidic foods consumed in the US. When you consume acidic foods (dairy, soda, animal protein, and refined sugar), your body leaches calcium out of your bones to counteract the acidity and maintain a comfortable level of PH in the bloodstream. Newer calcium balance studies suggest that the calcium requirement for men and women is lower than previously estimated.[64] The World Health Organization, for example, indicates the daily requirement of calcium for people eating less meat and dairy is more likely in the range of 600 to 800 mg.[65] The recommended daily amount for adults in the UK is 700mg.

Eating calcium rich foods alone is not enough to ensure strong bones. The body cannot absorb and use calcium at all without other nutrients. Vitamin D is the most significant nutrient for the proper absorption of calcium. Vitamin C, vitamin E, magnesium, boron and exercise also help the body absorb calcium. To maximize the absorption of calcium, make sure that your body has adequate levels of vitamin D.

It's also important to recognize that our bones are made of many nutrients besides calcium, so a well–rounded diet with lots of high–nutrient vegetables is essential for bone health.

Here are some recommendations to help you manage your calcium intake on a plant–based diet:

- Consume calcium-rich foods throughout the day because the maximum amount of calcium that the body can absorb at one time is about 500–600mg.[66]
- Consume two or three calcium–rich greens a day.
- Avoid calcium–leaching beverages such as soda and caffeinated drinks.
- Choose foods naturally high in calcium such as collard greens, curly kale, turnip greens, arugula, watercress, and mustard greens.
- Choose foods fortified with vitamin D and calcium, such as soy and other nut milks, orange juice, breads, and cereals (check the labels).
- Eat calcium–rich tofu products (tempeh, tofu).
- Stock up on calcium–rich snacks: dried kiwi, almonds, almond butter, sun–dried tomatoes, figs, and cooked edamame (soybeans).
- Get 10 to 20 minutes of direct sunlight a day when possible to help your body create the vitamin D it needs for bone health.
- Perform daily weight bearing exercise to maintain bone health.

You might think that an easy way to get more calcium is via a calcium supplement. Don't do it! Government panels that previously recommended calcium supplementation now recommend avoiding calcium supplements. This is backed by an increasing body of research.[67] This research shows that users of calcium supplements tend to have increased rates of heart disease, stroke, and death. So, look to your diet to meet your daily calcium needs rather than supplements.

Calcium intake is often cited as the most important factor for healthy bones; however, the importance of weight–bearing exercise in maintaining healthy bones cannot be emphasized enough. Numerous studies have shown that while calcium intake had only a modest effect on bone health, weight–bearing exercise has a significant effect on bone strength.[68]

Vitamin B–12

Most nutrients are readily available from plant sources. Vitamin B–12 is an exception. It is possible to get vitamin B–12 from fortified foods such as fortified nut milks, breakfast cereals, nutritional yeast, and mock meats. The drawback of this approach is that you'd have to eat several servings a day to get enough B–12. A more convenient and less expensive approach is to take a supplement. Supplements are available in pill form or as a liquid. It's best to take B–Complex supplement that contains other important B vitamins like biotin, thiamine, niacin, and riboflavin. Adults under the age of 65 can take one supplement each week containing 2,500 mcg of B–12 (in the form of cyanocobalamin), or a daily dose containing 250 mcg of B–12. Adults over the age of 65 should increase the dosage significantly, because your ability to absorb vitamin B–12 tends to decline with age.

In case you are wondering if you really need to make sure that you get enough B–12 in your diet, the answer is a resounding yes. A reliable source of vitamin B–12 is essential for anyone on a vegan or plant–based diet. Symptoms of B–12 deficiency may take years to develop, but the results can be disastrous. Prolonged vitamin B–12 deficiency can result in nerve damage resulting in confusion or even dementia, depression, loss of balance, and numbness and tingling of hands and feet.[69] There are cases that include paralysis, psychosis, blindness, and even death.[70] So, this is not something you can take lightly. Take a vitamin B–12 supplement, either a sublingual liquid, or pill form.

So, why would anyone consider a diet that isn't a significant source of a key nutrient like vitamin B–12? The answer is simple. If you adopt a diet full of B–12, you'll be eating red meat, fish, and dairy products. On such a diet, you'd be getting plenty of B–12, but you also would be getting cholesterol, casein, hormones, and other toxins that have been shown to lead to heart disease, cancer, and a number of other chronic diseases. In addition, the production of these products is polluting our environment, depleting our natural resources, and harmful to animals. When you compare this to a plant–based diet that is extremely nurturing to your body, makes efficient use of the environment, and saves animals, the choice is clear. It's worth taking a supplement to reap all the benefits of a plant–based diet. Even omnivores tend to be deficient in vitamin B–12, especially as they age. A vitamin B-12 supplement can make a difference.

Zinc

Zinc is an important mineral for overall health. It supports the immune system, wound healing, and blood sugar control. It protects against oxidative stress and helps the body repair genetic damage. The recommended dietary allowance is between 8 and 11 mg, depending on your age and gender. Zinc deficiency is more common in developing countries, but about 12% of the population in the US may be at risk. As much as 40% of the elderly might be at risk, due to insufficient dietary intake and a reduced ability to absorb zinc.[71] So, it's important to manage your dietary intake of zinc. Good sources of zinc include whole grains, tofu, tempeh, seeds, beans, nuts, peas, and legumes. Nutritional yeast and fortified breakfast cereals are also good sources of zinc. Soaking beans, grains, and seeds for several hours before cooking will help with the absorption of zinc in the body.

Iron

Iron plays an important role in the transportation of oxygen from the lungs to the rest of the body. Iron is an essential component of hemoglobin, the substance in your red blood cells that carries oxygen. Clearly, it's important to ensure that our bodies are getting enough iron. Fortunately, iron deficiency anemia is relatively uncommon in the United States (with the exception of some young children and females aged 12 – 49).[72] On the other hand, if we absorb too much iron, we may be increasing our risk of colorectal cancer, heart disease, infection, neurodegenerative disorders, and inflammatory conditions.[73] The RDA for iron is between 8 to 18 mg for most adults; the RDA for pregnant and lactating females is 27 to 32.4. You can have your iron levels tested with a simple blood test to see if you are at risk for too little or too much iron.

To ensure that you are getting enough iron, be sure to include iron–rich foods in your diet. These include spinach, Swiss chard, soybeans, lentils, quinoa, whole–grain breads and cereals, nuts, and seeds. Also, some foods are fortified with iron. Since plant–based iron is absorbed up to six times better when vitamin C is present, be sure to eat vitamin C–rich foods, such as citrus, tropical fruits, broccoli, tomatoes, and bell peppers, at the same meal as your iron food sources. Also note that drinking tea, coffee, or sodas with your meals can impair iron absorption.

Our bodies do a good job of regulating the absorption of iron. If our iron stores are low, our intestines boost the absorption of iron. If our iron stores are adequate, our bodies block the absorption of iron to keep our iron levels in an acceptable range. However, this mechanism only works with the non–heme iron found in plant foods. Our digestive system cannot regulate the heme iron found animal foods. The human body can't protect itself from absorbing too much heme iron, and it has no mechanism to rid itself of excess iron. Consuming animal products puts us at risk of iron overload. Iron overload favors the production of free radicals, fat oxidation, DNA damage, and may contribute to the development of cancer.[74]

In most cases, iron levels can be easily maintained by consuming iron–rich, plant–based foods. Check with your physician before taking iron supplements.

Iodine

Iodine is a trace mineral essential for thyroid function. Most people get plenty of iodine in their food, but pregnant and breast–feeding women should check with their doctor about taking a daily supplement. Good food sources of iodine include seaweed, such as nori, dulse, and arame, garlic, lima beans, sesame seeds, soybeans, spinach, Swiss chard, summer squash, and turnip greens. Iodized salt is a ready source of iodine, but this is not recommended due to the significant health risks associated with excess salt.[75] Since I've cut back significantly on my iodized salt consumption, I take a liquid iodine supplement.

Foods to Avoid or Minimize

Just as there are nutrients that you want to include in a vegan diet to ensure good health, there are foods that you want to minimize or eliminate to ensure good health.

Animal Products

Animal products should be at the top of your list of foods to avoid. Meat, dairy and egg products may have some redeeming qualities, but there are just too many negatives. Besides the harm to the environment and the suffering of animals caused by the production of these products, they pose a significant risk to your long–term health. To start with, they contain the wrong balance of the three macronutrients. They are very high in fat and protein, and low in carbohydrates; just the opposite of what our bodies need for optimal health. And the protein in animal products is the wrong kind. There is a big difference in how our bodies react to animal and plant protein. For example, animal protein causes our liver to raise the level of IGF–1 production, whereas plant protein does not increase IGF–1 production.[76] This is significant, because it has been well documented that IGF–1 promotes the growth of several types of cancers.[77] So, consuming animal protein over plant protein raises your risk of cancer.[78]

Inflammation

Consuming animal products causes inflammation in our bodies within a short amount of time. A study published in 1997 showed that a single meal of sausage and egg muffin can stiffen the endothelial cells that line your arteries within hours, and cut their ability to relax normally in half.[79] Repeated application of animal products in meal after meal wears down our immune system and promotes atherosclerosis.

Toxins

Animal products are also loaded with toxins that are harmful to humans. A very high percentage of flesh from animals including cows, fish, and chickens is contaminated with dangerous bacteria such as Listeria in deli meats, and Salmonella and Campylobacter in poultry. Ingesting these bacteria can cause food poisoning. This is nothing to be ignored, because there are thousands of cases of food poisoning in the U.S. every year, and ingesting animal flesh causes 70 percent of these cases.[80]

Eggs do not fare any better. Eggs can contain bacteria called Salmonella that can cause food poisoning. It is estimated that about 79,000 Americans are stricken each year with food poisoning specifically from eggs infected with Salmonella.[81] And if you think that thoroughly cooking the eggs will protect you from infection, think again. Researchers showed that Salmonella can survive many of the common cooking methods including cooked omelets and eggs boiled up to eight minutes.[82] Why risk it?

Food animals are regularly treated with antibiotics to promote growth and prevent disease. Approximately 80% of the antimicrobial drugs sold in the US each year go to the meat industry. These animals then produce antibiotic–resistant bacteria. The antibiotics and the resistant bacteria in meat can have a damaging effect on our gut microbiome.

Dairy products can contain toxins as well. A 2012 study of children in California investigated food contaminant exposure. The children were eating the standard Western diet, and cancer benchmark levels were exceeded by all of the children. In particular, dairy products proved to be the number one source of lead, banned pesticides, and dioxins.[83]

Even without the toxins, dairy products are dangerous for human consumption. If you stop and think about it, cow's milk is designed to turn a small calf into a 700–pound cow as quickly as possible, normally in about 2 years. All of the ingredients in that liquid, the lipids, the hormones, the proteins, and the growth factors, are there to support that rapid growth. Humans grow at a much slower rate. It takes up to 18 years or longer for a human to reach their full height. So ingesting dairy products unnaturally stimulates enzymes and growth hormones that increase the risk of myriad diseases. For example, casein, the primary protein in cow's milk, has been shown in numerous studies over decades to cause cancer in laboratory tests. In his video, "Dairy Protein Causes Cancer," Dr. T. Colin Campbell explains his view that casein "is a far more relevant carcinogen than any pesticide, herbicide, food additive, or other noxious chemical ever tested."[84]

Diseases

The list of diseases and conditions that have been associated with animal products is extensive. Here are just some of them:[85]

- Autoimmune disorders
- Cancer
- Cataracts
- Declining sperm counts
- Dementia
- Diabetes
- Gallstones
- Gout attacks
- Inflammatory disorders
- Neurological disease
- Rheumatoid arthritis

Another problem with animal products is that they do not contain some of the key nutritional elements found only plants. In particular, animal products do not contain any fiber. Fiber is essential for our gut microbiome and bowel health. People who consume healthy levels of dietary fiber have a significantly lower risk of developing coronary heart disease, stroke, hypertension, diabetes, obesity, and gastrointestinal diseases.[86] Unfortunately, less than 3 percent of Americans meet the minimum daily requirement for fiber (14 g/1,000 kcal). The only way to get enough fiber is to eat plants, and lots of them.

Nutrients

Animal products are also very low in vitamin C, phytonutrients, antioxidants, and other protective nutrients, some of which are found exclusively in plants. The more meat, eggs, and dairy that you consume, the less room on your plate for the beneficial and protective nutrients in plants.

Processed Foods

The healthiest populations on the planet eat very little processed foods, yet, in the West, processed foods have become part of the fabric of our daily lives. You can't open a fridge or a pantry without finding processed foods. We are talking about breakfast cereals, bread, crispy snacks, fried foods, meat products such as deli meat and bacon, cheese, refined sugar and flour, convenience foods such as microwave meals, and soft drinks. In general, the more processed the food, the less healthy. Some foods are minimally processed such as cut vegetables and roasted nuts. Foods that are lightly processed include pasta sauces with little or no added oil, plant milks, oil–free salad dressings, whole–grain breads, cereals, pastas, and pita pockets. These are still healthy.

The nutritional value of grains depends on how they are processed. Whole grains are incredibly healthy, but refined grains such as white flour have been processed to remove the bran and the germ from the whole plant. The refining process gives a finer texture and improves the shelf life, but it removes the fiber, phytonutrients, and many of the vitamins and minerals. The finer powder of the flour is digested quickly, triggering inflammation and spiking the blood sugar levels. This paves the way to insulin resistance and diabetes.

As discussed earlier, there is a way to determine just how intact the whole grains are in products like breads, tortillas, breakfast cereals, and English muffins. Read the nutrition label and make a note of the number of grams of carbohydrates and the number of grams of fiber. Divide the grams of carbohydrates by the grams of fiber. If the result is 5 or less, the grains are reasonably whole, with the nutrition intact. It passes the Five–to–One Test. If the result is 6 or more, the grains are more processed and less healthy. For example, if the label shows 28 grams of carbohydrates and 4 grams of fiber, divide 28 by 4 to get 7. Seven is greater than five, so this product doesn't quite pass the Five–to–One Test. Examples of foods that pass the test are Ezekiel breads and Uncle Sam cereal. Some people find the Five–to–One Test a bit restrictive, so they use a Ten–to–One Test instead. This might be a good starting point for someone just beginning their plant–based journey.

Some of the more heavily processed foods are combined with ingredients for flavor and texture along with preservatives for longer shelf life. Among these ingredients are sugar, fat, and salt. Food companies have discovered that this trifecta of ingredients stimulate people to buy their processed food products. These companies are driven to achieve the greatest allure for the least possible cost. This pursuit leads them inevitably to the same three enticing ingredients. Sugar may be the all–star. It ratchets up the allure with sweetness, but can also replace more costly ingredients to add bulk and texture to a product. Fats are also relatively inexpensive, and they can stimulate overeating and improve the way the product feels in your mouth. Salt is extremely inexpensive, and it has the amazing ability to increase the appeal of processed food. It is the combination of these three ingredients that makes processed foods so irresistible.

Creating alluring processed foods is not a casual endeavor. Unilever alone invested $30 million to study the sensory powers of food using advanced brain imaging and other neurological tools.[87] Many companies in the food industry contribute funding to and benefit from research on "food attraction" done at the Monell Chemical Senses Center in Philadelphia.[88] Over the past few decades, hundreds of top food scientists at Monell have investigated the mechanisms of taste and smell along with the psychology that determines our love for food. They have discovered the protein molecule in our taste buds that detects sugar. They have helped discover the "bliss point" of many ingredients. For each ingredient in a food, there is an optimum concentration at which the sensory pleasure is maximal. This optimum level is called the bliss point. The bliss point of sugar is the most powerful of all. Knowing the bliss point of sugar in a food, a food manufacturer can ensure that the food delivers the maximum attraction without sensory overload.

The food industry naturally uses every advantage to sell its products including the pleasure centers of our brains. In the early days of mankind, food was scarce and difficult to procure. So, our brains developed a way to ensure that we search for the most energy rich food available. When we eat something sweet, our brains release dopamine to stimulate our pleasure center. This stimulation encourages us to keep eating until we get signals that we are full. This adaptation was successful at keeping our focus on food and helping to perpetuate our species.

The problem is that food manufacturers have hijacked this direct link to our pleasure center. Processed foods have been optimized for maximum allure. That is, manufacturers have isolated sugar from the whole foods in which it was originally packaged (bananas, dates, etc.), so we get high doses of sugar without the fiber and the rest of the whole food that signals our bodies to stop eating when we get full. So, we tend to overeat, and the food companies sell more products.

Sugar stimulates the pleasure centers of the brain in the same way as some drugs. In fact, it uses the same mechanism. And like a drug addiction, the more obese an individual is, the less responsive they are to dopamine, and the more they have to eat to get the same stimulation. Fat stimulates the brain in the same way. PET scans reveal that fat also produces strong reward effects on the brain. [89]

So, many processed foods are designed to be as irresistible as possible, and incessant advertising further entices you to indulge. How does a person resist this two–pronged onslaught? First, be aware of the strong forces at work inducing you to eat processed foods. The better you understand how the food companies have hijacked your basic biology to sell their products, the more you can protect yourself by consciously making other choices. Keep in mind that junk food is not purposed with *sustaining* us, it is purposed with *entertaining* us. Second, value your health over instant gratification. Don't shop in the processed foods aisles; shop in the produce aisle instead. As you eat more healthy whole foods, your dopamine sensitivity will return to normal levels, so that your taste buds will once again appreciate natural foods.

Oil

Fat is an essential part of a healthy diet. There are many sources of healthy fats including leafy greens, seeds, nuts, soy products, avocado, and olives, but refined vegetable oil is not one of them. Added oil belongs on your list of foods to minimize or avoid.

The problem with oils is that they are 100% fat calories. They are the most calorie dense food, by far. Vegetables typically have about 100 calories per pound, and fruits have about 300 calories per pound, but oil has a whopping 4,000 calories per pound. There is no contest. It doesn't matter whether it is olive oil, coconut oil, canola oil, or any other kind of oil. All oils are calorie dense and nutritionally bankrupt. They do not contain fiber, minerals, or any other type of nutrients. Even worse, the fats contained in refined vegetable oil are harmful to the lining of our arteries (the endothelium).[90] Damaged endothelial cells pave the way to cardiovascular disease. So, avoid added vegetable oils as much as possible.

How do you avoid added oils from a practical standpoint? Sauté onions and another foods in water or vegetable broth instead of oil. Use herbs and spices to replace the flavor lost by removing the fat from a recipe. Use no–oil salad dressings; there are plenty available commercially, or you can make your own. Be aware of oil contained in packaged foods; read labels! Choose low oil or no oil versions. If you're baking, find recipes with minimal oil. Bake, broil, grill, or steam instead of frying. Or, you can get an air fryer and learn to "fry" foods without oil. Avoid processed foods. Request low oil or no oil meals in restaurants. Look up vegan recipes with no added oil online, and use the oil–free recipes in chapter 8.

Sweeteners

It is well documented that intake of excess sugar increases your risk of obesity, diabetes, and heart disease. So, you can cut out all sweets and be done with it, but this may be easier said than done. As we know, sugar can be quite addictive.[91]

There are other strategies. One is to use foods that are naturally sweet to enhance your creations rather than sugar. Add berries, banana, and pineapple to your smoothies to balance out the flavor of leafy greens (see *Donna's Green Plant Power Smoothie* in "Beverages"). Use dates, raisins, and coconut for making granola or energy bars (see "Snacks" and "Templates" in Recipes). Dates are loaded with fiber, vitamins, and minerals (especially iron) and digest slowly. They have antioxidant properties, and are loaded with phytonutrients. Use applesauce, apple juice, and orange juice in baking. You can even make your own syrup by soaking either dates or raisins, then blending them with filtered water.

Another strategy is to find products that contain more natural and less refined sugars, or take total charge and make your own desserts. If you choose the later approach, there are definitely some choices for sweeteners that are preferable to refined table sugar.

Agave is a substitute for honey for strict vegans and somewhat low on the glycemic index, but still a sugar. There is some controversy about the health value of agave. Use it sparingly. I use agave in soups and tagine when the flavor balance needs just a touch of sweetness.

Blackstrap molasses contains many nutrients (namely calcium), but it has a fairly strong flavor, so use it with caution.

Brown rice syrup is a fairly neutral flavored sweetener. It's about half as sweet as sugar.

Brown sugar is just refined, white sugar sprayed with molasses, so it is not really a more natural choice than table sugar.

Coconut sugar is made from air–dried coconut nectar. This process makes a granulated sweetener that is nutrient rich, with a lower glycemic index than table sugar.

Coconut nectar is a distinctly flavored liquid sweetener that retains many nutrients. It has a low glycemic index.

Date sugar is ground dried dates, so it has the same beneficial nutritional profile as dates. It doesn't dissolve in liquids, but can be used in baking. It has a thickening quality, so if replacing sugar, you may need to add a bit more liquid.

Erythritol is an interesting alternative. It is sugar alcohol naturally occurring in pears and other fruits. It can be purchased online if you can't find it in a local market. It is not as sweet as sugar, so you'll need to use a bit more to get a similar effect. It can't be used as a direct substitute for sugar in all cases, but I find it useful when combined with other sweeteners. I wouldn't recommend erythritol for baking. Unlike artificial sweeteners, erythritol is absorbed in the colon and has no known side effects. In fact, studies show that it has antioxidant properties.

Maple syrup contains vitamins, minerals, and numerous antioxidants. It is somewhat lower on the glycemic index than table sugar, yet is should still be used in moderate amounts.

Sucanat is a granular sweetener that is just as sweet as sugar and retains most of the vitamins and minerals of the sugar cane. I prefer it to table sugar and as a substitute for brown sugar.

Stevia is a powdered sweetener that has a slightly bitter aftertaste that some people can detect. It is sometimes combined with another sweetener to balance out the flavor. Mega doses of stevia can be harmful, so moderation is the key.

Xylitol is a granular sugar substitute that occurs naturally in the fibers of fruits, vegetables and tree bark. It is just as sweet as sugar, if not more so, and it has a slight aftertaste. It is used commercially in small amounts to sweeten chewing gum, but it is not recommended in large quantities because it has a laxative effect.

Sodium

Sodium is an essential mineral. It performs several functions in our bodies including regulating blood pressure and kidney function, assisting in the absorption of nutrients, and assisting in muscle contraction. The National Heart, Lung, and Blood Association states that a safe minimum intake of sodium is 500 mg per day. In fact, in a moderate climate, an average adult may be able to thrive on as little as 115 mg/day. However, the average sodium intake for adults in America is over 3,400 mg per day according to the National Heart, Lung, and Blood Association. This is over twice the recommended maximum of 1,500 mg per day for people over 40, people with hypertension, people with diabetes, or African–Americans. It is nearly seven times the safe minimum of 500 mg per day.

How is this huge discrepancy between the daily minimum requirement and actual intake amount possible? Table salt is about 39% sodium, but it's not the main source of sodium in the Western diet. The main source is sodium that is routinely added to processed foods and animal products. Approximately 75% of dietary sodium comes from processed foods. Some of the common foods packed with sodium include pizza, bread, chicken, and cheese. So, how do we cut down on our sodium intake if it is an integral part of the foods we consume? Or maybe a better question is – do we really need to cut down on our sodium intake? In other words, are our bodies able to handle the excess sodium without issue?

The answer is a resounding NO! No, our bodies cannot handle the excess sodium. There are serious health consequences to ingesting too much sodium. Excess sodium in the system causes the heart to work harder and leads to high blood pressure. High blood pressure, in turn, accounts for two–thirds of all strokes and half of all heart disease.[92] This means that high sodium intake is a major contributor to heart disease and stroke.

There are other consequences of excess sodium consumption, and not just in the American diet. Sodium is also considered to be a likely cause of stomach cancer worldwide.[92] In fact, excess sodium is considered to be the second–leading dietary killer in the world.[94]

Clearly, reducing salt and sodium should be a major dietary goal for anyone interested in achieving optimal health. Given the overwhelming influence of salt–laden processed foods in our food landscape, the best way to avoid excess sodium in your diet is to take charge of your own nutrition. Read Nutrition Facts labels, and choose brands with less sodium. Prepare most of your meals at home and emphasize whole foods rather than processed foods. You'll find that flavoring your food with others spices will cut down the need for salt. There are many salt–free spice blends readily available. Look to *The Vegetarian Flavor Bible* or vegancoach.com for recommended herbs and spices that match the foods you are preparing.

Foods for Thought

Just as some foods provide much needed nutrition, and other foods are to be minimized or avoided, there are some foods like soy and wheat products that are somewhat controversial. Soy, for example has many health benefits, but too much soy can create health issues. Wheat is generally beneficial in its whole grain form, but less so when it is processed. Even though it is rare, there are some people that are allergic to one or the other of these foods.

Soy

Soy tends to be controversial. Some people report allergic reactions, but the truth is that only 1 in 2,000 people have soy allergies.[95] As for other accusations, you will be hard pressed to find scientific evidence that soy in reasonable amounts is harmful to humans. It has been cultivated for over 10,000 years and there are thousands of research studies supporting the benefits of soy in the diet. Soybeans have more digestible protein than any other legume. Soy is a wonderful source of phytonutrients, fiber, iron, potassium, folate, and magnesium. Soy intake is associated with increased bone density and less bone fracture, lower cholesterol, and protection from breast cancer. As with any food, excessive amounts may have negative consequences. Some studies show that more than 7 servings of soy a day could negate some of the benefits of soy and increase levels of IGF–1. So, a moderate amount of 3 to 5 servings a day would give you the benefits of soy without any adverse effects.

Soy milk and tofu are typical sources of soy, even though about half the nutritional value is lost during processing. A better source would be tempeh, which is a type of fermented soybean patty. It contains whole soybeans, which contain more than 100 times total phytoestrogens than sprouted soybeans. Miso and edamame are also good sources of soy.[96] It is preferable to purchase organic soy products when possible to avoid contamination from pesticides.

A study published in 2004 showed that drinking two glasses of soy milk daily prevented bone loss in postmenopausal women over a two-year period.[97]

A meta–analysis of related studies published in 2009 concluded that soy intake is protective against the risk of endocrine–related gynecological cancers.[98]

If you have a confirmed allergic reaction to soy, then, of course, avoid it. If not, a moderate amount daily will add to your nutrient profile.

Wheat

Whole wheat contains a wealth of nutrients including calcium, magnesium, potassium, zinc, manganese, vitamin B, and vitamin E. Consumption of whole wheat can improve conditions like anemia, gallstones, breast cancer, inflammation, and obesity. It can regulate blood glucose levels in diabetics, and lower the risks of heart disease. Yet some people experience digestive and other health problems when eating wheat. There are three different medical conditions that can cause these issues: celiac disease, wheat allergy, and non–celiac gluten sensitivity.

Celiac disease is an autoimmune disorder in which your immune system reacts strongly to gluten, which is the general name given to the proteins found in wheat, barley, and rye. About 1 in 100 people are genetically predisposed to celiac disease, and you have a higher risk if you have a close relative with the disease. When people with celiac disease eat gluten, their immune system reacts and attacks the small intestine. Repeated exposure can lead to some serious health problems including type I diabetes, multiple sclerosis, osteoporosis, epilepsy, migraines, and intestinal cancer. The only treatment is lifelong adherence to a strict gluten–free diet. Children and adults exhibit somewhat different symptoms. Children are more likely to experience abdominal bloating, vomiting, weight loss, fatigue, irritability, and Attention Deficit Hyperactivity Disorder. Adults may experience bone or joint pain, arthritis, depression or anxiety, seizures or migraines, missed menstrual periods, or canker sores in the mouth.

Wheat allergy is an allergic reaction to foods containing wheat. Common symptoms included itchy rash, hives, asthma, itchy or watery eyes, diarrhea, abdominal cramps, nausea, and vomiting. An allergic reaction can be triggered by ingesting anything containing wheat, but also by inhaling wheat flour. Treatment is to avoid foods containing wheat, including many cereals, beer, pastry, pizza, salad dressings, most baked goods, and many bottled sauces such as soy sauce and ketchup. The prevalence of wheat allergy is not yet clear. Some studies estimate around 0.5 percent to 1 percent. One study estimated a prevalence of up to 9% worldwide.

Gluten sensitivity is a reaction to gluten with symptoms somewhat similar to celiac disease, but without the same antibodies and intestinal damage as seen with celiac disease. Individuals with non–celiac gluten sensitivity would be more likely to exhibit non–GI symptoms such as headache, joint pain, and numbness in the legs, arms, or fingers. Symptoms would appear hours or even days after eating food containing gluten.

Gluten sensitivity is probably more common than either celiac disease or wheat allergy. Estimates range as high as 6 to 7 percent of the population. However, self–diagnosis is not always accurate. A study in the Journal of Digestion discovered that 86 percent of 392 individuals who believed they were gluten sensitive could tolerate gluten with no ill effects.[99]

Because of the confusion, many people are choosing to avoid gluten in their diets. As a result, we see the expected proliferation of gluten–free products. This is a good thing for those with a gluten–related condition, but unnecessary for the majority of the population. If you suspect you have one of these medical conditions, it's probably best to work with a doctor to increase or decrease the gluten in your diet, then get a formal diagnosis regarding your bodies' ability to tolerate gluten.

CHAPTER 4: DAILY HEALTH

Live a healthy lifestyle by creating time for good nutrition.

— Dave Shepp

Daily Nutrition

With all the nutrition information from the previous chapter buzzing in your head, you may be wondering what to eat on a daily basis. Here are some guidelines to keep in mind as you shop and prepare meals.

Guidelines:

Strive for variety. Each plant brings unique nutrients to the table. The more variety you bring to the table, the better.

Eat the rainbow. Color in food equates to nutrition. Select dark and vibrant colors.

Strive for macronutrient balance. A healthy target based on the latest research would be 80% complex carbohydrates, 10% protein, and 10% fat. The important health factor is to keep protein and fats to a minimum. See Chapter 3 for information on macronutrients and recommended amounts.

Let your daily food intake evolve toward better health. Gradually replace transitional processed foods with whole foods. If you are eating heavy protein or heavy fat, replace those foods with complex carbohydrates – sweet potatoes, other veggies, and fruit.

Minimize oil (both processed and in foods), sugar, processed food, and junk food.

Daily Food Choices

Another day vegan. . . Still haven't died of nutrient deficiency.

— @incogneato_vegan

There are plenty of food pyramids to use as a guide in choosing your daily fare. See VeganFoodPyramid.com, SustainablePowerPlate.org (Physicians Committee for Responsible Medicine), FoodChoicesAcademy.com, veganpeace.com, and ordinaryvegan.net to mention a few. I'm not a big fan of the pyramid format because the most important foods are at the bottom of the pyramid, and we tend to read from the top down. The Plant–Based Food Choices diagram below presents the foods with the most servings listed at the top. The recommended daily amounts are compiled from several sources and based on the nutrition information in the previous chapter. The diagram is followed by descriptions of each food category. Note that the recommendations are designed for an optimally healthy diet – a whole food, plant–based diet with minimal oil and processed foods. Think of it as a goal – something to work toward as you make the transition away from the Standard American Diet.

Plant-Based Food Choices

Water and other healthy beverages
5 twelve-ounce glasses of water per day
Drink more if exercising heavily, ill, or pregnant

5 Servings

Vegetables - cruciferous, leafy greens, other veggies
Serving: 1/2 cup leafy greens, 1 cup other veggies
Eat extra green leafy veggies for heart health

5 Servings

Fruit - berries and other fruit
1 cup berries, 3 whole or 3 cups other fruit
Berries are especially high in antioxidants

4 Servings

Legumes - beans, lentils, tempeh
Three 1/2 cup servings cooked legumes
Choose rich colors. Legumes each meal

3 Servings

Grains - cereal, pasta, & rice
1/2 cup cooked, 1 cup cold
Focus on whole grain. Every meal.

3 Servings

Nuts & Seeds
1/4 cup, 1 Tbsp ground
Longevity

2 Servings

Herbs & Spices

1 Serving (for health and flavor)

The intent of the Plant–Based Food Choices plan is to give general guidelines, not for rigid compliance at each meal. For example, the food choices diagram suggests 5 servings of vegetables, but that's just a starting point. In truth, the more veggies, the better. And if you have a history of cardiovascular events, Dr. Esselstyn (see Reverse Heart Disease in Chapter 3) recommends that you eat 6 servings of leafy greens daily in addition to your other vegetables. That's a lot of vegetables! Also, no one eats the same thing every single day. You might have more beans or lentils one day and more grains and veggies the next. So use the diagram as a general guide, but take it with a grain of salt (a small grain).

Water

There doesn't seem to be any consensus on the amount of water our bodies require each day. A reasonable strategy would be to simply listen to your body and drink when you are thirsty. Easy, right? However, for many people, drinking enough water tends to get lost in the shuffle of daily activities. I'm one of those people, so I find it useful to establish habits that make drinking water part of my daily routine. This includes habits such as drinking water before each meal and carrying a water bottle with me, especially when I travel. I also set up a little tea station in my office with a countertop water heater and an assortment of teas, to add to my daily water intake.

The advice that many of us heard as children is to drink 8 eight–ounce glasses per day. Another recommendation is to drink 5 to 7 twelve–ounce glasses of water per day. Either of these recommendations should get you in the ballpark, with adjustments for your body weight and your gender. It's important to understand that these recommendations indicate total liquid intake from all sources. So, if you drink tea, coffee, juice, or any other beverages, they all count toward your daily water intake. Also keep in mind that about 20% of your water intake (more if you eat plant based) comes from the food you eat. So your water needs can be reduced, depending on the other beverages you drink and the types of food that you consume. On the other hand, you'll need to drink more water if you do vigorous exercise, or the weather is very warm, or you are ill or pregnant. See the discussion on water in the previous chapter.

Vegetables

Vegetables are packed with nutrients; they provide vitamin C, beta– carotene, riboflavin, iron, calcium, fiber, and other nutrients. There are a few special types of vegetables worth knowing about. Cruciferous vegetables are those of the family Brassicaceae. The flowers of these plants resemble a cross; hence the name cruciferous. Cruciferous vegetables include arugula, broccoli, bok choy, Brussels sprouts, cauliflower, cabbage, collard greens, horseradish, kale, mustard greens, radishes, turnip greens, and watercress. There are nearly 300 studies on PubMed that research the antioxidant nature of cruciferous vegetables. One of the possible reasons is that cruciferous vegetables contain very high amounts of glucoraphanin. When cruciferous veggies are either chopped or chewed, a chemical reaction takes place that converts glucoraphanin to sulforaphane. Sulforaphane is becoming known as an anticancer compound due to its potent antioxidant and anti–inflammatory properties.[1] Include about ½ cup of chopped cruciferous vegetable in your daily diet to enjoy the health benefits. To get the most health benefit, eat these veggies raw, such as broccoli sprouts. If you cook them, try the following. Cut up the veggies and let them sit for 30 or 40 minutes. This gives the sulforaphane a chance to form (from the cutting process), and it is resistant to heat. Then you can cook away as you see fit, and still enjoy the health benefits.

Another distinctive type of vegetable is leafy greens. This category includes arugula, beet greens, collard greens, kale, mustard greens, salad greens, spinach, Swiss chard, and turnip greens (note the slight overlap with cruciferous vegetables). The reason that you want to be aware of leafy greens as a unique grouping is that they offer the most nutrition per calorie. They are so protective against chronic diseases that studies from Harvard showed about a 20 percent reduction in risk for both heart attacks[2] and strokes[3] for every additional serving. That's amazing! Each additional serving lowers your risk by an additional 20%. Dr. Esselstyn concurs. Dr. Caldwell Esselstyn is an expert on arresting and reversing heart disease in clinical trials.[4] He is adamant that patients who have significant cardiovascular issues must eat 6 fist–sized servings of leafy greens every day. Chewing leafy greens will produce nitrites, which are converted to nitric oxide. Nitric oxide is the key to repairing oxidative damage to the lining of our arteries. This powerful antioxidant can diminish the oxidative inflammation in plaques and foam cells, minimizing the chance of rupture and blockage of the arteries.[5]

So, how does this apply to the rest of us? Do we really need to eat six servings of greens every day? We may not have had cardiac events, but every one of us over the age of ten who was raised on the Western diet has at least the beginnings of atherosclerosis.[6] The least we can do for our beleaguered arteries is to treat them to frequent doses of leafy greens. Add leafy greens in your meal planning as often as you can. They can be added to stir–frys and soups, or simply steamed or sautéed. Leafy greens tend to have a strong flavor on their own, but you can add balsamic vinegar, lemon juice, coconut aminos, nutritional yeast, and/or spices to enhance the flavor. I put some Worcestershire sauce or liquid smoke into a small spray bottle and spray it on the leafy greens. One of my favorite ways to enjoy leafy greens is topped with a creamy sauce. You won't believe what difference it makes in the flavor. See the Recipe chapter for a variety of sauce recipes.

One of the hallmarks of a whole food plant–based diet is rotating the food so that you get a variety of flavors and nutrition. In addition to the cruciferous vegetables and leafy greens, be sure to include an assortment of other vegetables, such as asparagus, beets, bell peppers, carrots, corn, mushrooms, onions, sea vegetables, squash, sweet potatoes, tomatoes, and zucchini. Select vegetables with bright and vibrant colors because that's where the nutrients are. Mushrooms are special because they are the only vegetable food source of B–12 and they contain the highest amount of the beneficial amino acid ergothioneine. Sweet potatoes also deserve a special mention. They are considered by many to be one of the healthiest foods on the planet. Their skin is extremely high in antioxidants, and recall that they were the primary vegetable food source of the very long-lived Okinawans (Chapter 1).

Fruits

A good rule of thumb is to eat one serving of berries per day and three servings of other fruit. For berries, a serving would be ½ cup fresh or frozen, and somewhat less for dried berries. For other fruits, a serving would be one medium fruit or a cup of cut–up fruit; ½ cup for dried fruit. As with vegetables choose colorful and vibrant fruit for its high nutritional value and strive to rotate fruits to get the benefit of all the nutritional profiles. Fruits tend to have shorter shelf life than some other produce, so you are best off eating fruits in season as much as possible.

Berries are particularly high in antioxidants; hence the recommendation of 1 cup each day. A study ranked the antioxidant properties of over 3100 food items from around the world.[7] Berries are quite high compared to other fruits. Measured in millimoles per 100 grams, blackberries come in at 4.02, raspberries 2.33, strawberries 2.16, and blueberries 1.85 whereas apples, bananas and red grapes are all around 0.3. Who knew that blackberries were so potent? Even so, any of the berries pack an antioxidant punch. Although not as common in the US, Indian gooseberries (amla) are perhaps the most antioxidant-rich fruit on the planet. The above study found whole or canned amla to be 13.27 mmol/100g. Impressive! Be sure to also include fruits that are high in vitamin C — citrus fruits, melons, and strawberries are all good choices.

Legumes

The legume food category includes beans, peas, and lentils. All of these are good sources of fiber, protein, iron, calcium, zinc, B vitamins, folate, and potassium. Legumes are naturally low in saturated fat and free of cholesterol. This group also includes chickpeas, baked and refried beans, soy milk, tempeh, miso, and tofu.

Legumes offer plenty of health benefits. They are reputed to help regulate blood sugar, insulin levels, and cholesterol. They may reduce the risk of stroke, depression, and cancer. A study published in 2004 examined dietary factors for survival of older individuals in four different countries. The only food group to be a significant predictor of longevity was legumes. In fact, the results showed a 7–8% reduction in mortality hazard ratio for every 20 gram increase in daily intake of legumes.[8] So, legumes definitely have something going for them.

Eating a ½ cup serving of cooked legumes with each meal will provide a healthy dose of these nutritious foods. Keep in mind that hummus and soy milk count toward your daily intake of legumes. Tempeh is a very good whole–food source of soybeans, and a reasonable substitute for some of the mock meats. When I first started my plant based journey, I pretty much avoided beans, not being a big fan of the flavor or texture. Then I acquired a taste for three–bean salad, and began to experiment with adding beans to soups, stir–fry, and even spaghetti sauce. I found that beans added substance to the texture without derailing the flavor. Then there is hummus. Homemade hummus is a delightful and fun way to enjoy beans as well as exploring a variety of different flavorings. Lentils are interesting because they tend to have a milder flavor than beans, and they can easily be sprouted, which improves their antioxidant properties immensely. If you are a dessert fan, you can even enjoy beans in *Peanut Butter Black Bean Brownies* in "Desserts." Bet you didn't see that coming.

Grains

Grains include bread, rice, pasta, hot or cold cereal, corn, millet, quinoa, barley, bulgur, buckwheat groats, and tortillas. Quinoa is technically a seed, but it acts like a grain, so it is included here. Quinoa has become my go-to grain. Build each of your meals around a hearty grain dish. Grains are rich in fiber and other complex carbohydrates, as well as protein, B vitamins, and zinc.

From a health standpoint, the key is whole grains. Processed or refined grains have been milled to remove the bran and germ. That gives the grains a longer shelf life and finer texture, but it removes most of the fiber and many nutrients. If you eat pasta or bread, make sure they are primarily whole grain. Cook up some grains as a breakfast cereal or make sure that your cold cereal is using whole instead of refined grains (see the *five-to-one* test in the previous chapter).

Throughout history, grains have been cultivated by and associated with cultures from every corner of the world. Rice has been a staple in Asia, the Inca revered quinoa, amaranth was central to the Aztec culture, and kamut was a staple in the Nile region. There is good reason for the popularity of grains. Whole grains are associated with reduced risk of heart disease, stroke, obesity, and type 2 diabetes. In addition, two large scale (74,341 and 43,744 participants) and long–term (26 and 24 years) studies in US men and women found that a higher whole grain intake was associated with significantly reduced mortality, especially deaths due to cardiovascular disease.[9]

It's pretty easy to include 3 servings of grains in your daily meals. ½ cup hot cereal or 1 cup cold cereal can be eaten at breakfast. A slice of bread or a tortilla can be used to make a sandwich or wrap for lunch. ½ cup of cooked grains makes a wonderful base to be topped with stir–fry, soup, and steamed or roasted veggies for dinner.

Nuts and Seeds

Nuts and seeds are amazing. They are packed with a generous arsenal of micronutrients including dietary fiber, omega-3 fatty acids, antioxidants (carotenoids, flavonoids, Vitamin E, resveratrol, and more), minerals (calcium, potassium, zinc, magnesium, manganese, and selenium), phytosterols, and arginine (an amino acid that promotes circulation).

There are several studies that show how eating nuts can confer increased longevity and reduced risk of disease. The Adventist Health Study showed that eating a handful of nuts five or more times a week could add up to two years to your life.[10] In the Nurses' Health Study, nuts were indicated as a dietary factor related to reduced risk of cardiovascular disease and cancers.[11] In a PREDIMED study, nut consumption was associated with a significantly reduced risk of all–cause mortality as well as a protective effect against cardiovascular and cancer mortality.[12]

That's terrific news for nut lovers, but what about the notion that nuts and seeds are too fattening for those who want to lose weight or even maintain their weight? Since nuts are high in calories and fat, you would think that they automatically lead to weight gain. Luckily, that's not the case. In fact, if you eat moderately, long–term studies have shown significantly less weight gain and reduced risk of abdominal obesity in participants who ate more nuts.[13] It turns out that nuts have a couple things going for them to counteract weight gain. For one, nuts are very filling. When you eat nuts, you feel full faster and as a result, you tend to eat less food overall. Score one for nuts! Best of all, nuts help boost your metabolism, so that you burn more of your own fat. A 2009 study on overweight individuals showed that the group eating walnuts burned about 50% more fat in an 8–hour period.[14] The combined effect of appetite suppression and elevated metabolism means that you eat moderate amounts of nuts without gaining weight.

Some of the popular nuts and seeds include almonds, Brazil nuts, cashews, chia seeds, flax seeds, hazelnuts, hemp seeds, macadamia nuts, pecans, pistachios, pumpkin seeds, sesame seeds, sunflower seeds, and walnuts. A suggested daily serving amount would be ¼ cup nuts or seeds or 2 tablespoons nut or seed butter. One to two cups would be a reasonable daily serving of nut milk.

Each of the nuts and seeds has their own nutritional profile.

Almonds are rich in antioxidants. Chia and hemp seeds are rich sources of omega–3 fatty acids. Hemp seeds are also high in protein. Pistachios have the highest levels of plant sterols. Sterols may lower cholesterol levels and reduce inflammation. Pumpkin seeds are rich in iron, calcium, and phytonutrients. Sesame seeds are a good source of calcium. They also provide vitamin E and contain a lignin called sesamin, which protects against breast cancer.

Flaxseeds deserve a special mention. Ground Flaxseeds contain about 1.8 grams of omega–3 fatty acids per tablespoon. They also contain up to 800 times more lignans than other plant foods. Flaxseed lignans have a much higher antioxidant content than any other fruit or vegetable. Lignans may lower the risk of cancer and cardiovascular disease. Flaxseed is also a good source of fiber.

Grinding flaxseeds releases the nutrients and makes it easier to digest. Buy the seeds in bulk, and then use a coffee grinder or spice grinder to break down the hard shells. The ground flaxseed can be stored for weeks at room temperature, but I prefer to store it in an airtight container in the refrigerator (or freezer).

Flaxseed has so many health benefits, that you would be well served to find a way to include a tablespoon (or two) into your daily diet. Ground flaxseed can be used in a variety of ways. You can sprinkle it on your cereal or into your smoothies. You can add it to soups, stir-fry, veggie loafs, or other cooked foods. It can also be used in baking to replace eggs, though it will require some adjustments. Consider making your own crackers with flaxseed and a dehydrator. See *Raw Flaxseed Crackers* in "Snacks."

One of my favorite ways to ensure regular intake of nuts and seeds is to include them in the breakfast meal. I generally have cereal (see *David's Breakfast Bowl* in "Breakfast") with a lot of toppings including walnuts, raisins, pumpkin seeds, chia seeds, ground flax seeds, puffed amaranth seeds, and hemp seeds. Many of these nuts and seeds also find their way into my daily smoothie. Another favorite is to use nuts to make a variety of creamy sauces. Cashews, almonds, and pine nuts work particularly well. See Sauces in Recipes. Homemade sauces are a delightful way to add flavor and pizzazz to steamed veggies and other dishes.

Herbs and Spices

As my tastes have evolved, I've really come to understand and appreciate herbs and spices in an entirely new way. Herbs and spices are not only nutritious, they work in concert with the natural flavors of plant–based foods to create some amazing flavor combinations. I will cover how to use herbs and spices to balance and enhance flavors in chapter 7. For now, we will look at some of the more common herbs and spices and their nutritional values.

Since herbs and spices are well know for their antioxidant properties, I've listed some common herbs and spices with particularly high antioxidant content according to the 2010 study.[15]

Antioxidant content	mmol/100grams
Amla (dried powder)	301.14
Cloves (ground)	125.55
Thyme, dried)	42.00
Oregano (dried)	40.30
Rosemary (dried)	39.99
Cinnamon	17.65
Turmeric	15.68

High concentrations of antioxidants in foods doesn't guarantee that these compounds will absorb free radicals in our bodies as well as they do in lab tests. However, studies show some remarkable effects in human subjects for foods high in antioxidants. A 2011 study[16] showed significant reduction of about 40% of total cholesterol for participants in only 3 weeks by taking one-half teaspoon of amla powder daily. Wow! Other studies also show health benefits from taking various forms of amla.

It's pretty easy to add antioxidant-rich herbs into your daily routine. Consider adding cloves, rosemary, oregano, and turmeric to spice up your veggie dishes. Add amla, thyme, and cinnamon to your morning smoothie.

Some of the commonly used herbs and spices include Arrowroot as a thickener; Basil for practically everything; Cinnamon to add sweetness; Cumin (the worlds second most popular spice behind black pepper) to add a bitter/sweet flavor to African, Indian, Mexican, Middle eastern cuisines; Curry powder to add a little heat; Cayenne to add a lot of heat; Garlic as a strong flavor enhancer; mint to add a slightly sweet sense of freshness to dishes; Rosemary to enhance Mediterranean cuisine; Oregano for a slightly bitter flavor used in Greek, Italian, and Mexican dishes; Thyme for French and Italian dishes; and Turmeric to flavor Indian or Moroccan foods and for its medicinal properties.

As far as daily doses go, you can generally use herbs and spices freely, but for safety sake, keep your herb and spice usage in the general range that you would see in recipes that use spices. Go easy on the really pungent spices; a little bit goes a long way. Because of its extensive health benefits, Dr. Greger recommends ¼ teaspoon per day for turmeric.[17]

Other Foods

The Plant–Based Food Choices diagram is based on the end goal: eating a whole foods plant–based diet. So what do you use as a guide while you're in transition? How do you deal with meat and dairy substitutes, oil, sweets and other processed foods? Let's face it; the vast majority of people who adopt a vegan diet eat some processed foods. It's pretty rare that someone new to the vegan diet immediately eats nothing but whole foods. There is definitely an adjustment period. When I decided to go vegan, I was delighted to find out that there were non–dairy milks, chick'n strips, and veggie patties, as well as vegan sour cream, cream cheese, and shredded cheese. It made the transition so much easier. I could still have all my favorite meals; all I had to do was find vegan substitutes for the animal products. And the best part was the delicious frozen coconut and almond milk desserts. Hooray! They taste wonderful without any dairy whatsoever. These products and others were vital to enabling me to eat vegan, almost without skipping a beat. As time went on, I gradually started to eat more whole foods and rely less on these transitional products.

So, how does the Food Choices diagram apply to someone just starting out? Use Food Choices as a goal. Not eating many leafy greens? Figure out how to work it into your diet. Need more grains? Try out quinoa, millet, and buckwheat until you find something that you like and use it as a morning cereal or with roasted veggies. If you don't eat any legumes one day, get some the next day. As your tastes change (and they will) use the techniques in Chapter 6 to crowd some of the more processed foods off your plate with more healthy and satisfying whole food options. Adjust what you are eating with the Food Choice recommendations as the goal. Be gentle with yourself and go at your own pace. See the next chapter for more transition ideas.

WFPB Diet in a Nutshell

What is WFPB? It is an acronym for Whole Food Plant–Based. A whole food plant–based diet is the diet that best reflects evidence–based nutrition. In a nutshell, a whole food, plant–based diet is centered on whole, unrefined, or minimally refined plants. The diet is based primarily on whole foods, namely fruits, vegetables, tubers, whole grains, and legumes. It excludes any animal products, including meat, poultry, fish, dairy products, and eggs. It minimizes highly refined foods like bleached flour, refined sugar, and oil.

Here is a summary of the guidelines in list form:

- Embrace whole plants – eat as much as you want
- Eliminate animal–based foods, including meat, dairy, and eggs
- Avoid refined and processed foods, such as sugar, sweets, pastries, and processed pastas.
- Avoid or eliminate oil – even the best oil is concentrated fat, which injures the innermost lining of your arteries.
- Minimize salt and fat
- Drink water as your primary beverage
- Include moderate and regular exercise
- Take a vitamin B–12 supplement, and monitor vitamin D levels with your personal doctor.

Daily Choices

I don't want to wake up dead tomorrow and realize I didn't even try.

— *Ryan E. Day*

Making a successful transition to eating a plant–based diet is largely about taking charge of your own health on a daily basis. It's about the daily choices you make when shopping and preparing meals. A number of outside influences affect these choices. The more you become aware of these influences, the easier it is to make food choices based on health rather than temptation. The food industry spends billions of dollars every year to entice us to eat dairy, meat, fish, poultry, dairy products, and eggs as well as processed foods full of sugar, fat, and salt. This ceaseless onslaught provides persistent pressure to purchase and consume food that has lead to rampant obesity and rapid increase in the outbreaks of chronic diseases. Awareness can provide some measure of protection, because it establishes a context in which you can make intelligent, informed choices with your food dollar.

Another reason that you need to take personal responsibility for your own health is that there are very few entities that are motivated to protect your health. The U.S. Department of Agriculture is assigned the task of setting healthy dietary guidelines. Yet, its primary mandate is to protect the food and agriculture industries. It constructs nutrition guidelines that are protective of the food industry's bottom line, and these guidelines have historically set the stage for the poor health we see today. The American Dietetic Association is also influenced by the food industry. The insurance companies are in business to sell plans to the sick. The pharmaceutical industry makes billions of dollars annually from chronic illnesses. Hospitals depend on our diseases. Doctors and nurses receive very little training in nutrition and behavior modification, yet they are very well rewarded for prescribing and administering drugs. Again, it is up to you to educate yourself and transform your own diet. Make food choices based on the best available information and evidence–based nutrition. This book will support you in the process. If you want to be kept informed about the latest in evidence–based nutrition, visit NutritionFacts.org. "NutritionFacts.org is a strictly non–commercial, science–based public service provided by Dr. Michael Greger, providing free updates on the latest in nutrition research via bite–sized videos".

The Cost of Eating Healthy

Is it expensive to eat healthy? If you measure the cost per calorie, the way we did over 100 years ago, then the answer is yes. You can get 4,464 calories per dollar from flour and 2,854 calories per dollar from refined sugar, but only 929 from lentils and 287 from quinoa.[18] But stuffing our faces with calories is not really the goal. In primitive times, calories were difficult to obtain and highly prized commodities, but that has changed dramatically. Calories are easy to come by in our modern world. In fact, they are ubiquitous. Many of the readily accessible foods such as sodas, fast foods, and packaged foods are packed with calories, but devoid of nutrition.

So, cost per calorie is an outdated way of looking at food costs. A more useful way to measure the true cost of food is cost–per–nutrition. To put this into perspective, consider that a serving of vegetables may cost about four times the average serving of junk food; however, the veggies provide about twenty–four times the nutrition per dollar when compared to junk food and highly processed foods. If you do the math, you see that vegetables provide six times the nutrition–per–dollar. The comparison between meat and vegetables is even more astounding. Meat costs approximately three times more than vegetables. On the other hand, meat supplies sixteen times less nutrition.[19] The bottom line is that vegetables provide forty–eight times more nutrition per dollar than meat. That's incredible. If there were ever an argument for eating vegetables over meat, this is it.

There are other superstars in the cost per dollar game. Red cabbage for example contains more antioxidants per dollar than any other produce, and certainly more that anything in the meat counter. Some of the other low cost, high nutrient foods in order of least expensive include mustard greens, carrots, kale, collard greens, bok choy, romaine, cauliflower, Brussels sprouts, spinach, Swiss chard, arugula, and sweet potato.

If you want to know more about how the nutrition of food is measured, look up Dr. Fuhrman's ANDI Index. ANDI stands for Aggregate Nutrient Density Index. It reports nutrients divided by calories. This measuring system rewards foods that are high in micronutrients per calorie, and penalizes foods that are high in calories and low in nutrition. The foods from highest nutrition density to lowest tend to be leafy greens, other vegetables, fruits, nuts and seeds, beans, animal products, and finally junk food. We will take a look at eating plant–based on a budget in a later chapter, but you can get a good head start just by looking at the ANDI index.

Healthcare

"Let food be thy medicine and medicine be thy food.

– Hippocrates

No discussion of daily health would be complete without considering the health care system. After all, when you get sick, you put your health in the hands of your health care practitioner. As children, we put our complete faith in our doctor's ability to know what is best to keep us healthy. As adults, we owe it to ourselves to take an informed view of the health care industry, and decide for ourselves how it can best serve our healthcare needs.

The first step in gaining an informed perspective is to realize that healthcare in the US is big business. The cost of healthcare in the US reached $3.2 trillion in 2015, and it has gone from 5% of the Gross Domestic Product in 1960 to nearly 17.8% of the GDP in 2015.[20] Now, that's BIG business! This has huge implications for us as individuals, because with big money at stake, decisions made by healthcare institutions, the pharmaceutical industry, and others involved in healthcare are inclined to be profit–driven rather than patient–driven. As Medical journalist Shannon Brownlee put it, "We have a disease care system, and we have a very profitable disease care system . . . it doesn't want you to die and it doesn't want you to get well; it just wants you to keep coming back for the care of your chronic disease."[21]

Another shocking aspect of our national healthcare system is that medical care is the sixth leading cause of death in the US. Approximately 106,000 people die from side effects of prescribed mediations every year.[22] Some 7,000 die from receiving the wrong medication by mistake. An additional 20,000 people die from other hospital errors.[23] So, if a trip to the doctors' office or hospital puts us at risk, how can we avoid it? Fortunately, most trips to the doctor's office are for diseases that can be prevented by healthy diet and lifestyle.[24]

Doctors can be great resources for curing infections and repairing broken bones, but they are rarely trained in nutrition. This is surprising, because poor nutrition is the root cause of most of our chronic diseases.[25] Unfortunately, doctors are predominantly trained in medical school to prescribe drugs rather than prescribe healthy eating.

It wasn't always this way. In the early 1900s, nearly half of the medical practitioners practiced holistic medicine, from naturopathy to homeopathy to herbal medicine and more. Many of these modalities were taught in the medical schools of the time. But around that same time, business magnates discovered that there was big money to be made by manufacturing and marketing artificial substances (drugs) to mask or stop symptoms of disease. This was a huge business opportunity. Abraham Flexner was hired to conduct a comprehensive study of medical education in the United States and Canada. The results were published in 1910 in conjunction with the Carnegie Foundation. This report highlighted many of the inconsistencies in medical education, but it also concluded that the natural healing modalities were unscientific quackery. The report ultimately led Congress to declare the American Medical Association the only body with the right to grant medical school licenses in the United States. The report called for the standardization of medical education to ensure that only allopathic–based (pharmacology–based) medical schools would be accredited in the U.S. By 1935, more than half of the medical schools that had existed in 1904 had either merged or closed. To further ensure a uniform curriculum, tax–exempt foundations were used to offer huge grants to medical schools on the condition that only an allopathic–based curriculum be taught. This changed the course of medical education and practice in the U.S. Today, the focus of medical practice is on prescription of drugs, radiation, and surgery.

Today, even decades later, very little nutrition or alternative medicine is taught in medical schools. A survey published in 2010 revealed that only 25% of the medicals schools required a dedicated nutrition course. On average, medical students received 19.6 hours of nutrition education during their entire medical school careers.[26]

The answers to our leading health woes are not at the bottom of our pill bottle,
but on the end of our fork.

– Shushana Castle and Amy–Lee Goodman

This is the "healthcare" system with which we are faced today, based on allopathic medicine. Looking at the positive side, drugs can often treat symptoms effectively. Unfortunately, they don't generally cure the underlying causes, and many of them also have unwanted side effects. As a result, chronic conditions tend to persist and worsen. Over time, patients are often required to add more and more drugs to keep the symptoms at bay. It can be a vicious cycle, but there is something you can do about it. Educate yourself about how a plant–based diet can protect you from life–threatening diseases and keep you free of drugs. Search for doctors who understand the relationship between nutrition and disease. There are websites popping up such as plantbaseddoctors.org and VegDocs.com to aid in this search. As the public's awareness of these issues increase, we are starting to see more doctors with nutrition training. My wife and I recently found a plant–

based doctor in our local area. Even the nation's largest healthcare provider, Kaiser Permanente, has acknowledged the role of plant–based nutrition in the pursuit of health. In a message to physicians in 2013, it states that eating healthy may be "best achieved with a plant–based diet."[27]

Get off the Medical System and onto the Self Care System.

– Nina Leavins

In this chapter we investigated several aspects of maintaining your daily health. We looked at recommended daily food choices in the Plant–Based Food Choices diagram. We looked at the basic guidelines for following a whole food plant–based diet. We looked at how educating yourself to the influence of the food industry can help with your daily food choices. We looked at the cost of eating healthy from a cost-per-nutrition perspective. We looked at the healthcare industry as a business, and why it is in our best interests to take an active role in our own healthcare. The focus of the next chapter is on how to make the transition to a plant–based diet.

CHAPTER 5: MAKING THE TRANSITION

We've looked at why you might want to eat a plant–based diet, how it will affect your awareness, the nutritional and health implications, and a few considerations of your daily health. That laid the groundwork for this chapter: Making the Transition to Plant–Based Eating.

Everybody is different. There are some people who kind of drag themselves toward
a vegetarian or vegan diet very slowly, while there are others who take to it instantly.
There are some who need a lot of support, while others have no trouble at all.
It's like quitting smoking: there are some folks for whom it's really rough,
and there are others who say, "I've made up my mind this is it."[1]

– Dr. Neal Barnard

Making the transition to a sustainable diet is very doable, though it is not without challenges. At first, it may seem like a vegan or plant–based diet is more about what you can't have than what you can have. When I made the decision to eat vegan, I wondered what I would do without my familiar comfort foods. What would life be like with out my burgers, pizza, tacos, spaghetti, milk, ice cream, and pies? It was difficult to imagine. As it turned out, those fears were unfounded. With all the options that are available nowadays, it was easy to convert my favorite foods into vegan versions without the animal products. In fact, most of the new dishes are better tasting than the SAD versions. My journey to a plant–based diet has been full of amazing new flavors and taste sensations.

A few people make the transition overnight, but that is rare. Most people make the change gradually over time. Even the rapid adopters go through stages. This chapter is designed to help transform your eating style in a way that fits you. It will help you gain a new perspective on the issues involved, and find your own unique path to achieve your goal. It will enable you to redefine your food comfort zone to embrace a delectable variety of new foods and flavors.

Throughout the process, it is important to keep your focus on your goal – to develop a satisfying eating style that provides you with nutrition, protects you from disease, does not harm animals, and has minimal impact on the environment. Keep the pace comfortable and manageable; this is not a race. Strive for progress, not perfection. Every step forward gets you closer to your goal. Above all, your eating style must satisfy your palate and be one that you can maintain. This chapter emphasizes staying in your own food comfort zone and allowing your comfort zone to shift and expand as you make changes toward a more healthy diet. The next chapter, Chapter Six, covers ways to fit your new food choices into your lifestyle and to maintain it for the long term.

It's important to embrace the learning curve. Give yourself time to learn the ropes because there is a lot to learn. One idea is to find a mentor who offers an eating plan that sounds attractive and follow that plan. Check out the "Gurus" section in the Resources chapter. Speaking of resources, there are lots of other items in Resources that might be helpful as you get started: books, documentaries, blogs and other social media sites, meetups, recipes online, cooking classes, and more. I found local and online cooking classes to be a big help and a good networking opportunity. Above all, take your time and enjoy the journey.

Stages of the Journey

Your journey toward a whole food plant–based diet will be unique. Nevertheless, there are phases that most people pass through. It is worth noting these so that you will recognize them as you progress. You may be just taking your first steps, or already well along the path.

Awareness – Like most people, you may have been drawn to plant–based eating by some change in your awareness. It could have been precipitated by a person, an event, a documentary, or a change in circumstance that caused you to take a new way of looking at what you eat. This is the first step toward a higher health consciousness.

Investigation – Awareness leads to questions. How do I get started? What changes should I make in my shopping and food preparation? What's the best way to make the transition? In this phase, you'll seek answers to these initial questions, and plot your course for making the change.

Implementation – In this phase, you'll make some changes in your kitchen to support your transformation. You'll establish a network of people who will support your efforts, and help you learn more about the benefits of plant–based eating. You'll start eating more plant–based foods, and crowding out animal products and processed foods. At that same time, you'll manage the pace of your changes so that you remain satisfied with your food choices. That is, you want to stay in your food comfort zone, and let that zone gradually shift and expand as you experience new foods and taste sensations. Give your body and taste buds time to adjust to your new eating style.

Maintenance – As you continue the process, you'll develop systems for regular food preparation at home, preparing food for travel, and eating at work. You will integrate your new eating style into social situations with family, friends, and dining out. You will learn ways to save money and time as you continue your progress toward eating more whole foods. As before, you will allow your food comfort zone to expand to include new foods and tastes.

Thriving – As you become more comfortable with plant–based eating, you will refine the process so that it fits seamlessly into your lifestyle. You will develop even more flavor combinations that stimulate and satisfy your palette. You will continue learning about the specific foods that best help you combat chronic diseases. You will continue to refine your eating habits to fully embrace a whole food plant–based eating style. You will enjoy the rewards of increased mental clarity, physical vigor, and reduced dependence on medications. You will have more energy to incorporate regular exercise into your lifestyle. Chances are, you will be so thrilled with how you look and feel, that you may even be inspired to share your experience with others.

Behavior Change

Before we get into the details of the transition, we need to talk about behavior change. That's what you are proposing – changing your eating habits. There are many factors that can conspire to keep you from making any changes, especially with something as deeply entrenched and personal as eating habits. These factors might influence you to keep eating the same old thing rather than breaking out of the mold and testing uncharted culinary waters. And you might not even be aware of these factors. Here are some of the common roadblocks to making a change of diet.

1. **Affordability**. It may seem cheaper to eat your traditional fare.
2. **Familiarity**. You are comfortable preparing your traditional foods. Changing means overcoming that inertia.
3. **Medical condition(s)**. You might have an allergy or other condition that would preclude you from eating certain types of foods.
4. **Childhood foods**. The foods you ate growing up can have a strong affect on your food choices as an adult.
5. **Reluctant partner**. It may be that your partner prepares the meals or has a different eating style.

6. **Religious principles**. Religious practice may influence what or when you eat.
7. **Cultural food traditions**. Family and cultural food traditions can be deeply rooted.
8. **Frequent travel**. Frequent travel may limit your food choices and challenge you to learn how to eat healthy on the road.
9. **The Pleasure Trap**. We are confronted with super–concentrated calorically–dense foods all the time. Junk food and processed foods have become pervasive in our society. These are inherently attractive and addictive. Breaking out of the pleasure trap requires elevated awareness and purpose.

As you can see from this list, food choices can be complicated. So, making a decision to change means overcoming a lot of inertia. That's why it is so important to get clear on **why** you want to change. Establishing a firm connection with the reason(s) you want to change your diet can energize your resolve to overcome the inertia and change your eating habits. So, take a moment to ponder your reasons for wanting to change. Chapter 1 covered several reasons that people seek out plant–based eating – health, environment, animals, cost, inspiration. Which of these reasons mean the most to you? Or do you have other reasons? With **your reasons** firmly in mind, imagine what your life will be like a couple of years from now when you have a new eating style firmly established. Imagine how you will feel when you achieve your goal. If you are like those who traveled this path before you, you will feel lighter on your feet, more energetic, and taking a lot less medications. That's inspiring.

One of the best ways to achieve such a major behavior change is to set small achievable goals over a moderate timeframe. For example, your first goal might be to make a few better food choices each week over a six–week period. A more specific goal might be to convert three of your usual dinner meals from animal–based to plant–based. At the end of that six weeks, evaluate your progress. If you achieved your goal, set another goal for the next six weeks. If not, figure out what it was that got in your way first, then make adjustments and set your next goal. You can make tremendous progress by achieving a sequence of smaller goals without feeling overwhelmed by the big picture. Just take it one step at a time.

It may seem like we are talking about extremely long time frames – six weeks at a time and change over months or years. But think about what you are dealing with. This is a major lifestyle change, and it has a huge upside (transforming your health and that of the planet). If you look at the big picture, a few months (or even years) is actually a relatively short time to make such a major change. After all, how many years did it take to develop your current eating habits – 20, 30, 40, 50 years? You can afford a few months to develop some new effective habits.

If you want your newfound plant–strong diet to last, you need to make it something that satisfies your taste buds and comfortably fits into your lifestyle. The key is to stay in your food comfort zone at every stage of the process. You may start out eating more comfort foods. As you go through the process, consciously add more whole food veggies and fruits to your meals, so that they crowd out the processed foods. As time goes on, your food comfort zone will expand and your body will begin to crave more whole foods as your taste buds transform. You will need less and less processed foods to maintain that level of satiety.

It's important that you listen to your body and manage your own transformation accordingly. Give yourself time to adjust. At the start of my journey, I couldn't imagine that a simple bowl of steamed veggies over quinoa could ever taste so good, but that's because my taste buds were over stimulated with sugar, fat, and salt at that point. As I've eaten more whole foods in my diet, my tastes have reset. I can now appreciate the unique flavors of each steamed vegetable. If I want to enhance the flavors, I can add spices, liquid flavorings, or my own homemade sauces.

If you can go faster, great! But you don't want to rush it to the point that you feel uncomfortable and tempted to revert to old habits. Reaching any kind of goal is a process. Let's say your goal is to eat 100% plant based. That's great! However, you may need to give yourself time to work toward that goal. Give yourself credit for any improvements you make in that direction, and give yourself a bit of slack if you stray from the goal. The worst thing you could do is to become frustrated or disappointed and quit because you "can't make it work."

Studies show that the human body is amazing. Even after years of eating food detrimental to our bodies, relatively short periods of eating a plant–based diet can make a dramatic difference. Even elderly people can reverse chronic disease by changing their diet. A 2014 study showed that just 30 days on a whole food, plant–based diet resulted in significant reduction of body mass index (BMI), systolic and diastolic blood pressure, cholesterol, lipoprotein cholesterol, and triglycerides for participants.[2] Dr. Dean Ornish put cardiac patients on a mostly vegan diet (with some stress management) and achieved a 90% reduction of angina attacks in just 24 days.[3] Speaking of rapid healing, in another study, patients who had been diabetic for years (even decades) were able to reduce their insulin by about 60 percent (half were able to stop insulin completely) by eating a plant–based diet for an average of just 16 days.[4] Sixteen days! I witnessed something similar when my ninety–year–old Mother–in–Law went from 10 units of insulin per day down to zero units a day in about two months on a mostly vegan diet.

So, don't hold yourself to an impossible standard. Anything you can do to improve your diet can make a significant difference. It's very comforting to know that you can replace those old habits in a few short months, or even in a couple of years by just redefining your food comfort zone and replacing the deleterious products with healthy foods. Trust your body to respond to the healthy foods you will feed it.

Preparing Your Kitchen

Kitchen Tools

Setting up your kitchen with a few basic tools will make your transition so much easier.

Electric Appliances

Here is a list of appliances that have been very useful in preparing plant–based meals. Evaluate what you have on hand. No need to rush out or hop online to purchase everything immediately. Just keep them in mind as you start to explore new recipes and cooking techniques.

Blender – A blender is great for making smoothies, dressings, dips, creamy sauces, and hot soups. I had a middle of the road blender for quite a while, until my aging dad came for a visit. He took one sip of his green breakfast smoothie made in the blender and said "Hmmm... Kind of chewy." That was it! I bundled the blender off to a relative in need, and bought a high–speed blender. Now, the smoothies and cream sauces come out nice and smooth. No more chewy smoothies! A powerful blender will also stand up to the job of grinding seeds and grains as well as tough vegetables and frozen fruit. For the record, I bought a Blentec. The other top of the line blender is Vitamix. Both brands have loyal admirers.

Coffee grinder – A small grinder is useful to grind up grains and seeds. I use a coffee grinder to grind dehydrated moringa, basil, and mint leaves to make useful powders. I also grind flax seeds every few days to keep the flax meal fresh.

> Moringa is a tree native to Africa and Asia. It's packed with nutrients including antioxidants, vitamin A, vitamin C, calcium, potassium, protein, and more. I grow it in gardening pots (in Southern California) and keep the trees very small for easy harvesting. I use the tender leaves in salads and the dried powder in smoothies and on cereal.

Countertop steamer – Steaming is a great way to prepare vegetables. It increases the antioxidant levels of some vegetables, and it lets the inherent flavors pop. You can steam veggies in the microwave or in a steamer basket on the stovetop, but I found that a countertop steamer has some advantages. First, you can set it and forget it. Set the timer, and the steamer will turn off when the time is up. You'll learn the best times for different vegetables. Speaking of cooking times, if your steamer has multiple levels, you can use that to your advantage. Put the harder veggies in the bottom tray where they cook the fastest. Put the greens in the top tray. With some experience, the veggies will cook to perfection. You can add spices, sauces, and other flavorings to enhance the flavors after the veggies are steamed. My steamer has transparent trays. So, I can see the veggies as they cook and make adjustments on the fly if necessary. Cleanup is easy, and the cost was minimal — less than $50. Finally, there is the fun factor. It's so easy and fun to use, that it has become one of the most used appliances in my kitchen.

Dehydrator – There are many uses for a dehydrator. The units are somewhat pricey, so do your research before buying one that meets your needs. Dehydrating is one way to preserve excess produce from your garden. Some popular items to dehydrate include bananas, apples, pears, tomatoes, zucchini, cauliflower, and kale. I use my dehydrator to dry herbs and moringa tree leaves and grind them into powders for use in other dishes. I've also made flaxseed crackers. Enterprising users have made fruit leathers, granola bars, cookies, and even cake in their dehydrators.

Food processor – A food processor can quickly and easily chop, slice, shred, grind, and puree almost any food.

Pressure cooker – A pressure cooker is suited for cooking large batches of food: soups, beans, grains, and vegetables. It speeds up the cooking of beans significantly. Consider getting a multi–use appliance that is a pressure cooker, slow cooker, rice cooker, food steamer, sauté pan, and soup maker.

Rice cooker – A rice cooker is a labor saving device, easy to use, and easy to clean. It cooks a variety of grains such as quinoa and millet, not just rice.

Slow cooker – A slow cooker or Crock-Pot is great for making soups, stews, and casseroles. Just toss in the ingredients, set it, and forget it. Some people cook almost every meal in their slow cooker.

Microwave – A microwave is useful to reheat dishes, steam veggies in microwave–safe cookware, and for cooking frozen dinners. Make sure you cover the food so that it retains the heat and doesn't splatter.

Other Kitchen Tools

Colander – A colander is a bowl with narrow slots or holes used for draining pasta and rice.

Cutting board – There are many types of cutting boards: wood, plastic, glass, or stone. I prefer bamboo. Harder surfaces might be easier to clean, but they may dull your knife blade more quickly.

Glass dishes and bowls – Get an assortment of sizes and shapes of glass containers with covers. They are useful for mixing, soaking foods in marinades, and storage.

Grater – Use a grater for shredding root vegetables and more. I find a handheld microplane grater useful for collecting the zest of lemons and oranges.

Hot pads – Protect your hands by using hot pads to pull dishes out of the oven or microwave.

Knives – Knives are probably the most used tools in the kitchen. Find knives that fit your grip and cutting style. At minimum, you'll need a long chef knife for cutting larger items, and a short serrated knife for smaller foods that require more dexterity. Most chefs prefer blades that require sharpening (such as ceramic or high–carbon stainless steel), and they often keep a spare to use when they send their knives out for sharpening. Chefs are often very passionate about their particular choice of knife. Knock yourself out sorting through the online debate about which knives are superior. The rebel in me took an entirely different path. I ended up with a set of stainless steel knives that are laser cut, and never need sharpening. They are not the sharpest tools in the shed, but they are very sturdy and work well for everything I need. Both my wife and I have tried using sharper knives, and we always seem to end up with knife cuts. So, we stick with the tried and true.

Pots and pans – You'll need pots and pans of various sizes. Consider non–stick for ease of use and clean up. A large pot is useful for soups and big batches of spaghetti sauce. A sauté pan with high sides is useful sautéing garlic, onions, and other vegetables. A saucepan can be used for boiling water, making sauces, and cooking pasta. I also a non–stick wok for stir-fry and other dishes.

Measuring cups – You'll need measuring cups for measuring quantities for recipes.

Measuring spoons – You'll need measuring spoons for measuring small quantities for recipes.

Spray bottles – A small 2–ounce fingertip spray bottle can make all the difference if you have liquid flavorings that need to be used in small amounts. For example, liquid smoke should be applied by the drop, but the aperture on some bottles is way too large for that kind of portion control. But if you put it in a spray bottle, you can apply just the right amount. I find spray bottles useful for spraying lemon juice, beet juice, Worcestershire sauce, and liquid smoke. Be wary of super cheap spray bottles; they will clog up quickly, as I learned from first-hand experience.

Strainers – Strainers come in handy for sifting flour, rinsing quinoa, and straining off liquid from cooked ingredients.

Tongs – Tongs are useful for picking up steamed veggies, noodles, etc.

Vegetable brush – A nice stiff vegetable brush will come in handy to clean fresh produce, especially if harvested from your garden.

Whisks – Whisks are a must for hand mixing and blending powders.

Optional Tools

Citrus juicer – A handheld or electric juicer will make it easy to extract juice from citrus fruits.

Cookie sheets and baking pans – These are just the thing if you are into baking.

Freezer – If you have space in your garage, a standalone freezer can make a huge difference in your ability to purchase in bulk and cook large batches for freezing.

Garlic press – A garlic press is a nice time saver if you need minced garlic and want it fresh.

Hand mixer or countertop mixer – I find a countertop mixer (with balloon whip) essential for making whipped toppings from aquafaba (bean juice). See *Whipped Topping* in "Desserts".

Juicer – I have a slow juicer, which is designed to extract more juice than other kinds of juicers. From a whole food diet standpoint, the concern with juicers is that they remove the fiber, and with that, you also lose most of the phytonutrients. Blending is probably a better choice to preserve the nutrition.

Pizza stone – A pizza stone will give you a crispier crust when baking pizzas. Some people use their pizza stones for cooking other foods as well.

Plastic containers – I recommend large plastic containers with snap-on lids for organizing your food stores. Label one or more containers for your grains, nuts, and seeds in the freezer, and another container for beans and lentils in your pantry or cupboard.

Rolling pin – If you roll out pizza or cookie dough, a rolling pin beats doing it by hand.

Salad spinner – Many people find a salad spinner useful for cleaning lettuce and other veggies.

Spiralizer – A spiralizer can be used to shred and extrude veggies into different shapes. One popular use is to make zucchini noodles in place of pasta for spaghetti.

Toaster oven – I use my toaster oven for toasting the occasional bun for a burger. The small tray is perfect for roasting nuts to add to any dish.

Water filter – Water filters definitely deserve a mention because water intake is so vital to our healthy bodily functions. Tap water can be purposely treated with fluoride, and there is a risk of contamination from older plumbing. Filtering the water can reduce the risk of ingesting unwanted contaminants. The filter types range from simple countertop filters to elaborate whole house systems. I found a reasonably priced countertop filter with three types of filtration. See the discussion in the Macronutrient section of Chapter Three.

Wire racks – Wire racks are used for cooling baked goods.

Yogurt maker – When our local farmers market ran out of cultured coconut milk yogurt, my wife got creative and figured out how to make her own with a yogurt maker. The process is amazingly simple. See the recipe in the From Scratch section of the recipe chapter. It tastes very fresh when homemade. It works a bit like a sourdough starter. You use a little bit of the previous batch as a start for the next batch. Homemade non-dairy yogurt is a great source of probiotics.

Stocking Your Kitchen

Along with outfitting your kitchen with useful cooking tools, part of preparing for a transition to a more healthy eating style is purchasing foods that will support you in the journey. Below, I've provided lists of foodstuffs that can be helpful at every stage of the process. The categories are pantry, freezer, refrigerator, condiments and spices, and fresh produce. These are pretty extensive lists compiled from people who have traveled the road before you. They include foods, condiments, spices, and flavorings that you will find in many vegan and plant–based recipes. You do not need to go out and purchase everything immediately. However, the lists can be a good reference as you run across new and unfamiliar ingredients when you try out new recipes. Use them to build your shopping lists.

So, you have an interesting decision to make. Do you pull everything out of the pantry, freezer, and fridge, and give it to the neighbors so that you can start with a clean slate? Or do you toss a few items that you won't be eating, then make the replacement a gradual process? My friend, Albert, followed the later path. He continued to use his existing food stores. At each shopping trip, he replaced any used items with vegan alternatives, or with more healthy options. The whole process took several months, but in the end, he had eliminated all animal products from his kitchen. As you try out new recipes, you can let the ingredients drive your restocking process. If a recipe calls for lentils, for example, and you've never had a lentil in your life, add it to your shopping list and give it a try. You can, of course, buy dry lentils and cook them yourself, but Trader Joe's and other markets carry packets of precooked lentils. Just open the package, and they are ready to go. If a recipe calls for liquid smoke, give that a try as well. One of my cooking mentors, Patty Knutson (vegancoach.com), selected liquid smoke as one of her top 10 vegan flavoring ingredients. I can see why, because it can really transform a dish, but be careful – it only takes a couple of drops to work its magic.

Even if you prefer a gradual replacement process, it's worth getting rid of the least healthy food items to make room for the new items. You can donate these items to neighbors, friends, or a food bank. Consider replacing foods that are expired, contain white flour or white sugar, contain more than five ingredients, or contain high–fructose corn syrup. Removing these items will minimize the distraction from the healthy foods you want to eat. Do a little inventory and purging of your pantry, freezer, and refrigerator.

Shop Organic

One of the choices you make when shopping is whether or not to purchase organic produce. Organic produce is grown without the use of pesticides or synthetic fertilizers. Organic farming methods prohibit the use of genetic engineering, ionizing radiation, or sewage sludge. A meta–analysis of 343 studies, the largest of its kind, found the concentration of antioxidants to be between 18% and 69% higher in organically–grown crops. It also found significantly less of the toxic heavy metal cadmium and four times less pesticide residue.[5]

The health benefits of antioxidants in organic produce is undeniable, but you can get the same antioxidant benefit by eating an extra serving or two of conventional fruits and vegetables. The health implications of consuming toxins contained in conventional produce requires further study. According to Dr. Greger, "You receive tremendous benefit from eating conventional fruits and vegetables that far outweighs whatever little bump in risk you may get from the pesticides."[6] You always have the option to choose organic produce when it is available and your budget allows. And when it doesn't allow, you can follow the sage advice of mothers everywhere: **eat your veggies**! (whether they be organic or otherwise).

You can further prioritize your organic food choices by following the recommendations of the Environmental Working Group (EWG). This group ranks pesticide contamination of 48 popular fruits and vegetables. Their Dirty Dozen (highest pesticide levels) and Clean Fifteen (lowest pesticide levels) lists are updated annually. Visit ewg.org/foodnews to view the updated lists. Keep a list of the dirty dozen handy, and purchase any of the items on this list as organic whenever possible.

Dirty Dozen

strawberries	spinach	nectarines
apples	peaches	pears
cherries	grapes	celery
tomatoes	sweet bell peppers	potatoes

Clean Fifteen

sweet corn	avocados	pineapples
cabbage	onions	sweet peas (frozen)
papayas	asparagus	mangos
eggplant	honeydew melon	kiwi
cantaloupe	cauliflower	grapefruit

Pantry

The pantry is a great place to store many of the building blocks of plant–based meals. Potatoes can make a base for meal. The darker colors have more nutrition, especially sweet potatoes. You can store onions and garlic in the pantry as well. Pastas also store well in the pantry. What about grains? You can store grains in the pantry, but I prefer to store them in the freezer for longer shelf life and to kill any insect eggs that may have hitchhiked a ride on the way home from the market. See the Freezer section. Your pantry is an ideal place to store your beans, peas and lentils. I recommend storing them in a large plastic bin (with snap on top) and storing the individual legumes in labeled bags with a zip top. Purchasing dried beans, peas, or lentils, and then cooking them in a pressure cooker or slow cooker will save you money over just buying canned legumes. On the other hand, canned beans are very convenient. Just open a can, and you've got a good base for a meal. Dry lentils and peas can be stored in the same container as the dry beans.

Here is a reference list for stocking your pantry items:

Agave	Peas
Applesauce (unsweetened)	Pasta noodles (whole–grain)
Artichoke hearts	Pineapple (crushed, chunks)
Beans – canned (black, garbanzo, great northern, kidney, pinto)	Pumpkin (canned, pure)
Beans – dry (adzuki, black, garbanzo, great northern, kidney, navy, pinto, white)	Raisins
Coconut milk (canned)	Red wine vinegar
Corn (canned)	Rice vinegar
Dates	Roasted red peppers
Kombu (for cooking beans)	Seaweed (dried: kombu, nori)
Lentils – dry (all colors)	Tofu (silken)
Liquid aminos	Tomato paste (cans)
Liquid smoke	Tomato sauce (canned)
Maple syrup	Vegetable broth
Marinara sauce	Vegetable stock powder
Oats	Vinegars (apple cider, balsamic, white)
Oil (coconut, olive)	Whole wheat pastry flour
Olives (black, green, Kalmata)	Yeast, active dry
Peanut butter	

Freezer

A freezer is extremely useful for storing goods for plant–based meal preparation. In fact, it is so useful that I ended up purchasing an upright freezer unit for the garage. Now, I have plenty of room to store grains, nuts, seeds, bags of fruit for smoothies, cooked beans and lentils, precooked meals in individual portions for later use, excess fruit from the garden, and frozen meals from PlantPure Nation and other brands (See the Resources chapter).

For a time, I had trouble with moths showing up in my dried goods in a particular cupboard. It turns out that tiny insect eggs can be hidden in some dried goods that you bring home from the market. Freezing the product for 2 to 3 days will kill any insect eggs. Now, I make a regular practice of freezing any suspect products for several days, before moving them to the pantry or fridge. This eliminated the problem with insect eggs. Grains are permanently stored in the freezer. Flours are frozen first, then stored in the refrigerator.

I recommend purchasing three large plastic containers (with snap on top) similar to the container for lentils in the pantry. Label them Grains, Nuts, and Seeds (you can combine the nuts and seeds if space is a consideration).

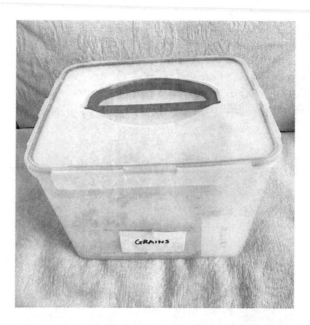

Store the individual items in bags with a zip top. You can label the outside of each bag or write the name of the item on part of a 3x5 card, and slip that into the bag. That way, your stored items will be easy to identify and locate. When you run out of quinoa, or walnuts, or chia seeds, simply add them to your shopping list and replenish.

When you purchase rice, be aware that the darker selections like wild rice, brown rice, and black rice will better support your health than heavily processed white rice. For other grains, quinoa is a great choice for its high protein content, but there are many other varieties to enjoy, including amaranth, barley, buckwheat, couscous, kamut, millet, oats, and wheat.

Here is a reference list for freezer items:

Burger patties (vegan)	Hotdogs (vegan)
Cheese (vegan)	Nuts (almonds, cashews, peanuts, pecans, walnuts)
Cooked beans, lentils (labeled)	Peas – dry
Edamame packages	Pineapple chunks
Fruit (mixed berry, mango, …)	Prepared meals (PlantPure, Amy's)
Grains – dry (amaranth, barley, buckwheat, couscous, kamut, millet, oats, and wheat)	Rice (black, brown, wild)
Greens – packaged (collards, kale, spinach, Swiss chard)	Seeds (chia, flax , pumpkin, sesame, sunflower)

Refrigerator

The refrigerator is used to store opened bottles or jars and many types of fresh produce. I also store flour in the refrigerator after first freezing for a few days.

Here is a reference list for refrigerator items:

Almond butter	Mayonnaise (vegan)
Bagels	Mint
Barbecue sauce	Miso (yellow or white)
Beef crumbles (vegan)	Miso paste
Bread	Mustard (Dijon, yellow,…)
Burger patty (vegan)	Non–dairy milk (almond, coconut, flax, hemp, oat, rice, soy)
Buttery spread (non–dairy)	Pasta
Cheese (vegan shreds or parmesan style)	Peanut butter
Coconut aminos	Pitas
Coffee creamer (soy)	Pre–chopped fruits and vegetables
Cream cheese (vegan)	Salsa (any variety)
Deli slices (vegan)	Seitan
English muffins	Sour cream (vegan)
Flour (almond, coconut, gluten free, spelt, unbleached all–purpose, whole–wheat)	Soy sauce (low–sodium)
Fruit preserves	Tahini
Garlic cloves	Tamari
Ginger root	Tempeh
Hot sauce (chili, Tabasco, …)	Tofu (Firm and extra–firm)
Hummus	Tortillas
Ketchup	Vegetable bouillon
Lemon juice	Worcestershire sauce (vegan)
Lime juice	Yogurt (almond, coconut, soy)

Condiments and Seasonings

Spices should be stored in a cool dry space away from light. Don't store them over a hot stove. Other condiments and seasonings can be stored in the spice cupboard or in the pantry.

Here is a reference list for condiments and seasonings:

Agar agar	Erythritol
Agave syrup	Garlic powder
Allspice	Ginger (ground)
Almond extract	Italian seasoning
Arrowroot	Maple syrup
Baking powder	Mint
Baking soda	Molasses
Basil	Nutmeg (Ground)
Black pepper (ground, whole)	Nutritional yeast
Black salt	Onion powder
Brown sugar	Oregano (dried)
Cayenne pepper	Paprika (regular and smoked)
Chili powder	Parsley
Chinese Five Spices	Peppermint extract
Chipotle powder	Poultry seasoning (granulated)
Chocolate (dark, vegan)	Pumpkin pie spice
Chocolate chips (vegan)	Red pepper flakes
Cilantro	Rosemary
Cinnamon (Ground)	Sage
Cloves (ground)	Sea salt
Cocoa (unsweetened)	Stevia
Coconut crystals	Sucanat
Coconut extract	Sugar (Organic)
Confectioners sugar (powdered)	Taco seasoning (packet)
Coriander (ground)	Thai seasoning
Cornmeal	Thyme
Corn starch	Turmeric
Cumin (ground)	Vanilla extract
Curry powder	White chocolate chips (vegan)
Date sugar	

Fresh Produce

Most fresh produce will be stored in the refrigerator. Garlic, onions, shallots, and sweet potatoes can be stored in the pantry. Avocado, bananas, pineapple, and tomatoes can be stored on a countertop. Some fruits, like grapefruit and oranges, can be stored on a countertop to ripen, then in the fridge.

Here is a reference list for fresh produce (remember to consult the Dirty Dozen list posted by EWG and purchase organic whenever possible):

Apples	Kiwis
Apricots	Lemons
Asparagus	Lettuce (romaine, butter lettuce, red leaf, green leaf, arugula)
Avocado	Limes
Bananas	Mangoes
Bell peppers (all colors)	Mushrooms
Blackberries	Nectarines
Blueberries	Onions (green, red, shallots, yellow)
Broccoli	Oranges
Cabbage (green, red)	Peaches
Cantaloupe	Pears
Carrots	Peppers (Anaheim, cayenne, jalapeño, Serrano, Tabasco, etc.)
Cauliflower	Plums
Celery	Potatoes (new, russet, sweet)
Cherries	Raspberries
Corn	Salad mixes
Cucumbers	Spinach
Fennel	Squash (acorn, butternut, spaghetti, yellow)
Garlic	Strawberries
Grapefruit	Sugar snap peas
Grapes	Tomatoes
Honey dew melon	Watermelon
Kale	Zucchini

Shopping

Compare the reference lists to the foodstuffs you have on hand, and decide what you would like to add or replace. Make a shopping list. This could be a handwritten list or using a shopping app on your smartphone. I use the Shopper app for several reasons.

- Lists can be shared across devices, so it doesn't matter if I'm using my iPhone or iPad.
- Lists can be shared with other people. This is key. If I'm out shopping at a particular store, my wife can update the list on her device, and I'll see the change while I'm still shopping.
- It allows for quick entry when selecting existing items or creating new items.
- Other features such as adding pictures, barcode scanning, and using coupons.

Make a list, and get ready to shop.

Where to Shop

The first and most rewarding stop in the shopping tour is your home garden. That's where you are guaranteed the freshest organic produce. For people with limited space, there are more options nowadays – indoor growing stations (such as Click & Grow, clickandgrow.com), hydroponic tower gardens for deck and patio, and vertical solutions for growing against a wall. I'm lucky enough to have more space, although much of it is on a steep slope. I've spent the last several years fashioning raised garden beds and pathways on the slopes. I've also built a couple of hydroponic towers. With the temperate Southern California weather, there is no shortage of herbs, leafy greens, and a few other vegetables coming out of the garden. When in season, there are several kinds of fruit. There is nothing like picking fresh produce right out of your garden. I encourage you to look at how you might grow your own food, even if it is a tomato plant outside, and a few herbs in an indoor growing station. Stacey Murphy of GrowYourOwnVegetables.org is a great resource for growing food in a limited space.

The next stop on the shopping tour is local farmers markets. Check to see if there is one near you. Generally, the produce is grown in the local area, and sold at a weekly market event. It is very rewarding to get farm–fresh produce and support your local growers.

There are a variety of different kinds of food markets, each with their unique appeal. Shopper's clubs like Sam's and Costco offer larger quantities at extremely good prices. They are increasingly embracing organic foods. In addition to bulk quantities of fresh produce, I look for non-dairy milks, quinoa, hemp seeds, walnuts, almonds, frozen fruits, and frozen vegetables. Other healthy chains, like Trader Joe's, tend to have really good prepared items such as packages of chopped vegetables, cooked lentils, and different types of mock meats and cheeses. Other stores like Wegman's and Whole Foods, may be a bit more expensive, but they have just about everything a plant–based shopper could want. Ethnic markets are worthy of consideration as well. You are likely to find unique vegetables, very ripe produce, and interesting herbs and spices at an ethnic market. Check to see if there is a food co–op in your area. Target has surprised me a couple of times. I couldn't find Gardein Savory Stuffed Turk'y Breast anywhere in town one Thanksgiving, but Target had plenty of them. While on vacation in Hawaii, I found an entire section in the frozen food aisle dedicated to plant–based alternatives. Target even launched their own line of vegan meats. Have a look at your local supermarket as well. These chains are responding to the changing food market with more organic produce and more vegan–friendly products.

That brings us to perhaps the most convenient way to shop – have the food delivered directly to your door. Having trouble finding erythritol, agar agar, or your favorite oil–free dressing at your local markets? Hop online, and you are likely to find just what you need. If you have an Amazon Prime membership, many products can be delivered to your door with no shipping charges. As I mentioned before, you can even order frozen meals from PlantPure Nation, and have them delivered.

Online shopping is not the only way to have food delivered. Some local markets and chains are featuring home delivery services. Another option is CSA (Community Supported Agriculture) in which you can also enjoy produce from a group of local farmers. You sign up for a weekly or bi–weekly box that is either delivered to your door or collected from a central distribution site. My service (Farm Fresh to You) delivers right to the door, and you can block any unwanted items using their website. I like the CSA service because it delivers fresh produce or a regular basis, and you get a chance to try out different kinds of fruits and vegetables that you otherwise might not have tried.

Reading Nutrition Labels

As you expand the repertoire of what you eat, you will be encountering new foods. If the food is somewhat processed, you'll want to determine how healthy it is. That's where nutrition labels come into play. Here are some guidelines to follow when reading nutrition labels.

INGREDIENTS: TOMATO PUREE (WATER, TOMATO PASTE), DICED TOMATOES (DICED TOMATOES, TOMATO JUICE, CITRIC ACID [ACIDITY CONTROL], CALCIUM CHLORIDE), SOYBEAN OIL, SALT, SUGAR, DEHYDRATED ONIONS, SPICES (PARSLEY, BASIL, OREGANO), GARLIC, CITRIC ACID (FOR TARTNESS), EXTRA VIRGIN OLIVE OIL, NATURAL FLAVOR.
CONTAINS SOY.

Ingredients1

INGREDIENTS: 100% WHOLE GRAIN ROLLED OATS.

Ingredients 2

First, look at the list of ingredients. It's often below or separate from the nutrition facts section of the label. The ingredients are listed in the order of the most common ingredient by weight at the top left, to the least common ingredient by weight at the end. Look at the ingredient list to guage how close the product is to being a whole food. The first ingredient list certainly contains a lot of tomatoes, but it includes quite a few other ingredients as well. You would probably be better off with a can of unseasoned tomatoes or use actual tomatoes. The second ingredient list only has one ingredient – whole grain rolled oats. That's as whole as it's going to get.

The next thing to look for in the ingredient list is oil. As you saw in chapter 3, oil is pure fat. All of us need to monitor our oil and fat intake. If you have heart disease, diabetes, or you want to lose weight, don't choose products with oil; put them back on the shelf. Notice in the first ingredient list that oil is listed in two places (soybean oil and extra virgin olive oil). This food is not a good choice if you have reason to pursue a low or no oil diet. The second ingredient list is perfectly free of added oil.

Next, you want to examine the Nutrition Facts portion of the label for evidence of the three most common ingredients in processed foods: fat, salt, and sugar.

The nutrition labels make it easy to determine the proportion of fat. In the first label, there are 180 total calories (per serving) and 15 calories from fat. So, divide 15 by 180 to get .083333 or 8.3%. Since **we want the fat in our diet to be less than 10% of our total calories**, this food fits in perfectly. 8.3% is less than 10%. How about the other label? There are 45 calories from fat out of a total of 90 calories (per serving). So, 50% of the calories are from fat. That far exceeds the ideal 10% level, and it is more than three times as much as the more generous guideline of 15%. The first label is a clear winner in the fat department.

Label 1   Label 2

To get a handle on the sodium (or salt) content, use this easy rule of thumb: **the number of milligrams of sodium should be less than the total number of calories per serving**. In the first example, 115 milligrams of sodium is much less than 180 calories per serving, so the sodium content is well within acceptable limits. Good job, product manufacturer! In the second label, 580 mg of sodium is over 6 times more than the total calories, 90 calories, so this product is loaded with sodium. See chapter 3 for health issues related to excess sodium in the diet.

For a healthy diet, **we want less than 5% of our total calories to come from added sugar**. For a 2,000 calorie diet, that means about 100 calories of added sugar, which is **about 25 grams of added sugar per day**. To put this in perspective, a can of coke has around 39 grams of added sugar. Oops, that's already way over the 25 gram daily target. For the products in the figure, one has 8 grams of added sugar per serving, and the other has 6 grams. Both are well under the 25 gram limit, but the 8 grams in the first item uses up about one third of the total daily allocation. So, that limits the amount of added sugar you should have for the rest of the day.

The nutrition label can be very helpful helping us avoid foods that are excessively high in sugar, salt, and fat. However, it may be reasonable to use a product that is high in sugar, for example, if it is combined with foods that are low in sugar. For example, if you put a slightly sweet cream sauce on a serving of steamed veggies that are relatively low in sugar, the sugar content of the dish taken as a whole could well be within the acceptable range.

The Nutrition Facts information can help you determine if you are dealing with a primarily whole food or one that has been refined. Remember the *Five–to–One Test* introduced in Chapter 3. **Divide the grams of carbohydrates by the grams of fiber.** If the result is 5 or less, the grains are reasonably whole, with the nutrition intact (*Five–to–One Test*). If the result is 6 or more, the grains are more processed. In the Label 1 product, 40 grams of carbohydrate divided by 13 grams of fiber gives just over 3. Three is less than 5, so this cereal definitely passes the test. The Label 2 product gives 11g divided by 3 g which equals 3.6. It also passes the test easily.

Another important fact listed on the nutrition label is the serving size. Does the serving size match the amount you would normally use? If not, you need to adjust the numbers to match your actual serving size.

Use some of these guidelines to examine the nutrition labels of products in your own pantry and fridge. It may give you a different perspective on the foods you have been eating. Take a closer look at food labels on your next trip to the market.

Walking the Aisles

Make a shopping list before entering the market. Consider items that you want to add to your pantry, freezer, or fridge from the reference lists above. Also consider ingredients from recipes that you want to try as well as foods for breakfast, lunch, snacks, and upcoming travel.

Eating plant–based changes your experience in the grocery store. Supermarkets are typically arranged with flowers and mouth–watering taste temptations near the entrance, and you have to wade through aisles of sugary snacks and processed foods to get to the healthy foods. Everything about the shopping experience is designed to get you to purchase more products, including the placement of tempting items at eye level, and the mood music. The best way to protect yourself from these influences is to maintain your focus on your well–prepared shopping list and bypass the distractions.

About eighty percent of the food on shelves of supermarkets today
didn't exist 100 years ago.

— *Larry McCleary*

When you enter the market, head directly for the produce section. You will find plenty of fruits and vegetables - things you can eat freely. So, stock up! Refer to the Fresh Produce list provided in this chapter for ideas and look for produce that is in season. Remember to shop for the rainbow. For the most nutritious produce, select the brightest, most vivid colors, because these foods contain the most antioxidants. Choose the darkest blackberries, the reddest cabbage, the reddest onion, the most scarlet tomato, and the darkest leafy greens you can find. Look for pre–chopped and ready–to–cook items as well. Remember to check the Dirty Dozen list and buy organic versions of the items on that list if possible.

Next, find the natural health foods section. Look for 100% whole grain products, non–dairy milks, and sauces that contain no added oil. Just be careful. There will likely be a lot of processed foods in this section as well. So, use your discretion, and practice your nutrition–label reading skills.

In the ethnic foods sections, you can find some specialty items like tamarind syrup, basmati rice, or specially flavored vinegars.

In the refrigerated section, you may find pre–chopped fruits and vegetables, sauces, nut butters, and vegan cheese. Refer to the Refrigerator list in this chapter for additional ideas.

You might be in for an awakening in the cereal aisle. Read the nutrition labels. You'll find that many of the cereals are loaded with sugar and most are not whole grain; that is, they don't pass the *Five–to–One Test*. There are some cereals that do provide a healthy balance of nutrition. Make a note of these when you find them for future reference. If you are at a loss, you can always go for the old fashioned oats. I've listed several healthy cereals and their nutrition information in the recipe *David's Breakfast Bowl* in "Breakfast" in the Recipe chapter.

Most markets have a section for spices. In my pre-vegan days, I didn't pay much attention to herbs and spices. Now that I'm eating more whole foods, I use them constantly. Herbs and spices not only add flavor to your dishes, they are full of nutrition as well. Turmeric, for example, is an extremely healthy spice. Also known as curcumin, it is very potent, so use small amounts. When you see a recipe with an unfamiliar spice, give it a try. See the Condiments and Seasoning list above for ideas. You may be able to buy small amounts in the bulk spice section to try out a particular spice. We will talk about using herbs, and spices to balance flavors of a dish in Chapter 7.

How about canned vegetables? Fresh is always preferable, of course, but canned vegetables can be a good backup. Since cooking dry beans from scratch is a lengthy process (soaking overnight, cooking, cooling, and storing), having some canned beans on hand can be a time saver. Just be careful to read the nutrition labels and be on the lookout for high sodium content. Refer to the Pantry list above.

> Note that rinsing canned beans can reduce the sodium content by up to one third.

If your market has a bulk section, you can stock up on nuts, seeds, grains, lentils, and beans. Just keep your attention on the task at hand, because there are a lot of sweetened and oily foods in that section as well.

The frozen foods aisle is great for frozen fruits and vegetables. You can find great blends for smoothies. Also look for frozen chopped vegetables that are very convenient. You'll likely find some frozen meat alternatives and some vegan frozen meals. These are not whole foods, but they can be an essential part of your toolkit when you are first starting out. I owe a lot to Gardein frozen foods. They helped me get through that first stage of transition. See the freezer list above.

> Tip: Keep insulated cold bags in your car to transport freezer items, especially if you have a long drive home.

Storing the Groceries

When you return from the market, you'll want to store your foodstuffs properly to get the most value from your purchases.

If you have any frozen foods, store them in the freezer first. Likewise, nuts, seeds, and grains go into the freezer. You can leave the foods in original packages or break them down into smaller quantities and store in plastic bags. Be sure to label each bag with the name of the item and the date. If you have space, the bags of nuts, seeds, and grains will go in larger plastic containers as described earlier.

Fresh greens are next. When harvesting leafy greens from your garden or bringing them home from the market, store them in a salad crisper or a plastic bag in the refrigerator. This will keep them as fresh as possible. When you are ready to use them, soak them in a large bowl or a salad spinner with a few tablespoons of apple cider vinegar for about 10 minutes. This will remove dirt and any unwanted insects. When done, rinse the leaves well in fresh water and shake them dry over the sink or dry in a salad spinner. Then, they are ready to cook or use raw.

For broccoli and cauliflower, store them in the fridge wrapped in a damp paper towel or in a plastic bag, with several holes poked near the head to allow good air flow. When you are ready to cook, cut into bite sized pieces, and soak in a vinegar/water solution for about 10 minutes as with leafy greens above. Rinse them well, then cook or use raw.

As for other fresh produce, see the discussion in the Stocking Your Kitchen section. Some of the produce will do well in the vegetable or fruit drawers in the refrigerator. Others can be stored on a counter for a few days, especially if they need to ripen a bit.

> Tip: Line the bottom of your vegetable and fruit drawers with a clean, dry, paper towel to absorb moisture. Change the paper towel weekly.

Condiments and seasonings will go in the spice cupboard, pantry, or refrigerator.

Legumes can be stored in the pantry, ideally in individually labeled bags inside a larger plastic storage container. If you have a large family, you might consider buying grains and legumes in larger quantities and then sealing them in vacuum bags ranging from 2 to 3 cups in size. These items will last an especially long time if they are vacuum–sealed. When you run out of an item in your freezer or pantry, bring out a vacuum–sealed bag. Store these bags in a cool dry place away from moisture, heat, and light. If you do this, be sure to label each bag, using a permanent marker, with the name and the date of the item. The date is very important to ensure that you use the older items first. If you accumulate a large number of sealed bags in the same place, both the name and the date will help you manage your stored items.

Transforming Your Meals

Recipe Substitutions

The first thing I did when converting to a vegan diet is to change out all the animal products in my favorite meals to plant-based alternatives, or at least to close approximations. It made the transition process so much easier. Here are some substitutions for commonly used recipe ingredients.

Meat, fish or poultry: There are more "meat substitutes" available today than ever before. You can find plant-based substitutes for chicken strips, bacon, sausage, hotdogs, hamburgers, deli meat, and more. Some of these substitutes can be pretty close approximations of their animal-based cohorts, such as the amazing Beyond Burger from Beyond Meat. Even though most of these products are highly processed, they can be an essential part of your initial transition because they allow you to stay in your food comfort zone. Later on, you can ease off on these transitional products as you move closer to a whole foods plant–based (WFPB) diet.

There are other less processed foods such as beans, lentils, and sweet potatoes that can be used for satisfying main dishes. Portobello mushrooms are often used in place of grilled meats, burgers, or steaks. Tofu is high in protein. It's relatively tasteless on it's own, but it picks up the flavors from other foods quite well. So, marinate tofu well before serving. Tempeh is a fermented soy product that also reacts well to marinade. Eggplant is a delicious alternative for sandwiches or Italian dishes.

Eggs: There is no single magic substitute for eggs, but you would be surprised how many dishes you can make without eggs. For baking, you can use "Egg Replacer" made from a mixture of flours by Ener–G Foods. You can also use other foods such as flaxseeds, chia seeds, and psyllium as binders in baking.

There is a surprisingly good substitute for egg whites: bean juice, also known as aquafaba. The most popular bean for this purpose is garbanzo beans, also called chickpeas, but juice from other beans can be used as well. Aquafaba is an amazing substitute for egg whites in making whipped topping and meringue cookies. See the Recipe chapter for sample recipes. In fact, aquafaba is so versatile that you can use it to make cheese, dressings, pancakes, quiche, meatloaf, mousse, non-dairy ice cream, macaroons, cookies, brownies, hummus and more. See the Facebook group and aquafaba book in Resources.

Perhaps the most challenging egg dish to replicate without actual eggs is a classic scrambled egg or omelet. The traditional way to make a vegan omelet is to cook crumbled tofu with spices and vegetables. You can make a very tasty dish with tofu, but no one will mistake it for a scrambled egg dish. However, technology never takes a day off. Recent entries such as VeganEgg by Follow your Heart, make it possible to make a dish that is vey similar to scrambled eggs. The texture is not exactly the same and you'll need to flavor it, but it is one step closer.

Here are some accepted plant–based egg replacement options to try:

1 egg = 2 Tablespoons potato starch	1 egg = ¼ cup mashed potatoes
1 egg = ¼ cup canned pumpkin	1 egg = ¼ cup puréed prunes
1 egg = ¼ cup oats or oat flour or bread crumbs in burger and loaf recipes	1 egg = 1 Tablespoon ground flaxseeds or chia seeds in 3 Tablespoons water
1 egg = 1½ teaspoons Ener-G Egg Replacer + 2 Tablespoons water	1 egg = 2 Tablespoons corn, arrowroot, or tapioca starch
1 egg = ½ banana	

Milk: Milk substitutes are readily available in almost any grocery store. Milk substitutes are made from soy, coconut, rice, almond, hemp, etc. These milks can be used in cereals, tea or coffee, and in both baking and cooking. They come in both regular and low–fat versions, as well as sweetened and unsweetened. Read the nutrition labels carefully. There is a lot of variation. Some are fortified with vitamins and minerals. Some are high in sugar while others may be high in fat. Although these non-dairy milks are preferable to cow's milk, keep in mind that they are processed to some degree.

Cheese: Cheese substitutes have come a long way. While plant-based cheeses may never taste exactly like the original, there are some satisfying substitutes. The substitutes can be made from cashew, soy, almond, and hemp as well as other ingredients. As with the non-dairy milks, the cheese substitutes are highly processed and contain added oils. Even so, for cheese lovers, these products can be helpful in the early stages of transitioning to a WFPB diet. There are other ways to add a cheesy flavor to recipes. Tofu or nut butters can replace cheese in some recipes. Nutritional yeast is a healthy way to add a cheesy flavor to sauces and other foods. Cashews, miso, tamari, and tahini are also used to replace cheese-flavored ingredients in some recipes.

Sweeteners: You can use foods that are naturally sweet as a healthier way to add sweetness to a dish compared to using honey or sugar. You can use fruit juice, applesauce, mashed bananas, fruit preserves, and dried fruits such as dates and raisins to replace added sugar in both cooking and baking. Shredded coconut adds a sweet flavor. There are some more processed sweeteners that are lower on the glycemic index and may contain more nutrients than sugar. These include agave syrup, blackstrap molasses, coconut sugar, date sugar, erythritol, maple syrup, Sucanat, and stevia.

Butter, Shortening, Fats, and Oils: For a healthy heart, you want to eliminate or minimize the use of added fats and oils. Fortunately, there are some alternatives. You can use vegetable stock, water, or wine to sauté or fry. For example, to caramelize onions, start with a warm pan, and heat the chopped onions, stirring constantly. Heat the onions until they start to brown, and only add the liquid in small amounts to keep the onions from sticking to the pan. With practice, you'll find that you can do this with other vegetables as well. Another way to get around the need for oil is to bake instead of fry. You can use an air fryer to make potato fries without any oil. See the Sweet Potato Fries recipe in "Snacks." For salad dressings use a base of vegetable stock, water or vinegar in place of the oil. You can also make creamy sauces using nuts, tofu, and spices as a topping for vegetable dishes.

For baking, you can replace processed fats with selected whole foods that have the double benefit of keeping the dish moist and adding nutritional value. This way, you can enjoy guilt-free baked goods on a regular basis. Try these replacements: mashed bananas, applesauce, ground nuts or seeds (e.g. almond, flax, or chia), pumpkin puree, nut or seed butters, and coconut butter (not coconut oil, which is 100% fat).

Salt: If you are looking to lower the salt content of your diet, there are many salt-free granulated spice blends to add flavor to your dishes. Other salt substitutes include fresh onion, garlic, lemon juice, salsa and hot sauces. Low–sodium soy or tamari sauce are good alternatives in some recipes.

Try some of these alternatives in your own dishes. It's probably best if you try one substitution at a time rather than several at once. Experiment and keep track of which flavor combinations you and your family prefer. Remember that your taste buds are replaced every few weeks and your taste preferences can change. So, keep trying.

3-3-3 Method

It's no secret that most American families tend to have a pool of favorite meals through which they rotate. It's usually about nine meals. You can use this as the basis for a clever strategy (inspired by Kaiser Permanente) to phase in plant–based eating and phase out whatever else you were eating. It is sometimes called the 3–3–3 Method because you transform the nine meal rotation in three phases, three meals at a time.

Phase 1

Phase 1 is identifying the three meals in your existing meal rotation that are already vegan or nearly vegan and refining them. If there are any animal products in the meals, remove them or replace with vegan alternatives. You can also ramp up the nutritive foods in the dishes. See the Plant–Based Food Choices section in Chapter 4 for recommendations on daily servings from the basic food groups – vegetables, legumes, whole grains, etc. In case you are short on nearly vegan dishes, I've included three examples for you to try. Follow the directions below. You'll find detailed recipes for all three recipes in the Recipe and Templates chapter.

> Note: if you are extremely limited on food–prep time, you can skip ahead to the Instant Gratification section below.

Stir-fry

I started with stir-fry because it is easy and one of my favorites. The basic idea is to cook up some vegetables quickly over a high heat until they are just barely done, and serve them over a bed of rice or other cooked grain. You can keep it to a few ingredients, or really pile them on for more flavors and textures. Keep in mind that this will be one of your go–to dishes, so you want to make it as flavorful and mouthwatering as possible. Bring on the veggies and spices!

Stir-fry is traditionally an Asian dish, so this version uses more Asian ingredients and flavorings. Naturally, you can change the flavors to Mexican, Italian, or any flavor profile you want. I find it easiest to prepare stir-fry in a non–stick wok, but you can use a large sauté pan as well.

Start by preparing a grain like brown rice or quinoa in a rice cooker. This will take about 20 minutes while you chop up and cook the veggies. I prefer quinoa because it works great in a rice cooker and adds more protein to the dish. Remember to rinse the quinoa before cooking it. If you are going to add tofu, or chick'n strips, or un–beef strips, you can chop them up and start them marinating now. For the record, chick'n means plant–based chicken strips, generally available in the refrigerated or frozen foods section of a supermarket, farmer's market, or health food store. Un–Beef strips are similar.

To begin the stir-fry process, add a little water or oil to the wok, and heat the minced garlic (and/or minced ginger) over medium heat. Water will work fine if you are limiting your oil intake; you just need to add more water periodically. Slice up some onion, and cook for several minutes until translucent. Stir occasionally, and add water as needed. While the onions are cooking, start chopping the hardest vegetables first, because they take the longest to cook. This means sweet potatoes and carrots. Set them aside until the onions are cooked. Chop the next hardest veggies and set aside. This might be bell peppers, zucchini, and yellow squash.

When the onions are done, stir in the other vegetables. You'll need to add more liquid until these cook down. It doesn't have to be water. You can add some sweet cooking rice wine, vegetarian stir-fry sauce, hoisin sauce, your favorite vinegar, coconut aminos, soy or tamari sauce. Stir as you add.

This might be a good time to add some flavorings. I use Chinese five–spice powder, a little Thai seasoning, turmeric, and a dash of sea salt and ground pepper. If you like a bit of heat, use some freshly chopped jalapeno or other pepper or use a ground spice like Chile pepper or cayenne pepper. For those who like it slightly sweet, you can add a touch of sweetener (like agave or one of the many sugar alternatives (date sugar, Sucanat, organic sugar, etc.). Stir in the spices, do a taste test, then add more spices or flavorings to adjust the taste. Note: Chapter Seven will cover flavor balancing and how to adjust flavors. Do your best for now. Let your taste buds be your guide.

Once you have the flavors adjusted to your liking, you can add the tofu or chick'n strips if you are using these. Then, it's time for the softer vegetables such as mushrooms, a little cabbage or bok choy, bamboo shoots, snow peas, or other leafy greens. These are added toward the end of the cooking process because they require less cooking time. Let these cook down briefly; it doesn't take long. When everything is nearly cooked, you can toss in small pineapple chunks, peanuts, or other nuts for crunch.

When everything is done, scoop some quinoa (or rice) into a bowl, top with the stir-fry and enjoy. There are so many things you can add to a stir-fry that it never seems to turn out the same.

Guess what? You just made your first plant–based dinner! For a more detailed directions, see *Stir-Fry Template* in "Templates."

> Tip – you can speed up the whole process by steaming a few of the harder veggies in the microwave for a couple of minutes, just enough to soften them. Then add to the stir-fry.

Veggie Soup

Veggie soup fits well within the plant–based profile. Pull out a large soup pot, and let's make some soup. The first decision is whether to use a soup base or flavor your soup from scratch. Let's use a carton of butternut squash soup for this round. Soups can be very satisfying, especially during cold weather. Be sure to pile on the veggies and flavor it to your tastes. Some suggested veggies would be sweet potatoes, onions, carrots, broccoli, cauliflower, celery, beets, bell peppers, yellow squash, zucchini, mushrooms, and tomatoes.

One of the great things about soups is that you can pretty much toss in anything. For example, I was not very enthusiastic about beans when I first changed to a vegan diet. But I discovered that you could add beans to soup with very little impact on the flavor. And beans make the soup a bit more robust. You can add corn to balance the beans. A nice touch for better nutrition is to add some chopped up leafy greens toward the end of the cooking process. Don't forget the spices. You can try out spice mixes or make your own combinations. Every soup should have its own unique flavor. Depending on your taste preferences, you can add a bit of heat with some hot spices, or add sweetener to brighten up the flavor. Sweetener made all the difference for me. I went from being soup–a–phobe to a soup aficionado by just adding a little bit of sweetener. Experiment with spices and flavorings until you find a combination that makes it taste delectable. Are we having fun yet? For a more detailed directions, see *Veggie Soup Template* in "Templates."

Did I see you scrunch up your face, wondering about the protein in this soup? Well, fear not. All vegetables have protein. See the discussion on protein in chapter 3. If you are concerned about protein or your body is adjusting from a typical protein-rich Western diet, you can easily ramp up the protein in this dish. Use tofu, tempeh, or a mock meat to add protein. Also add beans and corn. Some high-protein veggies include: peas, kale, mushrooms, spinach, collards, mustard greens, and broccoli. Don't forget herbs and spices as a protein source. Spices with high protein content include mustard seed, fenugreek seed, poppy seed, cumin seed, fennel seed, paprika, pepper, cardamom, ginger, and turmeric. By carefully selecting your ingredients, you can easily create a soup with 25 to 30 grams of protein or more. This is nearly half your protein requirement for the entire day.

Salad

I clearly remember the side salad served with my Bob's Big Boy hamburger when I was growing up. It was nothing more than some chopped iceberg lettuce smothered with Thousand Island dressing. Thank heavens for the dressing! But that's a pretty narrow view of what a salad can be. If you let your imagination loose (or just search the Internet), you can come up with a wide variety of salads that are deserving of top billing as a "main course." That's what we are going to create – a salad that you serve as a centerpiece of your dinner meal.

Consider the ways in which the following examples challenge the notion of a traditional salad.

- An Asian flavored tossed salad with shredded cabbage, carrots, and peanuts flavored with rice vinegar, soy sauce, cilantro, lemon juice, and green chilies, lightly cooked in a wok.
- A simple salad of greens (kale, collards, chard or other greens) sautéed with garlic and flavored with lemon juice or vinegar and a few spices. Top it with a sprinkle of sesame seeds.
- A salad featuring root vegetables (sweet potato, beets, carrot, fennel, etc.) flavored with spices and roasted for about 30 minutes. Add soy sauce and vinegar to taste.
- A more traditional salad with lettuce base containing an assortment of ingredients such as chopped carrots, celery, jicama, artichoke hearts, roasted red peppers, olives, tomatoes, avocado, basil leaves, croutons, sesame or other seeds, and topped with one or two oil–free dressings (readily available in many markets).

For this dish, we are going to make a very simple and delicious salad inspired by a local vegan restaurant. Call it a BBQ Chick'n Salad. Marinate chick'n strips in your favorite marinade, and heat it up, if necessary. Chop some lettuce, cube some jicama, dice some tomatoes, and slice some avocado. Open a can of beans and a can of corn; rinse and drain as necessary. Arrange the ingredients side by side on a plate. Flavor with vegan barbeque sauce, chipotle sauce, or vegan ranch dressing, and enjoy. This salad makes a very quick, satisfying, and healthy meal. See *Barbequed Chick'n Salad* in "Salads and Sides" for a detailed recipe.

At this point, you should have three plant–based dishes, whether you used the dishes suggested here or your own creations. That's three dishes to include in your meal rotation, and that's a good beginning. Don't worry if you didn't find all the ingredients on hand. You can build up your pantry and spices a few items at a time. Let the recipes that you use be your guide.

As you work these three meals into your rotation, you may notice that you feel weak for a few days. This happens in some cases because your body is having withdrawal symptoms from some of the more addictive foods. If that happens, just realize that your body has kicked into "house cleaning" mode, and it's working extra hard to rid itself of unwanted toxins. It is a natural reaction. Don't let it derail your commitment. On the other hand, the more you eat of these plant–based meals, the more you will start to feel lighter (plant–based foods don't "stick to your ribs"), and the more you will be regular (high fiber meals tend to flush out your system more easily).

What about the other six meals in your normal meal rotation? Keep them in place for now. Just intersperse the three new meals that we created with the others. Remember, we are making this change gradually so that your body and taste palette has time to acclimate to a new normal. You want to stay firmly in your food comfort zone as it gradually changes. Here's a tip for these other meals: eat your salad and/or veggies toward the beginning of the meal rather than after the bread and pasta. When you start a meal with high–fiber, high–water–content salads and vegetables, it will curb your appetite more quickly. You will also tend to eat more vegetables overall. Both of these factors will contribute to easier weight management.

Phase 2

Phase 2 is selecting three more meals that may not be vegan, but that you can readily adapt to be vegan. You already have a sense of where this is heading from the first three dishes. I selected three sample dishes that were favorites before I became vegan. It's easy to swap out the animal products in these dishes and replace them with vegan versions (meatballs, burgers, cheese, etc.) Note that the replacement foods do not contain animal products, but they are processed to a certain extent. In other words, they wouldn't fit into the whole food plant–based category, but that's okay. At this point in the journey, we are looking for dishes that are comfortable, tasty, and free from animal products. Moving toward more whole food plant–based cuisine will come later as your taste buds evolve.

Spaghetti and Sauce

The plan for this dish is to replace the meatballs, add additional veggies, and consider some alternatives to traditional spaghetti pasta. Let's start with the pasta. Traditional pasta is made from white flour, which is absorbed quickly into your blood stream. It tends to spike your blood sugar levels. Consider replacing this with noodles made from whole wheat, quinoa, kamut, spelt, or brown rice. There are also whole food options. My favorite is to steam or bake a spaghetti squash. When it is cooked, you can scrape out the tender insides with a spoon (use a hot pad to hold the squash, because it will still be hot). You end up with slender threads of squash that make a perfect base for the sauce. Some people prefer to process a raw zucchini with a spiralizer. This produces thin noodle–like strands of zucchini that can also be used as a spaghetti base. If you choose zucchini pasta, add the sauce just before eating.

Choose your "pasta" and let's move onto the sauce.

If you want meatballs in the sauce, you'll find plant–based options in the frozen section of most markets. Prepare according to the directions. If you want extra flavor, marinate the veggie meatballs in Worcestershire sauce, Bragg liquid aminos, soy sauce, teriyaki sauce, or any other marinade. Check the sodium levels of any marinade if you are sensitive to sodium.

To make the spaghetti sauce, use a large pot and sauté garlic, then onions in water until the onions are caramelized. Add water as necessary to keep the onions from burning. Add a jar of marinara sauce and a can of diced or roasted tomatoes. To flavor, add Italian seasoning, oregano, and a little lemon juice. For the veggies, slice up carrots, yellow squash, zucchini, green, red, yellow, and orange bell peppers, and mushrooms, and add them to the sauce. Let the sauce simmer uncovered for an hour or two until the vegetables become tender and the sauce thickens slightly. Add the veggie balls to the sauce. Do a taste test. Adjust the spices if necessary, and add sea salt and fresh ground pepper to taste. You can also add a little agave or other sweetener if you want it slightly sweet. You can also add dried chili, cayenne, or paprika if you like a bit of heat.

When everything is ready, scoop your noodle base into a bowl and top with generous helpings of the sauce. You can top the dish with vegan Parmesan if desired. This is a crowd pleaser, good for large gatherings. My friend, Rich, says he never met an Italian dish he didn't like, and this dish is no exception. You can prepare a large batch of sauce on a weekend, and enjoy it throughout the week. Freeze some for later use. For a more detailed directions, see *Spaghetti and Sauce* in "Makeovers."

Burgers

Burgers were my favorite food growing up – double deckers dripping with cheese and barbeque sauce. Oh my! There are three issues in "veganizing" a burger: the mayonnaise, the cheese, and the burger patty. The mayonnaise is easy; there are several brands of non–dairy mayo available, or you can make your own. See *Tofu-Cashew Mayonnaise* in "From Scratch." The cheese is fairly easy as well. It's just a matter of finding a vegan cheese that works for you. I tend to like the Follow Your Heart brand or Trader Joe's Mozzarella Shreds, but there are plenty to choose from in most supermarkets, health food markets, and even the refrigerated food section in Target. You can also make your own. See cheese recipes in "Dairy Alternatives."

Replacing the burger patty is interesting. I used to be quite particular about the type of veggie patty in my burgers. However, I found that as I added more ingredients and flavors to the burger, the patty played less of a role in the texture and flavor. Nevertheless, if the flavor of the patty is important to you, food scientists have you covered. They are developing vegetable–based patties that taste more and more like meat all the time. Frankly, it may taste too much like meat for some folks, so discretion is advised. For example, Beyond Meat came out with the Beyond Burger which "looks, cooks, and satisfies ... like beef..." The patty is quite realistic; however, it is very high in fat and sodium. The bottom line is that here are plenty of options to choose from in selecting a burger patty. Give them a try and see what works for you. Check the ingredients list to make sure that the patty does not contain animal products, and the nutrition facts for the usual suspects – sugar, salt, and fat.

Start the burger preparation by cooking the patty on a grill or in a pan, and add vegan cheese at the end to melt it slightly.

As I mentioned, the secret to a yummy burger for me is to pile up the other ingredients between the buns. I start with sautéed onions and mushrooms. Then I add other ingredients including roasted red peppers, lettuce leaves, basil leaves, fresh sprouts, and sliced avocado. Some people even include coleslaw. Then add your favorite condiments – non–dairy mayo, mustard, sweet relish, sliced pickles, ketchup, and barbeque sauce. Toast the buns lightly in a toaster oven or toaster, then apply the condiments, and pile on the ingredients until the pile just can't get any higher. Contain it all between the two buns, slice in half, and enjoy. For a more detailed directions, see *Burgers* in "Makeovers."

Tacos

I admit it. I've never been a huge fan of Mexican food. This is almost sacrilege for a Southern California native, but there it is. Imagine my surprise when I took stock of my favorite veganized comfort foods, and tacos were at the top of the list. I'm not saying that my tacos are whole food plant–based – far from it, but as a transitional food, bite for bite, they are about the tastiest for my palette. They are also not traditional tacos; they seem to have evolved of their own accord, borrowing several ingredients from the burger dish described above. But they hit the sweet spot in my taste buds.

Let's make tacos! Start by sautéing garlic, onions, and mushrooms in water, and set these aside. Open a package of un–beef crumbles, add in some salsa or other flavorings, and heat on the stove top or in the microwave oven. You can make your own crumbles, but they are also available refrigerated at Trader Joe's or in the frozen section of other markets. Chop some lettuce and basil. Slice tomatoes. Slice avocado. Open a can of sliced olives and a jar of fire–roasted peppers. Wash and rinse some fresh sprouts. Chop some fresh cilantro. Open a container of non–dairy sour cream. Arrange these ingredients on a plate or two. Open a jar of your favorite salsa and a bottle of sugar–free ketchup. I know it violates every rule in the taco maker's handbook, but for some reason, I need a dab of ketchup – maybe to tone down the spiciness of the salsa.

For the tortilla, you have options. Many people prefer corn tortillas. Others prefer the flour tortillas or variations. Remember that this is a transitional dish, so choose the one that tastes the best. I use a flour tortilla topped with non–dairy cheese shreds. Forty seconds in the microwave heats the tortilla and melts the shreds just enough. From there, add ingredients in any order that you choose. Fold the tortilla in half or wrap it like a burrito, and enjoy. For a more detailed directions, see *Tacos and Fixings* in "Makeovers."

Now that you have six vegan, primarily plant–based meals under your belt, you are well on your way toward edging any animal products off your plate and ushering in healthy alternatives. Work these into your meal rotation, and give your body time to adjust to these changes. Remember, you want to open yourself to new foods and flavors, but you also want to stay in your food comfort zone. So, experiment and go with the plant–based foods that taste the best.

Phase 3

Phase 3 is to find three additional plant–based meals that you can make and enjoy. You can convert some of your traditional dishes, or try out promising recipes from the Internet or from the recipes in this book, or you can make the three sample dishes described here. Think of it as an adventure with a tasty ending.

Monk Bowl

Monk Bowl is the name used by Mark Reinfeld of Vegan Fusion Academy for this dish, but you'll see similar dishes called dragon bowls or Buddha bowls if you look online. A monk bowl isn't a recipe so much as it is a template. A template lists the various components of the dish, leaving it up to you to pick specific ingredients from what you have on hand. For example, the monk bowl template has three components: greens, grains, and protein. For the greens component, you would select one or more green vegetables such as kale, broccoli, mustard green, and Swiss chard. Even though the name of the component is *greens*, you could optionally use another vegetable such as sweet potatoes, carrots, squash, etc. Go ahead; try something different. You would also decide how to prepare the greens or other veggies – raw, steamed, grilled, sautéed, baked, or roasted. For the grains component, you would select a grain from among brown rice, quinoa, millet, kamut, pasta, etc. For the protein component, you would select beans, lentils, tofu, or tempeh. These can be sautéed or grilled and made with a marinade of your choice. Add spices to the legumes to ramp up the flavor profile. You can garnish the bowl with nuts or seeds, and a sauce such as tamari, and/or nutritional yeast.

With all these choices, you can see that a single template can result in thousands of variations. Your tastes, your mood, and what you have on hand dictate each unique dish.

The beauty of monk bowls is that they can be created in 20 to 30 minutes. It helps to have the grains and legumes cooked in advance, then frozen and/or refrigerated for ready access.

Tagine

Tagine is interesting. Traditionally, it is a stew of meat and vegetables prepared by slow cooking in a shallow earthenware cooking dish with a tall, conical lid. It's a little bit like a stir–fry, but the spices and ingredients put it firmly in the Moroccan flavor zone. I discovered this dish when a group of 20 foodies descended on a Moroccan restaurant for a specially prepared plant–based multi–course dinner. Can you imagine a gang of vegans prowling the streets of San Diego? Well, it happened. All the dishes were delectable, but my favorite was the tagine. So, I decided to make my own. Even the first attempt was a savory success. Now, several versions later, tagine has become part of my regular meal rotation.

Cook a batch of quinoa, rice, or couscous. In a wok or large sauce pan, sauté some sliced onions with ginger and garlic for a few minutes. Then add 1–2 teaspoons each of lemon juice, turmeric, cumin, and cinnamon. A good strategy is to add small amounts of spice at first, then taste, then add more if needed. The basic recipe calls for cubed potatoes, cooked for 15 minutes, then put on simmer with chickpeas for about 25 minutes. I add in more veggies as they come off the cutting board: beets, carrots, zucchini, yellow squash, and even some greens like kale and Swiss chard. To enhance the nutrient profile of the dish, you can add half a can of rinsed and drained northern beans, and some lentils. To enhance the Middle Eastern flavors, you can add raisins, Turkish apricots, and dates. Add chick'n strips or tempeh if you want a meat substitute. Garnish with fresh cilantro, fresh thyme, and basil leaves.

You might want to make a large batch of tagine on the weekend, and portion it out throughout the week. You could also freeze some for later use. For a more detailed directions, see *Moroccan Tagine* in "Main Dishes."

> One of the essential ingredients of Moroccan cuisine is preserved lemons. They are made by immersing lemons in salt for several weeks. When the rinds soften, the seeds and pulp are discarded, and the rinds are used to add a special flavor burst to many savory dishes. Be careful; a little goes a long way. I use homemade preserved lemon in my tagine dishes rather than the lemon juice. You'll find the recipe of preserved lemons in the "From Scratch" section of the Recipe chapter.

Stuffed Squash with Cream Sauce

This is another template with plenty of possibilities for variation. The basic idea is to steam a squash, core out the center, and fill it with sautéed vegetables. Then top it with a cream sauce. For a more detailed directions, see *Stuffed Squash Template* in "Templates."

Soak about ¾ cup of cashews and/or almonds for about two hours. Cut a squash in half, and steam it until it is just tender. Avoid overcooking it; you don't want it to fall apart. You can use butternut, acorn, winter squash, or even potatoes or sweet potatoes. Hollow out the vegetable to make room for the filling. You can save this bit of squash for use elsewhere or try mixing it in with the cream sauce.

In a large pan or wok, sauté onions, garlic, and a bit of ginger in vegetable broth over medium heat. Start adding finely chopped vegetables from hardest to softest, adding water or more broth and stirring as needed. Suggested vegetables are sweet potato, beets, carrots, zucchini, yellow squash, broccoli, cauliflower, bell peppers (multiple colors), mushrooms, and greens (collard greens, kale, Swiss chard, and mustard greens). Cook the vegetables until almost tender, then reduce the heat.

Then add flavorings. Suggestions: nutmeg, cider vinegar, tamari, maple syrup, black pepper, a little nut milk (soy, almond, coconut, etc.), and just a dash of salt. Stir, and adjust the flavors to taste. Let it simmer for a few minutes while you assemble the cream sauce.

To make the cream sauce, drain the nuts and pour into a blender. Add a little bit of soy or almond milk and blend. You can add the scooped out squash if you like. It will enhance the texture and flavor of the sauce. Add lemon juice, a tiny bit of apple cider vinegar, miso, nutritional yeast, black pepper, and a dash of salt. Blend again and check the texture. Add water or non-dairy milk if it is too thick. Make sure it is well blended. If you like this sauce, make a double batch next time to use on other dishes.

To plate, scoop the veggies into the squash. Drizzle the cream sauce on top. Garnish with nuts or seeds.

Using this template, you can make a full and satisfying meal out of almost any potato or squash.

At this point, you've got nine vegan dinners added to your toolkit. Try out the recipes and tweak them to meet your tastes. Experiment and discover what variations work best for you. Continue to give your body time to adjust to this new normal.

Instant Gratification

For those moments when you are limited on time, there is a cost–effect way to eat plant–based practically without breaking a sweat. You can serve prepared meals from PlantPure Nation. These meals are whole food, plant–based meals that are low in added salt and sweetener and have no added oil. They are flash–frozen, packed with dry ice, and shipped to your door. The meals only take 6 minutes to prepare, then you are ready to eat. If you get the 20 pack, each carton runs less than $8 as of 2017, and shipping is free! Each carton contains two servings. That makes it just less than $4 a serving. Amazing! Toss in a side dish, some flavored water, and you are set. There are other brands of frozen dinners in local markets; just check the ingredients to make sure they are fully vegan.

If you are willing to do a little bit of cooking, Purple Carrot will deliver ready–to–cook meals to your door. Each shipment contains recipe cards and pre–measured ingredients of 100% plant–based meals prepared in 40 minutes or less.

PlantPure Nation does a lot more than make frozen foods. They are actively involved in raising people's health consciousness through a variety of programs: the PlantPure Nation documentary, wellness programs for companies and healthcare organizations, jumpstart programs, PlantPure Pods (for local education), and more. Visit Plantpurenation.com

That takes care of dinners. After that, breakfasts and lunches are easy.

Lunches

With so much care taken to prepare dinner meals, lunches can easily be built on the remains of dinner. This is especially true if a large batch of something (spaghetti, soup, stir–fry) was prepared on the weekend. There will be plenty to go around during the week. Lunches are also easier to make if you keep prepared ingredients in the fridge ready to go. I endeavor to keep a cooked grain (usually quinoa) and some cooked legumes in the fridge. The legumes are part of a longer process, namely soaking overnight, cooking, cooling, freezing in small portions, and keeping one portion in the fridge. I don't need to keep greens ready, because there are always some in the garden (kale and Swiss chard especially), and they cook quickly. So, with some leftovers from the previous dinner, I can assemble a healthy dish by adding greens, grain, legumes, and topping with a sauce.

Another good choice for lunches is salads. Salads can also be assembled quickly. I keep the lettuce in a crisper, so it stays fresh longer in the fridge. I also chop up salad ingredients in advance, and keep them in a separate container: carrots, celery, jicama, olives, and tomatoes. There are some other optional ingredients that you can add if you have some on hand: fresh sprouts, sauerkraut, three–bean salad, pre–cooked lentils, roasted red peppers, nuts, or seeds. To assemble, lay a bed of lettuce in a bowl, add the chopped ingredients, add optional ingredients, top with avocado and basil leaves, and use a combination of oil–free Walden Farms or homemade dressings.

Other lunch ideas include sandwiches, wraps, soups, tortillas with beans and salsa, and baked sweet potatoes. For lunch on the go, I make wraps, because they are delicious and travel well. See *Lunch Wraps* in "Sandwiches and Wraps."

Breakfasts

Who doesn't like a bowl of cold cereal in the morning? Cereal can get a bad rap because many of the boxed cereals are full of sugar to attract kids. Also, the cereals tend to be wheat–based, which is a problem for those with wheat allergies. But, you can find cereals that are whole grain and healthy for you if you search. Then, you can add all sorts of healthy ingredients to ramp up the nutrition and flavor.

I started with a simple breakfast called Rip's Big Bowl from the *Forks Over Knives* cookbook, and it evolved into something much more. See *David's Breakfast Bowl* in "Breakfast" for full details.

First, I swapped out the wheat–based cereals, partially to ensure that someone with wheat sensitivity could still enjoy it. Then, I added a collection of toppings. Each one was selected for something special that it brought to the table: walnuts, raisins, pea protein powder, amla powder, pumpkin seeds, hemp seeds, chia seeds, popped amaranth, homemade soy yogurt, and moringa powder. Use one or more non–dairy milks, and stir until the powders and other toppings are fully incorporated. Add more non-dairy milk if necessary. Then top it with an assortment of fresh fruits and enjoy. This is my go–to breakfast nearly every day, unless I swap out the cereal for oatmeal. As one of my friends said, "if you start your day with such a healthy breakfast, it seems like nothing could possibly go wrong the rest of the day."

Another great choice for breakfast is a smoothie. I'm blessed with a spouse who makes a smoothie almost every morning. So, I get a small serving of smoothie in addition to my breakfast bowl. See *Donna's Green Plant Power Smoothie* in "Beverages."

Other breakfast options include oatmeal or other porridge, tofu scramble, toast with almond butter and fruit preserves, occasional waffles, pancakes, or muffins.

Snacks

When you are preparing a meal, it's natural to want to nosh on something. Fresh vegetables to the rescue. Try a carrot, celery, a chunk of cabbage, jicama, red bell peppers, sugar snap peas, or a fresh cherry tomato from your garden. Enjoy them alone, or dip them in a little hummus.

Between meals, you may find yourself looking for a snack. Here are some quick snack ideas:

- Air–popped popcorn or corn kernels popped in a paper bag in a microwave
- Banana with nut butter
- Brown rice snaps with salsa
- Cereal with nut milk
- Cut veggies with hummus
- Dried fruit
- Fresh fruit
- Homemade trail mix
- Instant soups (vegan)
- Leftovers
- Toast (healthy) with fruit preserves

When you are on the road and have less control over your food sources, it helps to have some kind of snack on hand. I make a point to travel with plant–based granola bars or energy bars, nuts, and/or dried fruits. You have to be careful when selecting granola bars, but there are a few moderately healthy options on the market. A quick online search will reveal several options. You can also make your own. See 5-Ingredient Granola Bars in "Snacks" and 3-Ingredient Energy Bar Template in "Templates."

While we are on the subject of travel, what do you do when you are going to be out all day, or for an extended time, and you need to pack a full meal? My solution is to make a wrap in the morning, pack it in a cold bag when in the car, then carry it in a backpack when on foot. This works for amusement parks, picnics, sightseeing, airline flights, and more. See *Lunch Wraps* in "Sandwiches and Wraps." You can make it more of a meal by adding fresh fruit, packets of nuts and seeds, dried fruit, and a granola or energy bar.

My Transition to Plant-Based Eating

My transition in Fall of 2012 was perhaps a bit unusual. It turned out that I was primed to make the transition immediately, although the concept of changing my eating habits wasn't even on my radar at the time. On the recommendation of a co–worker, my wife and I watched *Forks Over Knives* on Netflix. That documentary was so compelling that we decided on the spot to eat a vegan diet from that day forward. It meant not eating any more meat or dairy, but it also meant trying out a host of new foods that we had pretty much ignored.

As luck would have it, I had recently retired from full time teaching. I was only teaching one class, so I had a lot more time on my hands. I turned my energies to learning as much as I could about plant–based eating – what to include, what not to include, how to prepare food, etc. I started attending some vegan cooking classes, and networking with those who were already well along the path to healthier eating. Of course, the Internet offered endless resources and recipes. I learned where to shop to obtain meat and dairy alternatives as well as organic produce. I learned that you can also shop online, and have products delivered right to your door. I cleaned out the pantry and fridge, and stocked up with more healthy foods.

I soon began to replace the animal products in all of my favorite dishes – tacos, spaghetti, burgers, pizza, stir-fry, and even soups. My wife started making daily smoothies. I found out about vegan restaurants in the area, as well as restaurants that offer some vegan–friendly alternatives. I discovered that planning ahead made everything easier. Preparing a large dish (soup, stir–fry, spaghetti, etc.) on Sunday simplified meal preparation during the subsequent week. I also learned to prepare food in advance for traveling, whether it was just a snack or two for an afternoon meeting, a picnic lunch for an all–day outing, or even packing selected food items for extended travel.

The entire transition seemed pretty easy, probably because I was very passionate about making the change, and I put a lot of energy into making it happen. I was mainly interested in the health benefits, but the more I learned about the awful things that happen to animals in the animal agriculture industry and the devastation it causes to our planet, the more passionate I became about eating a plant–based diet. Another factor was that I love a challenge. In an environment structured to guide us like lemmings into consuming the Standard American Diet (SAD), it can be a challenge to develop a different eating style. So, I embraced the challenge, and proved to myself that it could be done. Years from now, when a plant–based diet becomes mainstream, this will seem pretty ordinary. Until that day arrives, eating a plant–strong diet will require conscious food choices in the face of strong influences to the contrary.

Establishing a Support System

An important part of making and sustaining a major behavioral change is to establish a support system. I was lucky in that my wife agreed to make the journey with me. We have been able to support and encourage each other throughout the process. Even so, I made it a point to extend my support system by connecting with others. I joined several vegan meetups (meetup.com), and began to attend events. These included seminars, cooking classes, vendor fairs, and potlucks. I went to a lot of cooking classes to learn how to prepare vegan meals and to network with the participants. It wasn't long before my wife and I decided to invite some of these people to plant–based potlucks at our home. We now host about 3 or 4 potlucks a year. It gives us a chance to share recipes and experiences with like–minded people and sample new foods.

I reached out to friends and family to invite them to join with us in healthy eating. Some non–vegan friends are willing to meet at vegan restaurants and enjoy the food.

As I became more passionate about sharing the plant–based message, I created a business card containing resources that might be helpful to new vegans. It included videos on Netflix, local meetup groups, local vegan eateries, online resources, local markets, favorite brands and well as contact info. When I meet new people that express an interest in eating plant–based, I share the card with them. It's another good way to connect.

These are only some of the ways that you can strengthen your own support system.

Facebook is another option for support. There are numerous Facebook support groups for new vegans. In Facebook, do a search for new vegan, and you can pick and choose amongst the options. One of these groups has over 46,000 members as of this writing. Clearly, no one has to make this journey alone.

There are also dozens of vegan blogs. Some are listed in the Resources chapter. Check out some of the blogs in that chapter. Many of these have newsletters to which you can subscribe.

A great way for many people to make a transition is to fully commit to one of the structured online challenges, usually for a period of 21 days. These challenges are successful for several reasons. First, you have the support of the other participants as well as meal plans. Second, it takes about twenty–one days to form a new habit. Third, your taste buds go through a life cycle of 10 days to two weeks. New cells replace the old as the old ones die off. So, eating a new set of foods consistently for three weeks gives your taste buds plenty of time to adjust to new flavors.

You can set up your own challenge or join one of the many available online. It seems that nearly every individual or group that is passionate about plant–based eating has a jumpstart, or kickstart, or some kind of program to support you in the process of trying out a new eating style. Here are a few:

- Physicians Committee for Responsible Medicine 21–day Vegan Kickstart, 21DayKickstart.org
- Veg–Appeal Food Camps, https://veg–appeal.com/collections/classes/products/food–camp–weekly–meal–plans
- PlantPure Nation Jumpstart Kit, plantpurenation.com
- The Engine 2 Seven–Day Rescue Challenge, engine2diet.com
- Vegancoach.com Choose Vegan Basics: New Vegan?
- DrMcDougall.com Starter Kit (2 books and 2 videos)
- 7–Day Vegan Challenge, 7dayvegan.com
- 21-Day Food Day Challenge, ucdintegrativemedicine.com
- Kaiser Permanente 30–Day Challenge, https://share.kaiserpermanente.org/wp–content/uploads/2015/10/The–Plant–Based–Diet–booklet.pdf

The weekly meal plans and guides from Veg–Appeal are particularly "Appealing" and an inexpensive and effective way to get started with the transition to healthy eating. These guides leave nothing to chance. You download a Food Camp Guide for a specific theme (e.g. Asian), and you get a complete shopping list, a meal plan for the week, recipes, and step–by–step instructions. The plans include a Prep Day where you make the sauces and other basics for the week. That way, the individual meals only take 15 to 30 minutes to assemble throughout the week. You can get even more support via their Facebook page and food camp classes.

> Veg–Appeal is offering readers 25% off on the Food Camp Guides. Just use the code **HHHC** at checkout. Click on *Veg–Appeal*

If you prefer to follow your own path, here are a few different techniques for managing your transition to healthier eating:

Every Two Weeks Plan – Change at least one thing in your kitchen or your diet every two weeks that moves you closer to your ideal healthy eating plan.

One New Recipe Each Week – Try at least one new healthy recipe each week for a period of a year.

The 3–3–3 Method – This is the method used in Transforming Your Meals earlier in the chapter. Start by identifying 3 healthy meals that you already make (adjust if necessary). Then identify 3 meals that you can modify to make healthy. Then discover 3 new healthy recipes to enjoy. That gives you nine recipes that you can rotate through to provide plenty of variety.

Raising Your Health Consciousness

The important thing is not to stop questioning;
curiosity has its own reason for existing.

— Albert Einstein

While you are helping your body adjust to new taste sensations, keep asking questions. Questions that you asked earlier led to something that sparked your curiosity. The result is that you are now on a plant–based journey. Let that journey be a series of discoveries that broaden your understanding of the big picture – the relationship between nutrition and health, the politics of food and healthcare, the animal agriculture industry and its far–reaching influence on our daily lives, etc. Keep investigating and asking questions.

You can broaden your awareness in many ways. Subscribe to the nutritionfacts.org mailing list to keep up to date on the latest in evidence–based nutrition. Watch the growing number of vegan documentaries available on Netflix and elsewhere. See *Documentaries* the Resources chapter. Learn new cooking techniques by taking a live or online cooking class. You can even take a vegan cruise. Yes, you read it correctly. The Holistic Holiday at Sea is an annual cruise (14 years in 2017) in the Caribbean that is essentially a floating conference. You can eat plant–based fare as well as attend seminars on a broad array of topics relating to healthy eating. It's a great way to immerse yourself in learning while enjoying some enchanting ports of call. There are other vegan cruises starting to emerge. See the Resources chapter and do a search online.

As you learn, share your discoveries with others. You don't have to convince anyone that your way is the only way, but you can lead by being a positive role model. As you raise your health consciousness, you can help raise the health consciousness of others. That's what it is going to take – each of us doing what we can to raise the collective consciousness until we reach a tipping point.

CHAPTER 6: ESTABLISHING A SUSTAINABLE PLANT-BASED LIFESTYLE

Sustainable–nutritious eating/ living has a higher purpose.

– Elizabeth Salamanca–Brosig

You have made it this far down the path towards a whole food plant–based diet. This is a good time to take a look at ways to maintain the momentum. In this chapter, we will look at systems that you can put in place to support your success as well as dealing with obstacles that you may encounter.

A Lifestyle You Can Live With

It's important to make your new eating style one you can live with. The goal is to sustain your good eating habits and continue progress toward whole food eating. Here are some guidelines and tips to help you through the process. Select the ones that have the most meaning to you.

Guidelines

- As you transform your eating habits, it is very important to listen to your body. Your body will be adjusting to lighter food. You will be more regular and lighter on your feet. You will likely feel less aching in your joints, maintain lower blood pressure, and have more energy. Your tastes will also be changing. The more you include whole foods into your diet, the less your body will crave sugar, fat, and salt. But it's important not to rush it. Give yourself time to adjust. The last thing you want to do is adjust too quickly, then feel like the diet is not working for you. Introduce changes slowly, and make sure that you are satisfied at every point of the transition. Find your food comfort zone, and let that zone gradually expand to include new tastes.
- It's best not to think of your new eating style as a "diet". Diets are temporary. They are usually nutritionally skewed to exclude an important food group, and often result in short–term weight loss, but long–term weight gain. Instead, adopt an eating plan that is nutritionally balanced and permanent.
- Be true to your own best health; it's your **number one priority**. Embrace your new eating style. It's okay to eat differently from others.
- A vegan or plant–based eating style is often described in terms of what you can't eat. Try not to fall into that trap. Instead, focus on the incredible variety of foods and new flavors that you get to enjoy. Treat it like an adventure!

Tips

- Endeavor to fill up on low–fat, high–fiber, whole foods. Let the healthy foods crowd the other food off your plate.
- Put the less–healthy more tempting food products out of sight. Put the healthy choices front and center in your fridge, your pantry, and on your counter.

- Challenge yourself to continue learning about plant–based eating. Seek out new information to empower yourself. Stay current with the latest research, and use it to refine and improve your eating habits. See *Raising Your Health Consciousness* in the previous chapter.
- Identify your internal and external blockages – What is keeping you from reaching your health goals?
- Find a foodie friend, and attend healthy cooking classes. See Establishing a Support System in chapter 5.

Preparing for Success

There are several things you can do to prepare for a long and successful relationship with healthy eating.

Organize the Way You Store and Process Food

Most of us don't think much about how we store our food. Eating more plant–based gives you an opportunity to connect more with your food. If you incorporate a few simple guidelines, you can streamline the process and get more out of your food. It starts with selecting foods at the market. Check the ingredients and eschew items that contain excess sugar, salt, and/or oil. You can save money by purchasing dried beans and lentils rather than canned.

When you return from the market, store frozen foods in the freezer, and perishable items in the fridge. This is a good time to wash items like lettuce and put them in a lettuce crisper. You can repackage things in smaller quantities for lunches or travel. Store seeds and other items that attract pests or may contain eggs in the freezer for a few days. This will kill any insect eggs. Then you can move them to the fridge or pantry. You can also start soaking beans and lentils.

If harvesting from your garden, wash items thoroughly. Store greens in a crisper. You may want to steam some items. They will take less room to store, and you might even want to freeze some of them for future use.

It's a great idea to label items that you store in your pantry and freezer. Use rewritable labels. This will make it easier to identify items when you need them. Store food items in glass or non–BPA plastic.

Organize Your Reference Materials

As you progress on your journey toward plant–based eating, you are likely to come across information that would be useful to have on hand when shopping or preparing a meal. It might be cookbooks that you've collected, printed recipes, or tips that you find online or in a cooking class. Find a place in or near your kitchen for these items. Allocate enough space for your growing collection of cookbooks. Store stray bits of information in file folders and store in a file box. Organize your kitchen gadget manuals so that you can refer to that pressure cooker manual or stovetop steamer manual when you need them. I also found that a 3–ring binder containing key reference documents can be very helpful. I collected documents from online sources and cooking classes that would come in handy when shopping or cooking. Some of the documents include: cooking techniques, the Dirty Dozen, flavor balancing, international flavors, measurement conversions, and vegan flavor matching.

Another useful organizing tool is your handy dandy iPad or other tablet. You can use a recipe app to store recipes, then prop your tablet up and use it while you prepare your meal. You can edit the recipes on the fly, and make notes for future use. I use the app Evernote to store recipes, as well as notes on using the pressure cooker, successes and failures using aquafaba, and more.

Prepare a Large Dish Once a Week

Doing major food prep once a week on a weekend really helps cut down on the time spent during the week. On a typical weekend, I'll select a favorite dish on Saturday, depending on the season and my mood. Some of my favorites include stir–fry, soup, pizza, spaghetti, and tagine. All of these lend themselves to making large batches that are easy to store for future use. With the dish selected, I compare the necessary ingredients to my pantry, fridge, and freezer to make a shopping list. After shopping, I make the dish later that day or on Sunday. If you make enough, you can store some portions in the freezer as well as in the fridge. Be sure to label the items with a name and date so that you don't lose track of what they are.

During the week, you can rely on your prepared food but also mix it up. Variety is important, so every few days, make something different that is easy to prepare to keep it fresh.

Have Ingredients on Hand for Quick and Easy Meals

One of the secrets to making quick and easy meals that are affordable and tasty is to prepare some of the ingredients in advance. It doesn't take a lot of prep, just some planning. A little bit of planning goes a long way. Try this approach for a five-day cycle:

1. Shop to obtain fresh produce every 5 days (for optimal freshness). You can clean and store the produce right away, or refrigerate and clean just before you use it. Shopping idea: try out different types of produce each time you shop. That keeps your cooking experience fresh. Also, shop with color in mind. Dark colored fruit and veggies are packed with extra nutrition.
2. Prepare a grain dish and a dish of beans or lentils. It can be any grain you like, and you can try out different grains for variety. I tend to favor quinoa, but millet, barley, buckwheat, and couscous are other good choices. For beans and lentils, you can save time by purchasing them precooked. Beans are usually in cans; lentils can be in a vacuum sealed package. Or you can save money by purchasing dried beans and lentils, soaking overnight, and pressure cooking them. It's your choice. Speaking of choice, try out different beans or lentils – there are different colors of lentils, and a wide range of beans including adzuki, black, kidney, white, pinto, garbanzo, etc. Store your prepared grains and lentils in air–tight containers or bags in the freezer and the fridge. Label the items, especially if they are not easily recognizable.
3. Have salad ingredients ready to go. Wash lettuce and other leafy greens, and store in a crisper where they last a lot longer. Store sprouts and wash them just before you use them. I like to cut up the harder salad ingredients and store them in a separate container: carrots, celery, jicama, bell peppers, fennel bulb, and radishes. You can add other ingredients like avocado, sprouts, roasted peppers, and olives as you assemble the salad. One other thought on salad. You can prepare your own dressings or purchase them. Keep in mind, that you want to minimize oil. Some vendors such as Walden Farms make amazing salad dressings with no oil.
4. Now you can assemble a meal in minutes. Pull out the grain dish along with the dish of beans or lentils. Steam up a few veggies. Add some flavorings, striving for a balance of sweet, pungent, salty, sour, umami, and spicy. Toss a salad together. Voila!

If you follow this pattern of shopping, having ingredients on hand, and doing a bit of prep-work, you'll get into a nice rhythm. If you work during the week, you can modify the pattern as needed by using frozen meals from PlantPure Nation or going out to eat. For more in depth coverage of easy vegan meal planning and flavor balancing, see vegancoach.com, both the website and their marvelous online courses.

Food for Travel

You have the most control over your food preparation at home in your own kitchen. So, why ever leave home? Sometimes life intervenes, and you have to go to work, or to an all-day outing, or to a conference, or on vacation. Although there are more vegan and plant–based food options available on the road these days, you are still at the mercy of the food landscape when you travel. Yet, you can retain some measure of control by planning and packing a few essentials.

For travel to work, you can take food in an insulated food bag. Insulated bags are available at local stores or online. See what you can do to store things in the break or lunch room. I keep a box in a cupboard at work with utensils, paper bowls, tea bags and mug, and dry soup mixes. You may be able to carve out some space in the company fridge (or install your own mini fridge) for your favorite dressings, leftovers, or dishes that will last a few days. Be sure to stock up on snacks as well for your desk or lunch room – fresh fruit, vegetables, dried fruit, nuts, and energy bars.

If you travel by car, use an insulated food bag to store items such as sandwiches, wraps, fresh fruit, and baked potatoes. Make a point of keeping your car stocked with emergency rations. Keep a bag with dried goods such as energy bars, dried fruit, nuts, and seeds.

For day trips to picnics or amusement parks, I make lunch wraps in the morning (see the *Lunch Wrap* recipe in "Sandwiches and Wraps"), keep them in an insulated food bag in the car as long as possible, then transfer to a backpack for walking to the lunch site. I supplement the wraps with an assortment of dried fruit, nuts, seeds, carrots, celery, sugar snap peas, energy bars, apples, and any sweets.

For trips involving air travel, I bring fresh food for the flight, and pack some key items for the stay. If I'm staying at a timeshare or a place with reasonable kitchen facility, I pack some of the essentials that may be difficult or inconvenient to obtain in small quantities at the destination. Some of these items include a spice tower (small container with about 12 spices), extra 2"x3" bags of favorite spices, sealable bags of breakfast cereal, cereal toppings (nuts, seeds, dried fruit), protein powder, sweetener, snacks, tea bags, and extra resealable bags.

On arrival, I search HappyCow.net for vegan or vegan friendly restaurants in the area. You can often check menus online, and call ahead if you have any questions. Most restaurants will do their best to accommodate your needs. Fast food chains are a bit of a challenge, but UrbanTastebud.com has a complete rundown on what items are vegan at many of the popular fast food chains (45 at last count). Chipotle, for example has tacos, burritos, and sofritas that can be made vegan as well as a salad and tortilla chips.

For a week-long stay, I generally do a shopping trip on the first day to stock up on food for the week. Staying at a place with at least moderate kitchen facilities enables you to prepare breakfast and dinners as well as travel food for day trips.

Time-Saving Tips

Probably the most effective way to save time in assembling a meal is to use leftovers, frozen meals that you have prepared, or frozen meals that you purchased. Just take out the meal, heat it, and eat it.

In general, advanced meal preparation saves time in assembly. Chop up hard salad ingredients like carrots, celery, jicama, and bell peppers, and store in a container. Clean lettuce, basil, and other salad greens and store in a crisper. When it is time to prepare a salad, you can assemble it quickly. Lay down a bed of the greens, add the hard ingredients, add any other ingredients like avocado, nuts, seeds, fresh or dried fruit, then top with a salad dressing.

For warm meals, advanced preparation saves time as well. Make big batches of soups, stir–fry, and spaghetti sauce. Freeze these dishes in meal–sized portions. Then you can pull out portions as needed, heat them, and eat.

You can also pull recipe–free meals (see Chapter 7) together quickly with a bit of advanced preparation of the most time consuming ingredients. Cook large batches of dried beans or lentils in advance. Freeze portions and keep a portion in the fridge. Cook a batch of grains such as quinoa, millet, buckwheat, or kamut. Freeze some, and store a portion in the fridge for ready use. When it comes time to prepare a meal, you can pull out the prepared grain and legumes for heating. It doesn't take much time to sauté some greens and steam some other veggies. While they are cooking, whip up a flavorful sauce (see the Recipes chapter for examples). Add seasonings, nuts, and seeds, then garnish. In minutes, you will have a robust and satisfying meal.

If your taste buds are accustomed to foods containing animal products (meat, cheese, butter, etc.), it is especially important to season your plant–based foods well with herbs and spices. You can build your own flavor profiles one spice at a time, or you can save time by using seasoning blends. There are blends for all the international flavors (many of them salt–free) that can provide instant flavor and lots of variety. For soups, stir–frys, etc., you can use an instant vegetable stock powder for an instant flavor base. There are many brands available, or you can make your own.

I do spend a lot of time cutting vegetables on my trusty bamboo cutting board. I consider it a labor of love and health, but there are ways to speed up the process when time is of the essence. You can use a kitchen utensil or appliance like mandoline or a food processor to cut vegetables down to size quickly. You can save even more time by purchasing bags of veggies that are already cleaned and chopped for you – salad mixes, broccoli and cauliflower florets, coleslaw mixes, shredded carrots, and more. These are readily available from almost any market. They may not be quite as fresh as chopping raw produce yourself, but they will save you time if that is your goal.

Another time–saver is frozen vegetables. The vegetables won't be as fresh as raw produce, but it may be an acceptable tradeoff in a soup or stir–fry dish.

Money-Saving Ideas

There are numerous ways to save money eating a plant–based diet.

Eat with the Seasons

Seasonal produce will be less expensive than foods that are out of season. The savings can be significant.

Shop at the Edges

Shop at the edges of your market, where they keep the fresh produce and bulk items. The front and middle of the store are generally dedicated to pre–packaged foods and processed foods, which can be very expensive and not as healthy for you.

Buy in Bulk

One can of beans might cost around $2.00, but a whole pound of dried beans could cost less than $2.00.

Process your own Food

You can save money by doing some of your own food processing rather than buying foods processed by the food industry. Make your own flaxseed crackers and energy bars. Make your own salad dressings and sauces. Buy dried beans and lentils, and cook them yourself. Instead of buying sprouts, buy seeds and lentils, and sprout them yourself. See *Sprouts* in "From Scratch."

Dehydrate, Freeze, or Can

Dehydrate, freeze, or can excess produce. If you have fruit trees or bushes, you know that everything ripens in a short window of time. Don't let it go to waste. Eat what you can, then save the rest by dehydrating, freezing, or canning.

Late–Week Food Audit

Monitor the inventory in your refrigerator throughout the week. Make sure to use produce before it goes bad. If you end up with extra produce, you can throw it into a pot of soup or freeze it for later use. Be sure to adjust your shopping plan for the next week accordingly.

Pack Food and Water for Travel

Bring water, other beverages, and travel food from home rather than paying for food at concession stands.

Survival Budget

For some people, buying food on a limited budget is not a choice, it is a matter of survival. There are approximately 1.2 billion people on this planet that have only $1.50 or less to spend on food per day. To raise awareness of this fact, Darshana Thacker, a culinary project manager for Forks Over Knives, took up the challenge in 2013 to feed herself with plant–based foods on $1.50 per day for 5 days. Her focus was on foods that are inexpensive and provide the most nutrients and calories per dollar. This turned out to be lentils, beans, rice, potatoes, carrots, brown rice pasta, corn tortillas, oatmeal, tomato sauce, fresh spinach, a lime, and some spices. She purchased the majority of the items at a local 99–cent store to save money, and fed herself for 5 days on $7.50 total.

She spent some time cooking up some soup, a stew, a pasta dish, and baked potatoes. She even sprouted some of the lentils. She did not have a lot of fresh fruits and vegetables in this short trial, but could have worked in fresh seasonal items had the trial been extended. She had plenty of food to eat, and found it surprisingly satisfying.[1] Utterly amazing!

I'm not advocating that you adopt this kind of eating program, but this experiment clearly demonstrates that a diet consisting primarily of whole food plants can be extremely affordable.

You may have noticed that most of the money–saving tips above seem to be the exact opposite of the time–saving tips discussed previously. It's the old tradeoff between time and money. You can save money by purchasing raw whole foods, and cleaning, chopping, and cooking them yourself. You can save time by purchasing packaged fruits and vegetables that are already partially prepared. The choice depends on your priorities.

Grow your own Food

Growing your own food is something that can really enhance your connection with the food you eat. It can encourage you to cook more meals at home. With the rising costs of food, it can also make a serious dent in your grocery bill.

Limited space is no longer an excuse to opt out of growing your own food. You can grow food indoors, in hanging pots, in patio towers, in water (aquaponics), and more. There are plenty of do–it–yourself options as well as commercial systems that you can purchase. There is nothing like harvesting your own fresh produce, knowing exactly where it came from and how it was grown.

My backyard was pretty much unusable when I moved in seven years ago. It was primarily one extended steep slope. Over the years, I introduced pathways and raised garden beds on the slopes. Now, I have enough room to grow a robust variety of leafy greens, squash, beets, peppers, tomatoes, about 12 fruit trees, goji berries, fennel, kiwis, passion fruit, dragon fruit, and grape vines. On the deck, I have kumquats, a blueberry bush, and a moringa tree in a pot.

On a chance visit to Epcot Center in Florida, I discovered the world of hydroponics. They take their hydroponics seriously at Epcot Center. That visit inspired me to build a hydroponic tower and a couple of other experimental hydroponic stations. I installed two 530 gallon tanks to collect rainwater, and I use that rainwater for all the hydroponic water needs. Plants generally grow two to three times faster in the hydroponic tower because the roots are constantly bathed in nutrients. The tower is great for growing herbs like mint, basil, parsley, lettuce, and watercress. I can also start kale, Swiss chard, collards, peppers, amaranth, and even moringa tree seedlings until the

roots get too big. Then they have to be transferred to the garden. I also propagate seeds indoors under grow lights, and then transfer the seedlings to a hydroponic station or the garden.

It's wonderful to go "shopping" in the yard almost daily, especially for leafy greens and herbs. My wife loves to harvest fresh kale and mint for her smoothies. Growing your own produce also gives you some measure of food security against the possibility of natural disasters or a breakdown of the commercial food–production chain.

> *The stakes are pretty high because, let's face it, if you don't have your own food security,*
> *then your every day survival depends on large corporations*
> *who may be more interested in their profit than your health.*
>
> *– Stacey Murphy*

If you are growing your own produce in a backyard garden, you can significantly improve the soil in a number of ways. You can save your kitchen scraps and put them into a compost pile. Add leaves and other plant matter from the yard, turn it periodically, and in a few months you will develop rich compost material that you can mix into your garden soil. If you really want to speed up the composting process, run your vegetable and fruit left overs through an inexpensive juicer. Put the resulting pulp into the compost bin. The pulp will break down much more quickly than larger chunks of food matter. You can use the juiced liquid in a number of ways. Pour it directly onto the soil around your plants, or add it to the compost bin. You can even drink it, or use it as an extra source of cooking liquid, depending on what ingredients you use.

An added benefit of maintaining a compost bin is that you can use it to make compost tea (see directions below). This may be the best thing you can do for your garden. Spraying compost tea on your soil will nourish the rich microbial life that is so essential to healthy soil. In contrast, commercial fertilizers usually contain salts that kill this microbial life. With dead soil, you have to constantly add more fertilizer for the plants to thrive. Your plants become totally dependent on a constant supply of fertilizer. On the other hand, compost tea feeds the soil, and the soil nourishes the plants. Treat your garden soil with compost tea every month or two and you may never have to purchase commercial fertilizer again.

Look up how to make compost tea online and you will see plenty of variations. Here's a quick summary of how I make my compost tea. I fill a 5–gallon bucket nearly full of water. I insert a couple of bubbler stones (the kind you would use in a small aquarium) to let it aerate for a couple of hours to reduce the chlorine content. I then grab several handfuls of compost soil and place it in a paint sock or nylon stocking and suspend it in the bubbling water. Add a tablespoon or two of organic molasses, and let it bubble overnight. The good bacteria in the water feed on the molasses and will reach their maximum growth in about 12 hours. Pour some of the compost tea into a 3-gallon sprayer, and spray onto your soil and plant leaves. Repeat until all of the compost tea has been distributed. Do this every month or two, and your soil and plants will love it!

Physical Exercise

Diet is the major risk factor for death in the US by quite a margin over tobacco smoking, high blood pressure, and high body mass index. Physical inactivity is a distant fifth.[2] So, diet surpasses physical activity in terms of your overall health and longevity, yet physical activity does play a part. In fact, physical exercise can have a profound effect on your overall health.

The Centers for Disease Control and Prevention (CDC) recommends a minimum of 150 of minutes moderate–intensity exercise every week for adults. This is just over 20 minutes per day. Previous recommendations for daily exercise were higher, so consider this a minimum to maintain your good health. Moderate activities are those during which a person could talk, but not sing. Some of the moderate–intensity activities include bicycling, dancing, gardening, hiking, housework, swimming, doubles tennis, walking briskly, tai chi, qi gong, and yoga. Alternatively, you could engage in vigorous–intensity activities for 75 minutes a week. Again, this is a bare minimum.

In case you are wondering about the benefits of exercise, here are a few thoughts to chew on. Studies have shown that increased levels of physical activity are associated with decreased risks of a number of age–related diseases. Among these are type 2 diabetes, coronary heart disease, a number of cancers, and osteoporosis. Higher levels of physical activity have also been associated with overall improvement of general health and increased longevity.[3] In addition, many studies show that the more you exercise, the greater your life expectancy. For example, in a study of more than 650,000 adults, mostly age 40 or more, showed that life expectancy was 3.4 years longer for people who achieved the recommended level of exercise compared to people who were sedentary. People who exercised at twice the recommended level gained 4.2 years of life.[4]

Another beneficial aspect of exercise is that it activates the same regions of your brain as other mood enhancers. As you exercise, the levels of dopamine, serotonin, and other endorphins rise. These brain chemicals play an important part in regulating your mood. You can think of exercise as your personal anti–depression mechanism.

Exercise can also enhance brain function. Recent research indicates that exercise increases the levels of BDNF (brain–derived neurotrophic factor), which is a protein essential for maintaining healthy neurons and creating new ones. Increasing your level of physical activity not only supports brain cell growth and learning, it can potentially counteract depression and aging as well as combating Alzheimer's and Parkinson's diseases.

Once you decide to include more exercise in your lifestyle, the question is – how do you go about it? If you have been sedentary for some time, you don't want to overdo it and pull a muscle or get discouraged. Be smart about it. Start slowly. You might start with something as simple as standing and stretching for 5 minutes while you watch TV. You could go for a short walk. You could tend your garden for 10 minutes. Sneak in 5–minute activities throughout your day. The point is to introduce exercise into your life slowly, and build up the time and the activity level gradually as your body adjusts. Make small micro–changes in your activity level and string together a series of these small changes.

As you do this, notice how you feel. Even modest physical activity on a regular basis can improve your mood, your mental clarity and overall cognitive function, and increase your energy level and physical stamina. As your physical condition improves, you will get to a point where you are ready and able to take on more challenging activities. The great news is that you don't necessarily have to "join a gym" and limit yourself to walking on a treadmill and pumping iron. There are lots of fun things you can do to be more active.

Go dancing or join a dance class. Go on outings like a tourist: visit a museum, garden, or a park, and take pictures of your adventure. Take an exercise class (appropriate to your current fitness level) from a local adult or recreation center: Tai Chi, aerobics, chair exercise, local walks, stretching, zumba, pilates, or yoga. Pick fruit and make a pie with family or friends. Stretch while you are reading or playing video games. Lift weights while you watch TV. Play videos of yoga, aerobic exercise, or aerobic kickboxing and follow along. Go swimming. Bicycle around the neighborhood or to the local market. Go out for a short walk before breakfast, after dinner, or both. Be active in your garden: plant fruits and veggies, apply compost tea and mulch to the soil, harvest your produce, and trim trees and bushes as needed. Participate in a project to improve your household: paint, make minor repairs, or decorate a room. Join the local YMCA and participate in recreation activities such as cycling, hiking, and swimming, or in active sports such as tennis, basketball, and volleyball.

I maintain my fitness in a few ways. I work out with my wife most mornings to one of several half-hour aerobic exercise programs. Having an exercise partner helps keep it consistent, and I find that this is just enough to keep my muscles toned. Then I play doubles tennis twice a week. Donna and I do a lot of hiking whenever we travel, especially on mountain pathways or through tropical gardens.

A substantial portion of my physical activity comes from working in the garden. Not only is it a delightful place to catch some Southern California sunshine (and generate some vitamin D), but it also adds to my daily exercise. I'm not talking about casually picking a few flowers in the garden. Most of the time, I'm out there digging rocks to construct retaining walls for raised garden beds, laying pathways, constructing pergolas, creating ponds and stream beds, building a teahouse, and more. I've given myself 10 years to create the hardscape for the yard. Once that's in place, I'll spend even more time growing and harvesting crops.

These are the things that motivate me to keep active. Try out a few new activities and find the ones that stimulate you.

The following tips will help you fully integrate regular physical activity into your healthy lifestyle:

1. **Keep a record**. Write down why you want to exercise. Set some realistic goals, and record your achievements. Writing down your goals makes them more tangible and achievable.

2. **Establish a regular routine**. Add exercise activities to your diary or calendar. Schedule physical activity as you would any important appointment–and keep it.

3. **Make it fun**. Try out different activities and discover the ones that bring you the most joy and health benefit.

4. **Find a friend**. Schedule activities with family or friends who share your motivation.

5. **Figure it out**. There may be emotional issues that deter you from exercise. Figure it out! There may be logistical problems. Figure it out! There may be other pressing issues intruding on your exercise time. Think about the important contribution exercise makes to your health, and figure it out!

6. **If you drop the ball, pick it up**. If your exercise routine gets disrupted, don't get discouraged. Keep your eyes on the prize. Focus on the health benefit and reengage with renewed enthusiasm.

7. **Reward yourself**. As human beings, many of us tend to have a rather peculiar propensity to berate ourselves for the tiniest offense, yet we rarely remember to congratulate ourselves for our achievements. I see this all the time in my math students who frequently get down on themselves when they have trouble with a new concept, yet they seem to have difficulty acknowledging themselves for their successes. This is counterproductive, because acknowledging your achievements increases positive emotions such as self–respect, happiness, and confidence. This is just as important in learning math as it is in learning to exercise. Celebrating even small successes will help to keep you motivated and energized. So, think about where you started, and be mindful of congratulating yourself regularly as you progress. Reward yourself with a picnic with the family, a nice massage, reading a book, going to a movie, adding a charm to your charm bracelet or adding a stamp to your stamp collection.

Dealing with Cravings

Food is your emotional truth.

– Nigella Lawson

One of the challenges in making changes to your eating habits is dealing with cravings. After learning about the addictive nature of sugar, fat, and salt in a previous chapter, this shouldn't come as a surprise to any of us. Why do we crave meat and deep fried foods? Because of the fat. Why do we crave ice cream and chocolate? Because of the fat and sugar. Why do we crave soda? Because of the sweetener and the fizz. Why do we crave processed foods? Because food scientists have extracted the sugar, fat, and salt from whole foods, concentrated it, and put it into packaged foods. When we bite into such a morsel, the concentrated fats and sugars stimulate our pleasure centers, and drive our cravings for more. Unfortunately, the nourishing part of the whole food is stripped out. So, we are getting a lot of calories and stimulating flavors, but very little nutrition. These are aptly named "*empty calories.*"

These foods are designed to be addictive, and they are very successful at it. So, what can we do about it? The first step is to learn more about the nature of cravings. To understand cravings, we need to look at the big picture. You elected to follow a vegan diet in pursuit of a whole food plant–based eating style for optimal health. You've learned that the healthcare system operates more like a disease–care system, and that you need to take responsibility for your own health to avoid a life burdened with prescription medications and chronic illness. You want to live life fully, with all of your mental facilities and full physical functionality now, and into your later years.

Despite this intent, many of us have an internal conflict. There is a very powerful pleasure–seeking part of us that operates independently of our desire to be healthy. Our bodies developed in times of scarcity. We evolved the drive to seek out the most calorie-dense foods. This drive still operates, even though we are surrounded by calorie-rich foods. This pleasure-seeking drive may be like an inner voice tempting us to give in and eat foods that are unhealthy. The insidious thing is that this inner voice may be speaking in your *own voice*. The voice can sound like you, but it is really the addictive foods and food habits that are calling to you.

Sometimes you may feel that you are ravenous, and have to eat right now. Most likely, it's the cravings that are calling to you. In fact, you are probably not actually starving. Your fridge and pantry are stocked with plenty of foodstuffs. You have access to plenty of nutritious food, yet your body and taste buds are craving something salty, or sweet, or full of chocolate.

This struggle with cravings for unhealthy foods can derail your best intentions to pursue a healthy lifestyle. The key is to continue learning about nutrition and the consequences of food choices and to practice eating healthy foods until your taste buds adjust to prefer the healthy foods.

Learning how to deal with food addiction and cravings is an important part of your journey. Even though you value your health, your primitive brain doesn't want you to change. It wants to avoid the discomfort of withdrawal symptoms as well as the emotional anxiety associated with change. It will be looking for reasons to avoid any kind of major change in diet.

The only way to break free of this influence is to make a commitment to eat healthy foods and to avoid addictive processed foods until the cravings go away. Identify the food items that trigger your cravings. Ask yourself the question: "Who is in charge of my health, me or the doughnut?" Get rid of these "trigger" foods, and commit to change. You need to be fierce in your commitment. If you feel weak for a few days while your body adjusts, just realize that it is part of the healing process. Give your body (and mind) time to adjust. As you are healing, feed your body plenty of delicious plant–based foods. Establish routines that support healthy eating. Eliminate from your immediate environment any foods that have previously stimulated your cravings, and surround yourself with nutritious and tasty whole foods. Over time, your taste buds will adjust to whole foods, and you will arrive at a new normal in which you crave healthy foods.

Family and Social Challenges

Eating vegan or plant-based yourself is one thing. Cooking for a family or dealing with a reluctant partner can be a whole different kettle of fish, or should I say 'pot of potatoes'? Partners can be set in their ways and unwilling to try new things; they have their own food comfort zone. Kids tend to be finicky in their food choices. Let's look at the two issues separately.

Mixed Couples (Vegan/Non–Vegan)

If your spouse or partner is not fully on board with your plant–based eating style, you'll need to figure out how both of you can enjoy your own food preferences. You can start by having a discussion. Explain why you feel compelled to change your eating style. Express your interest in an arrangement that will allow each of you to pursue your own eating preferences. Listen to their concerns. See if you can both reach a consensus about how best to identify and build on the areas of common food interests and to accommodate both of your unique dietary preferences.

If your eating styles don't have much in common, you can start out with each person cooking their own meals. As time goes on, find opportunities to share your food with your partner. There are plenty of vegan dishes that many people can enjoy. Make smoothies, gourmet salads, spaghetti sauce, roasted vegetables with a cream sauce, tacos, fresh fruit, and tasty appetizers. Try some of the recipes in this book. Make extra, and offer to share. As your skills in flavor balancing and flavor matching improve (see Chapter 7), the dishes you share will become more irresistible. You may find that as your partner experiences the ever–changing variety of new flavors in your dishes, they will be more open to embracing plant–based dishes.

A good strategy for peaceful coexistence is to make meals to share with a vegan base, and let your partner add their own meat or dairy items as desired. Make a spaghetti sauce with lots of veggies, and let them add their own meatballs and parmesan cheese. You might even try plant–based meatballs and non–dairy parmesan (see recipe) to see if these are acceptable alternatives. Make well–seasoned steamed or roasted veggies on a bed of quinoa with a cream sauce and let your partner add their own meat. Again, you could let them try Gardein Chick'n Scallopini or Trader Joe's Chick'n with Mandarin Orange Sauce. As long as both parties get to eat foods that they like, you can still enjoy meals together.

Another strategy for expanding your partner's appreciation for plant–based eating is to find dishes or treats that both of you love. There are over 160 recipes in Chapter 8. Many of these have proven quite popular with both vegans and omnivores alike. Some of these favorites are listed in the table that follows. Give them a try.

Appetizers:	Salads and Sides
Italian Tofu Bites	Barbequed Chick'n Salad
Roasted Eggplant with Bruschetta	Garden Barley Salad with Italian Tofu Bites
Spicy Mini–Burger Bites	Heavenly Salad
Spring Rolls and Dipping Sauces	Not Refried Black Beans
	Roasted Vegetables
Breakfast:	Spanish Quinoa Pilaf
David's Breakfast Bowl	
High–Protein Vegan Waffles	**Sandwiches and Wraps**
Oatmeal–Maple Breakfast Cookies	Chickpea No–Tuna Salad Wraps
Raw Berry Compote	Lunch Wraps
	Mediterranean Bean Burgers
Dairy Alternatives:	Thai Peanut Burgers
Banana "Milk" Shake	

Chipotle Cheesy Sauce	**Sauces, Syrups, and Dressings**
Cherry Garcia Nice Cream	Cashew Cream Sauce
Double Chocolate Nice Cream	Dijon Ranch Dressing
Easy Cheesy Sauce	
Garlic–Herb Cream Cheese	**Makeovers:**
	Easy Portobello Fajitas
Desserts:	Spaghetti Sauce and Noodles
Cantaloupe Sorbet	Mushroom Cashew Gravy
Coconut Lemon Bars	Quick Balsamic Dressing
Date Sweetened Pumpkin Pie	Smoky BBQ Sauce
Decadent Chocolate Truffles	Smoky White Pizza Sauce
Meringue Cookies	Spicy Thai Almond Sauce
Mixed Berry Tart with Toasted Almond Crust	Spreadable Smoked Sharp Cheddar
No–Bake Dark Chocolate Pumpkin Pudding or Pie	Strawberry Vinaigrette
Peanut Butter Black Bean Brownies	Sweet Miso Lemon Dressing & Sauce
Watermelon Cake	
Whole Food Cookies	**Snacks:**
	Sweet Potato (Air) Fries
From Scratch:	
Tofu–Cashew Mayonnaise	**Tea Party:**
	Drop Scones
Main Dishes:	Mock Devonshire Cream
5–Layer Tamale Pie	Pineapple–Cream Cheese Tea Sandwich
Herbed Lentils and Roasted Butternut Squash	
Lazy Zucchini Lasagna	**Templates:**
Loaded Sweet Potatoes with Kale and Yam Black Bean Chili	3–Ingredient Energy Bar Template
Moroccan Tagine	5–Minute Creamy Dressing Template
Quinoa and Cranberry Stuffed Acorn Squash	Green Smoothie Template
Quinoa Power Bowl	Gourmet Salad Template
Simple BBQ Tofu	Stir–Fry Template
Sweet and Savory Veggie Stew	

There are many commercially available products that are sure to please as well. Frozen desserts are a good place to start. Can you imagine anyone turning down a So Delicious frozen almond milk bar covered with chocolate and nuts? In fact, any cookie, pie, or cake that is vegan will be a nice way to establish common ground. How about hamburgers as a shared food? The Beyond Burger patty from Beyond Meat is virtually indistinguishable from a beef patty. It was designed to be appealing to meat eaters, so it's a good bet for a food to share. Pile on fixings that you both like. Snack foods, such as mixed nuts, granola bars, peanut and almond butter are other good foods to share. Most people like to dip things, so serve chips or fresh cut veggies dipped in salsa, sauces, guacamole, or hummus. These commercial products will most likely not be as healthy, but your initial goal is to establish a list of foods that both of you can enjoy together. In time, you can include more healthy foods.

Here are a few things to consider when working out a comfortable agreement with a partner who has different food preferences.

- When going out to eat, look at menus ahead of time. Call ahead to ensure that the restaurant can provide something for everyone.
- Establish locations in the fridge for storing meat and dairy items. Keep these items separate from fresh fruit and vegetables.
- Discuss food handling policies. For example, let your partner know whether or not you are willing to cook eggs for them in the mornings. Address the issue of uncooked chicken in the kitchen. Several studies show that about 70% of store–bought chicken contains harmful bacteria. This bacteria can easily be spread through your hands, cutting boards, knives, kitchen cloths, dishes, tongs, basting brush, counter tops, etc.
- Stretch you partner's food comfort zone with a new dish from time to time, but don't push too much at once. There is no reason for food choices to become a divisive force in a relationship.
- Use vegan cooking as the base for all joint meals. Cook soups, pasta, curry, steamed or roasted veggies that are vegan, to which meat or cheese can be added. Make cashew sauce instead of a milk sauce. Use vegetable stock instead of beef or chicken. In this way, you can maintain a meal–time sense of unity while allowing your partner to satisfy their dietary preferences.

No single solution is going to work for everyone. There are "mixed" couples in which one person cooks all the meals, and prepares meat, dairy, and egg items separately. There are couples that love cooking together and enjoy the adventure of trying new dishes. There are couples that are both willing to eat primarily vegan at home, and choose other options as desired when dining out or at large gatherings. There are couples that have very different food preferences and end up cooking separate meals, yet eating together.

Keep in mind that only a small percentage of the population eats vegan, or even vegetarian. That percentage is growing at a rapid rate, but for now, vegan food may seem strange and even intimidating to people who are used to the more traditional Western diet. However, people's tastes and perceptions can change. A few bites of a well–seasoned, well–presented plant–based dish, can sometimes open people's eyes and taste buds to new and intriguing flavors. It is not uncommon for people who start out strongly opposed to anything that smacks of "rabbit food," to end up being open to vegan cuisine, or even embracing it.

Transitioning the Family

If you are the food preparer for the family, and you want to move toward more healthy meals, there is an effective strategy to use. It's based on the fact that human taste buds are constantly changing. The old cells die off and are replaced by new cells. In fact, all your taste buds are replaced within about 10 to 14 days. That's what allows people's tastes to change over time. When our taste buds are no longer assaulted with intense sugar, fat, and salt, they become more sensitive to natural flavors. So, the strategy is to ease your family off the intensely additive foods, while at the same time, introducing them to new healthier foods. Vary the dishes that you introduce, and change will happen over time.

Here are some guidelines to consider:

- Get kids involved in everything related to food: meal planning, shopping, and meal preparation (reading the recipe, stirring, mixing, adding ingredients, and taste testing). The more involved they are with the process, the more likely they will be to eat the "fruits" of their labor. The littler ones can stir and mix, while the older ones can plan and even cook whole meals. Pick age–appropriate cooking activities for them.

- Educate your kids about food sources. Pick fruit from a local orchard. Visit a farm or a farmer's market. Get the kids involved in planting and harvesting produce in your own yard. Help your kids understand the connection between animal food products and live animals. Take them to a farm sanctuary or petting zoo, and explain how we appreciate animals and that we don't eat meat because we don't want to harm the animals.

- Make healthy snacks visible and available. Keep the house well supplied with nutritious snacks. Good choices include sliced apples, carrot and celery sticks, whole grain crackers, popcorn without butter, raisins, nuts, seeds, and water bottles. Display healthy choices prominently and put less healthy choices away out of sight. Pack plenty of snacks when you travel.

- Freedom of choice makes a difference. Studies demonstrate that children will eat more vegetables if they have the freedom to choose.[5] An easy way to promote that is to develop meals that inherently have choices. For example, make a salad bar or a taco bar or a stuffed potato bar with lots of tempting options. On pizza night, provide a variety of toppings and let each person assemble their own pizza. Do the same thing on veggie burger night; let each person choose the fixings for their burger.

- Try out new recipes. Bring in new foods and new dishes. Learn about flavor balancing and flavoring blends. Find flavorful ways of introducing new foods. Introduce new foods in small amounts, or as part of larger dishes. You can start with a very tiny sliver of a new vegetable, and then increase the size over time. At the same time, gradually reduce the portions of meat, dairy, and eggs.

- Be a good example – Show your kids that you enjoy your healthy vegan meals and that you like trying out new food options. It will encourage them to follow suit.

- Persistence is the key. Children may require multiple exposures to new foods before they accept them. So, be patient and persistent about introducing healthy new foods. A good approach is to work new foods in gradually. Make the focus of each meal foods that have been accepted previously. Introduce new foods in small amounts or as a flavorful side dish.

- Establish healthy eating habits as early as possible. Children who are introduced to healthy eating early on are more likely to make better food choices as they get older.[6]

- Be prepared for some resistance. People get uncomfortable when you disrupt their food comfort zone. If one dish gets rejected, introduce something else next time, but be sure to try the rejected dish again later, maybe in a different form.

It may require particular care to encourage young eaters to try new foods. Here are some food ideas that may win them over.

Feed your kids whole fresh fruit. Slicing the fruit makes it easier to eat. Another kid–friendly way to give your kids a quick dose of nutrient dense fruit is to make fruit smoothies. Make smoothies on a regular basis. Use frozen fruit, ripe bananas, and pitted dates. Freeze smoothies into popsicles. You can even throw in a few veggies once they get used to drinking smoothies. It's a fun way to try out new fruits and veggies. See *Green Smoothie Template* in "Templates."

Leverage tastes with which your kids are familiar. For example, many kids enjoy the taste of peanut butter and jelly sandwiches. Use that to your advantage by using peanut butter in other dishes and sauces.

Tofu and leafy greens prepared without any seasoning can be pretty mundane. But you can really enhance the flavors by marinating them in soy sauce, tamari, Bragg Liquid Aminos, coconut aminos, or vegan Worcestershire sauce.

Some of the stronger spices like turmeric, ginger, cumin, curry, and garlic can be too bitter or spicy for the uninitiated. However, your kids can still benefit from the antioxidant properties of these spices if you mix them with something that will balance the flavors. Coconut milk can be a great solution. Add these spices to coconut milk to make a delicious base for curries and other spicy sauces.

Make food preparation and eating fun for your kids. Spiralize vegetables into interesting shapes. Put character stickers on fresh fruit slices. Come up with names for your creations, such as the Green Goddess or Incredible Hulk smoothies. Give your kids rewards for trying new foods. See who can make the most realistic or bizarre animal creations with their food. The book *Play with your Food*, by Joost Elffers, has loads of ideas.

Kids of all ages have fun eating fruits and veggies when they can dip them in yummy sauces and spreads. Make your own healthy tortilla chips (*Fat–Free Baked Tortilla Chips* in "Snacks") and dip in salsa or guacamole. Cut up carrots, jicama, celery, and bell peppers and dip in dressings or hummus (*Easy Hummus Dressing* in "Sauces, Syrups, and Dressings"). Make spring rolls to dip in different sauces.

Here are some sure–fire kid favorites:

Breakfast:
Bagels with cream cheese (*Garlic–Herb Cream Cheese* in "Dairy alternatives")
Cereal (*David's Breakfast Bowl* in "Breakfast")
Pancakes (*Blueberry Pancakes* in "Breakfast")
Waffles (*High–Protein Waffles* in "Breakfast")

Lunch/Dinner:
Burgers and Fixings in "Makeovers"
Mac n' cheese (*Mac and No–Cheese* in "Main Dishes")
Pasta and sauce (*Spaghetti Sauce and Noodles* in "Makeovers")
Peanut butter and jelly sandwiches
Pizza with toppings (*Pizza* in "Makeovers")
Spring Rolls and Dipping Sauces in "Appetizers"
Tacos and Fixings in "Makeovers"
Wraps or sandwiches (*Lunch Wraps* in "Sandwiches and Wraps")

Snacks:
Almond Oat Pumpkin Muffins in "Snacks"
Applesauce
Chips and salsa
Crackers (with or without peanut butter)
Dried fruit
Dried vegetables
Fresh fruit
Fresh veggies (with or without dip)
Granola bars (*5–Ingredient Granola Bars* in "Snacks")
Non–dairy yogurt (*Cultured Soy Milk (Yogurt)* in "From Scratch", with or without granola)
Nuts and seeds (*Nut Snack* in "Snacks")
Popcorn

Drinks:
Juice boxes
Smoothies (*Green Smoothie Template* in "Templates")
Soy milk
Water boxes

Social Situations

Family gatherings and holidays can be a challenge to someone newly adopting a vegan lifestyle. These gatherings are most often centered around food and tradition. Some family members may see your food choices as a challenge to the family status quo. Their reactions can vary widely. It can be anything from sidelong glances, to gentle teasing, to pushing food on you, to outright hostility. Realize that these reactions are often caused by feelings of insecurity. It is easy to interpret your new food choices as a criticism of their lifestyle. New ideas and new behaviors can be threatening to family members who fear that it may change the traditions and social structures. People are very protective of the patterns to which they have become accustomed.

Rather than provoke a confrontation, it is far more effective to downplay any attention on yourself. Redirect the conversation to another topic. Compliment the host on the foods that they prepared. After all, you are there to enjoy each other's company. Arguing about dietary choices is not on the menu. If someone confronts you about your food choices, state how good being vegan makes you feel, both physically and mentally, and leave it at that. If they continue to press, offer to share what you know about animal agriculture, but not at the dinner table. Postpone such discussions until later. Keep the focus on enjoying the family and celebration, not on meat eater vs. plant eater.

In general, it is best not to compromise on your food choices. Be true to your own moral compass. If you are confident in your food choices, people will be less likely to affect you. If someone pushes food on you, politely let them know that you no longer eat anything with animal products. On the other hand, if it is a well–meaning elder relative who is oblivious to your eating choices, you can gratefully accept the food, set it aside, and deal with it later.

Check with the host or hostess before hand to see if there will be plant–based food served. Even so, you will be well advised to bring your own food as well. Make it delicious, and bring enough to share. That way, you will be sure to have enough to eat, and you may open the eyes of some of the guests as to how tasty vegan food can be. Be enthusiastic about any effort that the host makes to accommodate your eating style.

If the issue of your eating style comes up away from the dinner table, be honest with your family. Share with them the reasons that you adopted a plant–based eating style. Explain that veganism isn't an attack against them. You are simply eating the foods that best support your own health.

Dining Out

It wasn't too many years ago that it was difficult to find plant–based food when dining out. Fast food eateries were serving meat and dairy products almost exclusively. All–vegan restaurants were rare, and it was pretty slim pickings at other establishments. Things sure have changed. There are all–vegan restaurants popping up like hot cakes in populous locations. Fast food places are also getting on board with vegan options. There are even cruises that offer meal plans that are 100% vegan cuisine. It's a definite trend, and it's all good news for the plant–based home chef who wants an occasional night off.

If you are eating with non–vegan friends or family, explore your vegan options before you go out to eat. If there are confirmed carnivores in the group, you'll need to find a place that serves standard fare, with ample vegan options. If the group is up for it, you can eat at a completely vegan restaurant. Do your research online. Check HappyCow.net for vegan friendly fare in the area. I use the HappyCow smartphone app whenever I travel. Urbantastebud.com has a list of 100% vegan restaurants across the country. It also has an extensive list of vegan options available at restaurant chains, both table service and fast food. If you have a specific restaurant in mind, look up the menu online. Call them if you have a question. Most eateries are motivated to accommodate your dietary needs.

If you are on the road and looking for fast food, peta.org has a long list of vegan options at nationwide fast–food chains. Onegreenplanet.org has a similar list, if a bit less ambitious.

Be an Example and Share Your Knowledge

Throughout this book, you've seen the intimate relationship between what you eat and the health consequences, good and bad. In Chapter 1, you read about the affect that animal agriculture has on our environment and the suffering that "food" animals endure. One or all of these factors influenced you to take an interest in plant–based eating. Now that your consciousness has been raised, there is no turning back. Even if you make a few questionable food choices down the road, the knowledge and awareness that you have attained are yours for good. The question is, what will you do with that knowledge?

Put that knowledge to good use as you continue on your path toward whole food plant–based eating. Expand your knowledge base as you expand your food comfort zone. Keep checking in with nutritionfacts.org to stay abreast of the latest news in evidence–based nutrition. Keep watching new health documentaries as they are produced. Connect with like–minded individuals through potlucks, meetups, and online communities.

Be willing to adapt your eating habits as you make new discoveries. For example, I recently found out some rice can contain high levels of arsenic. I investigated and discovered the best sources of rice with the least amount of arsenic. I found that rinsing or cooking the rice can reduce the risk. I also added other healthy grains to my meals. Another example is that I recently became aware that eating broccoli is perhaps the best way to help our livers remove toxins from our systems. So, I made an effort to include more broccoli in my weekly shopping list. Keep refining your food choices as you learn more about healthy eating.

You can also put your knowledge to good use by sharing it with others, even if you are just at the beginning of your journey. This is important because we are at a pivotal point in human history. With our population currently at 7.5 billion and our water and land resources stretched to the limits, we need immediate and decisive action to change the way we feed our global population. The safest and most effective way to do that is simple: vote with our dollars and eat more plant–based meals. More demand for plant–based meals, and less demand for animal products will have an immediate effect. It will minimize the need to clear more land for animal agriculture, enable us to feed more people worldwide, and reduce environmental pollution and animal suffering. It will also result in a healthier population.

To have a significant impact, the number of people eating plant–based meals needs to increase dramatically. Currently, the percentage of vegans and vegetarians in the general population is relatively small, but it is growing rapidly. A 2017 report by GlobalData indicates that 6% of US consumers now claim to be vegan compared to just 1% in 2014.[7] That's a 500% increase in just three years! This is just one of many signs that we are in the midst of a massive change. Celebrities, athletes, and other public figures are changing to plant–based eating. Restaurants are offering more plant–based options. We are seeing more organic foods and plant–based meat and dairy substitutes in grocery stores. In fact, data released by the Plant-Based Foods Association and the Good Food Institute show that the overall growth in plant-based foods was 8.1 percent in 2016. There is even a brick and mortar plant-based butcher shop in Minneapolis (TheHerbivorous Butcher)! There has been a dramatic shift in the USDA dietary recommendations away from meat and dairy over the last few decades. Similarly, the Canadian government recently issued a new draft of healthy eating recommendations that completely eliminated the milk category and elevated legumes above animal foods. In short, the awareness of plant–based eating is becoming more widespread. For the benefit of our planet, we need to accelerate that change and arrive at the tipping point as soon as possible. The tipping point will come when plant–based eating becomes the norm.

Each of us can make a contribution to raising people's awareness by simply sharing our knowledge. Every person who spreads the word now will affect hundreds or even thousands of people down the road as the message spreads.

How can you share your experience and knowledge with others? Let me count the ways.

1. Support an outreach group, such as veganoutreach.com, vegan.com, or the local pod of PlantPure Nation. Donate your time, money, or expertise.

2. Put a supportive reference in your email signature or elsewhere in your correspondence. It could be a quote or a statement about how many animals you saved today or how much water you saved today by eating plant based.

3. Wear a T–shirt that says "vegan," and have literature ready to hand out. Post flyers in public places such as campus bulletin boards. You can get literature from several outreach organizations.

4. Provide people with vegan food samples. Show how good plant–based food can taste. Bake muffins, make energy bars, cookies, or other snacks, and bring some to work or other gatherings to share.

5. Ask for vegan products everywhere you shop – cafés, restaurants, bakeries, shops, grocery stores. It will increase the awareness of the employees and perhaps the storeowner as well.

6. Start a blog and include your experiences, beliefs, and new things that you learn. Write articles in newsletters of local groups. Tailor the article to the audience. Start a podcast and interview others about their plant–based journey.

7. Organize a vegan potluck or a vegan group. You can create a chapter of an established vegan organization or start your own through something like meetup.com.

8. Speak about your experiences on social network sites. Share health and nutrition information, recipes, facts about animal suffering, and information about animal agriculture and the environment.

9. Lead by being a good example to your peers and family. Be a proud vegan. Eat healthy and share the food. Let your friends and family know what you are doing, why you are doing it, and how great it makes you feel.

10. Maintain a strong network with other vegans through meet–ups, email, blogs, Facebook, events, etc.

11. If you feel strongly about animal welfare, Mercyforanimals.org has an article on how you can use Facebook to share your advocacy.

Follow your strengths. Do what you can to pass the message on, and keep the movement growing. As you engage with other people, keep in mind that encouragement works better than guilt–tripping. Don't harangue or be pushy. People will come around when they are ready.

A man can do only what he can do.
But if he does that each day he can sleep at night
and do it again the next day.

– Albert Schweitzer

CHAPTER 7: RECIPE-FREE COOKING

The following chapter is about recipes and templates, but before we go there, have you ever considered cooking without recipes? It was sure a new concept to me when I began my plant–based journey. In fact, it was all I could do to muddle my way through a few recipes at the beginning. But I had the good fortune to attend an online food summit that introduced Patty Knutson (aka Sassy) of vegancoach.com several years ago. I ended up taking a few of her classes, and along the way, I learned how to cook without recipes. As she puts it, "recipes, shmecipes." Who needs them? Armed with this knowledge, I can go into my fridge (mindful of what's in the pantry and freezer as well), pull out seasonal produce and anything that needs to be used up, and create a meal on the spot. I can tell you, it is very liberating. You don't need to be a slave to any recipe. Of, course, you can still use recipes for inspiration, then create your own masterpieces.

I'll share a brief overview of the process in this chapter. If you want the full treatment, head over to vegancoach.com and put yourself in Sassy's capable hands (or oven mitts).

As my tastes have evolved, I've really come to understand and appreciate herbs and spices in an entirely new way. Herbs and spices are not only nutritious, they work in concert with the natural flavors of plant–based foods to create some amazing flavor combinations. There are two fundamental concepts that will help you bring out the best in your gastronomic creations – *flavor balancing* and *flavor matching*.

Flavor Balancing

So what is flavor balancing? Our taste buds perceive five basic flavors: sweet, salty, sour, bitter, and umami. Sweetness is the sensation you get when eating a ripe fruit, or maple syrup, or sugar. Salty is the sensation you get when eating salt, soy sauce, or sea vegetables. Sour is the sensation derived from lemons, grapefruit, or vinegars. Bitter is the sensation you get from eating black pepper, dark leafy greens, or dark chocolate. Umami is the yummy sensation you get when eating grilled foods, tomatoes, mushrooms, or nutritional yeast. The umami flavor really makes foods more satisfying.

Another "flavor" that is near and dear to many people's hearts is *spicy* or *pungent*. How many times have you seen someone pour gobs of hot sauce onto a dish or sprinkle hot red pepper flakes on their pizza (maybe you are one of these people)? Hot spicy food is an integral part of the flavor profile of many international cuisines. *Spicy* is not generally considered one of the core flavor categories, but so many people are attuned to the spicy heat level of their food that you would do well to consider the spiciness level of a dish when balancing flavors.

The essence of delicious cooking is to bring all of these flavors into a balanced harmony. Foods usually taste better if all of the flavors are represented. One dish might emphasize bitter and sweet, whereas another dish might be strong on umami, sour, and salty, but if all of the flavors are present to some degree, you'll generally get a more pleasing overall flavor. A dish that has a harmonious balance of all the flavors is more likely to taste good, from the first bite to the last. On the other hand. a dish that has a limited flavor profile might taste good for one or two bites, then fall flat after that. So, strive for a balance of flavors. Do a taste test of your food as you prepare it and think about all the flavors. Does it need a hint of sourness? If so, a slight squeeze of lemon juice could make all the difference. Does it have enough sweetness? If not, add some dried fruit, a sprinkle of cinnamon, or a little maple syrup. Is the flavor too mild? If so, add a bit horseradish or hot peppers to ramp up the heat.

You can also make corrections to the overall flavor of a dish by adding the "opposite" flavor to bring the flavors into balance. There are a few pairs of flavors that balance each other out. A good example is the infamous duo of sweet and sour. If your dish tastes a bit too sweet, adding something sour will downplay the sweetness. It works the other way as well. If your dish tastes too sour, add something sweet to balance it out. Other pairings that work in a similar manner are bitter and sweet (you've heard of bittersweet), and bitter and salty. If your dish tastes too strong in one of these flavors, you can add the opposite to balance the flavors.

Not every pairing works like this. For the pairing sour and bitter, sour tends to dominate. If you have a dish of leafy greens that tastes too bitter, adding some sour lemon juice will dampen the bitter flavor. But, it doesn't work the other way. If your dish is too sour, you can add bitter flavors all day long and it won't make much of a difference to the sourness of the dish.

In some cases, flavors can enhance or magnify the sensation of another flavor. Salty and sweet tend to enhance each other. That is, if you add salt to a dish, it makes the dish saltier, but it also brings out the sweetness. Likewise, adding a sweetener to a dish also enhances the salty flavor. Another flavor that enhances the salty flavor is sour. Adding the sour flavor of lemon juice or vinegar can bring out the saltiness of a dish. However, the opposite direction doesn't work as well; adding salt doesn't tend to enhance the sour flavor of a dish.

So, when you are tasting and balancing flavors, use this summary and diagram as a guide:

Sweet and sour balance each other
Bitter and sweet balance each other
Bitter and salty balance each other
Sour dominates bitter
Salty and sweet enhance each other
Sour enhances salty, but salty doesn't enhance sour.

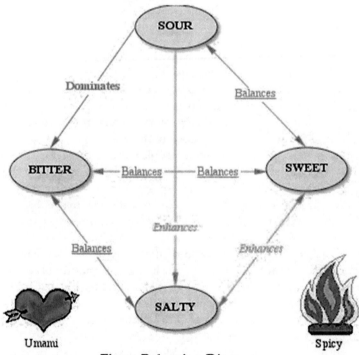

Flavor Balancing Diagram

With all this great information about balancing flavors, I'll bet you are wondering how you can determine which herbs, spices, and foods are sweet, which are salty, which are sour, etc. For some ingredients, it might be obvious, but for others, it might not be clear which flavor category fits best, or if the ingredient fits into more than one category. That's when you turn to *The Vegetarian Flavor Bible*, by Karen Page. I purchased a copy from an online source, and it has been extremely helpful. It lists almost every herb, spice, and food item you can imagine. For each item, it not only tells you the flavor category, but it gives the growing season, the nutritional profile, the calories, and tips. If you want to know the flavor category of any food, look it up. Dates, mint, and coconut nectar are sweet. Granny Smith apples, cream of tartar, and vinegars are sour. Olives and miso are salty. Kale, turmeric, and unsweetened cocoa are bitter. Hot peppers, garlic powder, and salsa are spicy. Tomatoes, nutritional yeast, and tamari are umami. Note that many food items fit into more than one category. Ginger is a combination of sour, sweet, and spicy. Adzuki beans are sweet, with a little bit of sour taste. Turmeric is mostly bitter, with a little sweet, and pungent notes. Knowing what flavor(s) each food component brings to the table will help you bring flavor balance to your dishes.

Perhaps the best feature of *The Vegetarian Flavor Bible* is that for each food, it gives a complete list of the other herbs, spices, and foods whose flavors match well with that food. In fact, that's our next topic – flavor matching.

Flavor Matching

A fundamental technique of recipe–free cooking is matching foods that have natural flavor affinities. Throughout time, chefs have been experimenting with flavor combinations. Many timeless combinations have emerged, such as apples and cinnamon, tomato and basil, and coconut, pineapple, and rum. *The Vegetarian Flavor Bible* has collected an amazing number of flavor matches and combinations from dozens of restaurateurs and chefs that you can use in your creations. For example, if you have a head of cauliflower and don't know what to do with it, *The Vegetarian Flavor Bible* has you covered. There are over 150 flavor matches for cauliflower, listing the favorites in bold type (bread crumbs, chiles, curries, garlic, lemon, …). There are nearly 30 flavor combinations such as cauliflower + capers + lemon + parsley, and cauliflower + coconut + curry. These food items are listed because they enhance the natural flavor of cauliflower. Using this to your advantage, you could start with a dish of plain steamed cauliflower, and enhance the flavor by adding cumin, garlic, some red onion, a few drops of lemon juice, and a dollop of non–dairy sour cream. Or you could combine cauliflower with Brussels sprouts, capers, lemon juice, and top with pine nuts. Or you could make a sauce with cauliflower, coconut, curry, and a few almonds. The point is, there are a countless number of delicious flavor combinations that you can make. Starting with proven flavor combinations puts you on the fast track to culinary bliss.

Another way to find flavor matching is to search online. You could search for vegan cauliflower recipes, and use the recipes to guide your flavor selections. Vegancoach.com also has excellent flavor matching lists for many popular fruits and vegetables. It's definitely enough to get you started.

Cooking Recipe–Free: The Process

So, you know about balancing the various flavor groups and choosing foods and spices that naturally complement each other, but how do you start from scratch to create a flavorful dish that you can be proud of? Here are some guidelines that you can use to create recipe–free masterpieces:

1. **Take an inventory** – See what you have on hand in your fridge or pantry. Lay out the seasonal produce on a counter. This is a great opportunity to use leftovers or produce that is getting long in the tooth. It's also a good time to think about flavor matching and flavor balancing. Once you identify a few key vegetables to be used, pull out some compatible herbs, spices, and other produce. Refer to the Flavor Bible or other flavor matching resource.
2. **Devise a plan** – Based on the main ingredients you intend to use, select a cooking style for the dish – blending, casserole, sauté, steamed, slow cooker, roasting, stir–fry, etc. You may decide to use a combination of methods. For example, you might decide to steam vegetables, and in the meantime use a blender make a creamy sauce. Consider cooking times for individual ingredients in your plan.
3. **Add ingredients and flavorings a little at a time** – You can always add more later.

4. **Taste throughout the cooking process** – Endeavor to include each of the flavor categories – sweet, salty, sour, etc. Use the techniques we have covered to balance the flavors. For example, if your dish is lacking a bitter component, add some leafy greens. Or if your dish could use a boost of both the sour and salty flavors, add a little bit of lemon juice. Recall that adding something sour also enhances the salty flavor. See the flavor balancing diagram above.

5. **Plate the dish** – Add a garnish or two for taste and texture, as well as visual appeal. Presentation is important. We eat with all of our senses including our vision.

6. **Make notes for future reference** - If the dish turns out great, make a note of the ingredients and flavor combinations that you used so that you can recreate it later.

Learning how to cook without recipes can save you time and money.

It will save you time in a couple of ways. It will save you time because you won't have to meticulously measure each and every ingredient before adding it to a dish. Experience will become your guide, and you can adjust amounts as you go. With a little bit of advanced preparation, you can make assembling a meal quick and easy. You just pull out the ingredients, combine them, and flavor the dish. To pull well balanced meals together quickly, you need to keep one portion of grains and one portion of legumes (beans and/or lentils) in the fridge ready to go. The secret is to prepare large batches of legumes and grains in advance, freeze most of it in portion sized bags or containers, and refrigerate just enough for the next meal. Whenever you use up a portion from the fridge, pull another portion out of the freezer and refrigerate. This gives you a good base for a meal. You don't really have to prepare greens in advance because they cook up so quickly. If you are using canned beans instead of cooking your own, that will make it even quicker.

Recipe–free cooking will also save you money. It will save you money because you'll be using more foods in season, and these are less expensive. You'll also use foods that you have on hand, so there will be less waste. You can save additional money by purchasing dry beans and lentils, and cooking your own.

In my book, (and, I do mean that literally) the biggest benefit of recipe–free cooking is that it makes it easier to eat more whole food plant–based meals.

When I first started this journey, I loved the fact that I could enjoy all my traditional favorite foods by just replacing the animal products with vegan substitutes. It meant that I could still enjoy my burgers, pizza, spaghetti with meatballs, tacos, and stir–fry, almost without skipping a beat. It made the transition from the SAD diet to eating vegan so much easier. It was also very satisfying because the meals tasted better and better as my cooking skills improved. I was very happy with my animal–free line up of meals. I was in a new and much more healthy food comfort zone.

This was a great first milestone in my journey to healthy eating, but it also meant that I was dependent on vegan cheese, chick'n, beef crumbles, un–meatballs, non–dairy cream cheese, and non–dairy sour cream. As you know, these products are not whole foods. They are processed, at least to a degree. To move toward a healthier WFPB diet, I began to ease off on these products and replace them with more whole food alternatives.

That's where recipe–free cooking came into play. Once I started taking recipe–free cooking classes at vegancoach.com, things started to change. I noticed that I began to rely more on seasonal produce. I started eating more beans and lentils (learning how to cook my own, rather than relying on cans or cartons). I began to include more leafy greens in my meals. I made a point to always have some cooked grains on hand. Once I learned how to make tasty sauces, which really added extra pizzazz to the meals, I noticed a strange thing – I was eating a substantially whole food plant–based diet. Without conscious intent, I got into the rhythm of pulling fresh produce, leftovers, and prepared components (primarily legumes and grains) out of the fridge and pantry, and whipping up meals on the fly. The regular rotation of traditional meals just sort of fell by the wayside. I still eat some of the traditional dishes, but primarily those that lend themselves to a whole food approach, especially, steamed veggies, stir–fry, soup, tagine, roasted veggies, and spaghetti sauce.

Give some of the techniques discussed in this chapter a try. You may find that cooking recipe-free will give you an extra boost toward your goal of eating a more whole food, plant–based diet.

CHAPTER 8: RECIPES AND FOOD TEMPLATES

In this chapter, you will find two types of guides for meal preparation. There are traditional *recipes*, with more specific directions, and there are *templates*, with structured guidelines for preparing an endless variety of dishes, depending on the ingredients you have on hand.

Some of the recipes and templates are transitional, using processed meat substitutes, oil, and/or processed sugar. These are a good place to start if you are used to the Standard American Diet, and you want to transition away from it. However, if weight loss or disease reversal is your goal, you'll want to focus on recipes that deemphasize these transitional products and emphasize whole foods. As your taste buds change, look for recipes and templates that have low or no oil and low sugar for optimal health. You can also adapt your favorite transitional recipes to more whole-food versions using the skills presented in the "Transforming Your Meals" section of chapter 5.

Many of the recipes and templates in this chapter were contributed by Tracy Childs. Tracy developed recipes that emphasize low-oil and low-sugar for her healthy cooking classes. To find out more about her work, go to Veg-Appeal.com and plantdiego.com.

> In the recipes that follow, Tablespoon is spelled with a capital T, and teaspoon is all lower case to emphasize the difference between the two and minimize confusion. No one wants a **Tablespoon** instead of a **teaspoon** of baking soda in their chocolate chip cookies.

Appetizers

Beet Hummus
Modified from Minimalist Baker

My usual market source was out of beet hummus, so I made my own. I removed the oil from this recipe, and it still turned out well.

MAKES 6 SERVINGS

2 precooked baby beets, about 3½ ounces

1 15-ounce can garbanzo beans, drained juice of three-quarters of a large lemon hefty pinch of sea salt

1 pinch of ground black pepper

3 teaspoons apple cider vinegar (or balsamic)

4 cloves garlic, minced

1 teaspoon mirin sweet cooking rice wine

1 teaspoon agave

4 heaping Tablespoons of tahini

⅔ cup water

1. Quarter beets and place in food processor. Blend until only small bits remain.
2. Add remaining ingredients, and blend until smooth.
3. Taste and adjust seasonings and/or flavorings as needed. If it's too thick, add a bit of water.

NOTE:

Will keep in the refrigerator for up to a week.

Creamy Artichoke Dip

Recipe adapted by: Tracy Childs of Veg-Appeal from a recipe by Teagen McLain

This dip is creamy and smooth. You can use it as you would hummus.

MAKES 4 SERVINGS

1 container of organic firm silken tofu (Mori-Nu), drained well (about 12 ounces)

1 can artichoke hearts stored in water, drained well and squeezed (or 1 cup steamed, frozen artichoke hearts, cooled)

¼ cup nutritional yeast

½ teaspoon salt (or less if artichokes are salted)

¼ teaspoon freshly ground pepper

1 teaspoon dill weed

1. Blend the ingredients until smooth in the blender.
2. Store in the refrigerator and serve with freshly toasted garlic bread or whole grain crackers or crudités.

Italian Tofu Bites

Recipe by: Tracy Childs of Veg-Appeal

These flavorful tofu bites are sure to be a hit any time for a substantial protein meal or salad addition, or a yummy appetizer.

MAKES 6-8 SERVINGS

1 16-ounce package organic extra firm tofu, drained and pressed if needed to remove excess moisture
1 Tablespoon red wine vinegar (or your favorite vinegar)
2 Tablespoons tamari, soy sauce, or Bragg Aminos.
1 Tablespoon mirin (rice wine) or your favorite sherry (or 1-2 teaspoons sweetener of choice)
2 teaspoons Italian seasoning
⅓ cup low-sodium vegetable broth
2-3 Tablespoons nutritional yeast
3-4 cloves garlic, minced
black pepper to taste

1. Cut the tofu into ¾-inch bite sized cubes.
2. In a skillet, stir together all of the remaining ingredients.
3. Add the tofu and toss to coat.
4. Bring to a boil on high heat.
5. Turn the heat down to a low boil and allow the mixture to cook down, stirring occasionally for about 20 minutes. The sauce should thicken and caramelize.
6. Serve with the sauce over mashed potatoes, pasta, or a cooked grain. Also great cold or warmed on salads!

Roasted Eggplant with Bruschetta

Adapted from Donna Pinto of Give Wellness by Tracy Childs of Veg- Appeal

1 medium eggplant, cut into about 9 ½-inch round slices
3 diced medium tomatoes, diced
2-3 cloves garlic, minced
3 Tablespoons minced fresh basil
Freshly ground black pepper and sea salt

1. Preheat oven to 425°F.
2. Coat a large baking sheet with coconut or olive oil spray.
3. Arrange eggplant rounds in a single layer. Sprinkle with sea salt and black pepper.
4. Roast for 15 to 20 minutes.
5. Carefully flip each piece: the undersides should be blistery, dark and a bit puffy and should release from the pan with no effort. If they're not, let them cook longer.
6. Once flipped, sprinkle them with additional salt and freshly ground black pepper and return the pan to the oven for another 5 minutes, until the undersides match the tops.
7. Meanwhile, prepare bruschetta topping in a bowl by combining the rest of the ingredients.
8. Move to a plate and spoon bruschetta mixture onto each piece of roasted eggplant.
9. Top each slice with a drizzle of *Low Fat White Bean Aioli* (in "Sauces, Syrups and Dressings")

Smoky Kale Dip

Recipe by: Tracy Childs of Veg-Appeal

This yummy, high-fiber dip is perfect for family gatherings or cocktail parties. I goes well with raw veggies, crackers, or crusty bread.

MAKES ABOUT 3 CUPS

¼ cup sun-dried tomatoes
1 ½ cups cooked white beans (any type), drained, liquid reserved
1 Tablespoon lemon juice
1 Tablespoon sesame tahini
2 cups blanched (hot water for 1-2 minutes – then drain), chopped kale or frozen kale, thawed and drained well
½ cup tomato salsa
1 Tablespoon light miso or Spike seasoning
salt and pepper to taste
1 teaspoon smoked paprika
½ teaspoon ground mustard powder

1. Soak the sundried tomatoes in hot water for at least 10 minutes, drain, reserving water and chop finely.
2. In a food processor, process the beans with 2-3 Tablespoons of the tomato soaking water, miso, tahini and lemon juice until smooth.
3. Pulse in the remaining ingredients and place in a bowl.
4. Serve immediately, or chill an hour before serving.

Spicy Mini-Burger Bites

Recipe by: Tracy Childs of Veg-Appeal

MAKES ABOUT 48 MINI-BITES

2 cups old-fashioned rolled oats
1 15-ounce can of black beans (drained and rinsed)
1 small jar of your favorite salsa (about 14 ounces)
2-3 cloves garlic, minced
3-4 scallions
1 cup finely shredded carrots
3-4 stalks of celery
¼ cup frozen corn, thawed
½ cup chopped cilantro
1 teaspoon cumin
1 jalapeño, optional
Salt, if needed
Additional salsa as a topping

1. Heat oven to 400°F.
2. Grease mini muffin pan.
3. Use a food processor to chop finely and mix all of the ingredients well. You may need to do this in batches for each ingredient if your food processor is small.
4. Spoon into the greased mini muffin pan and flatten the top with the spoon.
5. Bake for 15-20 minutes and then broil to brown the top (about 2 minutes, but watch for burning).
6. Serve cooled with salsa to spoon on top and eat!

Spring Rolls and Dipping Sauce

MAKES 8 SPRING ROLLS

8 rice paper wrappers
½ cup bean sprouts
½ cup fennel fronds, finely chopped
⅓ head of green or red cabbage, finely chopped
½ each green, red, and yellow bell peppers, shredded
½ jicama, shredded
5 green onions, chopped
½ cup fire roasted peppers
1 avocado, diced
1 cup quinoa, pre-cooked
¼ cup fresh herbs (use cilantro, basil or mint, your choice)
¼ cup carrots, grated or julienned
1 Tablespoon lime juice
1 Tablespoon soy sauce
½ teaspoon fresh ginger, grated

1. Place ingredients separately on plates.
2. Submerge rice paper wrappers in hot water on a large plate until almost pliable, about 12 seconds. Remove from water and place on a cutting board or large plate.
3. For each wrap, grab a selection of ingredients (about 3 Tablespoons), and place in the center of the wrapper.
4. Fold the left and right sides in slightly, about 1 inch or so. Then roll from the bottom until all the ingredients are enclosed.
5. Serve with dipping sauce and enjoy!

NOTES:

25 cm rice paper is easier to work with than the smaller sizes. Available at Asian markets and other stores.

Go easy on liquids inside the spring roll. The wrapper may get too wet, and rupture. Better to keep the insides relatively dry, and dip the rolls in dipping sauce.

DIPPING SAUCE

Use any of your favorite dipping sauces such as peanut, yakisoba, plum, sesame-ginger dressing, or tahini.

Alternatively, you can make your own sauce:

¼ cup soy sauce
¼ cup water
1 teaspoon corn starch
2 Tablespoons rice vinegar
2 cloves garlic, minced and crushed
2 Tablespoons sugar

1. Combine all ingredients in small saucepan and simmer for 3-5 minutes, stirring, until sugar dissolves and corn starch is well mixed.
2. Cool before serving.

Sweet & Spicy Red Lentil Dip

Recipe by: Tracy Childs of Veg-Appeal

½ onion, roughly chopped
½ large yam (orange flesh sweet
  potato), unpeeled, diced
1 cup dry red lentils, rinsed well
2 ¼ cups vegetable broth or stock
1 teaspoon smoked paprika
1 Tablespoon red wine vinegar
2 cloves garlic, pressed
2 teaspoons cumin
½ teaspoon ground coriander
½ teaspoon crushed red pepper
1 Tablespoon sesame tahini
1 Tablespoon lemon juice
⅓ cup roughly chopped fresh green
  herbs of choice (parsley, dill, thyme,
  scallions, cilantro, for example)
Salt and freshly ground pepper to taste
1 Tablespoon nutritional yeast, optional

1. In a medium saucepan, bring the onion,
   yam, lentils, and vegetable broth to a
   boil. Add a bit more broth if needed, to
   just cover the vegetables with liquid.
   Reduce heat, partially cover, and cook on
   low until veggies are soft, about 20
   minutes. Drain any excess liquid.
   Remove the pan from heat and allow the
   mixture to cool for a few minutes.
2. Stir in paprika, vinegar, garlic, cumin,
   coriander and crushed red pepper.
3. Add the mixture to a food processor with
   the tahini, fresh herbs and lemon and
   process until smooth. Taste and adjust
   seasonings, adding salt, pepper, and
   nutritional yeast if desired.
4. Chill for at least 1 hour (it will thicken)
   and serve with veggie sticks, whole-grain
   pita or crackers. This dip also makes a
   great sandwich spread or quesadilla
   filling.

Teriyaki Tempeh Tidbits

Recipe by: Tracy Childs of Veg-Appeal

These flavorful tempeh bites are sure to be a hit
any time for a substantial protein meal, or salad
addition, or a yummy appetizer.

MAKES ABOUT 4 SERVINGS

1 8-ounce package of tempeh
¼ cup coconut sugar (or maple syrup)
¼ cup soy sauce or tamari
3 Tablespoons rice vinegar
½ cup water
½-1 teaspoon spicy ingredient, optional
  (sriracha sauce or 1 hot chili, or ¼-½
  teaspoon red pepper flakes)
1 Tablespoon toasted, ground sesame
  seeds or 1 teaspoon toasted sesame
  oil (or both)
3 cloves garlic, minced
¾-inch piece of ginger, roughly
  chopped
chopped cilantro and minced red bell
  pepper garnish

1. Cut the tempeh block into ¾-inch square
   pieces (small because it expands)
2. Prepare the sauce by blending the
   ingredients in a blender, or in a bowl.
3. Pour the sauce into a skillet and add the
   tempeh. Stir to coat the tempeh.
4. Bring the mixture to a boil, coating the
   tempeh with the sauce.
5. Cook over medium high heat, stirring
   frequently for 4-6 minutes, until the
   sauce is reduced and thickened.
6. For an appetizer, transfer the mixture to
   a serving plate and sprinkle the edges of
   the platter with cilantro followed by
   minced red bell pepper.
7. This dish can also be served over a whole
   grain with veggies for a main dish or as a
   filling protein addition for salads.

Beverages

Donna's Green Plant Power Smoothie

A smoothie is a wonderful way to get your nutrition. A smoothie is easy to make, easy to digest, and it retains all the fiber and other nutrients of the original foods. You'll have fun with this because there are no rules – no measurements to cramp your style. This "recipe" is basically a list of ingredients that Donna typically uses when making her daily smoothie. She doesn't measure, and you don't have to either. Here are a few guiding principles to help you along.

- You'll need at least a cup or two of liquid to get things started.
- Use the smoothie setting on your blender, if available. Otherwise, start on low speed, and move up gradually. Pause to scrape down the sides and add more liquid as necessary.
- Most people start out heavy on the fruits and light on the leafy greens. When you find a balance that works, go with that. You can add more greens to future smoothies as your tastes adjust.
- Any blender will work, but your smoothies will turn out smoother in a higher powered blender.

MAKES 2-3 SERVINGS

INGREDIENTS

Water or any plant-based milk (e.g. almond, soy, coconut)
Coconut or soy yogurt
Organic protein powder
Flaxseed meal
Hemp seeds
Amaranth seeds, popped
Chia seeds
Frozen fruit: banana, berries
Kale or spinach
Tahini
Powdered greens
Drops of liquid kelp
Dropper full of liquid chlorophyll

OPTIONAL INGREDIENTS

Lemon juice (easy does it)
Mint leaves
Sweetener
Turmeric (not too much)
Cinnamon
Frozen kale and frozen fruit smoothie packs
Vanilla extract

1. Assemble the ingredients for your smoothie.
2. Add a cup or more of plant-based milk and/or filtered water to your blender.
3. Add fruits and vegetables. A banana makes a good base. Using frozen fruit and vegetables will make for a nice chilled result, but your blender needs to be strong enough to handle the frozen produce. Include more fruit in your first smoothies, to keep the flavor on the sweet side. Be sure to include berries, because they are very high in antioxidants. Gradually add more leafy greens to improve the nutritional profile as your tastes adjust. Spinach, kale, and bok choy are greens with relatively mild flavors.
4. With the lid in place, turn your blender on low, then increase the speed. When it is well blended, test the thickness. If it is too thick, add more liquid. If it is too thin, add nut butters, non-dairy yogurt, coconut meat, and chia seeds to make it thicker and creamier.
5. Enhance the flavor. Add spices such as vanilla extract, cinnamon, nutmeg, basil, and mint to ramp up the flavor. Add sweeteners such as maple syrup, dates, or erythritol. Blend it again and adjust the taste.
6. Boost the health factor by adding flaxseed, protein powder, goji berries, and sprouts.
7. Do final blending and flavor adjustments.
8. Serve.

Egg Nog

Recipe by: Patty (Sassy) Knutson of VeganCoach.com

MAKES 6 SERVINGS

4 cups unsweetened almond milk
½ cup date paste (see note below)
2 Tablespoons pure maple syrup
2 frozen bananas (can use unfrozen too)
2 teaspoons flax oil
2 teaspoons vanilla extract
¼ teaspoon nutmeg

1. Blend all ingredients except the bananas.
2. Blend bananas in at the end.
3. Serve immediately. Sprinkle with additional nutmeg.

NOTE:

To make date paste: Add ½ - 1 cup dates to a blender. Fill with water until water comes up to ½ to ¾ of the dates. Blend until smooth.

VARIATION:

Top with some non-dairy whipped topping.

Moringa Tea

The leaves of moringa trees are packed with nutrition. An equivalent weight (100 grams) of moringa leaves has over 3½ times the vitamin A as carrots, over 7 times the vitamin C as oranges, over 3½ times the calcium as cow's milk, over 6½ times the potassium as bananas, and over twice the protein as cow's milk.[1].

Moringa trees originated in the area of India, Pakistan, and Nepal, but they can be grown in a variety of climates. Store indoors or in a greenhouse during inclement weather. Trim your tree to less than five feet high for easy harvesting. The young tender leaves can be used as an additional green in salads, and all leaves can be used to make tea or nutrient powder.

1 bunch of fresh moringa leaves, enough to cover 3 or 4 trays in your dehydrator
Tea filter bags for loose tea (available online)

1. Harvest the leaves from the trees. It is okay to include branches and twigs.
2. Dry the leaves, option 1: place the leaves in a brown paper bag with some holes in it, and hang the bag in a cool area of your home. In about 10-14 days, your leaves should be dry enough to use.
3. Dry the leaves, option 2: Place the leaves, including the branches, on the trays of your dehydrator. Spread them out so that they are not touching. Dry on a low heat for a couple of hours until the leaves are brittle to the touch.
4. Crumble the dried leaves into a coffee grinder. Discard the branches and twigs.
5. Pulse the grinder briefly to break down the leaves.
6. Put the ground moringa in tea bags, and store in a cool, dry place.
7. To prepare Moringa Tea, just add hot water, lemon and sweetener to taste.

NOTES:

If you grind the leaves a little longer, it will form a powder that has many uses. See *Moringa Powder* in "From Scratch."

Breakfast

Blueberry Pancakes

Modified from Rochelle Harris

MAKES 6 - 8 PANCAKES

1 egg substitute (Ener-G Foods)
⅔ cup all-purpose whole wheat flour
2 Tablespoons baking powder
2 Tablespoons coconut sugar
pinch of salt
¾ cup coconut milk
2 Tablespoons melted non-dairy butter
½ cup blueberries
1 spritz of cooking spray

EGG SUBSTITUTE

1. Mix 1 ½ teaspoons of Ener-G Egg Replacer with 2 Tablespoons warm water in a small bowl. Mix thoroughly.

PANCAKES

1. Mix all dry ingredients.
2. Mix wet ingredients, including the egg substitute.
3. Pour wet ingredients into dry ingredients and mix well.
4. Gently fold in blueberries.
5. Rest batter 5-10 minutes.
6. Preheat skillet, and lightly spray oil when hot.
7. Portion pancakes in one-quarter cup servings, and place on the skillet.
8. Brown on both sides to desired doneness, and serve hot.

Breakfast Porridge

MAKES 3 SERVINGS

1 cup dry grain - amaranth, barley, buckwheat, kamut, oats, spelt, or wheat
1½ cups water
½ teaspoon salt, optional

1. Soak grain overnight in 3 cups water, optional.
2. Add 1 ½ cup of water and optional salt to a large sauce pan, and bring to a boil.
3. Drain and rinse the grain, and add to the sauce pan. Reduce the heat and cover.
4. Simmer, stirring occasionally, until all the liquid has been absorbed, for about 20–25 minutes.
5. Turn off heat, and let stand, covered, for 5 minutes.
6. Fluff with a fork.
7. Serve with nut milk and/or fruit.

NOTE:

Presoaking grains has a long tradition. The intent is to make the grains easier to digest and release any harmful elements. There is some debate about this, so it is your call.

David's Breakfast Bowl

This is my go-to breakfast. I swap the cereal out for oatmeal on occasion. The idea originated with Rip's Big Bowl in the Forks Over Knives cookbook, and evolved from there.

I've selected eight cereals for your consideration, based on their nutrition content using the guidelines developed in Chapter 5 for reading nutrition labels. Half are gluten-free and the other half contain wheat.

For each cereal, I've listed the total calories per serving, percent of fat, milligrams (mg) of sodium compared to total calories, grams (g) of sugar, and the carbohydrate/fiber ratio (Five-to-One Test).

Select four different cereals from the Gluten-Free Cereals and/or the Wheat Cereals categories below, and use about one-quarter cup each to make one cup total. Use your judgment on the serving sizes. Add toppings, fruit and non-dairy milk.

MAKES ONE SERVING

GLUTEN-FREE CEREALS:

Old-fashioned Oats 150 calories per ½ cup, 17% fat, sodium (0mg<150), 0g sugar, carb/fiber ratio: 7

Arrowhead Mills Organic Puffed Kamut 50 calories per 1 cup, 0% fat, sodium (0mg<50), 0g sugar, carb/fiber ratio: 5.5

Nature's Path organic whole O's (rice and corn) 120 calories per ⅔ cup, 1.3% fat, sodium (115mg<120), 4g sugar, carb/fiber ratio: 8.1

Arrowhead Mills Puffed Corn 60 calories per 1 cup, 2% fat, sodium (5mg<60), 0g sugar, carb/fiber ratio: 6

WHEAT CEREALS:

Uncle Sam Cereal 190 calories per ¼ cup, 3% fat, sodium (135mg <190), 1g sugar, carb/fiber ratio: 3.8

Post Shredded Wheat 170 calories per 1 cup, <1% fat, sodium (0mg<170), 0g sugar, carb/fiber ratio: 6.7

Post Grape Nuts Flakes 110 calories per ¾ cup, 1% fat, sodium (135mg>110), 4g sugar, carb/fiber ratio: 8

Arrowhead Mills Cereal, Puffed Wheat 60 calories per 1 cup, 0% fat, sodium (0mg<60), 0g sugar, carb/fiber ratio: 6

DRY TOPPINGS (COUNTER-TOP):

2 Tablespoons raisins
2 Tablespoons walnuts
1 Tablespoon pumpkin seeds
1 Tablespoon protein powder
½ teaspoon amla powder

TOPPINGS (REFRIGERATED):

1 Tablespoon ground flaxseed meal
1 teaspoon hemp seeds
1 teaspoon chia seeds
½ teaspoon moringa powder
1 Tablespoon puffed amaranth
2 Tablespoons cultured coconut milk or other non-dairy yogurt

FRUIT:

1 banana, sliced
Selections from fruit bowl (berries, grapes, apple, kiwi, and melons)

NON-DAIRY MILK:

1-2 cups non-dairy milk of choice (soy, almond, coconut, oat, quinoa, or hemp)

(Continues on next page)

David's Breakfast Bowl - continued

1. Select equal amounts of four of the cereals listed above (about ¼ cup each), and combine in a large bowl.
2. Add dry toppings.
3. Add enough non-dairy milk to moisten the cereal and powders. Mix well.
4. Add refrigerated toppings and mix. Add additional non-dairy milk to moisten thoroughly.
5. Cut up assorted fruit and add to the bowl. Slice up one banana in small chunks.
6. Add additional non-dairy milk as desired; the cereal and toppings will absorb quite a bit of liquid. Enjoy.

NOTES:

Most of the cereals listed can be purchased from local grocery or health foods stores. You can also purchase them online.

I combine four cereals ahead of time and store in a plastic container in a cupboard for convenience. The dry toppings are stored in canisters on the kitchen counter.

High-Protein Waffles

Recipe adapted by: Tracy Childs of Veg-Appeal from Dr. Barnard's Program for Reversing Diabetes.

People enjoying these waffles will never guess peas and oats were among the ingredients, making them low-glycemic and high fiber. You can keep soaked peas in the refrigerator and make the batter quickly in the blender. The batter keeps well refrigerated or frozen for fresh, light, crisp waffles anytime!

MAKES 7-8 WAFFLES

½ cup dry black-eyed peas, soaked overnight (1 ¼ cups after soaking)
2 ½ cups water
1 ¾ rolled oats
2 Tablespoons sugar or maple syrup
1 Tablespoon whole or ground flaxseed
1 Tablespoon baking powder
1 ½ teaspoons vanilla extract
¾ teaspoon salt

1. *The night before*: Place the black-eyed peas in a bowl and cover generously with water. Soak overnight or refrigerate for up to a week.
2. *In the morning*: Drain the peas, discarding the soaking water. Place in a blender with the remaining ingredients. Blend until smooth, light and foamy. Add more water by the tablespoon if needed.
3. Spray the hot, nonstick waffle iron with cooking spray. Pour in a generous ½ cup of the batter, close the iron, and cook for 5½ minutes.
4. Repeat with the remaining batter, blending briefly before pouring each waffle. If the batter thickens while standing, add enough water to return it to its original consistency. The waffles should be golden brown and crisp. Serve immediately or cool completely on a rack and freeze.
5. Serve with your favorite toppings, like fruit or Raw Berry Compote (see recipe below). For a savory dinner waffle, add less vanilla extract and sweetener and serve with ratatouille or other rich stews.

VARIATION:

Use white beans instead of peas.

Oatmeal-Maple Breakfast Cookies

Recipe by: Tracy Childs of Veg-Appeal

These heart-healthy "cookies" are a lot like an energy bar in taste and texture. They are very simple to make and are a great morning or afternoon snack with tea, coffee or a smoothie.

MAKES 24 SMALL COOKIES

1 ¾ cup old-fashioned rolled oats
2 Tablespoons flaxseeds, ground
1 cup non-dairy milk (*Quick Vanilla Almond Milk* in "Dairy Alternatives" works well)
½ cup raisins
3 Tablespoons maple syrup
1 teaspoon cinnamon
1 Tablespoon vanilla extract
¼ teaspoon salt

1. Preheat oven to 350°F.
2. Toast oats in a dry skillet using medium heat until golden brown (about 5 minutes). Watch carefully so they don't burn.
3. While oats are toasting, put remaining ingredients in the above order in a medium bowl.
4. Place the toasted oats in a blender or food processor and pulse to break down some of the oats into oat flour, leaving about ½ of the oats whole. Add the oats/oat flour to the other ingredients and mix well.
5. Let the mixture sit a few minutes to thicken, and stir again.
6. Form cookies by gently place tablespoons of dough (a melon baller works well for this) on a nonstick, parchment-covered or lightly greased baking sheet and flatten lightly with the back of a wet fork (to prevent sticking).
7. Bake for 20-25 minutes, or until slightly golden on edges. Check often to prevent burning.

Raw Berry Compote

Recipe by: Tracy Childs of Veg-Appeal

Satisfy your sweet tooth with this delicious, guilt-free berry deliciousness!

MAKES 32 ONE TABLESPOON SERVINGS

2 cups frozen mixed berries, thawed (at least mostly)
1 Tablespoon maple syrup
1 Tablespoon chia seeds
4 large dates, pitted
½ teaspoon vanilla extract

1. Combine all ingredients in a food processor until berries and dates are chopped.
2. Pour into a container and chill for an hour or two, until thickened. Serve with sweets for dessert, or with hot cereal or toast and nut butter for breakfast.

Spiced Chia-Oats Breakfast

Recipe by: Tracy Childs of Veg-Appeal

It doesn't get much simpler than this for a filling, delicious unprocessed breakfast! This is a great idea for breakfast on-the-go because the oats and chia will soften in about 1 hour or less. Chia and flax add omega-3 fatty acids to your diet.

MAKES 2 SERVINGS

1 cup rolled oats
½ teaspoon pumpkin pie spice (or cinnamon)
1 cup *Quick Vanilla Almond Milk* or *Banana Milk* in "Dairy Alternatives"
1 cup water
1-2 Tablespoons chia seeds
¼ cup fresh or frozen blueberries or *Raw Berry Compote* (previous recipe)
¼ cup raisins
2 Tablespoons ground flax seeds
nuts and/or seeds of choice and/or your favorite granola

1. Place uncooked rolled oats in a bowl with a cover. Sprinkle on the pumpkin pie spice or cinnamon (or both).
2. Pour almond milk and water over the oats along with the raisins, chia seeds, blueberries, flax and stir well.
3. Cover and refrigerate overnight, or allow it to rest for at least 20 minutes.
4. When ready to serve, top each serving with a splash of warm or hot water, and a small amount of nuts or seeds of choice: walnut, pumpkin, sunflower seeds. Stir in more almond milk as needed.

Sriracha Maple Tempeh "Bacon"

Recipe by: Tracy Childs of Veg-Appeal

MAKES 16 SLICES

1 package organic tempeh, cut into ¼-½ inch thick slices
½ cup water
1 Tablespoon maple syrup (plus a little more to taste)
1 ½ Tablespoons low sodium soy sauce or Bragg Aminos
1 Tablespoon apple cider vinegar
1 teaspoon onion powder
½ teaspoon garlic powder
1 teaspoon liquid smoke (or more to taste)
½ teaspoon Sriracha
nutritional yeast

1. Place all ingredients except tempeh and nutritional yeast in a sauté pan, and turn on the heat.
2. Place the tempeh slices in the skillet and bring the mixture to a boil, then reduce to medium-low so that the mixture is still bubbling. This will reduce the liquid and coat the slices.
3. Cook until the liquid has mostly dissipated. Turn off the heat.
4. Remove the slices to a parchment-lined baking sheet.
5. Sprinkle with nutritional yeast.
6. Broil the slices for 3 minutes.
7. Turn the slices over and sprinkle the other side lightly with nutritional yeast.
8. Broil another 2 minutes or until crispy.

Tofu Scramble

Modified from thespruce.com

Tofu scramble is a popular vegan breakfast alternative to scrambled eggs. This basic recipe lends itself to countless variations.

MAKES 2 SERVINGS

1 block organic firm tofu, drained and pressed
½ yellow onion, diced fine
½ green bell pepper, diced fine
2 Tablespoons water (or oil)
1 teaspoon garlic powder
1 teaspoon onion powder
1 Tablespoon soy sauce (or Bragg Liquid Aminos)
1 cup mushrooms, sliced
2 Tablespoons nutritional yeast
¼ - ½ teaspoon turmeric, optional
6 leaves fresh basil
½ cup non-dairy cheese, shredded
½ cup salsa, to taste

1. Press the tofu between paper towels to remove excess water.
2. Slice the tofu into approximately 1-inch cubes. Using either your hands or a fork, crumble it slightly.
3. Add onion, pepper, crumbled tofu and water to sauté pan. Sprinkle with garlic and onion powder, then sauté for 3-5 minutes, stirring often. Add more water if necessary.
4. Add remaining ingredients, reduce heat to medium and allow to cook 5-7 more minutes, stirring frequently, and adding more water if needed.
5. Add non-dairy cheese shreds to melt the last minute or so, and serve the dish when the cheese has melted.
6. Top with salsa and serve.

VARIATION:

Replace or enhance the tofu with the addition of VeganEgg by Follow your Heart, or similar egg substitute.

Dairy Alternatives

Banana Milk

Recipe by: Tracy Childs of Veg-Appeal

This is a great dairy alternative you can easily create yourself to use in oatmeal, on cereal, in recipes or as a yummy sweet beverage!

MAKES 1 SERVING

1 cup water
1 banana peeled and frozen (about 1 cup)
dash salt
dash cinnamon

1. Combine all of the ingredients and blend until smooth.
2. Add other flavorings if you wish (vanilla extract, nutmeg, peanut butter, or peanut powder for example).
3. Add more water if you want thinner milk.
4. Use immediately, or chill for a few hours before serving.

Banana "Milk" Shake

Recipe by: Tracy Childs of Veg-Appeal

Want a quick dessert? Try making a Banana "Milk" Shake. It's refreshing and a "no guilt" answer to your sweet tooth. You can add a teaspoon or two of cocoa powder to make a chocolate shake, or try the recipe below.

MAKES 1 SERVING

1 frozen banana
1 cup Quick Vanilla Almond Milk

1. Blend until smooth and creamy.

Cherry Garcia Nice Cream

Recipe by: Tracy Childs of Veg-Appeal

MAKES ABOUT 1 ½ CUPS

2 frozen bananas, sliced and thawed for a few minutes
¼ cup plant milk (almond, cashew, coconut, soy)
1 cup frozen cherries
¼ cup chocolate chips

1. Blend the bananas and plant milk in a blender (preferably high-speed) until smooth.
2. Pulse in the frozen cherries, leaving some chunks.
3. Add the chocolate chips and either blend to chop or leave them chunky.
4. Serve immediately or place in a covered container in the freezer for an hour to become firm.

Chipotle Cheesy Sauce

Recipe by: Tracy Childs of Veg-Appeal

This is a versatile sauce that can be used on nachos, enchiladas or used as cheese sauce for greens (or other) veggies, potatoes, or macaroni. It can be made smoky, spicy or kept mild.

MAKES: 3 CUPS

2½ cups diced potato, about 2+ medium potatoes of any variety
¾ cups carrots, sliced or diced small and packed to measure
¼ cup raw cashews
½ cup nutritional yeast
⅓ cup cooking water
1 Tablespoon lemon juice
1 Tablespoon light miso OR 1 teaspoon salt (or a bit more to taste)
1 teaspoon onion powder
½ teaspoon garlic powder
1 teaspoon smoked paprika, optional
½ or 1 small chipotle pepper in adobo sauce (or chipotle chili powder or hot sauce to taste)

1. Cover the carrots and potatoes with water and cook over medium-high heat, partially covered until tender, about 20 minutes.
2. Take 1/3 cup hot water out of the pot and set aside. Add cashews into the pot and cook for a few more minutes to soften them for blending.
3. Drain veggie/nut mixture.
4. Add the mixture, and the reserved hot water along with the rest of ingredients into a blender or food processor and blend well, scraping down sides of work bowl as needed.
5. Blend to a creamy, smooth texture. Serve warm. Refrigerate up to one week and reheat before serving adding water or lemon juice to thin.

Chocolate Nut Shake

Recipe by: Tracy Childs of Veg-Appeal

When you enjoy this "indulgent" shake, you will never know you are helping your heart by including a cholesterol-lowering power food, Brazil Nuts, and a good amount of blood-pressure lowering potassium (bananas and dates)! If you don't have a high-speed blender, chop the nuts beforehand and allow the mixture to soak a bit in the blender to soften and thaw before processing.

MAKES ABOUT 2 CUPS

1 cup water
1 large frozen banana
3 raw Brazil nuts
½ - 1 Tablespoon cocoa powder or 1 teaspoon cinnamon, optional
1 date, optional
3-4 ice cubes

1. Blend until smooth and creamy in a high-speed blender. Enjoy immediately.

Double Chocolate Nice Cream

Recipe by: Tracy Childs of Veg-Appeal

Bananas make amazing "Ice Cream!" You can make this any flavor – leave out the chocolate and add a teaspoon of vanilla extract to make Vanilla Nice Cream.

MAKES ABOUT 2 CUPS

2 Tablespoons-¼ cup non-dairy milk
2 cups frozen banana slices (about two medium sliced bananas)
2 Tablespoons cocoa powder
dash salt
1 teaspoon cacao nibs (raw chocolate pieces)

1. Allow the frozen bananas to soften for a few minutes for easier blending. The softer they are, the easier to blend and you need less non-dairy milk to help the blades turn.
2. Combine all of the ingredients except the nibs and blend until smooth.
3. Stir in the cacao nibs.
4. Use immediately, or freeze for an hour or so before serving.

Easy Cheesy Sauce

Recipe adapted by: Tracy Childs of Veg-Appeal from a recipe by Delisa Renideo of Yes to Life Solution.

Here is a very simple and easy way to create a cheesy sauce. It makes a great dip for chips, over taco salad, on tacos or burritos, over vegetables, and over baked potatoes. Try sautéing veggies, pouring cheesy sauce over the veggies and baked potatoes for a full meal. Yummy!

MAKES ABOUT 3 CUPS

⅓ cup raw cashews
2 cups water
½ - 1 teaspoon salt
1/4 cup nutritional yeast (flakes)
1 teaspoon onion powder
1/2 teaspoon garlic powder
3-4 Tablespoons corn starch or arrowroot
1 Tablespoon lemon juice or to taste. (More makes it a sharper cheese flavor, less is mild cheese flavor)
Optional: (for color) ⅓ cup red bell pepper, approximately, or 1 small jar pimentos

1. Blend all ingredients until smooth.
2. Pour into a saucepan and bring to a boil while stirring constantly.
It will thicken to nacho cheese consistency.
3. Serve hot.

NOTES:

For a great nacho-style cheese, blend in 1-2 teaspoons chipotle peppers in adobo sauce or sriracha or stir in salsa.

Garlic-Herb Cream Cheese

Recipe adapted by: Tracy Childs of Veg-Appeal from Artisan Vegan Cheese by Miyoko Schinner

This cream cheese has a delightfully light mouth feel. The xanthan gum is necessary to create the body we are used to in cream cheeses. You can leave the garlic and herbs out to create a plain cream cheese to use in recipes.

MAKES 2½ CUPS

2 cups raw cashews, soaked in water for 3 to 8 hours, then drained
¼-½ cup *Quinoa Rejuvelac* (in "From Scratch")
½ teaspoon salt
½ teaspoon xanthan gum
1 Tablespoon nutritional yeast
2-3 cloves garlic, pressed
1 teaspoon dried herb mix (Italian seasoning for example)
1/4 teaspoon freshly ground pepper
additional salt to taste

1. Put the cashews, salt, and quinoa rejuvelac in a blender (preferably high-speed)
2. Process until smooth and creamy, occasionally stopping to scrape down the blender jar and move the mixture toward the blades.
3. Transfer the mixture to a clean glass bowl or container, cover, and let rest at room temperature for 24 or more hours, depending on how sharp a flavor you want and the ambient temperature (fermentation will proceed more quickly at warmer temperatures).
4. Stir in the remaining ingredients. Taste and adjust seasoning.
5. Chill overnight and serve. The cheese will last for several weeks, kept covered and chilled.

Parmesan Cheese

Recipe by: Tracy Childs of Veg-Appeal

This makes a great substitution for Parmesan cheese – use on practically anything to add lots of flavor! Sliced almonds grind up easily, so use them if you have them.

MAKES 1 CUP

1/2 cup almonds, cashews, brazil nuts, walnuts, pecans, sunflower seeds or pumpkin seeds, roughly chopped if not using a high-speed blender
1/2 cup nutritional yeast
1 teaspoon onion powder
1 teaspoon garlic powder
½ teaspoon smoked paprika, optional
½-1 teaspoon salt

1. Grind all ingredients in a hi-speed blender or Vita-Mix.
2. Store in refrigerator.

Quick Vanilla Almond Milk

Recipe by: Tracy Childs of Veg-Appeal

This is a great dairy alternative you can easily make from almond butter! No need to soak almonds and strain the milk.

MAKES 2 SERVINGS

1½ cups water
1-2 pitted dates, soaked
2 Tablespoons almond butter
1 teaspoon vanilla extract

1. If dates are hard, place the water and dates in a bowl and allow the dates to soften for ½ hour to a few hours (or overnight in the refrigerator). Not soaking is fine with a high-speed blender, just blend longer.
2. Add the rest of the ingredients to a blender, along with the water and dates.
3. Blend until completely smooth.

Spreadable Smoked Sharp Cheddar

Recipe adapted by: Tracy Childs of Veg-Appeal from *Artisan Vegan Cheese* by Miyoko Schinner

You won't miss cheese if you have this on hand! Delicious on crackers, dried fruit, and veggies with wine or a refreshing beverage.

MAKES 2½ CUPS

2 cups raw cashews, soaked in water for 3 to 8 hours, then drained
⅔ cup nutritional yeast
½ cup *Quinoa Rejuvelac* (in "From Scratch")
2 Tablespoons light miso (chickpea or soy)
¾ teaspoon liquid smoke
¼ teaspoon probiotic powder, optional
Salt to taste, optional (Note that miso makes it salty)

1. Put all ingredients in a blender (preferably high-speed)
2. Process until smooth and creamy, occasionally stopping to scrape down the blender jar and move the mixture toward the blades.
3. Taste and add salt.
4. Transfer the mixture to a clean glass bowl or container, cover, and let rest at room temperature for 24 to 72 hours, depending on how sharp a flavor you want and the ambient temperature (fermentation will proceed more quickly at warmer temperatures).
5. Chill and serve. The cheese will last for several weeks, kept covered and chilled.

Sunny Probiotic Herbed Cheese Wraps

Recipe by: Tracy Childs of Veg-Appeal

This is a raw "cheese" that is so delicious. Serving it in collards is a delicious way to get your calcium and other vital minerals.

MAKES 3 CUPS

2 cups sunflower seeds, soaked 8 hours and sprouted if possible
2-3 cloves garlic, chopped
1 Tablespoon tahini
2 Tablespoons miso
2 teaspoons umeboshi vinegar
½ cup lemon juice
½ cup water (about)
1 cup fresh herbs of choice (can be a mix) dill/parsley/scallions/cilantro

1. Rinse the soaked seeds and drain and rinse well and drain again.
2. Place in a food processor with the tahini, miso, vinegar and garlic and start to process.
3. Keep the motor running and slowly add the lemon juice and water from the top. Add enough water to make the blades turn easily, and stop to scrape the sides and continue to process to create a smooth consistency (like hummus).
4. Add the herbs and pulse until they are finely chopped.
5. Enjoy in a collard or nori wrap with sprouts (see *Lentil/Mung Sprouts* in "From Scratch"), avocado/red bell pepper slices, on slices of cucumber, in celery or mini bell pepper boats, with raw (or other) crackers, or as a side with a green salad.

Tofu-Cashew Sour Cream

Recipe adapted by Tracy Childs of Veg-Appeal from *PlantPure Nation Cookbook*, by Kim Campbell.

This is a delightfully cool and creamy addition to complement most Mexican or spicy dishes. It has more flavor than any store-bought version.

MAKES 2 CUPS

½ cup raw cashews, soaked in plenty of water for 2-3 hours or overnight, drained and rinsed
1 10.3-ounce package silken tofu (Mori-Nu)
3 Tablespoons lemon juice
1 teaspoon sweetener of choice
1-3 teaspoons light miso paste
¼ teaspoon sea salt

1. Combine all ingredients in a blender and blend until creamy.
2. Allow the mixture to chill for 1 hour to thicken.

Tofu Feta Cheese

Recipe by: Tracy Childs of Veg-Appeal

You will love a vegan tofu feta cheese that has very little fat and is cholesterol-free. Make it several days before you need it. Use it in salads. It's really easy to make and will last in the refrigerator for about 2 weeks.

MAKES: 1 QUART

16 ounces super firm tofu
1 ½ Tablespoons light miso (chickpea is nice)
¼ cup lemon juice (about 1½ lemons)
½ cup water
½ cup apple cider vinegar
1 Tablespoon dried oregano
1 Tablespoon red wine vinegar
1-2 cloves garlic, finely minced
¼ cup minced Kalamata olives, optional
½ teaspoon maple syrup

1. If the tofu contains excess water, press the tofu, between clean towels with something heavy on top.
2. Cut the tofu into ¼ -½ inch cubes.
3. Place the miso in a small mixing bowl and add a few tablespoons of the water. Use a fork to break down the miso and incorporate it into the liquid.
4. Add the rest of the marinade ingredients to the miso, mix well and then add the tofu.
5. Cover and refrigerate for at least 2 hours. It will taste best after marinating for a few days.

Desserts

Apple Pie

Modified from Allen Prunty

MAKES 8 PIECES OF PIE

CRUST

10 graham cracker squares, 2 inches
  each
1 cup rolled oats
3 teaspoons egg replacer
4 Tablespoons warm water

FILLING

3 medium golden delicious apples
½ cup vegan butter
¼ cup golden raisins
½ cup dark brown sugar
1 ½ Tablespoons corn starch
1 ½ teaspoons cinnamon
1 teaspoon ground ginger
1 teaspoon vanilla extract
½ teaspoon ground nutmeg, optional

TOPPING

1 cup rolled oats
¼ cup vegan butter, melted
½ teaspoon sea salt, optional
⅛ teaspoon vanilla extract

1. Crush graham crackers with mallet. Combine with the oats in a medium-sized mixing bowl. In a small bowl, combine the egg replacer and warm water, and stir well. Add this to the crackers and oats.
2. Spray a baking dish or pie pan with oil. Put the crust mixture in the center. With a little cooking spray on your fingers, spread the mixture along the bottom and the sides. Make it about ⅛ inch thick.
3. Bake for 10 minutes at 350°F, then set aside.
4. Core 3 golden delicious apples, quarter them, and slice thinly.
5. Melt non-dairy spread in frying pan over medium heat, then add apples. Add the raisins and brown sugar and cook for about 5 minutes, stirring occasionally.
6. After 5 minutes sprinkle just enough corn starch in the mix to set it up. Add cinnamon, ginger, and vanilla extract (and nutmeg, if using). Stir well, then place on prepared crust.
7. Mix the topping ingredients, adding enough melted spread to make the oats wet. Add the vanilla extract and sea salt (if using).
8. Sprinkle the topping on top of pie. It doesn't have to cover completely.
9. Bake for 15 minutes 350°F or until the topping browns slightly.

Berry Cobbler

Modified from Mark Reinfeld

Gluten-free

MAKES ABOUT 12 SERVINGS

FILLING

1 cup dates, pitted & chopped
2 cups apple juice, fresh
3 cups blueberries, fresh or frozen
½ cup raisins
½ cup walnuts, chopped
¼ teaspoon cinnamon powder
⅛ teaspoon cardamom powder

CRUST - DRY

2 ¼ cups rolled oats
2 cups gluten-free flour mix
½ cup Sucanat (whole cane sugar)
½ cup pecans, finely chopped
½ teaspoon cinnamon powder
⅛ teaspoon nutmeg

CRUST - WET

½ cup safflower oil
½ cup water
1 ½ teaspoons vanilla extract

CRUMBLE

½ cup rolled oats
¼ cup Sucanat

1. Preheat oven to 350°F. Place Filling ingredients in a medium sized pot and cook over medium low heat until juice is absorbed and dates are softened, approximately 15 minutes, stirring frequently. Be careful not to burn. Remove from heat.
2. Place 2 ¼ cups of rolled oats, ½ cup Sucanat and remaining Dry ingredients in a large mixing bowl and mix well. Place Wet ingredients in another bowl and whisk well.
3. Add wet ingredients to dry ingredients and mix well. Place ⅔ of this mixture in a well oiled 9" x 13" casserole dish and press down firmly. Bake in oven for 10 minutes. Remove from oven and pour filling mixture on top of this.
4. Add ½ cup of rolled oats and ¼ cup Sucanat to remaining flour and oat mixture and mix well. Process slightly in a food processor and crumble on top of filing. Bake in oven until golden brown, approximately 25 minutes.

VARIATIONS:

Use blackberries or strawberries instead of blueberries.
Use brown rice flour instead of gluten-free flour.
Replace raisins with other chopped dry fruit, or fresh pear or apple.

"Buttercream" Frosting

This recipe is for those rare occasions when you need a creamy frosting.

MAKES 2 CUPS

½ cup non-hydrogenated shortening
½ cup vegan butter
3 ½ cups powdered sugar, sifted if clumpy
1 ½ teaspoons vanilla extract
¼ cup unsweetened soy milk

1. In an electric mixer, beat the shortening and margarine together on medium speed until well combined and fluffy.
2. Add the sugar, and beat for about 3 more minutes.
3. Add the vanilla extract and soy milk, and beat for another 5-7 minutes until fluffy.

NOTES:

This makes a lot, so you could make half a recipe.
You can order non-dairy shortening such as Nutiva and Spectrum online if you can't find it in your local market.

VARIATION:

Could use soy creamer instead of soy milk.

Cantaloupe Sorbet

Enjoy sorbet without the usual load of sugar.

MAKES 4 SERVINGS

Flesh of one cantaloupe
1 cup water
¼ cup erythritol
⅛ cup raw sugar
⅛ cup xylitol
2 sprigs of mint
⅛ cup (2 Tablespoons) lemon juice

1. Purée cantaloupe in food processor. Chill in fridge.
2. Heat water, erythritol, sugar, and xylitol in a small saucepan until dissolved. Bring to a boil. Simmer for one minute.
3. Remove from heat. Add sprigs of mint, and steep for five minutes.
4. Remove mint. Chill in the fridge until cool.
5. Combine melon, syrup, and lemon juice.
6. Freeze mixture in sorbet maker for 30 minutes.

Cashew Cinnamon Cream

Modified from Amy Chaplin, *At Home in the Whole Food Kitchen*

This dessert cream is an elegant way to dress up a simple dessert.

MAKES ABOUT 1 1/2 CUPS

1 cup raw cashews, soaked
¼ cup maple syrup
2 teaspoons vanilla extract
¼ teaspoon cinnamon
1 pinch sea salt
2 Tablespoons filtered water
¼ cup fresh orange juice

1. Soak cashews for 2 to 6 hours in filtered water.
2. Drain and rinse cashews. Place all ingredients in an upright blender and blend until completely smooth, scraping the sides as necessary.
3. Pour into a container and refrigerate until ready to use. The flavor and texture improve after a day in the fridge.

NOTES:

The cream will thicken slightly after it is chilled. If it thickens too much, use extra water or orange juice to thin it.
The cream will keep for up to five days in the fridge.

Chocolate Chip Cookies

Modified from Liz Gary

This version is modeled after a traditional chocolate chip cookie, using liberal amounts of oil and sugar. For a more whole food version, see *Oatmeal-Maple Breakfast Cookies* in "Breakfast".

MAKES ABOUT 2 DOZEN COOKIES

2 ½ cups gluten-free flour blend
1 teaspoon baking soda
1 teaspoon salt
1 cup vegan butter
¾ cup cane sugar
¾ cup packed brown sugar
2 Tablespoons egg replacer
¼ cup water
1 teaspoon vanilla extract
2 cups of non-dairy chocolate chips
1 cup chopped walnuts

1. Preheat the oven to 350°F.
2. In a small bowl, combine the flour, baking soda, and salt. Set aside.
3. In a large bowl, combine the vegan butter, sugar, and vanilla extract. Beat on high until fluffy.
4. Combine egg replacer with the water to dissolve, add to the creamed sugar mixture, and blend well. Gradually add the flour mixture and blend.
5. Stir in the chocolate chips and nuts.
6. Spoon out dough onto a silicone mat on a baking tray.
7. Bake 10-12 minutes or until lightly browned.
8. Transfer to wire rack and cool.

Chocolate Mousse

From Elizabeth Mansur

MAKES ABOUT 1½ CUPS

1 cup vegan chocolate chips
1 carton Organic Silken Tofu
1 Tablespoon maple syrup

1. Melt the chocolate chips.
2. Blend the tofu well in a blender, about 30 seconds.
3. Add the maple syrup.
4. Pour the melted chocolate over the tofu.
5. Blend well.
6. Chill for 2-3 hours or overnight.
7. Garnish with berries.

Coconut Sorbet with Creamed Coconut

Sorbets are a great summer dessert. Traditionally made with a sugar syrup, this recipe uses a combination of sweeteners to reduce the sugar impact.

MAKES ABOUT 6 SERVINGS

2 (13 ½ ounce) cans coconut milk
7 ounces (1 packet) creamed coconut
1 cup shredded coconut
2 Tablespoons raw sugar
2 Tablespoons xylitol
½ cup erythritol
1 drop of almond extract, optional
2 sprigs fresh mint

1. In a medium saucepan, combine the ingredients and bring to a boil, stirring until sugar is completely dissolved.
2. Remove from heat, steep with 2 sprigs of fresh mint for 5 minutes.
3. Remove mint, then refrigerate until fully chilled.
4. Freeze in an ice cream maker for 30 minutes.

NOTE:

If you don't have an ice cream maker, pour the mixture onto a cookie sheet, and freeze until set. Break it up, and blend in a food processor until smooth. Freeze and blend again for a smoother consistency.

Coconut Lemon Bars

Recipe by: Tracy Childs of Veg-Appeal

MAKES ABOUT 6 - 8 SERVINGS

FILLING

½ cup raw cashews, soaked overnight
½ cup millet soaked overnight in 1 ¾ cup water
¼ cup non-dairy milk
¼ cup coconut spread/butter
⅓ cup lemon juice (~1½ lemons)
zest from 1 lemon
⅛ teaspoon salt
⅓ cup maple syrup, add more to taste

CRUST

1 cup rolled oats
1 cup almond meal
⅛ teaspoon sea salt
2 Tablespoons coconut sugar
2-3 Tablespoons maple syrup
⅓ cup coconut spread/butter (See NOTES)

1. Soak the millet overnight in 1¾ cup water. Do not drain.
2. Soak the raw cashews overnight, covered in water, then drain thoroughly.
3. The next day, lightly grease a 9x9 inch square baking dish.
4. Place the millet and the water in a saucepan, bring to a boil, lower to simmer, cover and cook for 20-30 minutes until water is absorbed.
5. In the meantime, toast the ingredients for the crust. In a skillet, toast the oats over medium low heat stirring slowly until they start to become fragrant. Add the almond meal and toast that as well.
6. Add oats, almonds, sea salt, coconut spread and coconut sugar to a food processor and process into a dough, adding additional maple syrup or water if needed.
7. Transfer to the baking dish and with damp hands, press the dough firmly and evenly on the bottom.
8. Once millet is done and cooled for just a few minutes, add to a high speed blender along with the rest of the filling ingredients. Mix on high until very creamy and smooth.
9. Taste and adjust flavor as needed. You can add a bit more lemon zest and maple syrup. It should be very lemony, and not overly sweet.
10. Pour filling over the crust and spread into an even layer. Tap on counter to remove any air bubbles.
11. Let rest on the counter for about 10 minutes to cool then cover and, chill to firm, at least 4 hours, preferably overnight.
12. Slice to serve and store leftovers in the refrigerator, covered, up to 4 or 5 days.

NOTES:

Coconut butter is available in stores, usually with other coconut products on the shelves. You can also make it from scratch. Here is a good recipe for coconut butter:
https://wholenewmom.com/whole-new-budget/make-your-own-coconut-butter/

Date Sweetened Pumpkin Pie

Recipe adapted by Tracy Childs of Veg-Appeal from One Green Planet

MAKES ONE PIE

10 Medjool dates (about 1 cup), pits removed, room temperature
1 ¼ cups raw cashews (unsoaked)
1 ½ cups unsweetened non-dairy milk
1 15-ounce can pumpkin puree
2 Tablespoons tapioca flour (or corn starch)
2 teaspoons pumpkin pie spice
¼ teaspoon salt
1 9-inch unbaked pie crust

1. Preheat oven to 350°F.
2. In a high-speed blender, blend dates, cashews, and milk until smooth.
3. Add the remaining ingredients, and blend well.
4. Pour into the pie crust to the top and smooth the top.
5. Bake for 45-50 minutes, or until firm.
6. Allow it to cool completely and refrigerate overnight before serving.

Decadent Chocolate Truffles

Source: The Vegan Table

MAKES ABOUT 18 – 24 TRUFFLES

3 cups non-dairy semi-sweet chocolate chips
1 container (8 ounces) non-dairy cream cheese
3 cups powdered sugar
1 ½ teaspoon vanilla extract

Ingredients for coating truffles: finely ground nuts, sifted cocoa powder, cinnamon, toasted coconut, raw coconut, sifted powdered sugar, crushed peppermint, or candy sprinkles

1. Melt chocolate chips in a glass measuring cup in the microwave for 2 minutes at power level 7, stirring every 30 seconds.
2. In a counter top mixer, beat the cream cheese until smooth. Add powdered sugar 1 cup at a time until well blended. Add melted chocolate and vanilla extract and stir until thoroughly combined.
3. Cover and refrigerate at least one hour or overnight.
4. When chilled, shape into 1-inch balls and coat with any of the toppings.

VARIATION:

To moderate the sugar impact, replace some of the powdered sugar with erythritol, powdered in a coffee grinder.

Lemon Meringue Pie

MAKES 6 – 8 SERVINGS

FILLING

1 ¼ cup sugar
½ cup corn starch
¾ teaspoon agar flakes (or ¼ teaspoon agar powder)
¼ teaspoon salt
1 ¼ cup non-dairy milk (coconut or almond milk)
1 cup water
¾ cup lemon juice (about 5 lemons)
1 ½ Tablespoons lemon zest (about 5 lemons)

CRUST

1 pre-cooked pie crust

TOPPING

Whipped topping (in "Desserts" or "From Scratch")

1. Add the filling ingredients to a sauce pan and bring to boil. Whisk for 4-5 minutes. It will turn into a pudding like mixture.
2. Once it thickens, pour it into the pie crust, then cool for an hour or two.
3. Add the whipped topping to the top of the pie and serve.

VARIATIONS:

Use coconut sugar or Sucanat instead of sugar.
Make your own pie crust using one of the recipes in this chapter.

NOTE:

Best to add the whipped topping to portions of the pie as you serve them. Some whipped toppings do not hold up well when stored for extended periods of time.

Meringue Cookies

This recipe is based on the discovery in 2015 that bean juice can be whipped up very much like egg whites. This idea has become so popular, that bean juice acquired a special name – aquafaba.

MAKES 18 – 24 COOKIES

1 batch of whipped topping using aquafaba

1. Make a batch of whipped topping. See *Whipped Topping from Aquafaba* in "From Scratch."
2. Preheat the oven to 200°F.
3. Use baking sheets covered with nonstick silicone mats or parchment paper. Place about ¼ cup of the whipped topping on the mat for each cookie, leaving adequate space between the cookies for expansion. You can use a spoon, a pastry bag, or even a turkey baster to place and shape the cookies.
4. Place the baking sheets in the oven and set the timer for two hours. Rotate the baking sheets half way through. You may prefer the cookies chewier or more crunchy. Make a note of the time and results. Then, adjust the cooking time for future batches.
5. Leave the cookies in the oven for about half an hour as it cools down.
6. Place the cookies in an airtight container and store in the fridge. They will last for weeks that way. Don't leave the meringue cookies out on the counter any longer than necessary, because they will get soft and disintegrate, depending on the humidity. Take them out of the refrigerator just before serving.

NOTE:

If you want crispier meringues, try putting them in a dehydrator at 160°F for a few hours.

Mixed Berry Tart with Toasted Almond Crust

Modified from Amy Chaplin,
At Home in the Whole Food Kitchen

MAKES ONE 9" TART

CRUST

3 Tablespoons extra virgin olive oil,
  plus more for oiling the pan
¾ cup toasted sliced almonds, divided
½ cup regular rolled oats
¼ teaspoon sea salt
¾ cup whole spelt flour
4 Tablespoons maple syrup
1 teaspoon vanilla extract
½ teaspoon almond extract

1. Toast the almonds in oven, and set aside.
2. Line the bottom of a spring form pan with parchment paper. Turn the bottom upside down. Place a parchment sheet on top. Clamp into the sides of the pan, keeping the paper flush against the base. Fold the excess paper into the center.
3. Lightly oil the sides of the pan.
4. Preheat oven to 350°F.
5. Use a food processor to grind ½ cup of the almonds, oats, and salt until coarsely ground, about 20-30 seconds. Transfer to a small glass bowl and stir in the spelt flour. Roughly hand-chop the remaining almonds. Add to the bowl, and mix well.
6. Drizzle in olive oil, and mix with a fork or your fingertips until all flour is moistened. Add maple syrup, vanilla extract, and almond extract; mix until evenly incorporated. Dough should be moist but not sticky. Wash and dry your hands, then press crust evenly into prepared pan. Press crust only ½ inch up sides, leaving the top edge uneven. Prick bottom of crust several times with a fork, and bake for 18 minutes or until golden brown and fragrant. Remove from oven, and set aside to cool.

FILLING

¾ cup plus 1 Tablespoon apple juice,
  divided
¾ teaspoon agar flakes (or ¼ teaspoon
  agar powder)
1 teaspoon arrowroot
1 Tablespoon maple syrup
½ teaspoon vanilla extract
3 ½ cups mixed fresh berries -
  blueberries, sliced strawberries, etc.

1. Combine ¾ cup apple juice and agar flakes in a small, heavy-bottomed pot, and bring to a boil over high heat. Whisk, cover pot, reduce heat to low, and simmer for 5 minutes or until agar has completely dissolved.
2. In a small bowl, dissolve arrowroot in 1 Tablespoon apple juice and slowly drizzle into hot agar mixture, whisking constantly until mixture returns to a simmer and has thickened slightly. Remove from heat, and whisk in maple syrup and vanilla extract. Set aside, uncovered, for about 5 minutes or until mixture has thickened a little, but not begun to set.
3. Place berries in a bowl and pour in warm agar mixture. Stir gently with a rubber spatula or with your hands to combine. Working quickly, transfer the mixture to the baked tart shell, and carefully spread out the filling in an even layer. Refrigerate for 20 to 30 minutes, or until the filling is completely set. Serve topped with whipped topping or *Cashew Cinnamon Cream* in "Desserts."

No-Bake Dark Chocolate Pumpkin Pudding or Pie

Recipe by: Tracy Childs of Veg-Appeal

Nobody will believe that this dessert contains cancer-fighting pumpkin!

MAKES 1 PIE

2 soaked dates
1 cup vegan chocolate chips
1 can (15oz) pureed pumpkin
1 Tablespoon pure vanilla extract
1 heaping teaspoon cocoa powder
¼ teaspoon (level) salt
additional sweetener, optional
1 pre-cooked pie crust, if using

1. Soak dates in water to cover for 2 hours, then drain.
2. Gently (on low heat) melt the chocolate (either on the stove or in the microwave), then put all ingredients into a blender or food processor and blend until super-smooth.
3. Taste test for sweetness. Add more sweetener if necessary.
4. Pour into a piecrust or container and refrigerate until chilled. The longer it sits, the firmer it gets.
5. Top your pudding with a dollop of *Cashew Cinnamon Cream* (in "Desserts") for a special treat!

VARIATION:

Replace dates with 1 Tablespoon of another sweetener such as coconut sugar or maple syrup.

Peanut Butter Black Bean Brownies

Recipe by: Tracy Childs of Veg-Appeal

These brownies have so many redeeming qualities with black beans and oats as ingredients!

MAKES 16 SMALL BROWNIES

1½ cups black beans (1 15-oz can, drained and rinsed very well)
2 Tablespoons cocoa powder
⅓ cup rolled or quick oats
¼ teaspoon salt
⅓ cup pure maple syrup or other liquid sweetener
2 Tablespoons coconut sugar or other dry sweetener
¼ cup peanut butter or other nut butter
2 teaspoons pure vanilla extract
1 teaspoon baking powder
½-⅔ cup chocolate chips (not optional)
More chips, for presentation, optional
¼ cup pecans, roughly chopped, optional

1. Preheat oven to 350°F.
2. If using rolled oats, place them in the food processor and process for a few seconds to reduce size.
3. Combine all ingredients except chocolate chips & pecans in a food processor, and blend until completely smooth. Pulse in the chocolate chips and pecans, and then spread the thick batter into a lightly oiled 8×8 pan.
4. Cook the black bean brownies 15-20 minutes, (they will be slightly cracked on top). Then let cool at least 10 minutes before cutting and serving.

Pecan Pie

This recipe uses a premade pie shell. You can definitely make your own crust using one of the recipes in this chapter if you prefer.

MAKES 6 – 8 SERVINGS

4½ teaspoons egg replacer
6 Tablespoons warm water
¼ cup brown sugar
¼ cup erythritol
1 cup agave syrup
⅓ cup vegan butter, melted
½ teaspoon salt
2 teaspoons vanilla extract
1 9-inch pie shell, frozen or graham cracker crust pie shell
1 cup walnuts, coarsely chopped
¾ cups pecans halves, to decorate the surface of the pie

1. Preheat oven to 350°F.
2. In a very small bowl, heat the water in the microwave for 30 seconds. Whisk in the egg replacer until thoroughly mixed.
3. In a counter top mixer, vigorously mix together the egg replacer mixture, brown sugar, erythritol, agave syrup, melted vegan butter, salt, and vanilla extract until smooth.
4. Spread the chopped walnuts over the bottom of the pie shell. Pour the filling over the walnuts. Arrange the pecan halves on the surface in a decorative pattern. Just dip them below the wet filling and let them rise again so they get coated with the filling.

5. Bake for 30 minutes. After 30 minutes tent the pie loosely with aluminum foil to prevent the crust and pecans from getting too browned. Bake for another 30 to 40 minutes until the filling has set. The pie should be just barely wiggly in the center.
6. Remove from oven and let cool completely. Note that the pie will be puffed up a bit when you first take it out of the oven, it will settle as it cools.

NOTES:

Earth balance is a popular vegan spread used to replace butter.
Ener-G is a popular egg replacer brand.
This recipe uses erythritol to reduce the sugar impact.

Pecan Snowballs

MAKES 18 – 24 SNOWBALLS

1½ cups vegan butter
⅔ cup powdered sugar, plus more for dusting the baked cookies
¼ teaspoon cinnamon
2 teaspoons vanilla extract
1 ½ cups chopped pecans
3 cups gluten-free flour blend

1. Preheat the oven to 350°F.
2. Using an electric mixer, combine the vegan butter, powdered sugar, cinnamon, and vanilla extract. Beat until fluffy.
3. Stir in the flour and pecans, and mix well.
4. Shape into 1 inch balls, and refrigerate for about 30 minutes so that they hold their shape when baking.
5. Bake for 18-20 minutes or until lightly golden brown.
6. Roll the warm cookies in powdered sugar, and cool on a rack. After the cookies have completely cooled, roll in them in the sugar a second time.

VARIATION:

For less sugar impact, replace half of the powdered sugar with powdered erythritol. Use a coffee grinder or other grinder to grind the erythritol.

Pie Crust (Flaxseeds and Oats)

Recipe by: Tracy Childs of Veg-Appeal

This crust is lower in fat and calories than most, is still delicious, and also makes a wonderful crumble topping for oatmeal as well as any dessert! Adding ground flax increases the lignan content. Lignans are a nutrient linked with breast cancer reduction and prevention.

MAKES 1 PIE CRUST OR 1½ CUPS CRUMBLE TOPPING

¾ cup pecans or walnuts
¾ cup oats
2 Tablespoons fine, unsweetened coconut
3 large dates, pitted
¼ cup raisins
¼ cup ground flaxseeds
1 teaspoon cinnamon
¼ teaspoon nutmeg
⅛ teaspoon sea salt, optional
1½ Tablespoons maple syrup

1. In a dry skillet, toast the pecans on medium-low until they start to brown – about 5 minutes. Add the oats and allow them to toast for about 2 minutes. Finally, add the coconut, stir and remove from heat (coconut should brown in the hot pan).
2. In a food processor, process the dates into chunks along with the raisins.
3. Add the toasted mixture, ground flaxseeds, the seasonings, and drizzle in the maple syrup.
4. Pulse to process, until it holds together well for pie crust. Process less if you are using this recipe as a delicious crumble topping.
5. Transfer mixture to an 8 or 9-inch pie tin and press to line the bottom and sides. Crust should be between 1/8-1/4 inch thick. Reserve any extra as a crumble for your oatmeal or to top the pie.

Toasted Almond Pie Crust

Modified from Amy Chaplin, *At Home in the Whole Food Kitchen*

This recipe is a crowd-pleaser.

MAKES 1 PIE CRUST

3 Tablespoons extra virgin olive oil, plus more for oiling the pan
¾ cup toasted sliced almonds, divided
½ cup regular rolled oats
¼ teaspoon sea salt
¾ cup whole spelt flour
4 Tablespoons maple syrup
1 teaspoon vanilla extract
½ teaspoon almond extract

1. Toast the almonds in toaster oven, and set aside to cool. Be careful not to overcook.
2. Line the bottom of the springform pan with parchment paper. Turn the bottom upside down. Place a parchment sheet on top. Clamp into the sides of the spring form pan, keeping the paper flush against the base. Fold the excess paper into the center.
3. Lightly oil the sides of the pan.
4. Preheat oven to 350°F.
5. Use a food processor to grind ½ cup of the almonds, oats, and salt until coarsely ground, about 20-30 seconds. Transfer to a small glass bowl and stir in the spelt flour. Roughly hand-chop the remaining almonds. Add these to the bowl, and mix well.
6. Drizzle in olive oil, and mix with a fork or your fingertips until all flour is moistened. Add maple syrup, vanilla and almond extracts; mix until evenly incorporated. Dough should be moist but not sticky. Wash and dry your hands, then press crust evenly into prepared pan. Press crust only ½ inch up sides, leaving the top edge uneven. Prick bottom of crust several times with a fork. Bake for 18 minutes or until golden brown and fragrant. Remove from oven. Set aside to cool.

Watermelon Cake

Watermelon cake is another sure crowd-pleaser – colorful and yummy. It looks like a traditional cake from the outside, until you discover the watermelon inside.

MAKES 8 SERVINGS

1 large seedless watermelon
3 cups non-dairy whipped topping
½ cup sliced almonds
Seasonal fresh fruit (strawberries, blueberries, and kiwi work well)
coconut shreds, optional

1. With a sturdy, long knife, remove the top and bottom from the watermelon, and remove the rind from the middle section. The result should be a cake-shaped piece of watermelon.
2. Cut the watermelon "cake" into slices prior to frosting – 6 to 8 slices, depending on the size of the watermelon. Leave the slices in place. Transfer to a cake plate.
3. Pat the outside of the watermelon dry with paper towels. The sides need to be as dry as possible for the whipped topping to adhere.
4. Cover the entire cake with whipped topping, just like frosting a cake, and put sliced almonds and coconut shreds on the sides.
5. Cut up your favorite fresh fruit and arrange it on top.
6. Serve or store in the refrigerator until ready to serve. Yummy!

Whipped Topping (Coconut Milk)

This whipped topping is a good alternative to dairy whipped cream. It's very high in fat and calories, but it's great as an occasional treat.

1 can coconut milk (full fat)
½ teaspoon vanilla extract

1. Refrigerate 1 can of full fat (not lite) coconut milk overnight.
2. Remove the can, and flip it upside down. Open the can, and pour off the liquid. Save the liquid for another use if you like. Scoop the thicker coconut cream off the bottom of the can into the bowl of an electric mixer.
3. Whip the cold coconut cream with a balloon whip until the cream is fluffy.
4. Add vanilla extract or a sweetener to flavor this whipped topping.

White Chocolate Amaretto Pie

MAKES 8 SERVINGS

13 ounces vegan white chocolate chips
⅓ cup amaretto liqueur
1 teaspoon vanilla extract
1 pound silken tofu, drained
1 Tablespoon agave
1 9-inch prepared graham cracker crust

1. Place enough water in the bottom of a 2-quart saucepan to come 1½ inches up the sides. Bring to a simmer over medium heat.
2. Melt the white chocolate chips with the amaretto and vanilla extract in a large metal bowl set over the simmering water, stirring often with a rubber or silicone spatula.
3. Combine the tofu, agave, and chocolate mixture in a blender or food processor and blend until smooth (about 1 minute).
4. Pour the filling into the crust and refrigerate for 2 hours, or until the filling sets firm.
5. Serve with a dollop of whipped topping and sliced fruit.

NOTE:

Non-dairy white chocolate chips are available online.

Whole Food Cookies

Recipe by: Tracy Childs of Veg-Appeal

These cookies are simple to make, absolutely delicious, and great to have around for a quick breakfast or snack!

MAKES ABOUT 18 COOKIES

1 Tablespoon ground flaxseed
¼ cup raisins or goji berries
½ cup warm water
½ cup almond butter or peanut butter
1 teaspoon vanilla extract
¼ cup maple syrup
1 cup rolled oats
1 cup oat flour (blend rolled oats in the blender to make oat flour)
1 Tablespoon raw pumpkin seeds
2 teaspoons chia seeds
1 Tablespoon hemp seeds
1 teaspoon cinnamon
⅛ teaspoon salt, optional
¼ cup chocolate chips, optional

1. Preheat oven to 350°F.
2. Lightly grease or line a cookie sheet with parchment paper.
3. In a medium bowl, add the ground flax and raisins, then pour in the warm water and give a gentle stir. Allow it to sit a few minutes to soften and thicken. Add in the almond butter, vanilla extract and maple syrup. Stir well.
4. In a large bowl stir together the rolled oats, the oat flour, along with the other dry ingredients.
5. Add the wet ingredients and mix well.
6. Using a cookie scoop or spoon, place 2 Tablespoons of the mixture on the cookie sheet about about 1 inch apart. Using wet fingers, or a spoon, press them into a nice cookie shape. (They will not rise.)
7. Bake for 10 minutes, until lightly browned on the bottom and allow to cool before eating.
8. Store in airtight container and enjoy within 3-4 days.

VARIATIONS:

If using peanut butter instead of almond butter, use ⅓ cup peanut butter and also add ¼ cup applesauce to the wet ingredients.
If you add the chocolate chips, you may want to leave out the raisins.

From Scratch

Anti-Inflammatory Quinoa

Recipe by: Tracy Childs of Veg-Appeal

Adding turmeric and black pepper increases the anti-inflammatory properties of any food. Adding them to the cooking water in this recipe creates a pleasing yellow color, and adds a savory flavor to the quinoa.

MAKES ABOUT 3 CUPS

1 cup quinoa, rinsed well and drained
2 cups low-sodium vegetable broth or water
¼ teaspoon salt
½ teaspoon turmeric
black pepper to taste

1. Bring all ingredients to boil in a medium saucepan. Stir well. Reduce the heat to a low-simmer. Cover and continue to cook for 15 minutes.
2. Fluff the quinoa with a fork, replace the cover and let it rest for a few minutes. Serve and enjoy or chill for salads.

Cleaner Cooked Brown Rice

Recipe by: Tracy Childs of Veg-Appeal

It is known that soaking and rinsing rice and cooking it similar to pasta will reduce our exposure to possible arsenic in the rice.

MAKES 4 SERVINGS

1 ½ cups Brown Rice
10 cups boiling water

1. Soak the rice overnight in plenty of water.
2. Drain and rinse the rice well.
3. Add the rice to the boiling water and cook on a low boil for 45 minutes.
4. Drain the rice through a sieve (it might fall through the holes of a colander) and allow it to rest, covered, for a few minutes before serving.
5. Fluff and serve.

NOTE:

See videos on NutritionFacts.org for additional information on the risks of arsenic exposure from rice and the different varieties.

Cooked Beans from Scratch

Recipe by: Tracy Childs of Veg-Appeal

Soaking and cooking your own beans is fairly easy; not a lot of effort is required. It will save you money and you might like the result better than canned beans.

MAKES ABOUT 4 CUPS

2 cups dried beans (black, garbanzo, pinto, kidney, etc.)
1 inch piece kombu, optional
water to soak
water to cook

1. Place the beans in a bowl and cover by a few inches of water. Soak overnight. Beans will more than double in size so make sure to use plenty of water.
2. Drain and rinse the beans.
3. Place the beans in a pot and cover with a few inches of water.
4. Bring to a boil, then reduce and simmer, partially covered, for 1-2 hours until soft.
5. Season to taste.

NOTE:

See Veg-Appeal's "Handy Bean Cooking Guide" in this section for more detailed information and quicker soaking options. If you have a pressure cooker or Instant Pot, this can speed up cooking time for beans.
Adding kombu helps to soften the beans and may reduce the gas-producing properties.

Cultured Soy Milk (Yogurt)

There are some commercial plant-based yogurts available, but there is nothing like fresh homemade yogurt. You'll need a yogurt maker for this recipe.

MAKES 3½ CUPS

1 packet vegan yogurt starter
3 ½ cups plain soy milk, room temperature

1. Shake up the carton of soy milk thoroughly before pouring. Then, add soy milk to the container that came with your yogurt maker, or use a clean jar with a lid.
2. If this is your first batch, pour one full starter packet into the container. Otherwise, use 2 Tablespoons of your previous batch of yogurt in place of the powdered starter packet.
3. Whisk the ingredients thoroughly, then secure the container lid.
4. Place the container into the yogurt maker and fill with water to surround the container.
5. Incubate for at least 8 hours.
6. Remove the container, and allow it to cool.
7. Without stirring the yogurt, chill it in the refrigerator. It's best not to disturb the yogurt until it's had a chance to chill for several hours.

NOTES:

Cleanliness is important when making yogurt. The container should be washed with soap, hot water, and a clean sponge. Also, use a clean spoon each time you use it to avoid introducing unwanted contaminants.
It is critical to use soy milk that contains only organic soybeans and water.
Yogurt will stay fresh up to 2 weeks in the refrigerator.
You can try making yogurt with other nut milks; soy milk gave the best results in our testing.
You can use this yogurt in your morning cereal, in a smoothie, as a dessert topped with fruit, as a sour cream replacement for tacos, or in a salad.

Date/Fig Paste

Recipe by: Tracy Childs of Veg-Appeal

Keep this paste on hand to use as a sweetener in place of agave or any other liquid sweetener (you may need to add additional liquid as it is thicker than other sweeteners).

MAKES ABOUT ¾ CUP

1 cup pitted dried dates or figs (or a mix)
½ cup warm water

1. Soak the fruit immersed in the water for at least 2-3 hours (they should be soft).
2. Blend the fruit and the soaking water, adding more water as needed, to form a paste.
3. Store in the refrigerator until ready to use.

Easy Quinoa Flatbread, Wrap, or Pizza Crust

Recipe by: Tracy Childs of Veg-Appeal

These flatbreads are so easy to make and convenient to use for many applications! You may no longer need to purchase tortillas for wraps!

MAKES 4 MEDIUM (6-8 INCH) FLATBREADS

1 cup quinoa soaked for at least 4 hours, then drained, rinsed again, and drained well.
½ cup water (adjust as needed)
1 Tablespoon nutritional yeast
½ teaspoon baking powder
dash salt
1 teaspoon Italian seasoning, optional

1. Preheat oven to 400°F.
2. Place the soaked quinoa in the blender with the other ingredients. Start the blender and add water until the batter is the consistency of slightly runny pancake batter (it should pour easily).
3. Pour about ¼ of the batter in a circular motion onto parchment paper, then spread with a spatula to about ⅛ inch thickness, about the size of a small flour tortilla. Continue with the rest of the batter to form 4 or more flatbreads.
4. Bake on parchment paper for 15 minutes – until the breads start to brown around the edges and some on the top and also starts to pull away from the paper. The smaller or thinner rounds will cook faster than larger, thicker ones. Allow them to cool on the sheet for about 10 or so minutes, and are easier to handle. They should be fairly easy to remove.
5. Use as you would pizza crust or serve alone alongside a meal or as a wrap.

NOTE:

These are great stored in a Ziploc bag for future use, and are very versatile. Simply warm to soften a bit before use.

Four Thieves Tonic

Modified from thegrownetwork.com

The story goes that during a time when the bubonic plague ravaged Europe, four thieves concocted a tonic that was extremely potent; it gave them immunity from the disease. They used this immunity to rob stricken victims with impunity. Whether you believe the story or not, there is magic in the power of suggestion, and I hope there is magic in the protective powers of the tonic you create from the following recipe.

The idea is to prepare this recipe at least a month before the flu and cold season and the holiday season, when you will be exposed to larger crowds of people. If you take a teaspoon or two of tonic a day during your peak exposure, perhaps it will confer immunity from disease to you as it did for the four thieves.

MAKES ABOUT 1½ CUPS

INGREDIENTS

Garlic
Ginger
Horseradish Root
Rosemary, finely chopped
Juniper Berries
Apple cider vinegar

OPTIONAL INGREDIENTS

Mint
Coriander
Cloves
Black Peppercorns

1. Wash and rinse all ingredients.
2. Chop up several cloves of garlic. Since you are only going to retain the liquid, you don't need to worry about getting all of the skin off each piece.
3. In a similar fashion, chop about 3 inches of ginger into small pieces. You don't need to peel the skin.
4. Cut up the horseradish. The more surface area you expose, the more the horseradish essence will infuse into the liquid.
5. Assemble the ingredients, in a mason or other small jar as follows. Take a small handful of each item and put in the jar. Press down. Then do another round of each item, and press down. Continue until the jar is full.
6. Pour in the vinegar until the jar is full. Seal the jar with the lid. Turn the jar upside down a couple of times to let the vinegar permeate the mixture.
7. Write the date on the jar and place it in a cupboard for a month. You can shake it up periodically.
8. After a month, strain off the liquid and store it in the fridge. That's your tonic! You can toss the solids into your compost bin.

NOTES:

Take a teaspoon or two a day to boost your immunity and to ward off disease during flu and cold season.

You can also add it to salads as part of a dressing. I find the taste of the tonic surprisingly refreshing. I make a point of using it when I expect to encounter large crowds – family gatherings, cruises, airplanes, amusement parks, etc.

Handy Bean Cooking Guide

Courtesy of Veg-Appeal

Beans are nutritious and a great addition for protein, fiber, weight loss, digestion and disease prevention. They are also an inexpensive way to fuel your body, especially when cooked from scratch! Use this guide to make sure you get easy-to-digest, flavorful beans every time! If pressure cooking, consult your manufacturer's directions. These methods may be used to speed soaking time.

SOAK YOUR BEANS

It's important to soak larger beans (garbanzo, kidney, pinto, red, black) before cooking them. Soaking has two major benefits: It reduces the cooking time and it breaks down the compounds in beans that cause flatulence. The longer beans soak, the more the gas-producing compounds break down. Beans will double or triple in size, depending on which soaking method you use, so use a large pot. There are three soaking methods you can use, the Hot Soak/Quick Soak Method, the Traditional Soak Method, and the Super Quick Baking Soda Soak and Cook Method. The Hot/Quick Soak Method (with over 4 hours soaking) is the recommended method. It reduces cooking time and gas-producing compounds the most, and it produces consistently tender beans.

THE HOT/QUICK SOAK METHOD

1. Place beans in a large pot and add 10 cups of water for every 2 cups of beans.
2. Heat to boiling and boil for an additional 2-3 minutes.
3. Remove beans from heat, cover and let stand for 1-24 hours (over 4 hours is preferred for best digestion and flavor).
4. Drain beans and discard soak water.
5. Rinse beans with fresh, cool water.

THE TRADITIONAL SOAK METHOD

1. Pour cold water over beans to cover by at least 2 inches.
2. Soak beans for 8 hours or overnight.
3. Drain beans and discard soak water (NOTE: cold water starts but does not complete the rehydration process so the beans will appear wrinkled after soaking. They will fully rehydrate during cooking.)
4. Rinse beans with fresh, cool water.

THE SUPER QUICK BAKING SODA SOAK AND COOK METHOD

1. Pour cold water over beans to cover by at least 2 inches.
2. Add 1 Tablespoon of baking soda per cup of beans. Soak for at least 1 hour.

Pour off the water and rinse the beans. (Beans will cook faster using this method, so check after cooking for 1 hour, especially for large beans.)

COOK YOUR BEANS

Now that you've cleaned, drained, rinsed, and soaked your beans, you can cook them, which is as easy as simmering beans in plenty of fresh water (cover by an inch or two). Beans generally take 30 minutes-2 hours to cook, depending on the variety.

COOKING WATER ADDITIONS

Some cooks swear by certain additions to the cooking water to speed cooking, add nutrition and create delicious beans. You can try 1-2 inches of kombu or wakame seaweed, or a pinch of baking soda. A small amount of oil will help keep the foam down. Onions and herbs may be added towards the end of cooking, but acidic additions (lemon, tomato, vinegar) should be avoided until after the beans are fully cooked. For more information on cooking times for specific beans:

http://beaninstitute.com/recipes/cooking-with-dry-beans/

Kasha (Roasted Buckwheat)

Recipe by: Tracy Childs of Veg-Appeal

MAKES ALMOST 3 CUPS

Purchase toasted, hulled kasha for a nutty flavored, quick cooking whole grain that is easy on the digestive system. Despite the name, buckwheat is not related to wheat and is often sought as a gluten-free alternative to wheat. High in protein, iron, manganese, magnesium, phosphorus, copper, and zinc, buckwheat is a healthy addition to any salad, soup, or great as a side.

2 cups water
1 cup kasha
½ teaspoon salt, optional

1. Bring 2 cups of water to a boil.
2. Place the dry kasha in a sieve and shake it over the sink to remove excess crumbs.
3. Add the kasha to the boiling water, put on the lid, and turn the heat down to simmer.
4. After 15 minutes remove from heat and let sit for another 5-10 minutes.
5. Fluff with a fork.

Lentil/Mung/Adzuki Sprouts in a Sieve

Recipe by: Tracy Childs of Veg-Appeal

Legume sprouts are very simple and easy to sprout and are an excellent source of raw and digestible protein, vitamins and minerals. They are also a great source of fiber!

1. **Start with ⅓-½ cup of beans. They expand quite a bit from the soaking and sprouting.**
2. **Soak the beans overnight in plenty of water.**
3. **Drain into a sieve and spread them to create a thin layer with your fingers.**
4. **If you are gone most of the day, cover loosely with a dampened dishtowel and place the sieve over a bowl or plate to drain.**
5. **Rinse every 3-8 hours or so, or whenever you can. Sprout for 1-3 days. That's it!**
6. **Refrigerate in a closed container to arrest them from growing too large and tough.**

NOTES:

Use sprouts in salads/sandwiches/wraps. They are high in protein, and very alkaline.
Here is a great video on making your own sprouts:
www.naturalvita.net/how-to-sprout-food-easily-without-a-jar-only-a-sieve-bowl/

VARIATION:

You can also use sprouts to make a pâté in the food processor using fresh lemon juice and herbs. Use alone or in combination with sunflower seed sprouts.

Moringa Powder

Moringa powder sells for up to $2 or more per ounce online. But why pay that when you can easily make your own? It may be easier than you think. Moringa seeds are just a few dollars a packet, and they grow quite well from seed. They do best in a warm climate (having originated in India), but they can be grown in a colder climate if you keep them in a large pot and store the plant in a greenhouse or inside during the winter months. (Note: the plant will lose its leaves in the winter.) Your efforts will be worth it because moringa leaves are packed with nutrition.

MAKES 1½ TABLESPOONS

1 bunch moringa leaves, fresh off the tree, enough to cover 3 or 4 trays of your dehydrator

1. Follow the directions in the Moringa tea recipe in Beverages to harvest, dry, and grind the leaves.
2. Continue grinding in a coffee grinder until the leaves become a powder.

NOTES:

You can store the powder in the fridge and sprinkle it on your morning cereal, in your smoothie, in stir-fry, or in other dishes to improve the nutritive value. Keep your tree trimmed to less than head height for easy harvesting.

Preserved Lemons

I first discovered preserved lemons in a Moroccan dish called tagine. Used as a flavor enhancer in a wide variety of dishes, it is heavy in sodium content, so use sparingly.

8-10 lemons
½ cup-1 cup of kosher salt
Extra fresh squeezed lemon juice, if needed

1. Put 2 Tablespoons of kosher salt at the bottom of a sterilized quart-sized canning jar.
2. Clean the lemons well, because you will be using the rinds. Cut off and discard any stems and 1/4-inch from the tip of the lemons.
3. Cut the lemons lengthwise in half, but keep the lemon attached at the base, do not cut all the way through. Then make another cut the same way, as if you were cutting the lemons into quarters, but not all the way through.
4. Gently pull open each of the lemons and sprinkle well with kosher salt, inside and out.
5. Put the prepared lemons in a canning jar, and press them down hard so that their juices rise to the top. Continue adding lemons and pressing, making sure that they are covered with juice. Add more lemon juice as needed.
6. When the jar is full, add a couple more Tablespoons of kosher salt to the top.
7. Close the lid to the jar and let it sit at room temperature on the counter for a few days. Turn the jar upside down occasionally. After a few days, refrigerate for at least 3 weeks, until the rinds of the lemons soften. Continue to occasionally turn the jar upside down.
8. To use preserved lemons in cooking, remove a lemon from the jar and rinse it to remove the salt. Discard any seeds. Scrape off the pulp, leaving only the rind. Thinly slice or chop the preserved lemon rind to use in a recipe.
9. Can be stored refrigerated for up to 6 months.

VARIATIONS:

Experiment with adding spices to the preserved lemons such as bay leaf, cardamom, cinnamon stick, cloves, coriander seeds, peppercorns, or vanilla extract.

Quinoa Rejuvelac (Probiotic Water)

Recipe by: Tracy Childs of Veg-Appeal

This probiotic water can be used as the base of vegan cashew cheese recipes (which aids in the curing of the cheese) and also as a probiotic supplement beverage.

1. Start with ½ cup quinoa
2. Soak the quinoa for 8-12 hours in a sprouting jar.
3. Drain off water, place the jar tilted to drain and rinse 2-3 times a day until little sprout tails appear in 1-3 days.
4. Add 3 cups water and let sit on the counter or a warm place overnight.
5. You will notice that the water will get cloudy and little bubbles will start forming.
6. Taste. It should taste clean and fresh with a hint of lemon, and a bit bubbly. If it's ready, strain the rejuvelac off of the sprouts and store in covered glass container in the refrigerator. It will keep for about 2-3 weeks. You can drink it as a probiotic beverage and/or use to make cheese.

NOTE:

You can use the sprouted quinoa to make Quinoa Flatbread. It will have a slightly "sour dough" flavor due to using fermented quinoa.

"Scrappy" Vegetable Broth

Recipe by: Tracy Childs of Veg-Appeal

Don't throw away valuable vegetable scraps! Make them into delicious broth that can be used for soups, chili, stir-fries and sautés! Keep broth handy for sautéing by freezing in ice cube trays and storing in a container or bag in the freezer. Not only does it taste great, it's "free!"

MAKES ABOUT 2 QUARTS

4 quarts frozen vegetable scraps (see notes)
Filtered water to barely cover
12 peppercorns, optional
2 bay leaves, optional
4 dried juniper berries, optional
A handful or two of brown lentils, optional
Salt to taste, optional

1. Place the ingredients in a large pan and add water to barely cover.
2. Cover the pan and bring to a boil.
3. Leave the cover ajar and cook on simmer for 45 minutes-1½ hours, adding additional water as needed to keep the vegetables submerged.
4. Remove the pan from the heat and allow it to cool for about an hour.
5. In the sink, place a colander over a bowl and empty the contents from the stockpot. Squeeze or press down to remove any liquid from the vegetables. Freeze the collected liquid (in ice cube trays for sauté cubes!) or refrigerate until ready to use. Homemade vegetable broth will last up to 1 week, unfrozen. If you can, compost the cooked veggie scraps.

NOTES:

When preparing vegetables, keep the parts you may ordinarily throw away. Examples: ends and greens of root veggies, celery, collards and kale stems, onions, beets, outer cabbage leaves, cabbage cores, organic potato ends/ peelings, stems of parsley, cilantro and other herbs. Place them in a large bag in the freezer and add to it every time you prepare vegetables. When the bag is full (about 1 gallon) you can make broth.

Sesame Salt Sprinkle

Recipe by: Tracy Childs of Veg-Appeal

MAKES ABOUT ½ CUP

3 Tablespoons unhulled sesame seeds
½ teaspoon salt

1. In a warm skillet, place the sesame seeds and turn up the heat to toast them, moving them around to avoid burning.
2. Put the seeds, along with the salt into a blender and blend to grind. This will bring out the nutrition and flavor in the seeds.
3. Store in a covered container in the refrigerator if not using within a few days.

Sprouts

Sprouting of grains and seeds is becoming more mainstream. Sprouting increases the nutritive value and health qualities of foods in a natural way.[2] From a nutritional standpoint, the sprouting process has an amazing effect including an increase in protein quality, increase in fiber content, increase in vitamin content (sometimes dramatically), and increase in essential fatty acids.

Some of the health benefits associated with sprouting include improved digestion, boosting metabolism and immune system, protecting against cancer, and promoting heart health.

Most seeds and legumes can be sprouted. Some of the most popular items to sprout include alfalfa, pea, lentil, chickpea, mung bean, soybean, quinoa, amaranth, buckwheat, sesame, broccoli, and radish.

It's easy to sprout seeds at home.

1. Rinse the seeds thoroughly.
2. Soak seeds 8-12 hours/overnight in a sprouting jar.
3. Drain water and rinse with fresh water once or twice.
4. Rest the sprouting jar at an angle in a bowl or tray, with the screen cover pointing down, so that water can drain.
5. Every morning and night rinse with fresh water, to keep the sprouts wet and clean of mold.
6. Repeat the process until the sprouts are ready for use. The time will vary depending on the type of seed or legume you prefer (e.g. alfalfa sprouts are ready in 4-5 days, while lentils are ready in 1-2 days).
7. Rinse out with fresh water, and dry the sprouts on a paper towel. Then store on a paper towel in a plastic container with a lid in the fridge.
8. Eat within 2-3 days. Enjoy in salads, wraps, sandwiches, smoothies, juices, soups, and stews.

NOTE:

The soaking and sprouting times vary depending on the seed or legume. Search online for individual times.

Tofu-Cashew Mayonnaise

Recipe by: Tracy Childs of Veg-Appeal

MAKES ABOUT 2 CUPS

1 package silken tofu (Mori-Nu)
¼ cup cashews, soaked for 4 hours, drained and rinsed then drained well
2 Tablespoons apple cider vinegar
1 Tablespoon light miso
1 Tablespoon Dijon mustard
¼ teaspoon probiotic powder, optional

1. Place all ingredients in a blender and blend well.
2. Place in a covered jar or other container and chill until ready to use.
3. Use any way you use mayonnaise.
4. Use within about 7-9 days.

Whipped Topping from Aquafaba

Whipped topping using aquafaba (bean juice) is one of my favorite things to make for several reasons. One, the technique was first discovered in 2015, so it still has the novelty factor. Two, it's an easy way to make whipped topping without using eggs. Three, you can also use it to make meringue cookies as well as a host of other items.

So what is **aquafaba**? It is nothing more than bean juice, usually garbanzo beans (also known as chickpeas), but some people have had success using the juice of other beans. It turns out that if you whip the bean juice, it will whip up much like egg whites, although more slowly. If you want to dig deeper into this, there is a Facebook group that was formed called Vegan Meringue - Hits and Misses! Aquafaba enthusiasts post the results of their experience with this mysterious substance. Aquafaba can be used in many recipes including pancakes, cheese, brownies, and chocolate mousse. For more ideas, see the book *Aquafaba* by Zsu Dever, or other books on the subject.

I've tried three sources for garbanzo bean juice: pressure cooking, slow cooking, and bean juice from a can. The juice from pressure cooking didn't work well unless I cooked the juice down over the stove to make a more concentrated liquid. Slow cooking with a little bit of kombu (seaweed) worked better. Juice from canned garbanzo beans has been the most reliable and convenient source. I use the juice from canned beans in the instructions below.

½ cup aquafaba
¼ teaspoon cream of tartar
1 teaspoon vanilla powder
½ cup powdered sugar

1. Open a can of garbanzo beans, low-salt is preferable. Drain the liquid into a small container. It should yield about ½-¾ cup. Store it in the fridge until it's chilled.
2. Then pour ½ cup chilled aquafaba into the mixing bowl of a counter top mixer. If you use more juice, adjust the other amounts accordingly.
3. Use a balloon whip attachment, and start it on the lowest setting so that it doesn't splatter. Add the cream of tartar. Gradually increase the speed. Be patient, because it takes a lot longer to firm up than egg whites. It may take 10-15 minutes in some cases.
4. When it starts to firm up, add vanilla powder. Don't use liquid vanilla extract if it contains alcohol. Alcohol will defeat any attempts at making meringue cookies.
5. Gradually increase the speed and sprinkle in powdered sugar slowly to taste.
6. When it reaches the desired consistency, you can use it as a whipped topping on pies, cakes, and frozen desserts. You can also use it to make meringue cookies. See the recipe in Desserts.

NOTES:

Some people are very sensitive to the "bean" flavor of aquafaba. The vanilla flavoring and sugar can help mitigate the effect to the point that most people can barely detect it.

I've experimented with other sweeteners for whipped aquafaba, namely erythritol and cassava syrup. Erythritol deflated the cookies, and cassava had a strong after taste when cooked.

Left over whipped aquafaba doesn't hold its shape for long in the fridge. It will dissolve back into a liquid. However, you should be able to re-whip it in a mixer.

Use a sturdy counter top mixer. If you use a hand mixer, be prepared for a workout.

Main Dishes

5-Layer Tamale Pie

Recipe by: Tracy Childs of Veg-Appeal

MAKES 8 SERVINGS

1 prepared recipe Spanish Quinoa Pilaf (in "Salads and Sides") or packaged Spanish rice, prepared

1½ cups cooked black beans seasoned with 1 teaspoon each onion powder and cumin. Then add salt, pepper, and chili powder to taste

1 onion, cut into thin slices

1 bell pepper (any color), cut into thin slices

2 cups mushrooms, sliced

1 10-ounce package frozen spinach, thawed and seasoned with salt, pepper, cumin, chili powder

½ bunch of cilantro, chopped

1 cup *Tofu-Cashew Sour Cream* (in "Dairy-Alternatives")

1 tube prepared polenta, crumbled in the food processor or by hand

Warmed enchilada sauce, optional

Chopped fresh cilantro, optional

1. Prepare a 9x13 inch casserole dish by spraying lightly with cooking spray.
2. Preheat oven to 375°F.
3. In a heated dry skillet sauté the onion, bell pepper, and sliced mushrooms, adding water or vegetable broth as needed to prevent sticking. Season with salt and pepper to taste.
4. In a bowl, stir together the beans and seasonings.
5. In another bowl stir together the spinach, seasonings, cilantro and *Tofu-Cashew Sour Cream*.
6. Layer the prepared dish as follows:

Layer 1: Spanish Quinoa or prepared package of Spanish rice

Layer 2: Seasoned Black beans

Layer 3: sautéed onions, peppers & mushrooms

Layer 4: seasoned creamy spinach and cilantro

Layer 5: 1 tube of polenta, crushed in the food processor and spread on top.

7. Cover and bake in the preheated oven for 30 minutes, until hot and bubbly.
8. Uncover and bake for about 10 minutes to brown the top.
9. Optionally serve with warmed enchilada sauce, fresh chopped cilantro for garnish.

Collard Quinoa Tacos

Recipe by: Tracy Childs of Veg-Appeal

Collards are an amazing source of plant-based calcium as well as a potent cancer-fighter! Using them as a wrap or taco is an easy way to include them in your diet. Traditional tortillas may also be used — just heat them over a flame or in a toaster oven.

MAKES 4 SERVINGS

4 large collard leaves, washed and dried
1 recipe *Spanish Quinoa Pilaf* (in "Salads and Sides")
1 recipe *Not Refried Black Beans* (in "Salads and Sides")
***Tofu-Cashew Sour Cream* (in "Dairy Alternatives")**
Toppings of choice: chopped cilantro, tomatoes, red cabbage, onions, mung bean sprouts (in "From Scratch"), salsa or hot sauce of choice

1. Lay a collard leaf on a cutting board. Slice on both sides of the stem to remove it. Cut each half into halves to make 4 pieces from one leaf. Repeat for the remaining leaves.
2. For each taco, place about 2 Tablespoons each of the pilaf and beans. Add a dollop of sour cream and a sprinkling of toppings of choice.
3. Fold the leaves in half like a taco shell, and enjoy.

NOTE:

This recipe depends a great deal on the size of the collard leaves you can find because they vary in size tremendously. Using large leaves, you can make 4 small tacos (just a few bites each), almost like sliders. Feel free to indulge in several tacos. If you have smaller collard leaves, you can make a larger taco from each leaf (with the thicker stems thinned in the center and ends removed) and double or triple the filling. Also, note that many different fillings are great in collards; use your imagination!

Eggplant Beanballs and Spaghetti

Recipe by: Tracy Childs of Veg-Appeal

These beanballs resemble meatballs in shape and color. They are a wonderful, filling accompaniment to any pasta meal. The recipe makes a lot of beanballs and they reheat easily so be sure to freeze some for later. Your heart will be happy you chose these over the meat version!

MAKES 4 SERVINGS (ABOUT 36 BEAN BALLS)

2 Tablespoons vegetable broth (or water)
1 onion, chopped
1 pound eggplant (1 medium/large) unpeeled, cut into small cubes
¼ cup water
1 teaspoon salt, or to taste
½ teaspoon pepper
1 Tablespoon garlic, minced
1½ cups cooked or canned white beans (any kind), drained and rinsed
½ cup pecans, roughly chopped
¼ cup chopped fresh parsley and fresh oregano
Pinch of red chili flakes, optional
1 cup breadcrumbs, preferably whole wheat or gluten-free
1 jar of your favorite vegan marinara sauce
1 package of spaghetti, cooked al dente according to package directions

1. Heat the oven to 375°F.
2. Lightly oil a baking sheet, or line with parchment paper.
3. Heat the vegetable broth in a large skillet over medium-high heat. Add the onion and sauté until soft, adding additional broth/water as needed.
4. Add the eggplant and garlic and ¼ cup water. Sprinkle with the salt and pepper. Cover, but watch it to make sure it doesn't burn. Cook, stirring occasionally, until the eggplant is tender and beginning to brown, about 10 minutes.
5. Transfer the eggplant and onion to the bowl of a food processor and add the beans, pecans, breadcrumbs, red chili flakes and fresh herbs. Pulse until well combined and chopped, but not completely pureed.
6. Use a melon baller to scoop the batter into about 36 balls about 1 inch in diameter onto the prepared baking sheet.
7. Bake for 30 minutes.
8. Check to see if they feel firm to the touch. If they don't bake for another 5 or so minutes.
9. Meanwhile, warm the marinara sauce. Place the pasta on a plate. Top the pasta with the meatballs and marinara sauce. Do not immerse the bean balls in the sauce for long, or they may fall apart.

Herbed Lentils and Roasted Butternut Squash

Recipe by: Tracy Childs of Veg-Appeal

A most delicious way to enjoy fresh herbs, roasted veggies and lentils, all in one very flavorful dish. You could adjust the garlic if you prefer, or add more herbs if you want the greenery, or add more curry if you like it spicy. However, note that the curry should not be an overpowering flavor; it's intended to complement the other flavors.

MAKES 4 SERVINGS

4 cups butternut squash cubed into ½ - ¾ inch pieces
¾ cup vegetable broth, divided use
2 teaspoons curry powder
½ Tablespoon oregano
salt and pepper
2 cups cooked beluga lentils, drained and rinsed well (or use store-bought cooked or canned lentils, drained and rinsed well)
2 Tablespoons minced garlic (about 4-5 large cloves)
½ cup chopped basil
⅓ cup chopped parsley
2 Tablespoons apple cider vinegar
1 Tablespoon Dijon mustard
Salt and Pepper to taste
Parmesan Cheese (in "Dairy Alternatives") to taste, optional

1. Preheat oven to 450°F.
2. In a large bowl, toss the squash with about ¼ cup vegetable broth, curry powder, oregano, salt and pepper. Line a baking tray with parchment paper, or lightly oil a with natural oil spray. Spread out the squash, in a single layer with as much space between possible to allow for even browning. Roast in hot the oven for about 16-20 minutes, until starting to brown on some sides.
3. While the squash is cooking, put ¼ cup vegetable broth and minced garlic in a pan over medium heat. Shake it around a few times, and allow the garlic pieces to brown up a bit.
4. Add ½ of the herbs and sauté for a few seconds. Add the lentils and the remaining broth and stir to warm through.
5. Add apple cider vinegar, Dijon mustard and the remaining herbs. Stir. Add the squash chunks and stir. Add fresh ground pepper and a bit of salt, as needed. Garnish with vegan parmesan, if using.

VARIATION:
Try other vegetables in place of the squash: pumpkin, delicata squash, yams or sweet potatoes.

Italian Beans and Greens

Recipe by: Tracy Childs of Veg-Appeal

This is a delicious way to get some great, healthy servings of beans and greens!

MAKES 8 SERVINGS

¼ cup vegetable broth
1 large bunch of kale, chopped finely (or 10 ounces bagged greens like kale or collards)
4 garlic cloves, very finely minced or pressed
1 teaspoon dried oregano (or 2 Tablespoons fresh)
3 Tablespoons balsamic vinegar
1 Tablespoon Dijon mustard
3 Tablespoons tomato paste
1½ cups white beans of choice (cannellini is nice - white kidney beans), drained, rinsed
¼ cup pitted Kalamata olives, chopped coarsely or halved
1 large tomato, chopped, optional
Pepper to taste
Salt to taste, if needed
Additional vegetable broth, as needed

1. Heat a large saucepan or wok. Add a splash of the vegetable broth, and allow it to heat. Quickly add the remaining broth, chopped kale and cover. Lower heat and cook over medium-low heat, until the kale is soft (about 5 minutes).
2. Meanwhile, make a dressing by mixing together the garlic, oregano, vinegar, mustard, and tomato paste.
3. Add the beans and olives to the pan. Cook another 2-3 minutes over medium heat to blend flavors, adding additional splashes of vegetable broth as needed.
4. Stir the dressing into the kale mixture.
5. Add the chopped fresh tomatoes if using, and stir well.
6. Taste and add salt and pepper to taste (though you will probably not need more salt).
7. Serve immediately by itself or over pasta, brown rice, or some other grain or crispy whole grain garlic bread. You can also refrigerate and toss just before serving, as a cold side dish.

Kale and Sweet Potato Black Bean Chili

Recipe by: Tracy Childs of Veg-Appeal

MAKES 6 - 8 SERVINGS

1 onion, diced
3–5 Tablespoons water
1 Tablespoon minced garlic
2 Tablespoons chili powder
1 Tablespoon ground cumin
1 cup sweet potato, cut into ½ inch pieces
1 cup water
1 (28 ounce) can crushed tomatoes
2 cups chopped kale, packed
1 cup frozen corn
2 cups cooked black beans
¼–½ teaspoon salt, to taste
Pinch ground chipotle, optional
Optional garnishes: vegan sour cream, cilantro, green onions, toasted pepitas

1. Heat 3-quart saucepan. Add the onion and cook over medium heat until softened, adding water by the tablespoon as needed to prevent burning. Add the garlic and cook for one minute.
2. Add the chili powder and ground cumin. Stir and cook for 30 seconds or until fragrant.
3. Add the sweet potato pieces and 1 cup water and increase the heat to high to bring to a boil. Cover and cook for about 5 minutes to soften the yams.
4. Add the crushed tomatoes to the pan and stir well. Bring to a simmer and let cook for 5 minutes for flavors to blend.
5. Add the kale, corn and black beans. Cook, stirring occasionally, for 10-15 minutes. Taste and add salt, if needed.
6. Ladle into bowls and garnish with vegan sour cream, cilantro, green onions and toasted pepitas.

Lazy Zucchini Lasagna

Adapted by Tracy Childs of Veg-Appeal from a recipe in "The Cancer Survivor's Guide" by Jennifer Reilly

Your days of boiling lasagna noodles and eating high-fat lasagna are over. Enjoy this filling and cholesterol-free meal, which also boasts tons of fiber and cancer-fighting nutrients. Top this dish with nutritional yeast or Vegan Parmesan for a cheesier flavor and for added vitamin B-12. Try adding shredded carrots for extra beta-carotene!

MAKES 8 SERVINGS

10 ounces frozen, chopped spinach, thawed and drained

1 package (14-16 ounces) firm tofu

¼ cup non-dairy milk (such as rice, oat, soy, almond, or hazelnut), as needed

½ teaspoon garlic powder or 2 peeled garlic cloves, minced

Juice from ½ lemon (about 2 Tablespoons)

2 Tablespoons minced fresh basil

1 teaspoon salt (or to taste)

2 large jars pasta sauce of your choice (or equivalent of tomato sauce and add Italian seasonings)

8 ounces lasagna noodles (uncooked - you might not use all)

1-2 zucchini sliced thinly, lengthwise

1 large carrot, shredded, optional

1. Preheat oven to 375°F.
2. Blend tofu, nondairy milk, garlic, lemon juice and salt in a food processor or blender.
3. Stir in chopped basil and spinach.
4. Spread about ½ cup of the pasta sauce on the bottom of a 9x13 inch baking dish and place a layer of 4 lasagna noodles.
5. Spread ½ of the tofu mix on top of the noodles.
6. Follow with a layer of zucchini slices or shredded carrots if using.
7. Layer in a coating of the sauce.
8. Layer in 4 more noodles.
9. Follow with the rest of the tofu mixture then sliced zucchini if you used carrots.
10. Layer in 4 more noodles.
11. Cover with PLENTY of sauce!
12. Cover the dish TIGHTLY with foil.
13. Bake at 375°F for about 1 hour, test the top noodles for tenderness. Add more sauce if necessary (and return to oven for a few minutes).
14. Allow it to cool for a few minutes before serving with homemade *Parmesan Cheese* (in "Dairy Alternatives").

Loaded Sweet Potatoes with Chili

Recipe by: Tracy Childs of Veg-Appeal

MAKES 4 SERVINGS

4 large sweet potatoes, baked at 375°F in the oven until fork tender (about 35-50 minutes)

2 cups *Kale and Sweet Potato Black Bean Chili* (recipe in this section)

1 cup *Tofu-Cashew Sour Cream* or *Chipotle Cheesy Sauce* (in "Dairy-Alternatives")

½ cup sliced scallions

1 cup or more finely chopped spinach and/or cilantro

½ cup *Mung Bean Sprouts* (see recipe in "From Scratch")

4 slices *Maple Tempeh Bacon*, crumbled (in "Breakfast")

Toasted pepitas (pumpkin seeds)

Other toppings of choice

1. Split the sweet potatoes down the center and create a wide opening for your ingredients.
2. Pour in ½ cup chili per potato.
3. Top with the rest of the ingredients.
4. Enjoy!

Mac and No-Cheese with Broccoli Florets

Recipe by: Tracy Childs of Veg-Appeal

MAKES 4 SMALL SERVINGS

1 8-ounce package whole grain macaroni

1 recipe *Easy Cheesy Sauce* (in "Dairy Alternatives")

¼ cup *Spreadable Smoked Sharp Cheddar* (in "Dairy Alternatives"), optional

4 cups broccoli florets

1. Prepare the cheesy sauce, stir in the smoked cheddar (if using) and keep it warm.
2. Cook the macaroni according to the package directions.
3. During the last minute of cooking time, add the broccoli florets and allow them to cook together for a minute, or until the broccoli turns bright green. Drain well.
4. In a bowl, stir together the cheesy sauce, the broccoli and the macaroni and serve immediately.

Moroccan Tagine

A Moroccan Tagine dish was introduced as one of the sample dishes in *Transforming Your Meals* in Chapter 5. This is a more specific recipe.

MAKES 8 - 10 SERVINGS

4 Tablespoons water to cover onions

1 large sweet onion, thinly sliced

3 cloves garlic, minced

1 Tablespoon fresh grated ginger or minced ginger

2 teaspoons turmeric

1-2 teaspoons cumin

1 teaspoon cinnamon

6 dates, pitted and chopped

½ cup raisins

1 sweet potato, unpeeled, rinsed, and diced

½ cup carrots, sliced

1 teaspoon coarse sea salt

½ to 1 cup large green olives (pitted, and cut in half)

juice of 1 lemon

3 - 4 cups water (divided use)

1 teaspoon fresh thyme (3 or 4 sprigs)

1 can chickpeas, rinsed and drained

½ cup mushrooms, cleaned and sliced

fresh cilantro, thyme, and lemon slices (optional garnish)

1. Heat 3 Tablespoons of the water (reserve 1 Tablespoon for later) in large wok and sauté the sliced onions for a few minutes.
2. Add the fresh grated ginger and garlic; stir.
3. Add the turmeric, cumin, cinnamon; stir.
4. Add dates and raisins; stir. Add more water if necessary.
5. Add the potatoes, carrots, and salt, and gently stir to coat the potatoes with the spices and water.
6. Add olives, lemon juice, fresh thyme and 3 cups of the water (reserve remaining water for later).
7. Cook, uncovered for 15 minutes, until the potatoes are just tender but not cooked through; add the chickpeas, mushrooms, and remaining water.
8. Turn down the heat and simmer for an additional 25 minutes, until the potatoes are tender and the juices have thickened, stirring occasionally.
9. Garnish with fresh cilantro, fresh sprigs of thyme and lemon slices.
10. Serve over rice or quinoa or other grain.

VARIATIONS:

You can try out different veggies including yellow squash, zucchini, beets, leafy greens. Try Turkish apricots and other dried fruits. Use Basil as a garnish.

If you have preserved lemons, use a small amount in place of the lemon juice.

Quinoa and Cranberry Stuffed Acorn Squash

Modified from Liz Gary

This dish is terrific for special occasions, with its holiday-style flavors.

MAKES 4 SERVINGS

¾ cup white quinoa, rinsed
¾ cup red quinoa, rinsed
1 cup orange juice
2 cups apple juice
1 teaspoon ground cinnamon
½ teaspoon ground allspice
¼ teaspoon ground nutmeg
¼ teaspoon salt
½ teaspoon pepper
2 acorn squash
3 Tablespoons water
1 medium onion, diced
1 carrot, diced
1 celery rib, diced
½ cup dried cranberries
½ cup dried apples, diced
2 Tablespoons maple syrup
½ cup sliced almonds, toasted
¼ cup chopped fresh parsley

1. Toast quinoa without liquid in rice cooker for about 3 minutes. Add orange juice, apple juice, cinnamon, allspice, nutmeg, salt, and pepper. Cover and cook in rice cooker, about 25 minutes. (If you don't have a rice cooker, you can use a saucepan.)
2. Meanwhile, preheat oven to 350°F. Cut each acorn squash in half and steam in vegetable steamer. (Or, bake in oven.) While squash and quinoa cook, sauté onion, carrot, and celery in 3 Tablespoons water over medium heat for 8 to 10 minutes. Add sautéed vegetables to the simmering quinoa, along with the dried cranberries, apples, and maple syrup.
3. Simmer the aromatic mixture for 10 more minutes, at which point the quinoa should be fully cooked and hold together like sticky rice. Remove from heat and stir in sliced almonds and parsley.
4. Turn the squash cut-side up. Fill each half with ¼ of the quinoa mixture and return to the oven for 10 minutes, or until the squash is tender when pierced with a fork.

Quinoa Power Bowl

Recipe by: Tracy Childs of Veg-Appeal

MAKES 2 SERVINGS

¼ cup raw pumpkin seeds
5-6 cups chopped greens or baby greens (mix of romaine lettuce, chard, kale, spinach, cilantro, beet greens, broccoli for example)
½ cup chopped red cabbage
½ cup chopped cucumbers
½ cup cherry tomatoes, halved
1 cup great northern beans, drained and rinsed (or your favorite bean)
2 cups cold, cooked *Anti-inflammatory Quinoa* (in "From Scratch")
¼-½ avocado, cubed
½ cup *Sweet Miso Lemon Dressing* (in "Sauces, Syrups, Dressings"), thinned to desired consistency

1. Toast the pumpkin seeds in a skillet over medium-low heat until browned and crunchy, about 5 minutes.
2. Meanwhile, place all of your salad ingredients in a large bowl and toss well.
3. Add the dressing and toss again.
4. Sprinkle with the freshly toasted pumpkin seeds.
5. Serve immediately, or chill for about an hour. This salad is also delicious the next day!

Simple BBQ Tofu

Recipe by: Tracy Childs of Veg-Appeal

The tofu is baked in plenty of your favorite BBQ sauce to assure a moist, flavorful and heart-healthy substitute for meat!

MAKES 4 SERVINGS

1 14-16 ounce package firm tofu cut into 5 or 6 rectangular slices
1 ½ cups vegan BBQ sauce (or more to taste)
¼ cup tomato juice (or water)
1 Tablespoon Dijon mustard or red wine , optional
1 Tablespoon maple syrup, optional
1 Tablespoon red wine vinegar, optional

1. Preheat oven to 400°F.
2. If your sauce is too sweet or too tart, add the optional ingredients to balance the flavor, also adding the tomato juice to thin it and mellow it.
3. Drain well and cut the tofu into ¾ inch steaks/rectangles, about 5 or 6 total.
4. Pour about ½ cup of the sauce into a 9x11 inch casserole dish, and spread to cover the bottom. Lay the steaks side by side in the sauce, then turn them over.
5. Pour another layer of sauce over the top of the tofu and spread to make sure all pieces are coated well with the sauce.
6. Cover the dish with foil and place in the oven for about 25 minutes or more, until it is bubbling well.
7. Uncover, flip the tofu and put it back in the oven, uncovered and bake for another 20 minutes until sauce is thickened.
8. Allow it to cool a bit and serve as steaks, or sliced/cubed for salads.

Steamed Veggies

Some people might not consider steamed veggies as a main course, but it has definitely become a favorite in my household. With a side of beans or lentils, served over a bed of cooked grain (often quinoa), flavored with a variety of flavorings (herbs, spices, coconut aminos, tamari, Worcestershire sauce, nutritional yeast, liquid smoke), and topped with a tangy sauce, steamed veggies more than hold their own at center stage.

Not only is steaming one of the purest ways to enjoy the flavor of vegetables, it is easy and fun to prepare. I purchased an inexpensive counter top steamer with three transparent trays. It has a timer and shut-off feature, so your dinner won't overcook if you walk away. Since the trays cook at three different rates (the bottom tray cooking the fastest), it's very convenient to put the harder vegetables such as potatoes, carrots, and beets in the bottom tray, medium density vegetables such as squashes and bell peppers in the middle tray, and more delicate vegetables such as mushrooms, onions, tomatoes, and leafy greens in the top tray. Since the trays are transparent, you can monitor the cooking process and make adjustments on the fly.

Give steamed vegetables a chance. As you follow the path away from processed foods towards a more whole food plant-based diet, steamed vegetables will become more and more attractive.

Sushi Bowl with Creamy Wasabi Sauce

Recipe by: Tracy Childs of Veg-Appeal

MAKES 4 SERVINGS

4-5 cups warm *Cleaner Cooked Brown Rice* (in "From Scratch"), seasoned with 2 teaspoons rice vinegar
1 8-ounce package baked tofu (or bake your own), cut into sticks
3 Persian cucumbers, cut into sticks and halved
2 large carrots, cut into sticks and parboiled to soften for 2 minutes
1 avocado, sliced
16 flavored nori sheets (or 4 sheets of nori folded into 4 x 4 inch squares)
***Creamy Wasabi Sauce* (in "Sauces, Syrups and Dressings")**
***Sesame Salt Sprinkle* (in "From Scratch")**
Low-Sodium Soy Sauce, optional
Pickled Sushi Ginger, optional
Wasabi paste, optional

1. Prepare your ingredients.
2. Place 1 cup of cooked rice into each of 4 large individual bowls.
3. Arrange the ingredients around the side: cucumbers, carrots, tofu, avocado.
4. Place 4 flavored nori sheets over the rice in each bowl, either whole or crumbled.
5. Drizzle the *Creamy Wasabi Sauce* over the top of the rice, veggies and tofu, then sprinkle with *Sesame Salt Sprinkle* and add optional flavors.
6. You can eat this dish by placing some of each of the ingredients into a small nori sheet to each like "tacos" or crumble the nori over the bowls.

Sweet and Savory Veggie Stew

Recipe by: Tracy Childs of Veg-Appeal

MAKES 8 SERVINGS

1 onion, chopped
2 medium potatoes, cubed
1 sweet potato, cubed
3 carrots, sliced
2 golden beets or turnips, optional
1 onion, diced
6 cloves garlic, chopped
4 cups low-sodium vegetable broth
1 cup garbanzo beans
1 28-ounce can of crushed tomatoes
6 dates blended with ½ cup water (use more water if needed)
1 teaspoon cumin
2 teaspoons Herbs de Provence (or an Italian herb mix)
1 teaspoon smoked paprika, optional
1 Tablespoon apple cider vinegar
salt and pepper to taste

1. Sauté the onions in 1 cup of the vegetable broth while you chop your other veggies, adding more broth if needed.
2. Add the veggies to the pot along with broth to cover (add water if needed).
3. Blend the tomatoes, dates, seasonings and water then add them to the pot.
4. Cover and cook for about 45 minutes until veggies are soft.
5. Season to taste with salt and pepper or your favorite seasoning.
6. With a potato masher, mash some of the stew to thicken the broth and create a chunky stew. You can also blend some of the soup in a blender, then add back into the stew to make it thicker.

Makeovers (Animal => Plant)

Burgers

MAKES 1 SERVING

1 veggie patty
½ onion, thinly sliced, sautéed
¼ cup mushrooms, sautéed
Hamburger bun, toasted
Condiments: mayo, mustard, relish,
  BBQ sauce to taste
Fixings: roasted peppers, sliced
  avocado, fresh sprouts, lettuce, basil
  leaves as desired

1. Sauté onions and mushrooms in water.
2. Cook patty on grill or in a pan.
3. Toast buns and spread with vegan mayo, mustard, relish, and BBQ sauce.
4. Add patty, onions, and mushrooms, roasted peppers, sliced avocado, fresh sprouts, lettuce, and basil leaves.
5. Place the top bun, cut in half, and serve.

Easy Portobello Fajitas

Recipe by: Tracy Childs of Veg-Appeal

MAKES 2 SERVINGS

½ onion, thinly sliced
About 3 Tablespoons of water
2 large Portobello caps, thickly sliced
2 cloves garlic, minced
½ teaspoon ground cumin
½ teaspoon chipotle powder
1 jar of roasted red bell peppers, sliced
fresh cilantro to taste, chopped
½ cup shredded cabbage (red or green
  or a blend)
2 corn or whole-wheat flour tortillas
¼ cup of your favorite salsa
¼ cup *Tofu-Cashew Sour Cream (in
  "Dairy-Alternatives")*
Avocado slices, optional
Lime wedges, optional
Salt, to taste

1. Heat a sauté pan and add the onion. Sauté until browned, adding water by the tablespoon as needed.
2. Add the garlic, Portobello slices and sprinkle with the dried spices and salt to taste. Add another tablespoon of water to prevent burning if needed. Lower the heat to low, and cover to brown and soften the mushrooms. Check after a few minutes and turn them over. Increase the heat to braise them.
3. Meanwhile, heat the tortillas individually over a flame, in the toaster oven, or in wrapped foil in a hot oven.
4. To make each taco, place a couple of mushroom slices in a tortilla and top with the red bell pepper slices, cilantro, cabbage, salsa and finally a dollop of *Tofu-Cashew Sour Cream*. Add the other toppings if using.

VARIATIONS:

Instead of tortillas, make lettuce wraps or serve the ingredients over a bowl of greens topped with *Fat-Free Baked Tortilla Chips* (in "Snacks").

Pizza

Pizza is a staple of college students and large families everywhere. This recipe is a makeover of traditional pizza using non-dairy cheese, veggie sausage, and no added oil. This is a transitional dish. Using a pizza stone means less cooking time.

1 package pizza dough
1 jar marinara or pizza sauce
1 teaspoon minced garlic
lemon pepper, oregano, Italian spices
1 package (8-ounce) non-dairy
  mozzarella style cheese shreds
½ large onion, sliced
1 green bell pepper, sliced into rings
1 red bell pepper, sliced into rings
2 tomatoes, sliced
1 small can of sliced olives
1 cup mushrooms, sliced
2 veggie sausages, sliced
1 small jar of artichoke hearts

1. Heat oven to 450°F. If using pizza stone, place it in the oven at this time.
2. Let pizza dough rise according to the directions, then roll it out on a floured wood cutting board.
3. If using one, carefully remove hot pizza stone from oven using oven mitts and set it on stove top or trivet. Transfer the dough to the pizza stone, or a round pizza pan.
4. Bake the crust alone for 7 to 8 minutes.
5. Remove the crust from the oven.
6. Spread sauce over the crust. Add minced garlic and spread around the top. Add lemon pepper, oregano and Italian seasoning. Then, add non-dairy cheese.
7. Add onions, bell peppers, sliced tomatoes, artichoke hearts, sliced olives and mushrooms and sliced veggie sausage pieces.
8. Sprinkle more Italian seasoning and top with more cheese if you like it real cheesy.
9. Return to the oven and cook for 15-20 minutes until cheese is melted. If using pizza stone, cook for only 8-10 minutes.

VARIATIONS:

Use a ready-made pizza crust instead of prepared pizza dough. Check the ingredients first. Many crusts contain dairy products.

Replace the sausage with vegan pepperoni, chick'n, Tofurkey, or other meat substitute. Or remove it to create an all-veggie pizza.

For Hawaiian pineapple pizza, include less veggies (such as onions and mushrooms), a vegan ham substitute, and small pineapple pieces.

Try the *Smoky White Pizza Sauce* (in "Sauces").

NOTES:

Using a pizza stone requires less cooking time overall. You may need to pre-cook the onions and bell peppers in the microwave for about three minutes to ensure that they cook fully.

Replacing the flavor of dairy-based cheese on pizza can be challenging. I found the mozzarella shreds from Trader Joe's to be acceptable. There are many more brands available in markets and online. Try them, and let your taste buds be your guide.

Spaghetti and Sauce

MAKES 8 - 10 SERVINGS

1 spaghetti squash, steamed
1 package Trader Joes Meatless meatballs or *Eggplant Beanballs* in "Main Dishes"
1 cup marinade (see recipe for marinade for grilled veggies, or use Tamari sauce)
1 teaspoon minced garlic
1 onion, peeled, halved, cored, & sliced
1 jar Trader Joes marinara sauce or Sprouts roasted tomatoes
½ lemon, juice of
1 teaspoon Italian seasoning
1 teaspoon oregano
1 Tablespoon olive oil (omit if you are limiting oil)
½ cup sliced baby carrots
1 yellow squash, halved & sliced
1 zucchini, sliced
1 green bell pepper, diced
½ each red, yellow, & orange peppers, diced
8-10 button mushrooms, cleaned & sliced
1 can (2.25 oz) sliced olives, drained
salt & pepper to taste
2 teaspoons monk fruit sweetener or agave, optional
Parmesan Cheese (in "Dairy Alternatives")

1. Cut the spaghetti squash in half and steam for 30 minutes or more until you can separate the fibers easily with a fork. Store collected squash in a bowl and set aside.
2. Place meatless meatballs in marinade while you prepare the sauce.
3. In a large pot, heat minced garlic briefly, then add onions, and sauté on medium heat until carmelized. Add water as needed to prevent burning.
4. Add marinara sauce to onions and flavor with lemon juice, Italian seasoning, and oregano to taste. Add olive oil, if using. Let simmer.
5. Meanwhile, chop carrots, zucchini, yellow squash, bell pepper, and mushrooms.
6. Stir in vegetables and sliced olives. Cook on medium for 1 to 2 hours to thicken.
7. Add meatless meatballs to the sauce in the last 10 minutes.
8. Salt and pepper to taste.
9. Adjust sweetness, with monk fruit sweetener, agave or other sweetener, if desired.
10. Place spaghetti squash strands on a large plate or bowl. Reheat if necessary.
11. Scoop generous portions of sauce on the squash base.
12. Top with vegan parmesan cheese if desired.

VARIATIONS:

Use traditional pasta or noodles made from whole wheat, quinoa, kamut, spelt, or brown rice.
Create "noodles" by processing a raw zucchini through a spiralizer.

Tacos and Fixings

See also Transforming your Meals, Phase 2 in chapter 5.

MAKES 4 SERVINGS

1 cup salsa - your choice, divided
1 ½ cups un-beef crumbles. The Trader Joe's brand works well.
1 tsp minced garlic
1 onion, sliced and sauteed in water or a bit of water or oil
4 mushrooms, sliced and sauteed in a bit of water or oil
4 leaves red lettuce, chopped
¼ cup fresh basil, chopped
1 roma tomato, sliced
1 avocado, sliced
½ fire-roasted pepper
1 cup fresh alfalfa sprouts
½ can black olives, sliced
½ cup Sour Supreme non-dairy sour cream
4 teaspoons Walden farms sugar-free ketchup
½ cup vegan cheese, such as Trader Joe's mozzarella style shreds
4 tortillas, corn or flour. Use burrito sized tortillas if you want large tacos.

1. Mix about 1/3 cup salsa with the unbeef crumbles and heat in a microwave safe covered dish for about 2 minutes.
2. In a sauté pan, heat minced garlic briefly, then add onions, and sauté on medium heat until carmelized. Add water as needed to prevent burning. Remove the onions, and sauté the mushrooms in the same pan, adding water as needed.
3. Prepare the fixings and assemble on a large platter or two. Chop some lettuce and basil. Slice some tomato and avocado. Cut up some fire-roasted pepper. Rinse some fresh sprouts. Open a small can of black olives. Pull out some non-dairy sour cream and ketchup.
4. Sprinkle some cheese style shreds on the tortillas and heat in the microwave or oven until the cheese begins to melt.
5. Add ingredients in any order that you choose, and enjoy.

VARIATIONS:

Tortillas come in many sizes and flavors. Look for tortillas made from whole-wheat or corn meal rather than white flour. There are tortillas made from almond flour, coconut flour, kale, brown rice, sprouted grains, chia and quinoa. Some are gluten-free; some are low oil. You can also use large leaves such as collards to contain the fixings.

Salads and Sides

Barbequed Chick'n Salad

Inspired by Native Foods Restaurant

This salad is quick and easy to prepare. See also Transforming your Meals, Phase 1 (Salad) .

MAKES 4 SERVINGS

12 ounces chick'n
1 cup marinade (in "Sauces, Syrups, and Dressings")
3 cups lettuce, torn
½ jicama, cubed
1 tomato, diced
1 avocado, sliced
1 can corn
1 can beans, rinsed and drained
¾ cup sauce (BBQ sauce, chipotle sauce, or ranch dressing)

1. Marinate the chick'n while preparing the other ingredients.
2. Tear the lettuce into bite-sized pieces.
3. Peel the jicama and cut into cubes.
4. Dice the tomato and slice the avocado.
5. Drain the can of corn.
6. Rinse and drain the can of beans.
7. Heat the chick'n according to the directions.
8. Arrange ingredients side-by-side on individual plates.
9. Top with the sauce and/or dressing and serve.

Garden Barley Salad with Italian Tofu Bites

Recipe by: Tracy Childs of Veg-Appeal

MAKES 8 SMALL SERVINGS

1 cup barley
1 cup *Italian Tofu Bites* (in "Appetizers") or cooked kidney beans, drained and rinsed
1 cup steamed carrots
2 cups steamed broccoli florets
1 cup cherry tomatoes, halved
½ cup green onions, sliced or chopped parsley, optional
1 Tablespoon balsamic vinegar
2 Tablespoons *Creamy Low-Fat Mayo* (in "From Scratch")
1 Tablespoon Dijon-style mustard
1 teaspoon oregano or Italian seasoning
Salt and pepper to taste
Other flavor additions/substitutions: chopped roasted or raw red peppers, sliced olives, drained artichokes, cubes of baked tofu, thawed frozen peas, broccoli and/or corn, other steamed vegetables like green beans. Change up the flavors!

1. Add 1 cup barley to 4 cups boiling water. Cook until tender (test it to make sure it's to your liking as far as tender/chewy).
2. Add the carrots and then the broccoli during the last few minutes. Drain well and allow to cool.
3. Combine the barley, beans or Italian Tofu Bites, broccoli, carrots, tomatoes, and green onion in a large bowl.
4. Stir in the mayonnaise, balsamic vinegar, mustard and oregano.

NOTE:

Trader Joe's has 10-minute barley. Regular pearled barley will cook in about 25 minutes.

Garlic Bread (Low-Fat)

Recipe by: Tracy Childs of Veg-Appeal

MAKES 4 SERVINGS

4 slices whole grain bread
**¼ cup homemade *Parmesan "Cheese"*
(from "Dairy Alternatives")**
**2-3 Tablespoons water (or enough to
make paste)**
1-2 cloves garlic, pressed
**1 teaspoon dried basil or Italian
seasoning**

1. In a small bowl, stir together the Parmesan "cheese", water, pressed garlic and basil adding more "cheese" or water to make a spreadable paste.
2. Spread slices of bread evenly with the paste. Broil or toast until browned on the edges, or to taste.

Garlicky Greens

This dish is a simple and tasty way to eat your greens.

MAKES 5 SERVINGS

5 garlic cloves, pressed or minced
**1 large bunch kale, stemmed, rinsed
well, and chopped into ½-inch pieces
(about 4 cups, tightly packed)**
2 Tablespoons fresh lemon juice
½ teaspoon sea salt, or to taste
¼ teaspoon fresh black pepper
**¼ teaspoon crushed red pepper flakes,
optional**
**1 Tablespoon olive oil or vegetable
broth, optional**

1. Place ¼ cup water in a large sauté pan and heat over medium-high heat. When water begins to simmer, add garlic and cook for two 2 minutes, stirring frequently.
2. Add kale, cover, and cook until just tender, about 5 minutes, stirring frequently with tongs. Transfer to a bowl.
3. Add remaining ingredients, and stir well before serving.

VARIATIONS:

Replace kale with other greens, such as collards, Swiss chard, mustard greens, etc.
Add apple cider vinegar, liquid aminos, nutritional yeast, and/or a few drops of liquid smoke to change up the flavor.

Heavenly Salad

Inspired by Loving Hut restaurants

This salad is a nice variation on coleslaw.

MAKES 8 SERVINGS

1 green cabbage (about 3 cups), shredded
2 cups (5 large) carrots, shredded
1 cup red cabbage, shredded
½ green bell pepper, sliced
½ red bell pepper, sliced
½ cup shredded jicama
½ cup chopped peanuts
1 cup baked tofu, sliced (or other mock meat)
½ cup Quick Balsamic Dressing (in "Sauces, Syrups, and Dressings") or to taste
1 small bunch mint leaves
1 small bunch basil leaves

1. Shred the veggies (except for mint, basil, peanuts and tofu) in a food processor. May have to do several batches.
2. Place the shredded veggies into a large mixing bowl.
3. Mix in the dressing.
4. Sprinkle peanuts and tofu on top. Garnish with mint and basil leaves.

Not Refried Black Beans

Recipe by: Tracy Childs of Veg-Appeal

There's no reason to add lard or oil to this flavorful and creamy "refried" bean recipe!

MAKES ABOUT 6 CUPS

2 cups black beans, soaked overnight (in plenty of water), drained and rinsed
1 onion, chopped
1 small bunch cilantro, chopped (OK to include stems)
¼ teaspoon chipotle powder
½ teaspoon cumin
2 cups water (or more if not using pressure cooker)
1 teaspoon salt (or to taste)
½ teaspoon black pepper (or to taste)

1. Heat a large pan and add the chopped onions, sautéing and adding water by the tablespoon, as necessary to avoid burning or sticking.
2. Add the cilantro and spices and sauté for a few more minutes.
3. Add the beans and water, covering the beans by a at least 1 inch of water.
4. If using a pressure cooker, cook the beans to manufacturer's directions (about 10-15 mins) and allow the pressure to come down naturally (about 25-35 mins). It should take an hour total.
5. If cooking in a pan, bring to a boil then reduce to simmer, partially covered until tender, about 1-1½ hours until beans are very tender, adding additional water if the beans look dry and are not covered completely.
6. Drain excess liquid (reserving it) and if you want "refried" beans, mash the beans using a potato masher, leaving some whole. Add reserved liquid if needed. The beans tend to thicken as they cool but you can also drain some excess liquid.
7. Add salt and pepper and adjust to taste.

4

Potato Salad

MAKES 6 SERVINGS

6 medium new potatoes
⅓ cup finely chopped onion
½ teaspoon salt
¼ teaspoon ground pepper
¼ cup Italian dressing
½ cup non-dairy mayonnaise
2 teaspoon mustard
2 stalks finely chopped celery
1 small can sliced olives
¼ cup pickle relish
1 Tablespoon balsamic vinegar

1. Clean and boil potatoes in an uncovered saucepan for 20 to 25 minutes. Don't overcook.
2. Drain well, and let cool. Cube potatoes.
3. In a large bowl, combine all dressings and seasonings.
4. Add potatoes and toss lightly.
5. Chill for 6 to 24 hours.

Quinoa-Stuffed Bell Peppers

Modified from Diethood.com

MAKES 8 SERVINGS

Non-stick spray for baking dish
4 bell peppers, halved lengthwise, seeded
2 cups vegetable broth
1 cup uncooked quinoa, rinsed well
3 Tablespoons water
1 small yellow onion, diced
⅛ teaspoon salt
1 cup canned sweet corn
1 cup canned black beans
1 cup grape tomatoes, quartered
½ teaspoon chili powder, or to taste

Quinoa-Stuffed Bell Peppers (cont)

¼ teaspoon cayenne pepper
½ Tablespoon dried parsley
salt and fresh ground pepper, to taste
2 cups shredded non-dairy cheese, divided
non-dairy yogurt for garnish, optional

1. Spray a baking dish with non-stick spray.
2. Place halved bell peppers in casserole dish and set aside.
3. In a small saucepan, combine vegetable broth and (well-rinsed) quinoa, and bring to a boil. Lower to a simmer, cover, and continue to cook for 15 minutes.
4. Remove from heat, gently fluff with a fork, and set aside.
5. Preheat oven to 350°F.
6. In a sauté pan, heat water over medium heat. Add diced onions and add salt. Cook for 1 minute, or until translucent.
7. Stir in sweet corn and beans; continue to cook for 2 minutes, or until fragrant.
8. Stir in tomatoes and cooked quinoa; season with chili powder, cayenne pepper, dried parsley, salt, and pepper.
9. Add 1 cup non-dairy cheese; mix well and continue to cook for 3 to 4 minutes, or until everything is heated through and the cheese is melted.
10. Remove from heat.
11. Divide mixture evenly between peppers, packing the quinoa mixture tightly into the hollow pepper shells.
12. Bake for 30 minutes.
13. Remove from oven, and top each pepper with remaining cheese.
14. Put back in the oven and continue to bake for 5 minutes, or until cheese is melted.
15. Remove from oven and let cool 5 minutes.
16. Serve with a dollop of non-dairy yogurt, if desired.

Roasted Vegetables

Roasting is a tasty way to prepare vegetables. Use the *Marinade for Roasted Vegetables* (in "Sauces, Syrups, and Dressings"), or make your own.

MAKES 6 SERVINGS

1 large head of broccoli, florets chopped off from the stalk
1 sweet potato. sliced
1 large zucchini, sliced and cut into half moons
1 large yellow squash, sliced and cut into half moons
1 cup cherry tomatoes, sliced in halves
2 golden beets, sliced
½ pineapple, cut into spears
1 green bell pepper, sliced
1 red bell pepper, sliced
1 medium onion, sliced
3 carrots, sliced
¾ cup mushrooms, sliced
1 cup marinade

1. Chop and slice the vegetables and fruit. Place in a large bowl.
2. Add marinade to vegetable bowl and mix well to coat veggies. Let sit for 30 minutes, stirring on occasion.
3. Preheat oven to 425°F.
4. Prepare cooking pans with non-stick spray or use silicone mats.
5. Divide the vegetables among two or three or four pans so that they are in a single layer.
6. Roast vegetables for 15 minutes. Remove from oven and stir.
7. Return to oven and roast for another 15 minutes for a total of 30 minutes. Keep an eye on them, though, so they don't burn. Some ovens run hotter than others!

Spanish Quinoa Pilaf

Recipe by: Tracy Childs of Veg-Appeal

MAKES 4 SERVINGS

1½ cups quinoa rinsed well and drained
1¾ cups water or vegetable broth
1 can diced & fire roasted tomatoes with green chilies
¼ teaspoon salt, optional (can leave out salt if it's in broth or tomatoes)
1 teaspoon garlic powder
½ teaspoon onion powder
1 teaspoon cumin
½ cup frozen sweet corn, optional
½ cup frozen peas, optional

1. Heat water or vegetable broth until boiling.
2. Add the quinoa and the rest of the ingredients, except corn and peas.
3. Bring back to a boil and turn down to low heat.
4. Allow the mixture to simmer for about 15 minutes, until soft.
5. Turn off heat and add the optional corn and peas.

Spicy Greens Salad with Strawberry Vinaigrette

Recipe by: Tracy Childs of Veg-Appeal

MAKES 4 SERVINGS

5 or more cups mixed spicy and mild greens (such as arugula, chard, spinach, and kale)
1 Asian pear, cored and diced
⅓ cup fresh blueberries or sliced red grapes
2 Tablespoons chopped brazil nuts
1 blood (or other) orange, diced
1 recipe *Strawberry Vinaigrette* (in "Sauces, Syrups and Dressings")

1. Toss the salad ingredients together.
2. Add about half of the dressing, and toss gently, adding more dressing as needed.

Sweet and Spicy Kasha Vegetable Salad

Kasha is one of the healthiest foods available today. In fact, the nutrition in kasha is naturally high, earning it the coveted "superfood" title. One 1¼ cup serving of this recipe contains nearly 6 g of protein, 5 g of fiber, nearly 306 mg of potassium (essential for muscle strength). Plus, one serving contains only 132 calories, so it's perfect for those on a weight loss plan. Serve it as a side with a low-calorie wrap, green salad, and fruit for a complete meal.

MAKES ABOUT 4 SERVINGS

1 cup cooked and cooled *Kasha* (in "From Scratch")
1 cup garbanzo beans, cooked
1 small yellow or red bell pepper, chopped
1 medium cucumber, peeled, seeded, and diced
1-2 large tomatoes, diced
½ cup green onions, chopped
½ cup parsley, coarsely chopped
½ cup fresh mint, coarsely chopped
¼ cup lemon juice
1 Tablespoon maple syrup or other sweetener
1 Tablespoon Sriracha
1 Tablespoon water
½ teaspoon sea salt

1. Place the cooled kasha in a large bowl.
2. Add the chopped vegetables, herbs, and garbanzo beans to the kasha. Toss well.
3. Add the lemon juice, sriracha, sweetener, sea salt, and water. Toss to combine.
4. Chill for about an hour to allow the flavors to combine and serve.

Wok-Tossed Cabbage Salad

Modified from Mark Reinfeld

Stir-frying the ingredients in this recipe unlocks a much deeper flavor than the average salad. Heating cabbage in the wok for a minute or two gives it a softer texture.

MAKES ABOUT 7 CUPS

2 Tablespoons toasted sesame oil
1 Tablespoon brown mustard seeds
15 curry leaves, optional
1 pinch garlic salt
1 pinch onion salt
1-2 green chilies, seeds removed, and thinly sliced
3 Tablespoons fresh lemon juice
½ teaspoon sea salt, or to taste
6 cups finely shredded green cabbage
1 cup shredded carrot (about 1 large carrot)
2 Tablespoons rice vinegar
1 Tablespoon soy sauce, or to taste
2 Tablespoons fresh cilantro, minced
½ cup roasted peanuts

1. Heat a wok or pot over medium heat. Add the oil and heat it for 1 minute, then add brown mustard seeds. When they start to crackle, add the curry leaves (if using), garlic salt, onion salt, and chilies. Stir for 1 minute.
2. Add lemon juice and salt and stir. Add cabbage and carrot, and toss quickly for 1 to 2 minutes, just enough to coat the cabbage and soften it slightly. Add rice vinegar and soy sauce, to taste.
3. Turn off the heat, and transfer to a serving bowl. Top with cilantro and peanuts, and serve.

Sandwiches and Wraps

Basil Pinwheels

Basil pinwheels are basically lunch wraps sliced into sections, and served as appetizers. (See *Lunch Wraps* in this section.)

MAKES 24-30 PINWHEELS

1. Prepare lunch wraps per recipe below, except do not fold sides in.
2. Fill lettuce and basil all the way to the sides.
3. Roll the tortillas tightly.
4. Cut into 1½-inch segments, using toothpicks to secure the tortilla. The end segments will have lettuce protruding.
5. Place on platter and serve.

Chickpea No-Tuna Salad Wraps

Recipe by: Tracy Childs of Veg-Appeal

MAKES 6 SERVINGS

One 15-ounce can garbanzo beans (chickpeas); drained and rinsed
1 celery stalk, finely chopped (or 2 stalks if you'd like more crunchiness)
½ cup onion, finely chopped
1 Tablespoon capers
¼ cup homemade *Tofu-Cashew Mayonnaise* (in "From Scratch") or fat-free or low-fat vegan mayonnaise (low-fat Veganaise and Nayonaise brands are good)
1 Tablespoon lemon juice
1 Tablespoon mustard of choice (stoneground is delicious)
1 teaspoon dulse (seaweed) flakes, optional (for a fishier taste)
6 large Romaine leaves, whole grain bread or wraps/tortillas to serve

1. Coarsely chop beans in a food processor or mash beans with a potato masher. Do not over process to a smooth consistency; you want it to have some texture.
2. Place beans in a bowl and mix with chopped celery, capers, and onion.
3. Add the mayo, and other dressing ingredients to the chickpea mixture. Mix well and chill.
4. Serve on romaine leaves with grated carrots, beets and/or zucchini garnish, as a sandwich on whole wheat, rye or pumpernickel bread, in a wrap or with whole grain crackers or cut veggies as a snack.

Easy Meatless Meatball Sandwich

Inspired by Native Foods Restaurant Italian Sub sandwich

MAKES 6 SERVINGS

6 mini sandwich baguettes
1 bag Trader Joe's frozen meatless meatballs
1 sweet onion, sliced
12 ounce jar roasted red peppers
1 jar Trader Joe's organic marinara sauce
Non-dairy Parmesan style topping

1. Sauté onions in water or veggie broth until tender.
2. Slice red peppers into thin strips. Add peppers to onions, and cook for about two minutes. Set aside.
3. Pour marinara sauce into medium sized saucepan.
4. Add frozen meatballs, and cook over medium heat until meatballs are warmed (about 10 minutes).
5. Meanwhile, slice baguettes (not all the way through) and heat in toaster oven.
6. Spoon meatball mixture and onion/pepper mixture into baguettes.
7. Sprinkle with Parmesan topping, if desired, and serve.

Eggless Salad Rainbow Wraps

Recipe by: Tracy Childs of Veg-Appeal

These tasty wraps have the flavor and appearance of egg salad without the saturated fat and cholesterol. This versatile spread can also be used in sandwiches, stuffed in celery, along with crackers or on a toasted rice cake. It can be easily put together using a food processor!

MAKES 5-6 WRAPS OR ABOUT 2 ½ CUPS

14-16 ounces firm tofu, drained and pressed between paper towels, if necessary (to remove excess moisture)
1 green onion, finely chopped
2 stalks celery, finely chopped
1 Tablespoon chopped parsley, optional
2 Tablespoons pickle relish (or 1-2 small dill pickles, chopped – or use both!)
2-3 Tablespoons *Tofu-Cashew Mayonnaise* (Recipe in "From Scratch)
1 Tablespoon prepared mustard of choice
2 teaspoons lemon juice
½ teaspoon salt or black salt (kala namak)
½ teaspoon ground cumin
1 teaspoon turmeric
½ teaspoon garlic powder
freshly ground pepper to taste
½ teaspoon curry powder, optional
5 whole grain tortillas, collard leaves, or romaine lettuce leaves
baby spinach
cherry tomatoes
2-3 cucumbers, thinly sliced lengthwise
grated carrots

1. Mash the tofu with a fork or potato masher or in the food processor.
2. Stir in green onion, celery, relish, mayonnaise, mustard, lemon juice (if using) and seasonings.
3. Taste and adjust seasoning if necessary.
4. Spread ½ cup on each wrap on the side nearest to you and garnish with spinach, cucumbers, cherry tomato and grated carrots.
5. Roll up and serve!

NOTE:

Using black salt adds and "eggy" flavor to to the dish.

Lunch Wraps

These lunch wraps are great for travel. If you make a wrap in the morning and keep it as cool as possible, it can make a handy lunch when you are on the go.

MAKES 6 SERVINGS

6 (10-inch) flour tortillas, burrito or grande size burrito

1 (8 ounce) package non-dairy cream cheese, softened

1 cup cooked quinoa

3 ripe avocados

12 small pieces of chick'n

6 2-inch pieces roasted red peppers

1 cup sun-dried tomatoes

1 small can sliced olives

4 ounces fresh basil

1 small bunch of sprouts

12 leaves red leaf lettuce, rinsed

Optional: shredded carrots, jicama, red cabbage, non-dairy cheese, hemp seeds, or hummus

1. Spread cream cheese on each tortilla. Cover the tortilla completely, but lightly. Spread quinoa horizontally across the center of each tortilla. Spread avocado, and mix with the quinoa to hold in place.
2. Arrange chick'n across the middle of each tortilla.
3. Add roasted red peppers, sun-dried tomatoes, and olives. Be careful not to fill too full.
4. Finish with basil, sprouts, and lettuce on top of the other ingredients across the center of each tortilla. Do not place ingredients too close to tortilla edges.
5. Fold the two sides in toward the center, about an inch or so.
6. Starting at the bottom, tightly roll up each tortilla, incorporating all the contents and maintaining the folded sides.

VARIATIONS:

Replace chick'n strips with precooked lentils, beans, or other protein source.
Use cranberries instead of sun-dried tomatoes.
Use two pieces of rice paper instead of the tortilla. It needs to be a double layer to make it strong enough for transporting them.

Mediterranean Bean Burgers

Recipe by: Tracy Childs of Veg-Appeal

MAKES 6-7 BURGERS

2 cans (or 3 cups cooked) kidney beans, drained and rinsed

1-2 medium to large cloves garlic, roughly chopped (use 1 for kid-friendly burgers)

2½ Tablespoons tomato paste

1½ Tablespoon red wine or balsamic vinegar

1 teaspoon (a little generous) Dijon mustard

¾ cup green onions, sliced (using mostly green portion, and less white)

¼ cup fresh parsley, roughly chopped

2 Tablespoons fresh oregano, chopped (fresh is best, but if you don't have it, substitute about 1½-2 teaspoons dried oregano)

½ teaspoon (rounded) sea salt

freshly ground black pepper to taste

1¼ cups rolled oats (use certified gluten-free if possible)

⅓-½ cup Kalamata olives, roughly chopped

¼ cup diced red bell pepper

1. In a food processor, combine the kidney beans, garlic, tomato paste, vinegar, and mustard. Pulse until puréed.
2. Add the green onions, parsley, oregano, salt, and pepper to taste, and process to break up and blend. Add the oats and pulse to begin to incorporate.
3. Transfer the mixture to a large bowl (or remove the blade) and stir in the olives and red bell pepper.
4. Refrigerate the mixture for 30-45 minutes, then shape into patties with your hands.
5. To cook, brush about ½ teaspoon of oil over a heated skillet on medium/medium-high heat. Cook the patties for 6-8 minutes per side, or until golden brown. Alternatively, bake the patties for about 15-20 minutes at 400°F, flipping once through cooking.

Thai Peanut Burgers

Recipe adapted by Tracy Childs from a recipe by Kim Campbell of PlantPure Nation

MAKES 10 BURGERS

1 small onion, roughly chopped
5 cloves garlic
2 cups greens (can be mix of spinach, kale, arugula, cilantro, mint)
1 cup cooked sweet potato chunks
1½ cups cooked chickpeas
1½ cups quick cooking oats (or rolled oats)
2 Tablespoons flaxseeds, ground
1 Tablespoon green or red Thai curry paste (Thai Kitchen is a good brand)
½ cup peanut butter powder (low fat)
1 Tablespoon Bragg Liquid Aminos
Juice of 1 lime
Garnish: *Creamy Thai Peanut Sauce* (in "Sauces, Syrups and Dressings")

1. Preheat the oven to 375°F.
2. If using rolled oats, process them quickly in a food processor or blender to break them down, making it easier for them to act as a binder to hold your burgers together.
3. In a food processor, pulse-chop the onion, garlic, greens, sweet potatoes, and chickpeas into small pieces.
4. Add the other ingredients and process so that everything is evenly chopped but not completely smooth.
5. With wet hands, form 10 patties, and place them on a large parchment-lined cookie sheet. Bake the patties for about 30 minutes, until browned on the bottom, then flip and cook for another 10 minutes, until firm and lightly browned.
6. Allow them to cool for 5-10 minutes before serving.
7. Serve each burger with a dollop of *Creamy Thai Peanut Sauce* on a toasted whole-grain bun, or on a large piece of romaine as a lettuce wrap.

Sauces, Syrups, and Dressings

Cashew Cream Sauce

This sauce is easy to make and works as a topping to almost any vegetable dish.

MAKES 2 CUPS

2 cups cashews
1¼ cup almond milk
1 clove garlic, minced
1 teaspoon lemon juice
1 teaspoon apple cider vinegar
½ teaspoon miso
1 teaspoon nutritional yeast
½ teaspoon salt
¼ teaspoon black pepper

1. Place cashews in a bowl. Cover with water and soak for about 2 hours. Drain and rinse thoroughly.
2. Place rinsed cashews in the bowl of a food processor or blender with the other ingredients. Puree until very, very smooth. Thin out with more almond milk to desired consistency.
3. Serve it right away, and store excess in fridge for 3-4 days or freeze.

Creamy Thai Peanut Sauce

Recipe by: Tracy Childs of Veg-Appeal

MAKES A LITTLE OVER 1 CUP

1 cup *Tofu-Cashew Mayonnaise* (in "From Scratch")
1 Tablespoon peanut butter powder
1 teaspoon red Thai curry paste
1 teaspoon lime juice
dash sriracha

1. Stir together all of the ingredients in a bowl.
2. Taste and adjust seasoning.

Creamy Wasabi Sauce

Recipe by: Tracy Childs of Veg-Appeal

This sauce can be made spicy or not and can be used as a dipping sauce, for vegan sushi, on Asian noodle bowls, or used in the *Sushi Bowl with Creamy Wasabi Sauce* (in "Main Dishes")

MAKES A BIT OVER 1 CUP

1 cup *Tofu-Cashew Mayonnaise* (in "From Scratch")
2 cloves garlic
3 teaspoons wasabi powder
1-2 teaspoon low-sodium soy sauce or Bragg Liquid Aminos
2 teaspoons lime juice
1 ½ Tablespoons pickled ginger
1 teaspoon juice from the pickled ginger
1 Tablespoon rice vinegar (or other light vinegar)
1 handful roughly chopped cilantro or fresh basil

1. Combine all of the above ingredients in a blender and blend into a smooth and creamy texture.
2. Taste and adjust flavor and spice levels – see NOTES.
3. Chill for an hour or so for flavors to develop.

NOTES:

When adjusting flavor, keep in mind: flavor develops over time so you may want to wait before adjusting. Ginger and wasabi add pungent spice, lime and vinegar add tartness, soy sauce adds saltiness, and pickled ginger juice adds sweet/spice. See Chapter 7 for more on flavor balancing.

Dijon Ranch Dressing

Recipe by: Tracy Childs of Veg-Appeal

This dressing is reminiscent of a (mild) blue cheese knock-off, especially when paired with a salad containing sauerkraut!

MAKES ABOUT 1 CUP

½ cup low-fat *Tofu-Cashew Mayonnaise* (in "From Scratch")
3 Tablespoons to ⅓ cup unsweetened plant milk (use less milk to make a dip, and more to make a dressing)
2 teaspoons Dijon mustard
¼ teaspoon mustard powder
½ teaspoon garlic powder
½ teaspoon onion powder
⅛ teaspoon salt
2 teaspoons lemon juice
fresh ground pepper to taste

1. Place all ingredients in a jar and stir well.
2. Chill well to let flavors develop before serving.

Easy Hummus Dressing

Recipe by: Tracy Childs of Veg-Appeal

MAKES ABOUT ½ CUP

½ cup garlic hummus
2 Tablespoons orange juice
1 Tablespoon Dijon mustard
splash of vinegar of choice

1. Whisk the ingredients together and
    enjoy.

Low Fat White Bean Aioli

Recipe by: Tracy Childs of Veg-Appeal

Traditionally aioli is a white sauce made from
mayonnaise, garlic, and other flavors. This
version cuts the fat dramatically by using silken
(smooth textured) tofu. It also has fiber and
protein from the beans – so it's a win-win,
adding lots of flavor. Use it as you would
mayonnaise, on top of potatoes, grilled or
roasted veggies, or as a creamy topping for
Roasted Eggplant with Bruschetta (in "Appetizers"),
pasta, pizza, falafel or veggie burgers.

MAKES ABOUT 2½ CUPS

½ cup silken tofu, drained
1 ½ cups cooked or 1 can great
    northern beans, drained, reserve
    cooking liquid
2 Tablespoons lemon juice
½ teaspoon lemon zest, optional
¼ teaspoon smoked salt (to taste – can
    use regular salt)
pepper to taste

1 Tablespoon nutritional yeast
½ teaspoon liquid smoke, optional (to
    add smoky cheesy flavor)
2 Tablespoons sesame tahini, optional
    (to create a richer sauce)
2-6 cloves raw or roasted garlic
    (depending on how garlicky you like it
    – if you have roasted garlic, the
    amount can be increased because the
    flavor is much milder).
Water as needed

1. Combine all ingredients in a blender and
    purée until smooth.
2. To achieve a pourable consistency, add
    reserved bean cooking liquid.
3. Taste and add additional garlic and other
    seasonings to taste.
4. Transfer to a jar, cover and chill until
    ready to heat gently to use.
5. The sauce will thicken as it chills – just
    add a bit of water to thin.

NOTE:

To make a richer and cheesier sauce for pizza,
add ¼ cup tahini and ½ teaspoon liquid smoke.
If your beans are already salted (from a can),
consider omitting the salt.

Marinade for Roasted Vegetables

How do you make a tasty marinade with minimal oil? Simple – by replacing some of the oil with veggie broth, and adding plenty of herbs and flavorings.

MAKES 1¼ CUPS

⅓ cup olive oil
⅓ cup veggie broth
⅓ cup balsamic vinegar
¼ cup minced onion
1-2 Tablespoons chopped fresh basil
1 teaspoon minced garlic
½ teaspoon kosher salt
¼ teaspoon fresh ground black pepper
1 teaspoon Worcestershire sauce,
½ teaspoon ginger paste, optional

1. Combine all ingredients in a bowl and mix well.
2. Marinate veggies for 3-4 hours, and then roast or grill.

Mushroom Cashew Gravy

Recipe by: Tracy Childs of Veg-Appeal

MAKES ABOUT 2½ CUPS

2 Tablespoons raw cashew pieces
1 small onion, chopped
1½ to 2 cups sliced mushrooms
3 cloves garlic, chopped
2 cups water or low-sodium vegetable broth
1-2 Tablespoons soy sauce, tamari, Bragg Liquid Aminos or shoyu (add more to taste, if needed)
1 Tablespoon mirin or cooking sherry, optional
2 Tablespoons garbanzo bean flour, whole wheat flour, or potato flour
2 Tablespoons nutritional yeast, optional
1 Tablespoon onion powder
1 teaspoon garlic powder (or 2 cloves garlic, chopped)
1 teaspoon Italian or poultry seasoning
freshly ground pepper to taste

1. Soak cashews for 3-8 hours.
2. In a heated medium saucepan, place the chopped onions and start to sauté. Add the mushrooms and garlic and add splashes of broth to continue cooking until tender without burning.
3. Meanwhile, combine the rest of the ingredients in a blender and process until completely smooth.
4. Transfer this mixture to the saucepan; add to the sautéed vegetables. Simmer, stirring constantly until thickened, adding additional water if needed. Taste and add additional soy sauce if needed.

Quick Balsamic Dressing

Recipe by: Tracy Childs of Veg-Appeal

MAKES ABOUT ⅓ CUP

¼ cup balsamic vinegar or apple cider
  vinegar
1 Tablespoon maple syrup
1 Tablespoon of Dijon mustard
Salt & pepper to taste

1. Whisk all ingredients together.

Quick Cheezy Sauce

MAKES ABOUT 1¾ CUPS

1 cup raw cashew pieces
3 Tablespoons nutritional yeast
½ teaspoon sea salt, or to taste
½ teaspoon ground turmeric, optional
⅛ teaspoon freshly ground black
  pepper
Pinch of cayenne pepper or chipotle
  chile powder
¾ cup filtered water

1. Place the cashews in a bowl with ample water to cover. Allow to sit for 2 hours or more to soften. Rinse and drain well.
2. Transfer to a blender along with the remaining ingredients, including the filtered water.
3. Blend until creamy. Use immediately.

VARIATIONS:

Add 1 Tablespoon of an ethnic spice blend.
Add 1 Tablespoon of minced fresh cilantro, basil, or flat-leaf parsley, or 2 teaspoons of minced fresh dill.
Blend the cheese with 1 cup of raw or roasted red bell pepper.
Toss with elbow pasta for a delicious spin on mac 'n' cheese.

Roasted Vegetable Sauce

This makes a delicious sauce to pour over steamed veggies or another vegetable dish.

MAKES ABOUT 3 CUPS

VEGETABLES

2–3 medium tomatoes, quartered (3 cups)
1 large onion, chopped (2 cups)
1 medium zucchini, chopped (1½ cups)

FLAVORINGS

6 large garlic cloves
2 teaspoons sea salt or to taste
¾ teaspoon fresh ground black pepper
4 teaspoons balsamic vinegar
2 Tablespoons basil, minced
2 Tablespoons fresh flat-leaf parsley, minced
2 Tablespoons nutritional yeast
¾ teaspoon oregano, dried
¼ teaspoon crushed red pepper flakes, optional
1 Tablespoon soy sauce, optional

OIL

3 Tablespoons olive oil

1. Preheat oven to 400°F.
2. Place tomatoes, onion, zucchini, in a mixing bowl. Put the flavorings in a second small mixing bowl, and mix well. Then pour the flavorings over the veggies. Stir the veggies and liquid well.
3. Arrange the veggies on a silicone mat on a baking sheet.
4. Coat veggies with oil and roast for 30 minutes or until vegetables are soft.
5. Let cool briefly, then place in a blender, and blend well.

Smoky BBQ Sauce

Modified from Vegan Fusion

MAKES 2 CUPS

1 6-oz. can unsalted tomato paste
½ cup filtered water
¼ cup molasses
2 Tablespoons raw unfiltered apple cider vinegar
2 Tablespoons maple syrup
1½ teaspoons chili powder
½ teaspoon Chinese 5 spices
1 teaspoon sea salt
1 teaspoon soy sauce
½ teaspoon ground black pepper
¼ teaspoon all-natural liquid smoke
⅛ teaspoon clove powder

1. In a large bowl, prepare the BBQ sauce by combining all ingredients and whisking well.
2. Use immediately.

Smoky White Pizza Sauce

Modified from Patty "Sassy" Knutson at vegancoach.com

This is not a recipe or a template. This is an opportunity for you to take a list of ingredients and make a wonderful recipe-free pizza sauce using the skills presented in Chapter 7.

MAKES ABOUT 1 CUP

Cashews (approximately 3 handfuls)
Lemon juice
Coconut nectar
Nutritional yeast
Onion powder
Garlic powder
Tamari soy sauce
Extra-virgin olive oil
Liquid Smoke
Sea salt & freshly ground black pepper
Filtered water, to desired consistency

1. Soak the cashews in water for 1 to 2 hours to soften.
2. Drain and rinse the cashews, and place in a blender.
3. To the soaked cashews, add a Tablespoon or two of lemon juice, coconut nectar, and nutritional yeast. Then add lesser amounts (a teaspoon or two) of the onion powder, garlic powder, Tamari, and olive oil. The goal is to build the overall flavor one ingredient at a time, taste-testing as you go. By adding ingredients in small increments, you can always add more later to balance the flavors. If you add an excessive amount of something potent like lemon juice or liquid smoke, for example, you may not be able to bring the flavors into balance.
4. Add ¼ teaspoon or less of the Liquid Smoke. It is very potent.
5. Add ¼ teaspoon of ground black pepper. (Hold off on the salt for the moment.)
6. Now, blend your creation (add a little water if necessary) and give it a taste. If it needs to be more sweet, add some coconut nectar. If it needs to be more sour, add a little bit of lemon juice. If it needs to be more salty, add more Tamari or sea salt.
7. Add water VERY slowly. You only need enough water for your sauce to blend easily. If you make it too thin, it won't firm up in the heat of the oven.
8. Continue adding ingredients until you have the taste just right. Add water slowly to make the sauce just thin enough to pour.
9. Pour the sauce onto your pizza and top with your favorite ingredients. You can freeze any leftover sauce for later use.

Spicy Thai Almond Sauce

Recipe by: Tracy Childs of Veg-Appeal

This sauce can be made spicy or not and can be used as a dipping sauce, Asian noodle sauce, or salad dressing or over veggies. Very versatile! The sauce may thicken over time, and you can add additional water before serving if using as a dressing.

MAKES 2 CUPS

3 dates, pitted
¾ cup water
¼ cup lemon or lime juice
2-inch piece of fresh ginger
2 Tablespoons Thai red curry paste
½ teaspoon crushed red pepper flakes
One handful of cilantro and/or chopped green onion
1 ½ Tablespoons Name Shoyu or Bragg Liquid Aminos (raw soy sauce)
½ cup almond butter

1. In blender, combine all ingredients and mix well until smooth.
2. Add additional water as needed to reach the desired consistency.
3. Serve immediately, or store for ready use.

Strawberry Vinaigrette

Recipe by: Tracy Childs of Veg-Appeal

MAKES ABOUT 1 CUP

1 cup sliced strawberries (about 7 medium strawberries)
¼ cup water
1 Tablespoon apple cider or balsamic vinegar
1 Tablespoon chopped white or yellow onion
1 Medjool date, pitted and chopped (or 2 smaller dates)
1 heaping teaspoon Dijon mustard
1 teaspoon chia seeds
salt and ground black pepper to taste
1 teaspoon chopped fresh rosemary or thyme, optional

1. Blend until smooth (or to your desired consistency).

Sweet Miso Lemon Dressing & Sauce

Recipe by: Tracy Childs of Veg-Appeal

This sweet-tangy sauce is great on salads but can be a topping for steamed veggies, cooked grains, or baked potatoes. Blending in zucchini lowers the fat, and replaces the oil in the dressing, along with adding nutrition.

MAKES ABOUT 2 CUPS

2 large dates, pitted and soaked (if hard)
1½ cup chopped fresh zucchini (large chunks)
½ cup water
2 large cloves garlic
2 teaspoons coconut or apple cider vinegar
⅓ cup lemon or lime juice (if you prefer it less tangy, reduce the amount and make up the difference with water)
¼ cup sesame tahini
½ cup nutritional yeast
½ teaspoon salt or 1 Tablespoon light miso

1. If the dates are hard, soak them in the ½ cup water for about ½ hour, using warm water if you are in a hurry. Do not drain.
2. Add the water and dates to a blender along with rest of the ingredients, except for the herbs, and blend.
3. Add more liquid (water or lemon juice) to desired consistency.
4. Serve, or refrigerate for up to one week, adding more lemon/water as it thickens over time.

Snacks

5-Ingredient Granola Bars

Modified from Minimalist Baker

Healthy, no bake granola bars with just 5 ingredients and a sweet, crunchy texture. Almond butter and maple syrup complement each other perfectly in this ideal portable breakfast or snack.

MAKES 10 BARS

1 heaping cup packed dates, pitted
¼ cup maple syrup
¼ cup almond butter
1 cup roasted unsalted almonds, loosely chopped
1½ cups rolled oats
optional additions: chocolate chips, dried fruit, nuts, banana chips, vanilla
  extract, shredded coconut, etc.

1. Process dates in a food processor on medium until small bits remain (about 15 seconds). It should form a dough-like consistency.
2. Optional step: Toast your oats (and almonds if raw) in a 350°F oven for 10-15 minutes or until slightly golden brown. Toasting adds a special flavor. Don't let them burn!
3. Place oats, almonds, and dates in a large mixing bowl, and set aside.
4. Warm syrup and almond butter in a small saucepan over low heat. Stir and pour over oat mixture and then mix, breaking up the dates to disperse throughout.
5. Once thoroughly mixed, transfer to an 8x8-inch baking dish or other small pan lined with plastic wrap or parchment paper so they lift out easily.
6. Press down firmly until uniformly flattened. Use something flat, like a drinking glass, to press down and really pack the bars, which helps them hold together better.
7. Cover with parchment or plastic wrap, and let firm up in fridge or freezer for 15-20 minutes.
8. Remove bars from pan and chop into 10 even bars (or 9 squares). Store in an airtight container for up to a few days. You can also store them in the freezer to keep them extra fresh.

NOTE:

Select dates that are sticky and moist if possible. This will help hold the bars together better. If not, you can soak them in water for 10 minutes to soften, then drain before processing.

VARIATIONS:

Use agave nectar instead of maple syrup if you don't want the strong maple flavor.
Use creamy peanut butter instead of almond butter.

Almond Oat Pumpkin Muffins

Recipe by: Tracy Childs of Veg-Appeal

These muffins are made with whole foods, but you would not know it from the taste! They are gluten-free if you use gluten free oats to make the oat flour.

MAKES 30 MINI-MUFFINS OR 20 MEDIUM SIZED MUFFINS

1½ cups pumpkin puree, 1 can
3 Tablespoons ground flax
2 teaspoons vanilla extract
⅓ cup maple syrup
¼ cup non-dairy milk
1½ cups almond meal
¾ cup oat flour (grind rolled oats in the blender)
½ teaspoon salt
1 teaspoon baking powder
¼ teaspoon baking soda
2 teaspoons pumpkin pie spice
2 ½ Tablespoons hemp seeds, optional

1. Preheat the oven to 350 degrees.
2. Lightly grease muffin tins.
3. Place the pumpkin purée into a mixing bowl and stir in the ground flax, along with the vanilla extract, maple syrup and non-dairy milk, and mix well.
4. Add in the rest of the ingredients, and stir well.
5. Fill about 30 mini muffin tins or 20 medium muffin tins.
6. Bake for about 22-25 minutes for mini muffins and 30-35 minutes for medium muffins. Test for doneness by lightly touching the top of a muffin. It should feel fairly firm to the touch.
7. Remove from the oven and allow them to cool in the tins for about 10 minutes then cool fully on cooling racks before serving.
8. Store in the refrigerator after one day.

Banana Nut Oat Clusters

Recipe by: Tracy Childs of Veg-Appeal

Makes a great snack to freeze in baggies, and you have a nutritious and filling "grab and go" breakfast or snack.

MAKES 12-15 CLUSTERS

½ cup dried fruit: raisins, chopped dates, or dried cranberries
2 medium bananas, mashed
1 ½ cups old-fashioned oats
½ cup nuts or seeds: whole pumpkin, sunflower seeds or chopped pecans,walnuts, almonds, or peanuts
¼ cup unsweetened coconut
1 teaspoon vanilla extract
1 teaspoon cinnamon
¼ teaspoon salt, optional

1. Soak the dried fruit for 30 minutes, if needed. (If the dried fruit is moist, there is no need to soak it.)
2. Preheat the oven to 325°F.
3. Line baking sheet with parchment paper or lightly grease it.
4. Combine the mashed bananas, oats, vanilla extract, and cinnamon. Mix gently.
5. Add the nuts, coconut, and dried fruit to the banana oat mixture.
6. Scoop a heaping Tablespoon of mixture and place onto the prepared baking sheet.
7. Bake for 13-15 minutes or until golden brown.

Fat-Free Baked Tortilla Chips

Recipe adapted from a recipe by Julie-Marie Christiansen by: Tracy Childs of Veg-Appeal

MAKES 4 SERVINGS

1 package corn tortillas, frozen
salt or other seasonings to taste (Chili Lime Seasoning from Trader Joe's is great)

1. Preheat the oven to 380°F.
2. Separate the tortillas. They should separate easily with a table knife while frozen solid. As you separate them, break them into chips of desired size, and place them on one or two large, flat baking sheets. Do not let them overlap.
3. Season to taste.
4. Place in the preheated oven.
5. Bake for 18 minutes.
6. Allow them to cool on the baking sheet and store in an air-tight container. If the chips get tough or chewy over time, you can crisp them briefly in a toaster oven for a minute or two.

Mango-Lemon Chia Pudding

Recipe by: Tracy Childs of Veg-Appeal

This pudding can be a breakfast with granola, or a snack or a dessert and is a great replacement for yogurt! It's a great source of protein, fiber, and omega 3 fatty acids!

MAKES ABOUT 4 SERVINGS

1 heaping cup cubed mango (can be frozen mango, thawed)
1 Tablespoon freshly squeezed lemon juice
1 cup water
1 large or 2 small dates, softened (The dates can be softened in water for about ½ hour if needed.)
2 Tablespoons almond butter
½ teaspoon cinnamon
¼ cup chia seeds
Toasted coconut, optional

1. Add everything but the chia seeds and the toasted coconut to the blender.
2. Blend until smooth.
3. Stir in the chia seeds (do not blend) and transfer the mixture to another container.
4. Chill for 4-8 hours so that the chia can thicken the pudding.
5. Garnish with a sprinkle of toasted unsweetened coconut if desired.

Nut Snack

Recipe by: Tracy Childs of Veg-Appeal

Most nut mixes tend to be expensive, too salty, not fresh, or not what you prefer. You can save money and develop your own recipe including your favorites, using this as a guide. Trader Joe's has a great selection of organic nuts, seeds, and dried fruit.

MAKES 2 CUPS

½ cup unsalted & roasted Valencia peanuts
½ cup lightly salted & roasted Valencia peanuts
¼ cup raw cashews
½ cup raw pumpkin or sunflower seeds
¼ cup raisins
¼ cup dried cranberries

1. Stir together the ingredients.
2. Store in a covered container in the refrigerator or on the counter if you plan to snack soon!

Pizza Kale Chips

Recipe by: Tracy Childs of Veg-Appeal

MAKES 8 SERVINGS

1½ cup sunflower seeds, soaked for about 3-4 hours or overnight, drained and rinsed.
1¼-1½ cup water (or more)
5 sun-dried tomatoes, soaked to soften for a few minutes in warm water and drained
2-3 Tablespoons lemon juice or apple cider vinegar
2 Tablespoons nutritional yeast
1 Tablespoon sesame tahini
1-2 Tablespoons tamari soy sauce
½ teaspoon smoked paprika
½ teaspoon onion powder
½ teaspoon garlic powder
½ teaspoon ground turmeric
1 teaspoon Italian seasoning
¼ teaspoon freshly ground black pepper
2 bunches of curly kale, washed and dried well and tough stems removed

1. Select 5 large mesh-lined dehydrator trays. Non-stick liners are not required.
2. Process all ingredients except the kale in a blender until smooth, adding enough water to create a thick but pourable consistency.
3. Tear the kale into medium (2-3-inch) pieces.
4. Place in a large bowl (or two bowls) and pour the sauce over top and massage gently into the kale to distribute the sauce (without breaking down the kale). Your hands will be messy, but it's fun!
5. Place the kale pieces spaced evenly over dehydrator trays.
6. Dehydrate at 105°F for about 6-8 hours (until crisp).
7. Store in a sealed container to maintain crispness.

NOTE:

Save any extra sauce. It's great over potatoes, veggies, grains, or on pizza!

Raw Flaxseed Crackers

Modified from Nikki, Eating Vibrantly

MAKES 36 CRACKERS

1 cup flaxseeds
2 Tablespoons ground flaxseed
¾ cup filtered water
3 teaspoons tamari
3 teaspoons maple syrup
¼ teaspoon onion powder
¼ teaspoon garlic powder

1. Mix the flaxseed and flaxseed meal in a bowl.
2. Combine the water, tamari, maple syrup, onion powder, and garlic powder in a pitcher and mix until everything is thoroughly mixed.
3. Pour the water/tamari mix over the flaxseed mix and stir thoroughly.
4. Leave to sit for 15 to 20 minutes, stirring regularly, until the mix becomes thickened, but not too stiff.
5. Spread mix thinly over one dehydrator tray and score lightly with a spatula to define the individual crackers.
6. Dry for 12-36 hours at 105°F, flipping crackers once after 5-6 hours, optional.
7. Break crackers along score lines and store in an airtight container.

NOTE:

If you don't have a dehydrator, bake in oven at 400°F for twenty minutes.

VARIATIONS:

Use Bragg Liquid Aminos instead of tamari.
Try sun-dried tomatoes, basil, smoked paprika.

Spiced Energy Super Snacks

Recipe by: Tracy Childs of Veg-Appeal

MAKES 8 SERVINGS

5 large pitted dates
3-5 dried figs (depending on size)
⅓ cup golden berries (tart) or goji berries (sweet)
½ cup raw pumpkin seeds
½ cup apricots
½ cup Brazil nuts
⅓ cup rolled oats
⅓ cup flaked unsweetened coconut
2 Tablespoons hemp seeds
1 teaspoon cinnamon
¼ teaspoon nutmeg
¼ teaspoon ginger
pinch of pink Himalayan salt

1. In a food processor, process all ingredients until they hold together when pinched.
2. Roll into bite sized balls. A melon baller can be helpful for measuring the appropriate dough for each ball.
3. Chill and serve. Best kept chilled, but they great for hiking, travel and other activities.

Sweet Potato (Air) Fries

French fries and sweet potato fries are popular with kids of all ages. Unfortunately, they are not that healthy because they are usually deep-fried in lots of oil. This recipe brings you the same great taste with no oil by using an air fryer. An air fryer circulates hot air around the food, and crisps it up much like deep-frying in oil.

MAKES 2-3 SERVINGS

2 sweet potatoes, sliced into ½-inch square shafts. (Thinner cuts tend to burn or shrivel.)

1. Preheat air fryer at 370°F for a couple of minutes.
2. Slice raw sweet potatoes by hand or with ½-inch cut slicer. Raw sweet potatoes can be too tough for some slicers. If so, cook the sweet potato for a minute or two in a microwave or steamer to soften before slicing.
3. In a medium bowl, spray the sweet potato slices with water, veggie broth, aquafaba, soy sauce, or Bragg coconut aminos. Stir and spray some more to coat. The liquid will help the seasonings to adhere to the slices. See the comment below regarding spray bottles.
4. Sprinkle one or more of your favorite seasonings, for example: Chinese five spices, onion powder, pepper seasoning, garlic powder, poultry seasoning. If you like spicy, add some paprika or chili powder. Stir to coat evenly.
5. Bake for five minutes in the air fryer.
6. Remove the tray, shake or stir the fries, then air fry for another 2 - 3 minutes. The fries should be crispy on the outside and tender on the inside.
7. Best served immediately after it cools briefly.

NOTE:

You can find French Fry Cutter kitchen tools online.

> For applications like moistening the sweet potato cuttings, a fine mist spray is much more effective than brushing it on or dripping from a bottle. Invest in some good quality 2 ounce spray bottles. Use them to store and spray aquafaba, beet juice, coconut aminos, liquid smoke, veggie broth, Worcestershire sauce, etc.

Soups

Ginger Miso Noodle Bowl

Recipe by: Tracy Childs of Veg-Appeal

MAKES 4 SERVINGS

½ red or other onion, chopped

1 lb. of baby bok choy, separated and washed (cut any large leaves in half vertically)

4 ounces vermicelli or pad thai rice noodles

7-8 large shiitake mushrooms, sliced or use dried mushrooms soaked in warm water and drained, destemmed and sliced (frozen shiitake may also be used)

1 or more medium garlic clove, finely chopped

1 teaspoon fresh ginger, finely chopped

Pinch of red pepper flakes

4 sun-dried tomatoes, soaked for 10 minutes, rinsed and finely diced

4 cups water and/or ginger-miso/pho or other vegetable broth plus extra water

Juice from ½ fresh lemon

Fresh garnishes: scallions, cilantro, basil, bean sprouts

Season with 2 Tablespoons or more of miso paste (dissolved in water or broth before adding), hot sauce, soy sauce, salt and pepper, if desired

1. Place a large (12-14") deep sauté pan over medium/high heat. Add the chopped onions and sauté until browned and soft, adding splashes of water by the Tablespoon, as needed to prevent sticking. Add the mushrooms, garlic, ginger and pepper flakes and sauté for about 2 minutes.
2. Add the broth and the sun-dried tomatoes and cook for a few minutes until fragrant and the broth begins to bubble.
3. Break the rice noodles in half (or more) and add them to the soup and stir. Add the bok choy and lemon juice. Cook on medium until noodles are soft but still a bit firm. Add more water as needed.
4. Top each serving with a choice of fresh garnishes and season as desired with miso/broth mixture.

Golden Cream of Broccoli Soup

Recipe by: Tracy Childs of Veg-Appeal

MAKES 5-6 SERVINGS

4 cups water or vegetable broth
4 red potatoes, unpeeled and scrubbed, cut into chunks
1 onion, diced
3 whole garlic cloves, peeled
1 teaspoon whole celery seeds
1 teaspoon dried dill
½ teaspoon dried marjoram
½ teaspoon turmeric
¼ teaspoon ground black pepper
1 ½ cups cooked or canned chickpeas, rinsed and drained
¼ cup bean cooking liquid, vegetable broth, or water
4 cups chopped (½-inch pieces) broccoli florets
1 Tablespoon Bragg Liquid Aminos, tamari sauce or salt to taste
½ cup soy creamer or unsweetened non-dairy milk, optional

1. Combine the water, potato, onion, garlic, celery seeds, thyme, marjoram, turmeric, and pepper in a large pot. Place over medium heat, cover, and simmer for about 20 minutes, or until the vegetables are tender.
2. Stir in the chickpeas and the bean cooking liquid or broth. Remove from the heat and let cool slightly.
3. Transfer to a blender and process in several batches, filling the blender container no more than half full for each batch. Hold the lid on tightly and start the blender on the lowest speed. Process for 1 to 2 minutes, or until the mixture is completely smooth.
4. Return the blended soup to the pot and stir in the broccoli and Bragg Liquid Aminos. Cover and simmer for 5-10 minutes, or until the broccoli is fork-tender. Taste and add more seasoning and soy creamer if desired.

Red Lentil and Greens Dal

Recipe by: Tracy Childs of Veg-Appeal

This soup is so nutritious and so simple to prepare, you'll want to make it often. The flavor is exquisite. Make sure to add the black pepper to increase the disease-fighting power of the turmeric. The cooking directions are designed to protect the nutrient density of the greens and garlic.

MAKES 8 1-CUP SERVINGS

6 cups water or low-sodium vegetable broth

2 cups dry red lentils, rinsed until the water runs clear (or mostly)

1 large onion, chopped or minced

1 small sweet potato or yam, or 1 large carrot cut into 1 or 2-inch pieces

1 teaspoon turmeric

1 teaspoon ground cumin

1 teaspoon ginger powder (or 1 Tablespoon fresh ginger)

1 large pinch chili powder or small dash hot sauce

2-4 Tablespoons fresh lemon juice, optional

salt and/or Bragg seasoning to taste

2-3 Tablespoons nutritional yeast or to taste

1 cup frozen corn

4-5 cups chopped greens (spinach, collards, cilantro and/or destemmed kale – a mix is nice)

black pepper to taste

1 cup cubed tofu, optional

1. Combine water or broth, lentils, onion, turmeric, cumin, potato or carrot, and chili powder or hot sauce in a medium soup pot and bring to a boil. Reduce heat, partially cover, and simmer until lentils have disintegrated, about 30-60 minutes.

2. Chop the greens and garlic and set it aside while the lentils cook.

3. Stir in lemon juice, salt, nutritional yeast, garlic, corn, greens, and black pepper to taste and cook for an additional 5-10 minutes.

4. For a smoother consistency, before adding tofu, you can remove a few ladles-full of the dal (or up to about ½ of the dal) and blend in the blender then add back to the pot.

5. Finally add the cubed tofu and add additional water to thin, if needed, especially when reheating.

6. Serve over rice and/or with quinoa, or whole-grain pita bread. Store leftover dal sealed well in the refrigerator for up to 1 week, or 3 months frozen.

Simple Miso Soup

Recipe by: Tracy Childs of Veg-Appeal

There is nothing more welcoming or nourishing than a warm bowl of miso soup. In Japan this soup is consumed with every meal – and for good reason! Miso possesses strong probiotic qualities that help to digest your meal. But miso soup can also be a meal in itself! It is very surprising how filling it is, and it makes a great, savory yet hydrating breakfast. Mostly, it is made fresh and consumed, but you can make it ahead – just be sure to heat it gently.

MAKES 2-4 SERVINGS

4 cups water
1 cup mix of chopped raw hard veggies (daikon radish, carrots, onion, zucchini) - if already cooked, add them at the end with the greens
2 dried shiitake mushrooms
1-2 inch piece of wakame seaweed, sliced with scissors or crumbled
½ cup cubed baked or plain tofu, optional
1-2 cups greens (broccoli, kale, collards)
1-3 Tablespoons dark brown miso paste
2 scallions or ¼ cup parsley or cilantro, chopped for garnish

1. Bring the water along with the hard veggies, mushrooms and wakame to a boil. Boil gently for about 5 minutes, until the veggies are tender.
2. Remove the mushrooms to a cutting board and slice and remove and discard the tough stem after cooling. Place the slices in the pot.
3. Put the miso in a bowl and ladle in about ¼ cup of the warm broth. Stir to dissolve the miso.
4. Add the greens. If the greens are already cooked, turn off the heat and allow them to warm in the broth. If raw, cook on low boil for about 1 minute.
5. Add the dissolved miso paste and stir. Do not reboil the soup after the miso is added, as it will destroy the probiotic properties of the miso.
6. Serve garnished with fresh scallions or cilantro.

NOTE:

To make "Anti-inflammatory Miso Soup" add ½ teaspoon turmeric, 1 teaspoon grated ginger and ⅛ teaspoon freshly ground pepper in step 1.

Smashed Split Pea and Barley Soup

Recipe by: Tracy Childs of Veg-Appeal

MAKES 6 SERVINGS

1 cup split peas
5 cups water
1½ onions, chopped
2 stalks sliced celery
5 cloves garlic, minced
2 bay leaves
2 cups chopped kale
3 chopped carrots (¼-inch pieces)
¼ cup pearled barley
1 vegetable bouillon cube
3 Tablespoons nutritional yeast
2 Tablespoons Bragg Liquid Aminos or soy sauce
Pinch of salt
Pepper to taste

1. Bring the first 5 ingredients to a boil. Cover and allow to cook 50 minutes on low heat until the peas are starting to disintegrate.
2. Remove and discard the bay leaves. Add the kale and cook the soup 5 minutes to soften the kale.
3. Allow the soup to cool a bit and put in the blender. Cover and blend the soup until smooth.
4. Pour the soup back into the pan.
5. Add the carrots, barley, and the bouillon cubes. Add additional water as need to help the barley soften. Bring the soup back to a boil lower the heat and cover. Cook the soup on low for another 20-30 minutes.
6. Stir in the final ingredients and serve the soup with crackers or garlic bread or enjoy it as it is!

Tom Kha Soup

Modified from Taste of the East

Tom Kha is my favorite soup at Thai restaurants. The coconut base with the Thai seasonings is a great flavor combination.

MAKES 8 SERVINGS

1 cup filtered water

4 cups vegetable stock (one 32-ounce carton)

3 14-ounce cans coconut milk

1 2-inch piece ginger, peeled

1 stalk lemongrass, ½-inch pieces

2 kaffir lime leaves

4 cups assorted chopped vegetables (carrot, zucchini, broccoli, eggplant, mushrooms)

1 cup yellow onion, quarter moons

1 red or green serrano chile, seeded and diced

1 lime, juiced

¼ cup wheat-free tamari or soy sauce

¼ cup fresh cilantro, minced

4 cups Napa cabbage, shredded, lightly packed

1 cup mung bean sprouts, optional garnish

1. Place the water/vegetable broth in a large pot over medium heat. Blend about half of the coconut milk with the ginger, lemongrass, and lime leaves on high speed for 20 seconds until there are no chunks. Add the remaining coconut milk and blend again for 5 to 10 seconds to incorporate. Pour this mixture into the water and continue cooking over medium heat while you prepare the vegetables.

2. Place each vegetable into the soup pot as you go, starting with the hardest, longest cooking veggies. Add the onion and chiles, cover and heat for 10 minutes or until all the veggies are tender.

3. Add the lime juice and tamari and stir. Cook for 2 more minutes and taste. If you think the soup needs more lemongrass, ginger or kaffir lime, blend more now with ½ cup of the broth. Otherwise, add the cilantro and cabbage and serve immediately, garnished with mung bean sprouts, if using.

NOTE:

If you aren't serving all of this soup immediately, you may want to leave the cabbage on the side. Portion out some shredded cabbage to each bowl (remember it will shrink down quite a bit when it gets hot), add the soup and stir.

Zen Soup

Inspired by Plumeria Restaurant, San Diego

This soup is a variation the traditional Tom Kha soup served in many Thai restaurants. It's a bit more hearty with the addition of legumes and more vegetables.

MAKES 6-8 SERVINGS

6 cups filtered water or vegetable stock

2 14-ounce cans coconut milk, or lite coconut milk

1 piece of ginger, 2 - 4 inches, peeled

2 lemons, juiced

1 small jar of green curry paste

4 cups assorted chopped vegetables (carrot, zucchini, broccoli, cauliflower, green pepper, red pepper, mushrooms)

1 cup cooked adzuki beans or lentils

1 cup yellow or red onion, chopped or quarter moons

2 pieces chick'n scallopini or tofu, sautéed and cut into chunks

¼ cup tamari or soy sauce

¼ cup fresh cilantro, minced

4 cups Napa cabbage, shredded, lightly packed

1 cup mung bean sprouts, for garnish

¼ cup parsley for garnish

1. Place the water or vegetable stock in a large pot over medium heat.
2. In a blender, blend about half of the coconut milk with the ginger and lemon juice on high speed for 20 seconds until there are no chunks of ginger. Add the remaining coconut milk and blend again for 5 to 10 seconds to incorporate. Pour this mixture into the water/vegetable stock. Add the jar of green curry paste, and continue cooking over medium heat while you prepare the vegetables.
3. Chop the vegetables. Place each vegetable into the soup pot as you go, starting with the hardest vegetables.
4. Next, add the beans and onion. Cover and heat for 10 minutes or until all the veggies are tender.
5. Add the chopped chick'n and tamari and stir. Cook for 2 more minutes and taste. If you think the soup needs more lemon or ginger, blend more now with ½ cup of the broth. Otherwise, add the cilantro and cabbage and serve immediately.
6. Garnish with mung bean sprouts and parsley.
7. Serve over cooked quinoa if desired.

NOTE:

If you are only serving a portion of this soup immediately, keep the cabbage on the side. Portion out some shredded cabbage to each bowl, add the soup, and stir.

Tea Party

Curry Chick'n Salad Tea Sandwich | 218

Drop Scones | 219

Mock Devonshire Cream | 220

Pineapple-Cream Cheese Tea Sandwich | 220

Vegg Salad Tea Sandwich | 221

My wife and I discovered in our travels at home and abroad that we absolutely love the English-style afternoon tea. We encountered it in England, Canada, on cruise ships, locally in San Diego, at the Huntington Library, and in the most unlikely location - in the Chinatown district on Oahu, Hawaii. We started hosting tea parties, and indeed transformed our dining room to emulate some of the lavish settings that we encountered. Of course, this was before we learned about eating vegan. The traditional English Tea is full of butter and cream - great for clogging arteries; not so great for long-term health. So, we set out to transform the dishes so that we could continue to enjoy them as vegans. Of course, some of the dishes still contain oil, so they are not whole food, plant-based, but as an occasional treat, they are delicious.

Curry Chick'n Salad Tea Sandwich

MAKES 24 SANDWICH TRIANGLES

1 package Gardein chick'n scallopini or other chick'n
3- 4 Green onions
2 stalks of celery
½ cup non-dairy mayonnaise
1 teaspoon curry powder, adjust to taste
1 apple diced (Granny Smith or Crisp Red Apple)
½ cup raisins/cranberries mixture
½ cup slivered almonds
12 slices bread, thin sliced
¾ cup soft vegan butter

1. Sauté chick'n for 2 to 3 minutes on each side over medium heat until browned.
2. In a food processor, mince green onions and celery. Add chick'n, non-dairy mayo, and curry powder. Process on pulse until mixed. Stir in apple, raisins, and almonds.
3. Cut crust off stack of bread with bread knife first. Discard or set aside crusts.
4. Spread vegan butter on inside of bread slices.
5. Add sandwich ingredients.
6. Cut sandwich in quarters diagonally.
7. Serve or store in plastic tote with lid.

Drop Scones

MAKES ABOUT 12 SCONES (SERVING 6-8 PEOPLE)

vegetable oil or oil spray, as needed to grease cookie sheet
2 cups whole-wheat flour
⅓ cup sugar
2 teaspoons baking powder
¼ teaspoon salt
6 Tablespoons coconut oil
½ cup dates, chopped
½ cup almond milk
1 egg equivalent – using egg replacer
1 teaspoon vanilla extract
1 Tablespoon sugar to dust tops of scones

1. Heat oven to 425°F.
2. Grease a cookie sheet with vegetable oil and a paper towel, or spray with oil spray.
3. Mix flour, sugar, baking powder, and salt in a food processor.
4. Add coconut oil, and pulse until fine crumbs form.
5. Add dates.
6. Prepare egg replacer. Blend 1½ teaspoons egg replacer and 2 Tablespoons warm water. Mix well. Whisk until frothy.
7. Beat almond milk into egg replacer mixture with a fork.
8. Add milk/egg mixture and vanilla extract to flour mixture. Beat slowly until moistened.
9. Drop by 12 heaping portions, 2 inches apart onto prepared baking sheet.
10. Sprinkle scones with 1 Tablespoon sugar.
11. Bake 11-13 minutes, or until golden brown. Best if served warm!

VARIATIONS:

To minimize sugar use, replace the sugar with 2 Tablespoons Sucanat and 2 Tablespoons Erythritol. Replace dates with ½ cup cranberries or ½ cup raisins.

Mock Devonshire Cream

MAKES: 2 CUPS

2 eight-ounce containers of non-dairy cream cheese, softened
½ cup sugar
3 teaspoons of freshly squeezed lemon juice
2 teaspoons of vanilla extract
1 cup powdered sugar
1 cup non-dairy sour cream

1. In a counter-top mixer, beat non-dairy cream cheese, lemon juice, and vanilla extract.
2. Gradually beat in the powdered sugar.
3. Fold in the non-dairy sour cream.

NOTE:

Can also be frozen and thawed when ready to use.

Pineapple-Cream Cheese Tea Sandwich

MAKES 40 SANDWICH TRIANGLES

1½ cups non-dairy cream cheese, softened
½ cup pineapple, finely chopped
½ cup finely chopped nuts (e.g. walnuts)
¾ cup soft vegan butter
1 teaspoon cinnamon
20 slices bread, thin sliced

1. In a small bowl, soften the cream cheese by letting it come to room temperature or microwaving about 15-20 seconds. Stir in the pineapple and nuts.
2. Combine the vegan butter spread with cinnamon, and spread the mixture over 1 side of each slice of bread.
3. Spread the cream cheese mixture evenly over 10 slices of bread and top with the other 10 slices.
4. Remove the crusts and cut sandwiches in quarters diagonally.

VARIATION:

Cinnamon Raisin bread works well as the bread. You can replace cinnamon with 1 teaspoon nutmeg.

Vegg Salad Tea Sandwich

This recipe uses The Vegg, a plant-based egg yolk replacement.

MAKES 40 TRIANGULAR SANDWICHES

1 twelve-ounce block of extra firm tofu
½ cup non-dairy mayonnaise
1½ teaspoon of sea salt
¼ teaspoon turmeric
1 teaspoon yellow mustard
¾ cup soft vegan butter
20 slices bread, thin sliced

VEGG MIXTURE

1. Put 2 Tablespoons of Vegg and 1 cup water in blender and blend very well. Set aside. Measure out 1 Tablespoon and store the remainder of the Vegg mixture in the fridge for future use.

VEGG SALAD

1. To make the "egg" salad, drain the tofu and press out as much water out of the tofu as possible with paper towels, i.e. wrap the tofu in a paper towel and press between two plates. Repeat, if necessary, to get most of the moisture out of the tofu.
2. Put the tofu in a large mixing bowl and break it up really well with a fork or your with your hands.
3. Add 1 Tablespoon (only) of the Vegg mixture to the non-dairy mayo, and mix well.
4. Add all of the remaining ingredients to the tofu, and mix together well. Taste, and add more salt if needed.
5. Cut crust off stack of bread with bread knife first. Discard or set aside crusts.
6. Spread vegan butter on the inside of the bread slices.
7. Spread the Vegg salad mixture onto bread slices.
8. Cut sandwiches in quarters diagonally, and serve.

Templates

A template is a recipe that is broken down into distinct and well-defined components. By changing the ingredient(s) used for each component, you can create a multitude of variations for the dish. For example, a salad template might have a greens component, a nuts and seeds component, a sprouts component, a legume component, and a raw veggie component. You might use romaine as a green this time, arugula as a green the next time, and a combination of red leaf and bibb lettuce the following time. Mark Reinfeld and Vegan Fusion have championed the concept of a template.

3-Ingredient Energy Bar Template

Modified from The Kitchn

These energy bars are easy to make and travel reasonably well. The template consists of three components, along with optional add-on ingredients.

MAKES 8 BARS

1 cup nuts
1 cup dried fruit
1 cup (12-15 whole) dates, pitted
Optional: shredded coconut, chia seeds, chocolate chips, white chocolate chips, cocoa powder, crystalized ginger, ground cinnamon, ground nutmeg, or lemon zest

1. Select the nut(s) and dried fruit. This is the fun part of the template, where you select the individual types of nuts that you will use (cashew, almond, brazil, pistachio, hazel, walnut, pine nut, peanut . . .), and the types of dried fruit (raisins, apple, craisins, apricot, fig, mango, banana, pineapple . . .).
2. Select optional ingredients, if desired, to create a unique flavor profile.
3. Roast the nuts. This step is optional, but roasting the nuts really intensifies their flavor. Roast the nuts in a toaster oven for a few minutes at a time. Stir for more even roasting. Watch them closely; they will burn quickly. Cool before using.
4. Combine the core ingredients along with any optional ingredients in a food processor. Pulse a few times just to break them up. Separate the dates if they start to clump together.
5. Process continuously for 30 seconds. Scrape sides if necessary.
6. Process repeatedly in 30 second increments until all ingredients have broken down into crumb-sized pieces, scraping the sides as necessary.
7. Continue processing until the ingredients clump together and gather into a ball, approximately 1 to 2 minutes.
8. Transfer the ball onto a piece of plastic wrap or wax paper, and press with your hands to desired the thickness.
9. Wrap the dough in plastic wrap, and chill in the refrigerator for at least an hour or overnight.
10. Unwrap the chilled dough and transfer to a cutting board. Cut into 8 large bars (or smaller squares if desired). Wrap each bar in plastic wrap or wax paper.
11. Store the bars in the fridge for several weeks or in the freezer for up to three months.

NOTES:

The dough can optionally be shaped into small balls. Refrigerate in an airtight container or wrap in plastic for longer storage.

The bars can be taken on picnics or other outings, but will soften if not chilled.

5-Minute Creamy Dressing/Sauce Template

Recipe by: Tracy Childs of Veg-Appeal

Want to make an amazing, homemade dressing for every salad or bowl meal (beans, greens, veggies) in just 5 minutes? Here is a guide to make that happen. Use these ideas as a template (choose one option from each category and go ahead and get creative.)
It's all about the sauce for making food delicious! Get started by using the examples below.

MAKE IT CREAMY (CHOOSE ONE):

¼ cup *Tofu-Cashew Mayonnaise* (in "From Scratch")
1 Tablespoon sesame tahini + 3 Tablespoons water
1½ Tablespoons almond butter + 2½ Tablespoons water
¼ cup ripe avocado, mashed well with the tang ingredient of choice (see below)
¼ cup hummus
1 Tablespoon hemp seeds + 3 Tablespoons water (requires blender)
2 Tablespoons soaked raw sunflower seeds + 2 Tablespoons water (in blender)

GIVE IT TANG (CHOOSE ONE):

½-1 Tablespoon vinegar of choice (rice, balsamic, apple cider, etc.)
½-1 Tablespoon lemon, lime or grapefruit juice

ADD SOME FLAVOR (CHOOSE 1–3, BEING MINDFUL OF THE SALT CONTENT IN SOME OF THESE INGREDIENTS):

⅛ teaspoon salt
Zest of lemon/lime/orange
½-1 teaspoon Bragg Liquid Aminos, Shoyu, soy sauce, tamari sauce, or coconut aminos (all of these have a similar flavor)
1 teaspoon miso paste
½ teaspoon umeboshi vinegar
1 Tablespoon prepared mustard
dried herbs or minced fresh herbs (cilantro, scallions, dill)
½ Tablespoon nutritional yeast
½ teaspoon cumin

SWEETEN IT, OPTIONAL – (CHOOSE 0-1):

½ Tablespoon orange juice
½-2 teaspoons coconut sugar
2 teaspoons *Date/Fig Paste* (in "From Scratch")
2 teaspoons maple syrup

GIVE IT A KICK, OPTIONAL – (CHOOSE 0-3):

¼ teaspoon grated fresh or powdered ginger
¼-½ teaspoon pressed fresh or powdered garlic
¼-½ teaspoon Sriracha or other hot sauce
⅛ teaspoon cayenne or chipotle chili powder
1 Tablespoon salsa of choice

ADD OMEGA-3 FATTY ACIDS OR THICKENER, OPTIONAL – (CHOOSE 0-1):

½ teaspoon chia + 1 Tablespoon water (allow to thicken for about ½ hour)
1 Tablespoon hemp seeds + 3 Tablespoons water (requires blender)

MAKE IT ANTI-INFLAMMATORY, OPTIONAL – (CHOOSE 0-3):

½ teaspoon chia + 1 Tablespoon water (allow to thicken for about ½ hour)
1 Tablespoon hemp seeds + 3 Tablespoons water (requires blender)
¼ teaspoon turmeric
fresh ginger, peeled
Fresh herbs (cilantro, basil, scallions, parsley – requires blender)

LOWER THE CALORIES, OPTIONAL:

Add veggies like ½ cup chopped zucchini, red bell pepper, cherry or whole
  (chopped) tomatoes. You may need to increase the other flavors.

1. In a blender, place your chosen dressing ingredients and blend. If not adding
   ingredients requiring a blender, in a small deep bowl, stir together the creamy base (and
   miso, if using) with water if needed. Then add other ingredients of choice, stirring well.
2. If using a blender, you don't need to press or chop the herbs, garlic, ginger, etc. Just add
   all of the ingredients and blend until smooth. You may want to double or triple the
   recipe to make more for a few days of salads.
3. Drizzle your dressing/sauce over salad or bowl of beans, grains and veggies. Enjoy a
   different meal every time by changing up the ingredients!

IDEAS TO GET STARTED:

Get creative! Here are a few examples of some favorite combinations to get you started (can be
made without using a blender).

- Asian: Almond Butter | Lime | Coconut Sugar | Shoyu | Ginger | Garlic |
  Turmeric
- Greek: Tahini | Lemon | Salt | Nutritional Yeast
- Mexican: Hummus | Lime | Salsa | Nutritional Yeast | Cumin
- Italian: Tofu-Cashew Mayonnaise | Balsamic Vinegar | Italian Herbs | Dijon
  Mustard | Garlic

Bean Salad Template

Recipe by: Tracy Childs of Veg-Appeal

Beans are one of nature's most plentiful, sustainable, and amazing health foods with bountiful and filling fiber, protein, and minerals. Yet they are often forgotten and undervalued. Therefore, it compels us to create yummy dishes that feature beans! Bean salads are a great way to go, because they are ready to eat cold alongside almost any meal. Beans add fiber, protein, calcium, and other nutrients that enhance our health. They are especially good for our digestion! Your creations can be elaborate or simple, depending on the time and energy you have to create them. Adding grains along with the beans adds to the satiety and flavor. Get creative and have a new bean salad every week and see the notes below for some ideas to get you started.

MAKES ABOUT 4 ONE-CUP SERVINGS

1. CHOOSE YOUR BEANS

Use 1 ½ to 3 cups (use 3 cups if not using grain, see whole grain below). Note that a 15-ounce can of beans contains about 1 ½ cups. Or you can cook your own beans (in "From Scratch"). Either way, serve them cooked, drained, and rinsed. Some favorite beans include:

**Black beans
Garbanzo Beans (or Chickpeas)
Kidney Beans
Pinto Beans
Black-eyed Peas
Edamame (frozen green soybeans, prepared to package directions)
Baby Lima Beans (frozen), thawed
Cannellini Beans
Great Northern Beans
Lentils (brown or beluga. Trader Joe's carries cooked lentils for convenience)**

2. ADD A WHOLE GRAIN (CHOOSE 0-1) 1 ½ CUP OF COOKED AND COOLED:

Kasha **(in "From Scratch")**
Quinoa **(in "From Scratch")**
Cleaner Brown Rice **(in "From Scratch")**
**Barley
Bulgur Wheat**

3. ADD FRESH HERBS (CHOOSE 0-3) ¼ - ½ CUP COMBINATION OF CHOPPED OR SLICED:

Cilantro

Basil
Mint
Parsley
Scallions (green onions)
Red onion
Yellow onion

4. ADD SOME FRESH INGREDIENTS (CHOOSE 0 – 3) ¼ - ½ CUP, SLICED, DICED, HALVED (IF NECESSARY):

Cherry or whole tomatoes
Parboiled carrots or sweet potato
Peeled or Persian/English cucumber
Sugar snap peas
Radishes
Celery
Legume sprouts (Recipe in "From Scratch")
Red (or any color) bell pepper
Avocado
Herbs (listed above)

5. SWEETEN IT (CHOOSE 0-3):

1 peeled and seeded orange
½ cup thawed frozen corn
½ cup thawed frozen peas
1 handful red or green grapes
½ cup fresh or frozen pineapple, cut into bite sized pieces
½ cup fresh or frozen mango, cut into bite sized pieces
1 Tablespoon date/fig paste (recipe in "From Scratch")
1-2 dates (seeded and diced small)
2 Tablespoons chopped dried mango, prunes, pineapple, cranberries, apricot (diced) or raisins
1 teaspoon to 1 Tablespoon maple syrup or another sweetener

6. GIVE IT TANG (CHOOSE 1-2) ABOUT 2 TABLESPOONS OF (OR A COMBINATION):

Juice of lemon, lime or grapefruit
Your favorite vinegar (e.g. rice, red wine, apple cider)

7. ADD OMEGA-3 FATTY ACIDS (OPTIONAL – CHOOSE 0-1):

1 Tablespoon hemp seeds

8. MAKE IT ANTI-INFLAMMATORY (OPTIONAL – CHOOSE 0-3):

1 Tablespoon hemp seeds
¼ teaspoon turmeric + a grind of black pepper (enhances effectiveness of
  turmeric)
fresh ginger
Fresh herbs (as described above)

9. ADD SOME SPICES TO TASTE:

½ teaspoon cumin, oregano, basil, lemon zest, curry powder, garlic or onion
  powder
¼ teaspoon salt
¼ teaspoon pepper

10. GIVE IT SOME KICK/PIZZAZZ (OPTIONAL):

1 teaspoon grated fresh or powdered ginger
1 teaspoon pressed garlic
½ teaspoon crushed red pepper flakes, Thai chili paste, sriracha, or your favorite
  hot sauce
½ cup salsa
½ large jalapeño, diced finely
1 teaspoon to 1 Tablespoon prepared mustard
½ cup chopped artichokes
¼ cup sliced sundried tomatoes
¼ cup sliced olives of choice
1 Tablespoon capers
½ teaspoon toasted sesame oil

11. MAKE IT CREAMY (OPTIONAL):

½ cup Ripe avocado mashed with your tangy ingredients (citrus/vinegar)
½ cup Cashew-Tofu Mayonnaise (Recipe in "From Scratch")
1 Tablespoon Hemp seeds

1. Choose your ingredients and add them to a large bowl.
2. Fold or stir gently to combine.
3. Serve immediately or chill for an hour or so to allow flavors to meld.
4. The flavor of bean salads is best slightly chilled but not too cold, making them a great take-along lunch.
5. The flavor of bean salads is best within the first few days, but can be revamped by adding additional fresh ingredients.

Get creative! Here are a few examples of favorite combinations.

Simple Ideas to Get Started (add more spices to your taste):

- Mexican: Black or Pinto Beans | Quinoa | Mango | Corn | Salsa | Cilantro | Scallions | Avocado | Lime | Red Wine Vinegar | Garlic
- Asian: Great Northern Beans | Edamame | Cherry Tomatoes | Persian Cucumber | Sugar Snap Peas | Cilantro | Mint | Rice Vinegar | Toasted Sesame Oil
- Italian: Cannellini Beans | Peas | Cherry Tomatoes | Red Bell Pepper | Basil or Parsley | Scallions | Red Wine Vinegar | Artichokes | Sundried Tomatoes | Olives | Garlic
- Indian: Lentils | Brown Rice | Onion | Peas | Raisins | Lemon | Curry | Cumin | Tofu-Cashew Mayonnaise
- Moroccan: Chickpeas | Peas | Dates | Lemon | Red Wine Vinegar | Olives | Cumin
- Tropical: Chickpeas | Red Onion | Cubed Avocado, Dried or Fresh Pineapple | Rice Vinegar | Lime Juice | Cilantro

Gourmet Salad Template

You don't ever have to eat a boring salad again. Use this salad template as a guide to create an endless variety of delicious salads. This template consists of six core components and optional add-on ingredients.

GREENS COMPONENT

Select a salad green (buttercup, green leaf, red leaf, romaine, or mix), or other greens such as arugula, baby kale, or baby spinach.

RAW VEGGIE COMPONENT

Select a combination of avocado, beet, bell pepper (green, red, orange, yellow), broccoli, cabbage (red or white), carrot, cauliflower, celery, corn kernels, cucumber, jicama, onion (red, white, or green), sauerkraut, tomato, zucchini or other favorites. Use different cuts: chop, dice, grate, and slice.

COOKED VEGGIE COMPONENT

Add steamed, grilled, roasted, or sautéed veggies of your choosing including bell pepper, carrots, cauliflower, egg plant, onion, sweet potatoes, tomatoes, yellow squash, zucchini.

LEGUME COMPONENT

Add cooked beans (adzuki, black, edamame, fava, garbanzo, kidney . . .), lentils (any color), or roasted tofu cubes or tempeh cubes.

NUT AND SEED COMPONENT

Add a sprinkle of raw or toasted nuts (almonds, cashew, pecans, walnuts), or seeds (hemp, popped amaranth, pumpkin, sesame, sunflower, and more).

SPROUTS COMPONENT

Choose your sprouts: alfalfa, broccoli, clover, lentil, mung bean, pea, sunflower, and/or mixed sprouts.

DRESSING COMPONENT

Use freshly squeezed lemon juice, or any dressing.

OPTIONAL

Artichoke hearts, basil leaves, bite-sized pieces of baked tortillas or pita bread, caramelized onions, croutons, dried fruit, edible flowers (basil, chrysanthemum, fennel, fuchsia, garlic, and nasturtium, to name a few), fennel fronds, mint leaves, olives, parsley, roasted red peppers, sautéed mushrooms, sun-dried tomatoes (marinated) .

1. Assemble ingredients into a large bowl and mix well.
2. Have fun garnishing the top with nuts, seeds, mint or basil leaves, edible flowers.
3. Apply dressing of choice or serve on the side.

Green Smoothie Template

Recipe by: Tracy Childs of Veg-Appeal

If it's green and you have a high-speed blender, you can make a smoothie out if it! Use this template to make a different, healthy, anti-inflammatory, alkalizing and delicious smoothie every day! Adding something tangy (citrus) to your smoothie is important to help balance the flavor of green vegetables and to help preserve it if you make a large batch to have some for tomorrow. Tip: leave out the banana if you plan to store your smoothie.

Pick something from each of the categories below.

MAKES 2 LARGE SERVINGS

1. MAKE IT GREEN (CHOOSE 1-3 OR A COMBINATION):

2 cups kale, collards, spinach or baby greens mix
1 small/medium cucumber cut into chunks
2 stalks celery cut into chunks
1 small/medium zucchini
¼ cup mint leaves

2. MAKE IT CREAMY (CHOOSE 1-3):

1 banana
1 zucchini
¼ cup ripe avocado
½ cup tofu
1 Tablespoon almond butter
1 Tablespoon hemp seeds
2 Tablespoons soaked raw sunflower seeds
2 Tablespoons flaked coconut soaked overnight to soften
substitute non-dairy milk for all or some of the water
¼ cup rolled oats

3. GIVE IT TANG (CHOOSE 1-2):

1 peeled and seeded orange
Juice of ½ lemon or lime
½ peeled and seeded grapefruit

4. SWEETEN IT (CHOOSE 1-3):

1 banana
handful or more of berries (changes the color from green to brownish)
1 cup watermelon chunks
1 cup peach slices

1 peeled and seeded orange
1 handful red or green grapes
½ cup pineapple
½ cup mango
1 cored apple cut into chunks
1 cored pear cut into chunks
½-2 teaspoons coconut sugar
1 Tablespoon *Date-Fig Paste* (in "From Scratch")
1-2 dates
1 Tablespoon maple syrup
use coconut water or sweetened dairy alternative as a liquid

5. ADD A LIQUID (CHOOSE 1-2):

1 cup water
1 cup watermelon chunks + some liquid
1 cup ice + some liquid
1 cup coconut water
1 cup non-dairy milk

6. GIVE IT A KICK, OPTIONAL:

¼ teaspoon grated fresh or powdered ginger

7. ADD OMEGA-3 FATTY ACIDS/THICKENER, OPTIONAL – (CHOOSE 0-1)

1 Tablespoon chia
1 Tablespoon hemp seeds
1 Tablespoon ground flaxseeds

8. MAKE IT ANTI-INFLAMMATORY, OPTIONAL – (CHOOSE 0-3):

green vegetables (from #1 above)
1 Tablespoon chia
1 Tablespoon hemp seeds
¼ teaspoon turmeric + a grind of black pepper (enhances effectiveness of turmeric)
¼-½ teaspoon Matcha (green tea powder)
fresh ginger
Fresh herbs (cilantro, mint, parsley)
Green tea as liquid (see below)

9. LOWER THE CALORIES, OPTIONAL:

Add vegetables instead of fruit
Add less chia/hemp/flax
Use water instead of non-dairy milk

1. Add the soft fruit first to the blender, near the blades to help them move freely.
2. Add other ingredients.
3. Blend until smooth.
4. If it's too thick, add more liquid and blend again.

IDEAS TO GET STARTED:

Get creative! Here are a few examples of popular combinations to get you started.

- Orange | Kale | Cucumber | Celery | Grapes | Pineapple | Hemp | Water | Lemon
- Apple | Cucumber | Banana | Orange | Kale | Chia | Lemon
- Banana | Pear | Soy milk | Kale | Orange
- Grapes | Pineapple | Spinach | Soy Milk
- Mango | Mint | Lime | Cucumber | Water
- Watermelon | Mint | Coconut Water

Salad in a Jar Template

For this template, you can vary the ingredients to style the salad with international flavors (Greek, Asian, Mexican, etc.) or rotate in the ingredients that you like for variety.

Dressing component
Spices component
Legume component
Salad toppings component
Lettuce component
Garnish component

1. Using a Greek version as an example, start with a little red wine vinegar in the bottom of the jar.
2. Add oregano, then some chickpeas and tofu feta cubes (marinate the tofu in red wine vinegar, lemon juice, olive oil, oregano, garlic powder, salt).
3. Add sliced roasted red peppers, Kalamata olives, and artichoke hearts.
4. Top with romaine lettuce.
5. Place the top on the jar and store in the fridge. Make several variations on the weekend, and store for a quick lunch during the week.
6. To serve, turn the jar upside down and dump it into a bowl. The lettuce will be at the bottom, and all the wet ingredients go on top. Add sesame seeds or other toppings for garnish.

Stir-Fry Template

This template consists of five components.

VEGETABLE COMPONENT

Select from among onion, sweet potato, beets, bok choy, carrots, zucchini, yellow squash, broccoli, cauliflower, bell peppers, mushrooms, leafy greens, mung beans.

FLAVORINGS COMPONENT

Select from among black pepper, Chinese five spices, garlic, Thai seasoning, and just a dash of salt.

SAUCE COMPONENT

Select from among water (to start the onions), sweet cooking rice wine, stir-fry sauce, Bragg liquid aminos.

OPTIONAL INGREDIENTS

Select from among chick'n strips, tofu, water chestnuts, pineapple (small pieces), and cashews.

GARNISH COMPONENT

Select from among basil leaves, moringa leaves, sesame seeds.

1. Sauté onions in a wok with a little water.
2. Meanwhile, steam sweet potatoes to soften.
3. In a separate skillet, sauté chick'n strips.
4. When the onions are carmelized, add in items from hardest first (potatoes, carrots, beets, bell peppers) to the fastest cooking items last (water chestnuts, mung beans, pineapple, and leafy greens). Stir as you add items.
5. Add the chick'n strips or tofu.
6. Add flavorings and sauces to taste.
7. Mix together and simmer to let the flavors mingle.
8. Serve over quinoa or rice.

Stuffed Squash Template

This template consists of five components and a garnish.

LEGUME COMPONENT

Select dry or precooked beans or lentils (any color).

SQUASH COMPONENT

Select squash large enough to stuff – e.g. acorn, butternut.

COOKED VEGETABLE COMPONENT

Select from among sweet potato, beets, carrots, zucchini, yellow squash, broccoli, cauliflower, bell peppers, mushrooms, leafy greens.

FLAVORINGS COMPONENT

Select from among black pepper, garlic, ginger, liquid smoke, maple syrup, nutmeg, non-dairy milk, onion, tamari, vinegar, and just a dash of salt.

SAUCE COMPONENT

Use Cashew Cream Sauce (in "Sauces, Syrups & Dressings") or other sauce.

OPTIONAL GARNISH

Select from among basil leaves, edible flowers, mint leaves, nuts, or seeds.

1. Soak beans and lentils overnight. Cook in steamer or pressure cooker. Set aside. Or use pre-cooked beans or lentils.
2. Soak nuts for about two hours for the sauce.
3. Steam squash until tender (butternut, acorn, winter squash, etc.) Hollow out the squash to make room for filling. You can use the removed squash to add body to the sauce.
4. In a large pan or wok, sauté onions, garlic, and a bit of ginger in vegetable broth over medium heat. Start adding finely chopped vegetables from hardest to softest, adding water or more broth and stirring as needed.
5. Add flavorings. Let it simmer for a few minutes while you assemble the cream sauce.
6. Make *Cashew Cream Sauce* (in "Sauces, Syrups and Dressings") or other sauce, incorporating the removed squash.
7. To plate, add a small amount of beans and/or lentils into the hollow of the squash. Fill the hollow with drained veggies. Top with creamy sauce and add garnish.

Veggie Soup Template

See also Transforming your Meals, Phase 1 in Chapter 5.

MAKES 6-8 SERVINGS

BASE COMPONENT

Include 4-8 cups of the following in any combination – water, vegetable stock, a carton of soup (like carrot ginger, or butternut squash – check ingredients to ensure that they are non-dairy).

SEASONING COMPONENT

If using vegetable stock or a carton soup base, you may not need much extra seasoning. Otherwise, try out your favorite spices and flavorings: Chinese 5 spices, a dash of Thai seasoning, coconut aminos, and/or Worcestershire sauce. You could also add fresh or dried ground cloves, parsley, basil, oregano, cilantro, thyme, or turmeric. To increase the sweetness, add a splash of agave or a teaspoon or two of erythritol or Sucanat to taste. To increase the heat, add small amounts of chili powder, cayenne pepper, or paprika.

VEGETABLE COMPONENT

Chop fresh vegetables as needed: onions, sweet potatoes, beets, carrots, celery, bell peppers (all colors), yellow squash, zucchini, mushrooms, tomatoes, fennel, broccoli, cauliflower, cabbage, bok choy, kale leaves, Swiss chard, and collard greens. You can also add one can of sweet corn, drained, or frozen vegetables.

LEGUME COMPONENT

Beans – one or two cans should do it. Choose from kidney, black, garbanzo, pinto, or any other favorite bean. This adds some protein.

MEAT SUBSTITUTE COMPONENT (OPTIONAL)

For additional protein and texture, add your favorite meat substitute. Gardein's Chick'n Scallopini or Chick'n strips are good options. Cook according to the package directions.

Veggie Soup Template (continued)

1. In a large soup pot, sauté onions in some water (use a bit of oil if preferred). If you want to caramelize the onions, keep stirring until they are a nice golden brown color and the water is evaporated. Add water as needed to keep from burning. You can also add celery at this point.
2. Add soup base, and stir.
3. Add seasonings. Taste as you go, and adjust to balance flavors. See Chapter 7 for more on flavor balancing.
4. Add vegetables, putting in the hardest first (potatoes, carrots, and beets) and the tender vegetables last (leafy greens, mushrooms, and cabbage).
5. Add beans and/or legumes.
6. Prepare meat substitute, and add, it if desired.
7. You may need to add more liquid if it cooks down too much or if you want a thinner soup.
8. Cook until all vegetables are al dente, more or less, to your taste.

VARIATION:

Serve soup over cooked quinoa (more protein) or other cooked grain or spaghetti squash.

NOTE:

For efficiency, make a big pot of soup on the weekend. Refrigerate portions for meals during the week, and freeze in labeled containers for future use.

CHAPTER 9: RESOURCES

Listing resources in a book is a risky proposition because things change so quickly. Nevertheless, the resources listed here can be a good starting point for your investigations.

Apps For Smartphones

These are apps for your smartphone that relate to plant–based eating.

21–Day Vegan Kickstart – Supports kickstart program with recipes and resources
AirVegan – plant–based options at airport terminals
Animal–Free – large database of animal–derived ingredients
Bunny Free – check if a company is cruelty–free
Cruelty–Free – lists companies that do not test on animals
Easy vegan recipes – lots of easy vegan recipes
Forks Over Knives – recipes
Happy Cow – vegan restaurants nearby
Heart of Vegan – Lots of vegan info such as blogs, recipe sites, quotes, books, and education programs.
Gonutss – helps you translate your favorite foods to vegan
Is It Vegan? – scan the barcode, and the app tells you if the item has animal ingredients
Vegan Passport – find vegan food in restaurants around the globe
VeganXpress – vegan friendly restaurants
VeganYumYum Mobile – pick up ingredients on the go for included recipes
VegSafe – identifies elements of animal origin in products

Blogs

Allyson Kramer
Awesome Vegan Blog
Big Raw
Blog.fatfreevegan.com
Deliciously Ella
Fat–Free Vegan Kitchen
Fork & Beans
Ginger Is The New Pink
Gluten–Free Vegan Girl
Happy Herbivore
Hell Ya It's Vegan
I Eat Trees
I Love Vegan
Meet The Shannons
Minimilist Baker
My Whole Food Life
No Meat Athlete
Oh She Glows

Olives for Dinner
Rawsome Vegan Life
Seitan Is My Motor
So What Do Vegans Eat?
The Snarky Chickpea
The Vegan Stoner
Vegan Crunk
Vegan Dad
Vegan Eats And Treats
Vegan Richa
Vegan Yum Yum
Veganacious

Books

21 Day Weight Loss Kickstart by Dr. Neal Barnard
4Leaf Guide to Vibrant Health by Morris Hicks and Kerry Graff, MD
A Plant–Based Life by Micaela Cook Karlsen
Becoming Vegan by Brenda Davis and Vesanto Melinda
Blue Zones by Dan Buettner
Breaking the Food Seduction by Neal Barnard, MD
Dr. Neal Barnard's Program for Reversing Diabetes by Neal Barnard, MD
Eat *to Live* by Dr. Joel Fuhrman
Fast Food Genocide by Dr. Joel Fuhrman
Finding Ultra: Rejecting Middle Age, Becoming One of the World's Fittest Men and Discovering Myself by Rich Roll
Food Choice and Sustainability: why Buying Local, Eating Less Meat, and Taking Baby Steps Won't Work by Dr. Richard Oppenlander
Food Over Medicine by Pamela Popper
Healthy at 100: The Scientifically Proven Secrets of the World's Healthiest and Longest–Lived Peoples by John Robbins
How Not To Die by Dr. Michael Greger with Gene Stone
Keep it Simple, Keep it Whole by Alona Pulde, MD and Matthew Lederman, MD
I'm Mad as Hell, and I'm Not Going to Eat It Anymore!: Taking Control of Your Health and Your Life – One Vegan Recipe at a Time by Christina Pirello
Mad Cowboy: Plain Truth from the Cattle Rancher Who Won't Eat Meat by Howard F. Lyman with Glen Merzer
My Beef with Meat: The Healthiest Argument for Eating a Plant–Strong Diet by Rip Esselstyn
Power Foods for the Brain by Neal D. Barnard, MD
Prevent & Reverse Heart Disease by Dr. Caldwell Esselstyn Jr.
Shred It by Robert Cheeke
Skinny Bitch by Rory Freedman and Kim Barnouin
Surprises in Mili's Suitcase by Katherine Orr and Antonia Demas, PhD
The Campbell Plan by Thomas Campbell, MD
The Cancer Survivors Guide: Foods that Help You Fight Back by Dr. Neal Barnard
The Cheese Trap by Dr. Neal Barnard and Marilu Henner
The China Study by Dr. T. Colin Campbell
The China Study Solution by Thomas Campbell, MD
The Complete Idiot's Guide to Plant–Based Nutrition by Julieanna Hever
The Empty Medicine Cabinet by Dustin Rudolph
The End of Diabetes by Dr. Joel Fuhrman

The End of Overeating by David A. Kessler
The Food Revolution by John Robbins and Dean Ornish
The Good Carbohydrate Revolution by Dr. Terri Shintani
The Happy Herbivore Guide to Plant–Based Living by Lindsay S. Nixon
The Healthiest Diet on the Planet by Dr. John McDougall & Mary McDougall
The Low–Carb Fraud by T. Colin Campbell, PhD with Howard Jacobson, PhD
The Mindful Vegan by Lani Muelrath
The Plant–Based Journey by Lani Muelrath
The Pleasure Trap by Douglas Lisle, PhD and Alan Goldhamer, DC
The Starch Solution by Dr. John McDougall, MD and Mary McDougall
The Sugar Solution by Sari Harrar
The Sustainability Secret: Rethinking Our Diet to Transform the World by Kip Andersen and Keegan Kuhn
The Vegiterranean Diet by Julieanna Hever
The Whole Foods Diet by John Mackey, Alona Pulde, MD, and Matthew Lederman, MD
Thrive: The Vegan Nutrition Guide to Optimal Performance in Sports and in Life by Brendan Brazier
Whole: Rethinking the Science of Nutrition by T. Colin Campbell, PhD with Howard Jacobson, PhD
Why We Love Dogs, Eat Pigs, and Wear Cows by Melanie Joy

Cookbooks

1000 Vegan Recipes by Robin Robertson
Aquafaba: Sweet and Savory Vegan Recipes Made Egg–Free with the Magic of Bean Water by Zsu Dever
Artisan Vegan Cheese by Miyoko Schinner
Blissful Bites by Christy Morgan
Bravo! by Ramses Bravo and Alan Goldhammer, DC
But I Could Never Go Vegan by Kristy Turner
Eat Vegan on $4.00 a Day by Ellen Jaffe Jones
Eat, Drink, and Be Vegan by Dreena Burton
Forks Over Knives by Gene Stone
Forks Over Knives The Cookbook by Del Sroufe and Isa Chandra Moskowitz
How It All Vegan by Tanya Barnard and Sarah Kramer
Let Them Eat Vegan by Dreena Burton
Plant–Powered Families: Over 100 Kid–Tested, Whole–Foods Vegan Recipes by Dreena Burton
Plant–Strong by Rip Esselstyn
Prevent and Reverse Heart Disease by Caldwell B. Esselstyn Jr., MD
Quick–Fix Vegan by Robin Robertson
Short–Cut Vegan: Great Taste in no Time by Lorna Sass
The Book of Veganish by Kathy Freston and Rachel Cohn
The China Study Cookbook by LeAnne Campbell, PhD
The China Study All–Star Collection by LeAnne Campbell, PhD
The China Study Family Cookbook by Del Sroufe
The China Study Quick & Easy Cookbook by Del Sroufe
The Complete Idiot's Guide to Vegan Cooking by Beverly Lynn Bennett
The Engine 2 Diet by Rip Esselstyn
The Great Life Cookbook by Priscilla Timberlake and Lewis Freedman, RD
The Happy Herbivore Cookbook by Lindsay S. Nixon
The PlantPure Kitchen by Kim Campbell
The PlantPure Nation Cookbook by Kim Campbell

The Vegan Table by Colleen Patrick–Goudreau
The Vegetarian Flavor Bible by Karen Page
Unprocessed by Chef AJ and Glen Merzer
Veganomicon by Isa Chandra Moskowitz

Documentaries

The documentaries in this section are intended to provoke thought about the profound effects of our everyday food choices. Some may cause you to reevaluate your choices, while others may reinforce the choices that you have already made. Many of these documentaries are available on Netflix.

Carnage: Swallowing the Past (2017) – www.imdb.com/title/tt6667360/
Crazy Sexy Cancer (2007) – www.imdb.com/title/tt0960749/,
Cowspiracy: The Sustainability Secret (2014) – www.imdb.com/title/tt3302820/
Earthlings (2005) – www.imdb.com/title/tt0358456/
Eating You Alive (2016) – www.imdb.com/title/tt5241760/
Farm to Fridge (2011) – view discretion advised. www.imdb.com/title/tt1863233/
Fat, Sick & Nearly Dead (2010) – www.imdb.com/title/tt1227378/
Food Choices (2016) – www.imdb.com/title/tt6039284/
Food Matters (2008) – www.imdb.com/title/tt1528734/
Food, Inc. (2008) – www.imdb.com/title/tt1286537/
Forks Over Knives (2011) – perhaps the most influential of all the plant–based documentaries
        www.imdb.com/title/tt1567233/
Hungry for Change (2012) – www.imdb.com/title/tt2323551/
Live and let Live (2013) – www.imdb.com/title/tt3408558/
Meat the Truth (2007) – www.imdb.com/title/tt1341746/
Meet Your Meat (2002) – www.imdb.com/title/tt1667843/
Peaceable Kingdom (2009) – www.imdb.com/title/tt0435715/
Planeat (2010) – www.imdb.com/title/tt1467030/
PlantPure Nation (2015) – www.imdb.com/title/tt3699150/
Simply Raw: Reversing Diabetes in 30 Days – www.imdb.com/title/tt1587696/
Speciesism: The Movie (2013) – www.imdb.com/title/tt2359814
Super Size Me (2004) – www.imdb.com/title/tt0390521
The Engine 2 Kitchen Rescue (2011) – www.imdb.com/title/tt2234536/
The Ghosts in our Machine (2013) – www.imdb.com/title/tt2654562/
Unity (2015) – sequel to Earthlings. www.imdb.com/title/tt2049636/
Vegan: Everyday Stories (2016) – www.imdb.com/title/tt4805966/
Vegucated (2011) – www.imdb.com/title/tt1814930
What the Health (2017) – follow up to Cowspiracy – www.imdb.com/title/tt5541848/

Gurus

One of the most important things you can do as you start your journey toward plant–based eating is to find a guru who has a philosophy and eating style you can relate to. There are any number of similar, but unique plant–based eating programs. These are headed by intrepid leaders who have acted on evidence–based research to develop appropriate recipes and eating plans in spite of tremendous government and industry pressures to the contrary. Each of these leaders has their own version of what the most healthy diet should be. Even though there are some differences, the overriding belief is that a whole food plant–based diet with minimal oil, sugar, and processed foods is the best protection against the ravages of diet–caused diseases. Identifying one leader or eating program that you can relate to simplifies things and makes it easier to follow.

My wife follows the guidelines of Ann and Jane Esselstyn, the wife and daughter of Dr. Caldwell Esselstyn, and the authors of numerous cookbooks. This duo cook primarily whole–food plant–based with an emphasis on low oil. I greatly admire the efforts of Dr. Michael Greger to keep us informed of the latest research results by posting videos on nutritionfacts.org. I endeavor to keep up with his recommendations as the research evolves. I've been strongly influenced by the Certificate program created by Dr. T. Colin Campbell and his son, Dr. Thomas Campbell, though eCornell. I've also learned a lot about cooking and nutrition from Patty "Sassy" Knutson of vegancoach.com. Sassy taught me how to cook without recipes; it's very liberating. Dr. Neal Barnard has had a tremendous influence on the plant–based movement with his numerous books, his founding of the Barnard Medical Center in Washington, D.C., and his outreach as president of the Physicians Committee for Responsible Medicine (PCRM). Caldwell Esselstyn showed us how to reverse heart disease with his eating program as did Dean Ornish in his studies. Dr. Michael Klaper has been a strong advocate and practitioner of plant–only medicine since, well, maybe since time began (let me get back to you on that). Dr. John McDougall is also a strong proponent of a low–fat, whole foods, plant–based vegan diet. The McDougall Diet has been quite successful helping people lose weight, reduce cholesterol, reduce blood pressure, and more. Although not strictly plant–based, Dr. Joel Fuhrman coined the term "Nutritarian" for his nutrient–rich diet program and championed the concept of nutrient density with his ANDI (Aggregate Nutrient Density Index) scores. Rip Esselstyn has a following with his Engine 2 Diet. John Robbins has given us numerous books on diet and how to age gracefully, and serves as co–host of the Food Revolution Network with his son Ocean. Nelson Campbell created the documentary "PlantPure Nation," established the nationwide educational outreach system of pods in local communities, and pursues plant–based healthcare in hospitals and corporations. The website plantpurenation.com has a 10–day challenge and delivers frozen meals to your door.

There are plenty of other leaders and eating plans that are not mentioned here. The point is, if you are just getting started, do a little research, and find your own guru or eating plan to follow. It will make your transition that much easier.

Ann and Jane Esselstyn – planeat.tv/ann–esselstyn
Dr. Caldwell Esselstyn, Jr. – dresselstyn.com
Dr. Dean Ornish – deanornish.com
Dr. Joel Fuhrman – drfuhrman.com
Dr. John McDougall – https://www.drmcdougall.com
Dr. Michael Greger – nutritionfacts.org
Dr. Michael Klaper – doctorklaper.com
Dr. Neal Barnard – pcrm.org
Dr. T. Colin Campbell – nutritionstudies.org
Dr. Thomas Campbell – nutritionstudies.org
John Robbins – Foodrevolution.org
Nelson Campbell – plantpurenation.com
Ocean Robbins – Foodrevolution.org
Rip Esselstyn – engine2diet.com

Meetups (meetup.com)

Meetup is a social networking site that enables people to connect online with people of common interests and arrange offline group meetings. Search meetup.com for plant–based meetups in your local area. Some San Diego meetups are included here as examples.

Awesome Rawsome Lifestyle
East County Vegans
North County Vegans
PlantDiego
San Diego Raw Vegans
San Diego Vegans
San Diego Vegan Community
San Diego Vegan Networking Group
South County Vegans

Online Cooking/Nutrition Classes

Living Light Culinary Institute – www.rawfoodchef.com/classes/plant–based
Forks Over Knives – www.forksoverknives.com/cooking–course/online
Plant–Based Nutrition Certificate – nutritionstudies.org/courses/plant–based–nutrition
Plant–Based Pro Certification – https://rouxbe.com/plant–based–certification–course/
School of Natural Cookery – www.naturalcookery.com/
Vegan Coach – vegancoach.com
Vegan Fusion – veganfusion.com

Recipes Online

Some of these sites listed here have additional resources, but all of them are chock full of recipes.

Chocolate Covered Katie – ChocolateCoveredKatie.com
Fat Free Vegan Recipes – http://fatfreevegan.com
NutritionMD – nutritionmd.org
Plant Based on a Budget – plantbasedonabudget.com
Plant–Powered Kitchen – plantpoweredkitchen.com
Straight Up Food – straightupfood.com
The Compassionate Cook – thecompassionatecook.blogspot.com
VaVaVoom – eerainuh.com

Shop Vegan Food Online

Adrianascaravan.com – ethnic condiments and seasonings
CSA (Community Supported Agriculture) – farm fresh produce delivered to your door or a pickup location. Check online for services in your area.
Edenfoods.com – organic foods
Elpasochile.com – salsas, dips, and hot sauces
Goldminenauralfoods.com – organic ingredients
Kingarthurflour.com – large selection of baking flours and baking equipment
Pangea (TheVeganStore.com) – food, cosmetics, home, cleaning, etc.
PlantPureNation.com – frozen meals delivered packed in dry ice.
Ranchogordo.com – good selection of heirloom dried beans
Theherbivorousbutcher.com – vegan meats and cheeses
Thrivemarket.com – Food, beauty, health, etc.

Try.purplecarrot.com – portioned meal ingredients
Vegan.com – compilation of vegan foods from amazon.com
Vegan Essentials – food, beauty, clothing, home products, books, etc.

Social Media Resources

Facebook

Aquafaba (Vegan Meringue – Hits and Misses!)
Dr. Caldwell B. Esselstyn, Jr.
Dr. Garth Davis
Dr. Joel Kahn
Dr. John McDougall
Dr. Neal Barnard
Food for Life San Diego
Jeff Novick, MS, RD
Kathy Freston
Rich Roll
Veg–Appeal

Instagram

Go to Instagram.com and search for these accounts. Instagram is based primarily on pictures, but you may be able to find recipes through the author's Bio or website.

Bestofvegan
knfx
minimalistbaker
nomyourself
ohholybasil
plantbased_pixie
pureveganfood
slowclubcookery
sweetsimplevegan
thedreamyleaf
theveganpecan

Pinterest

Go to Pinterest.com and search for these boards.

A Rooted Kitchen
Chocolate Covered Katie
Engine 2 Diet
Finding Vegan Bloggers!
From A to Vegan
Healthy Snack Food Recipes
Kathy Patalsky of Healthy, Happy, Life.
Melissa Martin (Vegenista)
Plant–Based Bloggers
The Laziest Vegans in the World
Vegan Community
Vegan Recipes around the World
Vegansaurus
VegNews Magazine
Whole Food Mommies Recipes –
        https://www.pinterest.com/wfmommies/whole–food–plant–based–recipes/?lp=true
Your Daily Vegan

Reddit

Go to Reddit.com and search for these subreddits. Reddit is a place where people can meet on the internet and share information on topics of common interest. Reddit is like a front page to the internet. You can customize that front page by subscribing to subreddits that interest you. The posts are listed in order of popularity. You can upvote posts you like and downvote posts that you don't like. Clicking on a post generally takes you to another website. Here are some subreddits you may find of interest:

r/ForksoverKnives
r/grainfreeplantbased
r/plantbased
r/PlantBasedDiet
r/PlantBasedRecipes
r/vegan
r/Vegan_Food
r/veganfitness
r/veganrecipes
r/veganrunners
r/VeggieMeat
r/vegweightloss
r/wfpb
r/WFPBsupportgroup
r/WholeFoodsPlantBased

Tumblr

Go to Tumblr.com and search for these accounts. They are mostly pictures, but some accounts post links to recipes.

Aplantbasedworld
Br–avo
Healthyliveshealthyvibes
Lazyv
Loveveganaddict
The–veggiekitchen
Veganrecipecollection
Veganfoody
Veganjul
veganzoejessica
Veggie–ness

Twitter

is called a hashtag. It marks keywords or topics in a Tweet. Type a hashtagged keyword in the search bar to discover related content and accounts.
@ is used to call out user names in Twitter. @UserName becomes a link to a specific Twitter profile.
Go to twitter.com and type these into the search box.

#plantbased
#VeganCook
@AboutVeganFood
@CookVeganMag
@FindingVegan
@ItsEasy2bVegan
@PBforHealth
@PlantBasedNews
@Plantarian
@TheVeganKitchen
@TheVeganSociety
@Vegan
@VeganCook101
@VeganLifeMagazine
@VeganRadio
@Wholefoodrainbw

Websites

Blue Zones – bluezones.com
Campaign for a Commercial Free Childhood – www.commercialfreechildhood.org/
Child Nutrition Programs (USDA) – http://www.fns.usda.gov/cnd/
Center for Science in the Public Interest – https://cspinet.org/
Centers for Disease Control and Prevention. – www.cdc.gov

Corporate Accountability International –
   https://www.stopcorporateabuse.org/
Cowspiracy – cowspiracy.com/facts/
Dietary Guidelines for Americans –
   http://www.cnpp.usda.gov/DietaryGuidelines
Dr. John McDougall – https://www.drmcdougall.com
Dr. T. Colin Campbell – nutritionstudies.org
Economic Research Service (USDA) Food Choices and Health –
   http://www.ers.usda.gov/topics/food–choices–health.aspx
Engine 2 Plant–Strong – engine2diet.com
Factory Farming Awareness Coalition – http://www.ffacoalition.org
Farm Sanctuary – https://www.farmsanctuary.org/
Environmental Working Group – a complete list of food recommendations on organic produce without pesticides. Ewg.org

Dining Out
   HappyCow – HappyCow.net
   OneGreenPlanet – Onegreenplanet.org
   PETA – https://www.peta.org/living/food/chain–restaurants/
   UrbanTasteBud – urbantastebud.com/vegan–restaurant–list/
   VegGuide – VegGuide.org
   Yelp – Yelp.com, search for vegan
Fooducate – nutrition information. Fooducate.com
Food and Nutrition Information Center: Food and Nutrition Topics from A to Z (USDA) –
   http://fnic.nal.usda.gov/topics–z
Forks Over Knives – Forksoverknives.com
Food Safety Information – foodsafety.gov/
Foods (FDA) – https://www.fda.gov/Food/default.htm
Grow Your Own Vegetables – https://growyourownvegetables.org
Happy Herbivore – https://happyherbivore.com/
Dr. Joel Kahn – drjoelkahn.com
John Robbins – Foodrevolution.org
Medline Plus – https://medlineplus.gov /
Mercy for Animals – mercyforanimals.org
National Center for Health Statistics (CDC) – http://www.cdc.gov/nchs/
Nutrition – a service of the National Agricultural Library, USDA
   Nutrition.gov
Nutrition Facts – Nutrition info from current research. NutritionFacts.org
Office of Disease Prevention and Health Promotion –
   https://health.gov/dietaryguidelines
Office of Dietary Supplements (NIH) – https://ods.od.nih.gov/
Oregon State University Micronutrient Information Center –
   http://lpi.oregonstate.edu/mic
Organic Facts – Organicfacts.net
Plant Yourself – plantyourself.com
Plant–Based Dietitian – plantbaseddietitian.com
Plant–Based Nutrition Support Group – https://www.pbnsg.org
Plant–Based Pharmacist – PlantBasedPharmacist.com
PlantDiego – Example of local pod organization, Plantdiego.com
PlantPure Nation – plantpurenation.com

PlantPositive – Plantpositive.com

Rise of the Vegan – articles on the vegan movement. riseofthevegan.com.

Straight Up Food – straightupfood.com

The Good Food Institute – transitioning the global food system away from industrial animal agriculture. http://www.gfi.org/

The Herbivorous Butcher – meats and cheses online, brick and mortar store, blog, recipes, farm sanctuary kickstarter. theherbivorousbutcher.com

The Plant-Based Foods Association - https://plantbasedfoods.org/

The Plant–Based Diet Kaiser Permanente – https://share.kaiserpermanente.org/wp–content/uploads/2015/10/The–Plant–Based–Diet–booklet.pdf

The Plantrician Project – Plantbasedresearch.org

The Vegan Junction – Theveganjunction.com

The Vegetarian Flavor Bible by Karen Page

The Vegetarian Resource Group. Vrg.org

Thrive Market – vegan foods and products online. Thrivemarket.com

UC Davis Integrative Medicine - blog and recipes. ucdintegrativemedicine.com

Urban Tastebud – Urbantastebud.com

USDA Food Composition Databases – find nutrient information for your food items. https://ndb.nal.usda.gov/ndb/

USDA Nutrient Data Laboratory – http://www.ars.usda.gov/main/site_main.htm?modecode=80–40–05–25

Veg–Appeal – classes, services, resources. Veg–appeal.com

Vegan Coach – vegancoach.com

Vegan Cruise Planners – Vegancruiseplanners.com

Vegan kit – starter kit for going vegan. Vegankit.com

Veg Jaunts and Journeys – guided tours to vegan–friendly places. Vegjauntsandjourneys.com

VegNews Magazine – vegnews.com

VegWorld Magazine – vegworldmag.com.

Whole Food Mommies – Wholefoodmommies.com

Vegetarian Resource Group – Vegetarianism in a Nutshell, www.vrg.org

REFERENCE CITATIONS

Reference citations are organized by chapter and numbered sequentially in the order that they occur. References in the text are indicated by a superscript number enclosed in brackets. [23]

Preface

1. United Nations Department of Economic and Social Affairs, Population Division, "World Population Prospects: The 2015 Revision—Key Findings and Advance Tables" (PDF), July 2015 (Retrieved June 26, 2016).
2. Simon, S., "World Health Organization Says Processed Meat Causes Cancer," American Cancer Society, https://www.cancer.org/latest–news/world–health–organization–says–processed–meat–causes–cancer.html (October 26, 2015).

1. Why Eat a Plant–based Diet?

1. PCRM.org, "Lifestyle Intervention for Diabetes More Cost–Effective Than Drugs," http://www.pcrm.org/health/medNews/lifestyle–intervention–for–diabetes–more–cost.
2. Lenders, Carine, et al., "A Novel Nutrition Medicine Education Model: the Boston University Experience," *Advances in Nutrition* 4 (January 4, 2013): 1–7
3. US Burden of Disease Collaborators, "The State of US Health, 1990–2010: Burden of Diseases, Injuries, and Risk Factors," *JAMA* (2013); 310(6): 591–606
4. Orlich, Michael J., MD; Pramil N. Singh, DrPH; Joan Sabaté, MD, DrPH; et al., "Vegetarian dietary patterns and mortality in Adventist Health Study 2," *JAMA Internal Medicine* (July 2013); 173(13): 1230–8.
5. Spencer, E.A., P.N. Appleby, G.K. Davey, and T.J. Key, "Diet and body mass index in 38000 EPIC–Oxford meat–eaters, fish–eaters, vegetarians and vegans," *International Journal of Obesity* (June 2003); 27: 728–34
6. Kaiser Permanente, "The plant–based diet: a healthier way to eat," https://share.kaiserpermanente.org/wp–content/uploads/2015/10/The–Plant–Based–Diet–booklet.pdf.
7. Hicks, J. Morris, "Our own health, or the health of our ecosystem?" https://hpjmh.com/2016/09/06/our–own–health–or–the–health–of–our–ecosystem/
8. Truth or Drought, "'Save Water Eat Plants' Lawn Signs Show Going Vegan Saves 600 Gallons Per Day," https://www.truthordrought.com/single–post/2015/04/18/Save–Water–Eat–Plants–Lawn–Signs–Show–Going–Vegan–Saves–600–Gallons–Per–Day (accessed May 30, 2017).
9. McWilliams, James. "Meat Makes the Planet Thirsty." *The New York Times,* March 7, 2014. http://www.nytimes.com/2014/03/08/opinion/meat–makes–the–planet–thirsty.html?_r=1 (accessed April 27, 2016).
10. Livestock's long shadow, ftp://ftp.fao.org/docrep/fao/010/a0701e/a0701e07.pdf (accessed May 30, 2017).
11. Kanaly, Robert A., et al., "Energy Flow, Environmental and Ethical Implications for Meat Production," UNESCO Bangkok (2010), http://unesdoc.unesco.org/images/0018/001897/189774e.pdf.

12. Hyner, Christopher, "A Leading Cause of Everything: One Industry That Is Destroying Our Planet and Our Ability to Thrive on It," *Stanford Environmental Law Journal*, https://journals.law.stanford.edu/stanford–environmental–law–journal–elj/blog/leading–cause–everything–one–industry–destroying–our–planet–and–our–ability–thrive–it.

13. Margulis, Sergio, "Causes of Deforestation of the Brazilian Amazon," World Bank Working Paper, no. 22, http://documents.worldbank.org/curated/en/758171468768828889/pdf/277150PAPER0wbwp0no1022.pdf.

14. Ibid.

15. Machovina, Brian, et al., "Biodiversity conservation: The key is reducing meat consumption," *Science of the Total Environment* 536 (2015): 419–31 http://www.cof.orst.edu/leopold/papers/Machovina_2015.pdf.

16. Sheer, Roddy, and Doug Moss, "What Causes Ocean 'Dead Zones'?" Scientific American, https://www.scientificamerican.com/article/ocean–dead–zones/.

17. World Population Balance, "Current Population is Three Times the Sustainable Level," http://www.worldpopulationbalance.org/3_times_sustainable (accessed February 2017).

18. ABC News Staff, "100 Million Dieters, $20 Billion: The Weight–Loss Industry by the Numbers," ABC News, May 8, 2012, http://abcnews.go.com/Health/100–million–dieters–20–billion–weight–loss–industry/story?id=16297197.

19. Fung, Teresa T., Rob M. van Dam, Susan E. Hankinson, Walter C. Wilett, and Frank B. Hu, "Low–Carbohydrate Diets and All–Cause and Cause–Specific Mortality: Two Cohort Studies," *Annals of Internal Medicine* (2010); 153(5): 289–98.

20. Greger, Michael MD. *How Not to Die*. Flatiron Books, 2015: 403.

21. Robbins, John. *Healthy at 100: The Scientifically Proven Secrets of the World's Healthiest and Longest Lived Peoples*. Ballantine Books, 2007.

22. Stanger, Janice PhD, "What Do the Healthiest, Longest–Living People in the World Eat?" Forks Over Knives, www.forksoverknives.com/longevity–diet/.

23. Willcox, Bradley J., D. Craig Willcox, Hidemi Todoriki, et al., "Caloric Restriction, the Traditional Okinawan Diet, and Healthy Aging," *Annals of the New York Academy of Sciences* 1114 (2007): 434–55. http://www.okicent.org/docs/anyas_cr_diet_2007_1114_434s.pdf (accessed July 17, 2017).

24. Cusack, Leila, Emmy De Buck, Veerle Compernolle, and Philippe Vandekerckhove, "Blood type diets lack supporting evidence: A systematic review," *The American Journal of Clinical Nutrition* (2013); 98(1): 99–104

25. Larhammar, Dan, "Fakes and frauds in commercial diets," *Scandinavian Journal of Nutrition* (2005); 49(2): 78–80.

26. Greger, Michael, MD, "Blood Type Diet Debunked," https://nutritionfacts.org/2015/06/04/blood–type–diet–debunked/ (accessed July 17, 2017).

2. Higher Health Consciousness

1. PETA.org, "Meat and the Environment," https://www.peta.org/issues/animals–used–for–food/meat–environment/.

2. PETA.org, "Vegans Save 198 Animals a Year," https://www.peta.org/blog/vegans–save–185–animals–year/.

3. *Carnage: Swallowing the Past*, http://www.imdb.com/title/tt6667360/.

3. Nutrition and Health

1. Greger, Michael M.D., "Plant–based Diets," www.nutritionfacts.org/topics/plant–based–diets/ (updated November 30, 2016).

2. Tuso, Philip J., Mohamed H. Ismail, Benjamin P. Ha, and Carole Bartolotto, "Nutritional Update for Physicians: Plant–Based Diets." *The Permanente Journal* (Spring 2013); 17(2): 61–6.

3. NIH, "Overweight and Obesity Statistics," https://www.niddk.nih.gov/health–information/health–statistics/overweight–obesity.

4. Boston Medical Center, "Weight Management," https://www.bmc.org/nutrition–and–weight–management/weight–management (accessed January 18, 2017).

5. Pietiläinen, K.H., et al., "Does dieting make you fat? A twin study," *International Journal of Obesity* (2012); 36: 456–64.

6. Berkow, Susan E., PhD, CNS; and Neal Barnard, MD; "Vegetarian diets and weight status," *Nutrition Reviews* (April 2006); 64(4): 175–88. DOI: http://dx.doi.org/10.1111/j.1753–4887.2006.tb00200.x

7. Farmer, Bonnie, MS, RD; Brain T. Larson, PhD; Victor L. Fulgoni III, PhD; Alice J. Rainville, PhD, RD; and George U. Liepa, PhD; "A Vegetarian Dietary Pattern as a Nutrient–Dense Approach to Weight Management: An Analysis of the National Health and Nutrition Examination Survey 1999–2004," *Journal of the American Dietetic Association* (June 2011); 111(6): 819–27. DOI: http://dx.doi.org/10.1016/j.jada.2011.03.012.

8. Wang, Y., Beydoun M.A., "Meat consumption is associated with obesity and central obesity among US adults," *International Journal of Obesity* (June 2009); 33(6): 621–8. DOI: http://dx.doi.org/10.1038/ijo.2009.45

9. Rosell, M., P.N. Appleby, E. Spencer, and T. Key. "Weight gain over 5 years in 21,966 meat–eating, fish–eating, vegetarian, and vegan men and women in EPIC–Oxford," *International Journal of Obesity* (September 2006); 30(9): 1389–96. DOI: http://dx.doi.org/10.1038/sj.ijo.0803305.

10. Sabaté, Joan, and Michelle Wien, "Vegetarian diets and childhood obesity prevention," *The American Journal of Clinical Nutrition* (May 2010); 91(5): 1525S–29S. DOI: http://dx.doi.org/10.3945/ajcn.2010.28701F.

11. Turner–McGrievy, Gabrielle M., PhD, RD; Charis R. Davidson, MPH; Ellen E. Wingard, MPH, RD; Sara Wilcox, and Edward A. Frongillo, PhD; "Comparative effectiveness of plant–based diets for weight loss: A randomized controlled trial of five different diets," ScienceDirect, *Nutrition* (February 2015); 31(2): 350–58 http://www.sciencedirect.com/science/article/pii/S0899900714004237.

12. Centers for Disease Control and Prevention, "Long–term Trends in Diabetes." https://www.cdc.gov/diabetes/statistics/slides/long_term_trends.pdf (accessed September 3, 2017).

13. Tonstad, Serena, MD, PhD; Terry Butler, DrPH, Ru Yan, MSC, and Gary E. Fraser, MD, PhD; "Type of Vegetarian Diet, Body Weight, and Prevalence of Type 2 Diabetes," *Diabetes Care* (May 2009); 32(5): 791–6. DOI: http://dx.doi.org/10.2337/dc08–1886.

14. Zhu, Weifei, Stanley L. Hazen, et al., "Gut Microbe–Generated Trimethylamine N–Oxide From Dietary Choline Is Prothrombotic in Subjects" *Circulation* (2017); 135: 1671–73. https://doi.org/10.1161/CIRCULATIONAHA.116.025338

15. Cornell University, "Dietary compound linked to heart disease may be influenced by gut microbiome," *ScienceDaily*, August 11, 2016, http://www.sciencedaily.com/releases/2016/08/160811120408.htm.

16. Cleveland HeartLab, "TMAO Testing: A New Way To Assess Heart Attack And Stroke Risk," http://www.clevelandheartlab.com/blog/horizons–tmao–testing–a–new–way–to–assess–heart–attack–and–stroke–risk/.

17. Greger, Michael, MD, "Eggs vs. Cigarettes in Atherosclerosis," NutritionFacts.org, http://nutritionfacts.org/video/eggs–vs–cigarettes–in–atherosclerosis/.

18. Chen, Junshi, T. Colin Campbell, Li Junyao , and Richard Peto. *Diet, Life–Style and Mortality in China:*

A Study of the Characteristics of 65 Chinese Counties. New York: Oxford University Press, 1990.

19. Shaper, A.G., and K.W. Jones. "Serum–cholesterol, diet, and coronary heart–disease in Africans and Asians in Uganda: 1959," *International Journal of Epidemiology* (2012); 41(5): 1221–5

20. Voller, Robert D., Jr., MD; William B. Strong, MD; "Pediatric aspects of atherosclerosis," *American Heart Journal* (1981); 101(6): 815–36

21. Ornish, D., MD; S.E. Brown, MD; L.W. Scherwitz, PhD; et al., "Can lifestyle changes reverse coronary heart disease?" *The Lancet* (July 21, 1990); 336(8708): 129–33. DOI: http://dx.doi.org/10.1016/0140–6736(90)91656–U.

22. de Lorgeril, Michel, MD; Patricia Salen, BSc; Jean–Louis Martin, PhD; Isabelle Monjaud, BSc; Jacques Delaye, MD; and Nicole Mamelle, PhD; "Mediterranean Diet, Traditional Risk Factors, and the Rate of Cardiovascular Complications After Myocardial Infarction: Final Report of the Lyon Diet Heart Study," *Circulation* (1999); 99: 779–85. DOI: http://dx.doi.org/10.1161/01.CIR.99.6.779

23. Esselstyn, Caldwell B., Jr., MD; Gina Gendy, MD; Jonathan Doyle, McS; Mladen Golubic, MD, PhD; and Michael F. Roizen, MD; "A way to reverse CAD?" *The Journal of Family Practice* (July 2014); 63(7): 356–64.

24. Lim, Dr. Stephen S., PhD; Prof. Theo Vos, PhD; Abraham D Flaxman, PhD; et al., "A comparative risk assessment of burden of disease and injury attributable to 67 risk factors and risk factor clusters in 21 regions, 1990–2010; a systematic analysis for the Global Burden of Disease Study 2010," *The Lancet* (2012); 380(9859): 2224–60.

25. Donnison, CP, MB, BS Lond., "Blood pressure in the African native," *The Lancet* (1929); 213(5497): 6–7.

26. Lindahl, Olov, Lars Lindwall, Alf Spångberg, ÅKe Stenram, and Per Arne Öckerman, "A vegan regimen with reduced medication in the treatment of hypertension," *British Journal of Nutrition* (1984); 52(1): 11–20.
http://journals.cambridge.org/download.php?file=%2FBJN%2FBJN52_01%2FS000711458400067 2a.pdf&code=6e14372caf0bdba50e7fa9d615b280fd.

27. Centers for Disease Control and Prevention, "Sodium Intake Among Adults—United States, 2005–2006," *Morbidity and Mortality Weekly Report* (2010); 59(24): 746–9.
https://www.cdc.gov/mmwr/preview/mmwrhtml/mm5924a4.htm.

28. Duke University Medical Center, "Salt appetite is linked to drug addiction, research finds," *ScienceDaily* (July 29, 2011), http://sciencedaily.com/releases/2011/07/110711151451.htm.

29. SFGATE, "How Much Sodium Do Adults Need Daily?" http://healthyeating.sfgate.com/much–sodium–adults–need–daily–5362.html (accessed January 9, 2017).

30. National Cancer Institute, "Cancer Statistics," https://www.cancer.gov/about–cancer/understanding/statistics (updated March 14, 2016).

31. Twombly, Renee, "Cancer Surpasses Heart Disease as Leading Cause of Death for All But the Very Elderly," *JNCI: Journal of the National Cancer Institute* (2005); 97(5): 330–31. https://jnci.oxfordjournals.org/content/97/5/330.1.full.

32. Key, T.J., P.N. Appleby, E.A. Spencer, et al., "Cancer incidence in British vegetarians," *British Journal of Cancer* (2009); 101(1): 192–7.

33. Dinu, M., R. Abbate, G.F. Gensini, et al., "Vegetarian, vegan diets and multiple health outcomes: A systematic review with meta–analysis of observational studies," *Critical Reviews in Food Science and Nutrition* (2016); 57(17): 3640–9. http://www.ncbi.nlm.nih.gov/pubmed/26853923.

34. Allen, Naomi E., Paul N. Appleby, Gwyneth K. Davey, Rudolf Kasks, Sabina Rinaldi, and Timothy J. Key, "The Associations of Diet with Serum Insulin–like Growth Factor I and Its Main Binding Proteins in 292 Women Meat–Eaters, Vegetarians, and Vegans," *Cancer Epidemiology, Biomarkers & Prevention* (November 2002); 11(11): 1441–8.

35. Rowlands, Mari–Anne, David Gunnell, Ross Harris, et al., "Circulating insulin–like growth factor (IGF) peptides and prostate cancer risk: a systematic review and meta–analysis," *International Journal of*

Cancer (May 15, 2009); 124(10): 2416–29.

36. Renehan, Andrew G., PhD; Marcel Zwahlen, PhD; Prof. Chistoph Minder, PhD; Sarah T. O'Dwyer, MD; Prof. Stephen M. Shalet, MD; and Prof. Matthias Egger, MD; "Insulin–like growth factor (IGF)–I, IGF binding protein–3, and cancer risk: systematic review and meta–regression analysis," *The Lancet* (April 24, 2004); 363(9418): 1346–53.

37. Soliman, Sherry, William J. Aronson, and R. James Barnard, "Analyzing Serum–Stimulated Prostate Cancer Cell Lines After Low–Fat, High–Fiber Diet and Exercise Intervention," *Evidence–Based Complementary and Alternative Medicine* 2011 (2011), Article ID: 529053.

38. Thorogood, M., et al., "Plasma lipids and lipoprotein cholesterol concentrations in people with different in Britain," *British Medical Journal* 295 (1987): 351–3.

39. Song, Mingyang, MD, ScD; Teresa T. Fung, ScD; Frank B. Hu, MD, PhD; et al., "Association of Animal and Plant Protein Intake With All–Cause and Cause–Specific Mortality," *JAMA Internal Medicine* (2016); 176(10): 1453–1463.
    http://jamanetwork.com/journals/jamainternalmedicine/article–abstract/2540540.

40. Zeratsky, Katherine, RD, LD, "What is high–fructose corn syrup? What are the health concerns?" Mayo Clinic.

41. Tang, Gang, MD; Duan Want, BS; Jun Long, BS; et al., "Meta–Analysis of the Association Between Whole Grain Intake and Coronary Heart Disease Risk," *American Journal of Cardiology* (2015); 115(5): 625–9.

42. Anue, Dagfinn, Teresa Norat, Pål Romundstad, and Lars J. Vatten, "Whole grain and refined grain consumption and the risk of type 2 diabetes: a systematic review and dose–response meta–analysis of cohort studies," *European Journal of Epidemiology* (2013); 28(11): 845–58.

43. Cho, Susan S., Lu Qi, George C. Fahey, Jr., and David M. Klurfeld, "Consumption of cereal fiber, mixtures of whole grains and bran, and whole grains and risk reduction in type 2 diabetes, obesity, and cardiovascular disease," *The American Journal of Clinical Nutrition* (2013); 98(2): 594–619.

44. Greger, Michael, MD, "Where Do You Get Your Fiber?" Nutritionfacts.org,
    http://nutritionfacts.org/2015/09/29/where–do–you–get–your–fiber/.

45. Karlsen, Micaela, MSPH, "How Much Protein Do We Need? RDA vs. Dietary Guidelines," Center for Nutrition Studies, http://nutritionstudies.org/how–much–protein–do–we–need–rda–vs–dietary–guidelines/

46. Robbins, John. *Healthy at 100: The Scientifically Proven Secrets of the World's Healthiest and Longest Lived Peoples.* Ballantine Books, 2007.

47. Physicians Committee for Responsible Medicine, "The Protein Myth," PCRM.org,
    http://www.pcrm.org/health/diets/vsk/vegetarian–starter–kit–protein.

48. Song, Mingyang, MD, ScD; Teresa T. Fung, ScD; Frank B. Hu, MD, PhD; et al., "Association of Animal and Plant Protein Intake With All–Cause and Cause–Specific Mortality," JAMA Internal Medicine (2016); 176(10): 1453–1463.
    http://jamanetwork.com/journals/jamainternalmedicine/article–abstract/2540540.

49. Campbell, T. Colin, PhD, "A Fallacious, Faulty and Foolish Discussion About Saturated Fat," Center for Nutrition Studies, http://nutritionstudies.org/fallacious–faulty–foolish–discussion–about–saturated–fat/.

50. Barnard, Neal D., et al., "A low–fat vegan diet and a conventional diabetes diet in the treatment of diabetes: a randomized, controlled, 74–wk clinical trial,"
    https://www.ncbi.nlm.nih.gov/pmc/articles/PMC2677007/pdf/ajcn8951588S.pdf.

51. Esselstyn, Caldwell B, Jr., MD, "Best Results: Cleveland Clinic Study Stops Progress of Heart Disease with Diet and Cholesterol Drugs," http://www.dresselstyn.com/news_info.htm.

52. Papanikolaou, Yanni, et al., "U.S. adults are not meeting recommended levels for fish and omega–3 fatty acid intake: results of an analysis using observational data from NHANES 2003–2008," *Nutrition Journal* (2014); 13: 31. https://www.ncbi.nlm.nih.gov/pmc/articles/PMC3992162/.

53. Simopoulos, A.P., "The importance of the ratio of omega–6/omega–3 essential fatty acids," *Biomedicine and Pharmacotherapy* (October 2002); 56(8): 365–79. https://www.ncbi.nlm.nih.gov/pubmed/12442909.

54. HealthAliciousNess.com, "Top 10 Foods Highest in Omega 6 Fatty Acids," www.healthaliciousness.com/articles/high–omega–6–foods.php (updated June 22, 2017).

55. Thanopoulou, Anastasia C., MD, et al., "Dietary Fat Intake as Risk Factor for the Development of Diabetes," *Diabetes Care* (February 2003); 26(2): 302–7. https://doi.org/10.2337/diacare.26.2.302.

56. Sieri, Sabina, Paolo Chiodini, Claudia Agnoli, et al., "Dietary Fat Intake and Development of Specific Breast Cancer Subtypes," *Journal of the National Cancer Institute* (April 9, 2014).

57. Kroenke, Candyce H., Marilyn L. Kwan, Carol Sweeney, Adrienne Castillo, Bette J. Caan. "High– and Low–Fat Dairy Intake, Recurrence, and Mortality After Breast Cancer Diagnosis," *Journal of the National Cancer Institute* (March 14, 2013); 105(9): 616–23.

58. Fuhrman, Joel. *Nutritarian Handbook & ANDI Food Scoring Guide*. Gift of Health Press, 2012: 22.

59. Jiménez-Monreal AM, García-Diz L, Martínez-Tomé M, et al., "Influence of Cooking Methods on Antioxidant Activity of Vegetables." *J Food Sci.* (April 2009);74(3):H97-H103.

60. Holick, Michael, "Vitamin D is essential to the modern indoor lifestyle," *Science News* (October 23, 2010); 178(9): 32.
    https://www.sciencenews.org/article/vitamin–d–essential–modern–indoor–lifestyle/
    (accessed December 24, 2016).

61. Holick, Michael F., "Vitamin D: A D–Lightful Solution for Health," *Journal of Investigative Medicine* (August 2011); 59(6): 872–80.

62. Mitchell, Deborah, Maria Henao, Joel Finkelstein, and Sherri–Ann Burnett–Bowie, "Prevalence and Predictors of Vitamin D Deficiency in Healthy Adults," *Endocrine Practice* (November–December 2012); 18(6): 914–23.

63. Bischoff–Ferrari, Heike A., "Optimal Serum 25–Hydroxyvitamin D Levels for Multiple Health Outcomes," *Advances in Experimental Medicine and Biology* (2014); 810: 500–25.

64. Harvard Women's Health Watch, "How much calcium do you really need?" Harvard Health Publications, http://www.health.harvard.edu/staying–healthy/how–much–calcium–do–you–really–need (updated August 22, 2017).

65. "Calcium requirements and recommended intakes," Human Vitamin and Mineral Requirements, http://www.fao.org/docrep/004/y2809e/y2809e0h.htm#bm17.5.

66. "Calcium: Fact Sheet for Health Professionals," *National Institutes of Health*, https://ods.od.nih.gov/factsheets/Calcium–HealthProfessional/.

67. Greger, Michael, MD., "Are Calcium Supplements Safe?" http://nutritionfacts.org/video/are–calcium–supplements–safe/.

68. Penn State, "Exercise More Critical Than Calcium For Adolescent Bones," *ScienceDaily* (June 9, 2004), http://www.sciencedaily.com/releases/2004/06/040609070411.htm.

69. MedlinePlus, "Vitamin B12 deficiency anemia," https://medlineplus.gov/ency/article/000574.htm (reviewed February 1, 2016).

70. Greger, Michael MD. *How Not to Die*. Flatiron Books, 2015: 407.

71. Oregon State University, "Zinc deficiencies a global concern," www.oregonstate.edu/ua/ncs/archives/2009/sep/zinc–deficiencies–global–concern.

72. U.S. Department of Health and Human Services. *Healthy People 2010 – 2nd Edition*. McLean, VA: International Medical Publishing, Inc., 2002.

73. Greger, Michael, MD, "Risk Associated with Iron Supplements," https://nutritionfacts.org/video/risk–associated–with–iron–supplements/.

74. Greger, Michael, MD, "Donating Blood to Prevent Cancer?" https://nutritionfacts.org/video/donating–blood–to–prevent–cancer/.

75. Lim, Dr. Stephen S., PhD; Prof. Theo Vos, PhD; Abraham D. Flaxman, PhD; et al., "A comparative

risk assessment of burden of disease and injury attributable to 67 risk factors and risk factor clusters in 21 regions, 1990–2010; a systematic analysis for the Global Burden of Disease Study 2010," *The Lancet* (2012); 380(9859): 2224–60.

76. Allen, Naomi E., Paul N. Appleby, Gwyneth K. Davey, Rudolf Kaaks, Sabina Rinaldi, and Timothy J. Key, "The Associations of Diet with Serum Insulin–like Growth Factor I and Its Main Binding Proteins in 292 Women Meat–Eaters, Vegetarians, and Vegans," *Cancer Epidemiology Biomarkers Prevention* (November 2002); 11(11): 1441–8.

77. Rowlands, Mari–Anne, David Gunnell, Ross Harris, et al., "Circulating insulin–like growth factor (IGF) peptides and prostate cancer risk: a systematic review and meta–analysis," *International Journal of Cancer* (May 15, 2009); 124(10): 2416–29.

78. Chen, Junshi, Richard Peto, Wen–Harn Pan, Bo–Qui Liu, T. Colin Campbell, Jillian Boreham, Banoo Parpia, Patricia Cassano, and Zheng–Ming Chen. *Mortality, Biochemistry, Diet and Lifestyle in Rural China: Geographic Study of the Characteristics of 69 Counties in Mainland China and 16 Areas in Taiwan.* Oxford, UK; Oxford University Press, 2006.

79. Vogel, Robert A., MDa; Mary C. Coretti, MDa; and Gary D. Plotnick, MDa; "Effect of a Single High–Fat Meal on Endothelial Function in Healthy Subjects," *American Journal of Cardiology* (1997); 79(3): 350–4.

80. PETA.org, "Meat Contamination," https://www.peta.org/living/food/meat–contamination/ (accessed July 2, 2017).

81. U.S. Food and Drug Administration, "Egg Safety: What You Need to Know," https://www.fda.gov/Food/FoodborneIllnessContaminants/BuyStoreServeSafeFood/ucm077342.htm (accessed July 12, 2017).

82. Humphrey, T.J., M. Greenwood, R.J. Gilbert, et al., "The survival salmonellas in shell eggs cooked under simulated domestic conditions," *Epidemiology and Infection* (1989); 103(1): 35–45.

83. Vogt, Rainbow, Deborah Bennett, Diana Cassady, Joshua Frost, Beate Ritz, and Irva Hertz–Picciotto, "Cancer and non–cancer health effects from food contaminant exposures for children and adults in California: A risk assessment," *Environmental Health* (2012); 11: 83.

84. Campbell, T. Colin, "Dairy Protein Causes Cancer—Dr. T. Colin Campbell," Center for Nutrition Studies, http://nutritionstudies.org/provocations–dairy–protein–causes–cancer/.

85. NutritionFacts.org, "Animal Products," https://nutritionfacts.org/topics/animal–products/ (accessed July 14, 2017).

86. Anderson, J.W., P. Baird, R.H. David, Jr., et al., "Health benefits of dietary fiber," *Nutrition Reviews* (April 2009); 67(4): 188–205. https://www.ncbi.nlm.nih.gov/pubmed/19335713.

87. Moss, Michael. *Salt Sugar Fat: How the Food Giants Hooked Us.* New York: Random House, (2013): 149–50.

88. Ibid., 7.

89. Ibid., 149.

90. Rueda–Clausen, Christian F., Federico A. Silva, Manuel A. Lindarte, Cristina Villa–Roel, et al., "Olive, soybean and palm oils intake have a similar acute detrimental effect over the endothelial function in healthy young subjects," *Nutrition, Metabolism and Cardiovascular Diseases* (2007); 17(1): 50–57.

91. Avena, Nicole M., Pedro Rada, and Bartley G. Hoebel, "Evidence for sugar addiction: Behavioral and neurochemical effects of intermittent, excessive sugar intake," *Neuroscience & Biobehavioral Reviews* (2008); 32(1): 20–39. https://www.ncbi.nlm.nih.gov/pmc/articles/PMC2235907/.

92. He, F.J., and G.A. MacGregor, "A comprehensive review on salt and health and current experience of worldwide salt reduction programmes," Journal Human Hypertension (2009); 23: 363–84.

93. World Cancer Research Fund / American Institute for Cancer Research. Food, Nutrition, Physical Activity, and the Prevention of Cancer: a Global Perspective. Washington, D.C.: AICR, 2007.

94. Lim, Dr. Stephen S., PhD; Prof. Theo Vos, PhD; Abraham D. Flaxman, PhD; et al., "A comparative

risk assessment of burden of disease and injury attributable to 67 risk factors and risk factor clusters in 21 regions, 1990–2010; a systematic analysis for the Global Burden of Disease Study 2010," *The Lancet* (2012); 380(9859): 2224–60.

95. Vierk, Katherine A., MPH; Kathleen M. Koehler, PhD, MPH; Sara B. Fein, PhD; and Debra A. Street, PhD; "Prevalence of self–reported food allergy in American adults and use of food labels," *Journal of Allergy and Clinical Immunology* (June 2007); 119(6): 1504–10.

96. Thompson, Lilian, Beatrice A. Boucher, Zhen Liu, et al., "Phytoestrogen Content of Foods Consumed in Canada, Including Isoflavones, Lignans, and Coumestan," *Nutrition and Cancer*, 54(2): 184–201.

97. Zhang, Xianglan, MD, MPH; Xiao–Ou Shu, MD, PhD; Honglan Li, MD; et al., "Prospective Cohort Study of Soy Food Consumption and Risk of Bone Fracture Among Postmenopausal Women," *Archives of Internal Medicine* (September 12, 2005); 165(16): 1890–5.

98. Myung, S–K., W. Ju, H.J. Choi, S.C. Kim, The Korean Meta–Analysis (KORMA) Study Group, "Soy intake and risk of endocrine–related gynaecological cancer: a meta–analysis," *BJOG: An International Journal of Obstetrics and Gynaecology* (December 2009); 116(13): 1697–1705.

99. Capannoio, A., A. Viscido, M.A. Barkad, et al., "Non–Celiac Gluten Sensitivity among Patients Perceiving Gluten–Related Symptoms," *Journal of Digestion* (2015); 92(1): 8–13. https://www.ncbi.nlm.nih.gov/pubmed/26043918 (accessed July 18, 2017).

4. Daily Health

1. Zhang, Y., P. Talalay, C.G. Cho, G.H. Posner, "A major inducer of anticarcinogenic protective enzymes from broccoli: isolation and elucidation of structure," Proceedings of the National Academy of Sciences of the United States of America (March 15, 1992); 89(6): 2399–403.

2. Joshipura, K.J., F.B. Hu, J.E. Manson, et al., "The Effect of Fruit and Vegetable Intake on Risk for Coronary Heart Disease," *Annals of Internal Medicine* (2001); 134(12): 1106–14.

3. Joshipura, Kaumudi J., ScD; Alberto Ascherio, MD; JoAnn E. Manson, MD; et al., "Fruit and Vegetable Intake in Relation to Risk of Ischemic Stroke," *JAMA* (1999); 282(13): 1233–9.

4. Esselstyn, Caldwell B., Jr., MD, "Updating a 12–Year Experience With Arrest and Reversal Therapy for Coronary Heart Disease (An Overdue Requiem for Palliative Cardiology)," http://www.dresselstyn.com/site/study02/.

5. Esselstyn, Caldwell B., "A plant–based diet and coronary artery disease: a mandate for effective therapy," *Journal of Geriatric Cardiology* (2017); 14: 317–320.
http://www.jgc301.com/ch/reader/create_pdf.aspx?file_no=S_20170301008&flag=1.

6. Voller, Robert D., Jr., MD; William B. Strong, MD; "Pediatric aspects of atherosclerosis," *American Heart Journal* (1981); 101(6): 815–36.

7. Carlsen, M.H., B.L. Halvorsen, K. Holte, et al., "The Antioxidant Food Table," *Nutrition Journal* (2010); 9: 3. https://www.biomedcentral.com/content/supplementary/1475–2891–9–3–S1.pdf.

8. Darmadi–Blackberry, I., M.L. Wahlqvist, A. Kouris–Blazos, et al., "Legumes: the most important dietary predictor of survival in older people of different ethnicities," *Asia Pacific Journal Clinical Nutrition* (2004); 13(2): 217–20. https://www.ncbi.nlm.nih.gov/pubmed/15228991.

9. Wu, Hongyu, PhD; Alan J. Flint, MD, ScD; Qibin Qi, PhD; et al., "Association Between Dietary Whole Grain Intake and Risk of Mortality: Two Large Prospective Studies in US Men and Women," *JAMA Internal Medicine* (2015); 175(3): 373–84.

10. Fraser, Gary E., MB, ChB, PhD; and David J. Shavlik, MSPH; "Ten Years of Life: Is It a Matter of Choice?" *Archives of Internal Medicine* (2001); 161(13): 1645–52.

11. Baer, H.J., R.J. Glynn, F.B. Hu, et al., "Risk factors for mortality in the nurses' health study: a competing risks analysis," *American Journal of Epidemiology* (2011); 173: 319–29.

12. Guasch–Ferré, Marta, Mònica Bulló, Miguel Ángel Martínez–González, et al., "Frequency of nut

consumption and mortality risk in the PREDIMED nutrition intervention trial," *BMC Medicine* (2013); 11: 164.

13. Martinez–Gonzalez, M.A., M. Bes–Rastrollo, "Nut consumption, weight gain and obesity: Epidemiological evidence," *Nutrition, Metabolism, and Cardiovascular Diseases* (2011); 21(Supplement 1): S40–5.

14. Tapsell, Linda, PhD; Marijka Batterham, PhD; Sze–Yen Tan, MSc; and Eva Warensjö, PhD; "The Effect of a Calorie Controlled Diet Containing Walnuts on Substrate Oxidation during 8–hours in a Room Calorimeter," *Journal of American College of Nutrition* (2009); 28(5): 611–7.

15. Carlsen, M.H., B.L. Halvorsen, K. Holte, et al., "The Antioxidant Food Table," *Nutrition Journal* (2010); 9: 3. https://www.biomedcentral.com/content/supplementary/1475–2891–9–3–S1.pdf.

16. Akhtar MS, Ramzan A, Ali A, Ahmad M., "Effect of Amla fruit (Emblica officinalis Gaertn.) on blood glucose and lipid profile of normal subjects and type 2 diabetic patients." *Int J Food Sci Nutr.* 2011 Sep;62(6):609-16.

17. Greger, Michael, MD. *How Not to Die.* Flatiron Books, 2015: 352.

18. Efficiency Is Everything, "Calorie Per Dollar List—Eat for 21 Dollars a Week," Efficiencyiseverything.com/calorie–per–dollar–list/ (accessed December 4, 2016).

19. Connell C.L., J.M. Zoellner, M.K. Yadrick, et al., "Energy density, nutrient adequacy, and cost per serving can provide insight into food choices in the lower Mississippi Delta," *Journal of Nutrition Education and Behavior* (2012); 44(2): 148–53.

20. Centers for Medicare & Medicaid Services, www.cms.gov, (updated December 6, 2016).

21. González, Juan, "'Escape Fire': As Supreme Court Rules on Healthcare, Film Tackles U.S. Inefficiency, Spiraling Costs," https://www.democracynow.org/2012/6/28/escape_fire_as_supreme_court_rules.

22. Lazarou, Jason, MSc; Bruce H. Pomeranz, MD, PhD; and Paul N. Corey, PhD; "Incidence of Adverse Drug Reactions in Hospitalized Patients: A Meta–analysis of Prospective Studies," *JAMA* (1998); 279(15): 1200–5.

23. Starfield, Barbara, MD, MPH, "Is US Health Really the Best in the World?" *JAMA* (2000); 284(4): 483–5.

24. Egger, Garry J., Andrew F. Binns, and Stephen R. Rossner, "The emergence of 'lifestyle medicine' as a structured approach for management of chronic disease," *Medical Journal of Australia* (2009); 190(3): 143–5.

25. Murray, Christopher J. L., MD, DPhil; Charles Atkinson, BS; Kavi Bhalla, PhD; et. al., "The State of US Health, 1990–2010: Burden of Diseases, Injuries, and Risk Factors," *Journal of the American Medical Association* (2013); 310: s178–9.

26. Adams, K.M., M. Kohlmeier, and S.H. Zeisel, "Nutrition education in the U.S. medical schools: latest update of a national survey," *Academic Medicine* (September 2010); 85(9): 1537–42. https://www.ncbi.nlm.nih.gov/pubmed/20736683.

27. Tuso, Philip J., MD; Mohamed H. Ismail, MD; Benjamin P. Ha, MA, RD; Carole Bartolotto, MA, RD; "Nutritional Update for Physicians: Plant–Based Diets," *The Permanente Journal* (Spring 2013); 17(2): 61–6.

5. Making the Transition to Plant–Based Eating

1. Karen Page. *The Vegetarian Flavor Bible.* New York: Little, Brown and Company, 2014: 53.

2. Morton, D, P Rankin, L Kent, et al., "The Complete Health Improvement Program (CHIP) and reduction of chronic disease risk factors in Canada," *Canadian Journal of Dietetic Practice and Research* (Summer 2014); 75(2): 72–7. https://www.ncbi.nlm.nih.gov/pubmed/24897012.

3. Ornish, D., L.W. Scherwitz, R.S. Doody, et al., "Effects of stress management training and dietary changes in treating ischemic heart disease," *JAMA* (January 7, 1983); 249(1): 54–9.

https://www.ncbi.nlm.nih.gov/pubmed/6336794.

4. Anderson, J.W., and K. Ward, "High–carbohydrate, high–fiber diets for insulin–treated men with diabetes mellitus," *The American Journal of Clinical Nutrition* (November 1979); 32(11): 2312–21. https://www.ncbi.nlm.nih.gov/pubmed/495550.

5. Baranski, M. et al. "Higher antioxidant concentrations and less cadmium and pesticide residues in organically–grown crops: a systematic literature review and meta–analyses." *British Journal of Nutrition.* July 11, 2014

6. Greger, Michael MD. *How not to Die*. Flatiron Books. 2015: 337.

6. Establishing a Sustainable Plant–based Lifestyle

1. Thacker D. "My $1.50 a Day Challenge: Eating a Plant–Based Diet on an Austere Budget". https://www.forksoverknives.com/my–1–50–a–day–challenge–eating–a–plant–based–diet–on–an–austere–budget/#gs.ImHwkSY

2. Murray, Christopher J. L., MD, DPhil; Charles Atkinson, BS; Kavi Bhalla, PhD; et. al., "The State of US Health, 1990–2010: Burden of Diseases, Injuries, and Risk Factors," *Journal of the American Medical Association* (2013): 310(6): 591–608.

3. Reimers CD, Knapp G, Reimers AK. "Does Physical Activity Increase Life Expectancy? A Review of the Literature." *Journal of Aging Research.* Volume 2012(2012), Article ID 243958

4. Moore SC, Patel AV, Matthews CA, et al. "Leisure Time Physical Activity of Moderate to Vigorous Intensity and Mortality: A Large Pooled Cohort Analysis." *PLos Med* 9(11): e1001335. https://doi.org/10.1371/journal.pmed.1001335

5. University of Granada "Children Eat More Vegetables When Allowed to Choose, Spanish study finds." *ScienceDaily.* ScienceDaily, 2 June 2011.
www.sciencedaily.com/releases/2011/06/110602084232.htm

6. Cooke, L. "The importance of exposure for healthy eating in childhood: a review." *J Hum Nutr Diet.* August 2007. Volume 20, Issue 4, pages 291–400.

7. "Veganism has grown 500% since 2014 in the US." Rise of the Vegan. June 25, 2017. https://www.riseofthevegan.com/blog/veganism–has–increased–500–since–2014–in–the–us

8. Recipes and Food Templates

1. Gopalan, C., B.V. Rama Sastri, and S.C. Balasubramanian. *Nutritive Value of Indian Foods*. National Institute of Nutrition, Reprinted 2012. http://www.eeb.cornell.edu/biogeo/nanc/Food_Feed/table 1 gopalan et al 1989.pdf.

2. Plaza, Lucia, Begoña de Ancos, and Pilar M. Cano, "Nutritional and health–related compounds in sprouts and seeds of soybean (*Glycine max*), wheat (*Triticum aestivum.L*) and alfalfa (*Medicago sativa*) treated by a new drying method," *European Food Research and Technology* (July 15, 2002), http://link.springer.com/article/10.1007/s00217–002–0640–9.

GENERAL INDEX

in grains, 41

in legumes, 40

B-12. *See* Vitamin B-12

baking

    date sugar in, 33

    Egg Replacer, 67

    equipment, 54

    ground flaxseed in, 42

    healthy sweeteners, 33

    minimize oil, 33

    non-egg binders, 67

baking powder

    in recipes, 114, 117, 140, 149, 204, 219

baking soda

    in cookies, 133

    in muffins, 204

    soaking beans, 151

balsamic vinegar

    in recipes, 163, 178, 181, 190, 196, 197, 198, 200, 225

    to flavor leafy greens, 40

bananas

    antioxidants, 40

    dried, 53

    in recipes, 94, 112, 122, 123, 124, 204

    potassium in, 112, 123

    storage, 60

    whole food, 32

Barnard, Neal, xv

    books, 240

    influence, 243

    pcrm.org, 243

    program for reversing diabetes, 16, 117

    quote, 49

bay leaf, 153

bay leaves

    in recipes, 154, 214

BDNF

    brain–derived neurotrophic factor, 88

beans, 17, 170

    advanced preparation, 102

    aquafaba, 67

    cooking guide, 151

    cost, 85

    for quick meals, 83

    how to store, 56

    in recipes, 71, 105, 107, 117, 140, 159, 160, 161, 163, 164, 169, 171, 178, 181, 183, 186, 190, 195, 216, 226, 230, 235

    nutrition, 40

    protein, 21

    protein source, 74

    rinsing, 66

    soaking, 151

    source of iodine, 29

    source of zinc, 28

    sprouting, 152

beef

    animal suffering, 6

    omega-6 fatty acids, 23

    water footprint, 6, 13

beets

    in recipes, 105, 171, 234, 235

    roasted, 182

bell peppers

    in recipes, 108, 173, 174, 183, 190, 225, 227, 230, 234, 235

    snack, 77

    steaming, 69

    stuffed, 181

broccoli

    beta-carotene in, 24

    cruciferous vegetable, 39

    flavonoids in, 24

    in recipes, 166, 169, 178, 182, 211, 213, 215, 216, 230, 234, 235

    liver detox with, 11

    lutein in, 24

    sprouting, 155

    storage, 66

    sulforaphane source, 11

    vitamin C in, 28

broccoli sprouts

    health benefit, 39

    sulforaphane source, 11

brown rice, 58

    in recipes, 69, 72, 74, 147, 171, 226

brown rice syrup, 33

brown sugar

    in recipes, 130, 141

brownies, 140

Brussels sprouts

    cruciferous vegetable, 39

    detox with, 11

    nutrient dense, 45

buckwheat, 41, 43, 58, 83, 85

    in recipes, 114, 152

    sprouting, 155

butter

    substitutions, 68

butternut squash

    in recipes, 70, 162

C

cabbage

    cruciferous vegetable, 39

    in Clean Fifteen, 56

    in recipes, 71, 108, 160, 169, 173, 178, 180, 184, 189, 215, 216, 230

    liver detox with, 11

    red cabbage for antioxidants, 45

    select vivid colors, 65

    snack, 77

caffeinated drinks

    calcium-leaching, 27

calcium, 8, 24, 26, 27

    in beans, 226

    in collard greens, 127, 160

    in legumes, 40

    in moringa leaves, 52, 112

    in nuts and seeds, 41

    in pumpkin and sesame seeds, 42

    in wheat, 35

    vitamin D helps absorption, 26

calcium stones

    excess protein, 21

calories

    ANDI Index, 45

    cost-per-calorie, 7

    derived from fat, 17

    dietary guidelines, 20

    empty, 90

    energy required to produce, 5

    fewer with WFBP diet, 4

    from complex carbohydrates, 9, 20

    from fat, 22

    from nuts, 42

    from oil, 32

    from plant protein, 18

    from protein, 21

in recipes, 73, 107, 120, 160, 173, 225, 228

spicy, 101

salt. *See* sodium

sandwich

in recipes, 185, 186, 187, 188, 191

Sandwiches and Wraps. *See* Recipe Index

saturated fat, 21, 22, 23, 26, 40, 188

sauces, 35, 42, 51, 52, 53, 65, 68, 79, 85, 92, 93, 94, 102

in recipes, 108, 171, 191, 192, 193, 194, 195, 196, 197, 198, 199, 200, 201, 235

Sauces, Syrups, and Dressings. *See* Recipe Index

scallions

allium compounds in, 24

in recipes, 107, 109, 127, 166, 210, 213, 224, 225, 227

Schweitzer, Albert

quote, 98

sea salt

in recipes, 69, 72, 105, 106, 127, 130, 133, 135, 139, 142, 143, 167, 179, 183, 184, 190, 197, 198, 199, 221

seasonal produce, 85, 86, 99, 101, 102

seasonings

storage, 60, 67

seaweed

in recipes, 151, 157, 186, 213

iodine source, 29

seeds, 32, 41, 42, 84, 206

bulk, 66

garnish, 74, 75, 234, 235

grinding, 52

in recipes, 71, 76, 119

nutrition density, 45

propagating, 87, 153

snacks, 94

sprouting, 85, 155

storage, 58

travel, 84

seizures, 35

serotonin, 88

sesame seeds

in recipes, 155, 234

Shepp, Dave

quote, 37

shitake mushrooms

in recipes, 213

shoyu

in recipes, 196, 200, 224

smoking, 4, 16, 49, 88

smoothies, 91, 94, 95

in recipes, 111, 231

Snacks. *See* Recipe Index

soaking, 28, 33, 53, 66, 76, 82, 83, 114, 117, 126, 147, 148, 151, 155

sodium, 24, 34, 68, 115

blood pressure and, 17

excess, 34

minimum intake, 17, 34

rule of thumb, 64

soft drinks, 20, 31

Soups. *See* Recipe Index

in recipes, 209, 210, 211, 212, 213, 214, 215, 216, 236

soy, 8, 10, 26, 32, 34, 67, 68

allergies, 34

fermented, 25

isoflavones in, 24

sources, 35

soy creamer

RECIPE INDEX

CPSIA information can be obtained
at www.ICGtesting.com
Printed in the USA
LVOW09s1306151217
559854LV00002B/33/P

9 781976 480782